Unsuspected Eloquence

Music can noble hints impart,
Engender fury, kindle love;
With unsuspected eloquence can move,
And manage all the man with secret art.
—Joseph Addison

UNSUSPECTED ELOQUENCE

A History of the Relations between Poetry and Music

JAMES ANDERSON WINN

New Haven and London, Yale University Press

Published with the assistance of the
Frederick W. Hilles Publication Fund.

Designed by James J. Johnson
and set in Linotron 202 Baskerville type.
Printed in the United States of America by
The Murray Printing Co., Westford, Mass.

Acknowledgment is made to the following
publishers for permission to quote:
    "Warm are the still and lucky miles" from
W. H. Auden: Collected Poems, edited by
Edward Mendelson, Random House, Inc.,
New York. Copyright © 1940 and renewed
1968 by W. H. Auden.
    "In a Station of the Metro" from *Personae:
Collected Shorter Poems*, by Ezra Pound, New
Directions, New York, and Faber and Faber
Ltd., London. Copyright 1926 by Ezra Pound.

Library of Congress Cataloging in Publication Data

Winn, James Anderson, 1947–
    Unsuspected eloquence.

    Bibliography: p.
    Includes index.
    1. Music and literature. I. title.
ML3849.W58   780'.08   80–27055
ISBN 0–300–02615–3

    10   9   8   7   6   5   4   3   2   1

For Kathe,
who read the one about the boat

Sine musica nulla disciplina potest esse perfecta; nihil enim est sine illa.

—Isidore of Seville

Poets who will not study music are defective.

—Ezra Pound

Contents

Preface

In 1963, surveying the field of American literary scholarship, René Wellek pointed out some areas in which there was clearly work to be done:

> While some modern critics have brought to bear all kinds of other types of knowledge on the understanding of literature, they seem to have neglected the illumination which can be brought to literature from the two fields which seem the nearest to the art of words: linguistics and aesthetics, including the aesthetics of the fine arts. Linguistics is especially indispensable for a study of style, diction, and meter; and the relations of literature to music and painting have hardly begun to be studied by modern methods.[1]

In the seventeen years since Wellek wrote those words, scholarship and criticism have explored as never before the various kinds of light linguistics can shed on literature; the resulting work, highly theoretical and often controversial, has attracted more widespread attention than the less sensational, but to my mind equally important, advances on the aesthetic side. These have included both general and specific studies of the relations between literature and painting: the pioneering work of Jean Hagstrum and the recent work of Ronald Paulson, for example. And there have been admirable studies of the relations between literature and music, such as John Hollander's *The Untuning of the Sky*, which has made a generation of scholars more sensitive to the way both myths about music and technical lore drawn from Pythagorean music theory found expression in Renaissance poetry.

1. *Concepts of Criticism,* p. 312.

The question of "meaning" in music, an inevitable concern of such studies, has received increased attention in recent years from composers, musicologists, and theorists of music as well. Most of the resulting books have been more psychological than literary, concentrating on what happens to us when we listen to music: Leonard B. Meyer's *Emotion and Meaning in Music,* with its emphasis on "tension" and "release," and Victor Zuckerkandl's *Sound and Symbol,* a strangely mystical combination of Gestalt psychology and Schenkerian analysis, are typical. But a recent book by E. T. Cone, *The Composer's Voice,* gains a fresh perspective on the way composers express themselves, by borrowing ideas and terms from literary criticism—mainly from Wayne Booth's acute perceptions about *personae* in *The Rhetoric of Fiction.*

When I began the research and thinking that eventually led to this book, I considered reversing Cone's procedure: I hoped to explore the applicability to poems of some kinds of analysis practiced by musical theorists. But as I began to gather historical material from scattered sources, I recognized the more pressing need for an inclusive general account of the explicit historical relations between music and poetry. Some parts of the story have been told before, in far greater detail than is possible here, in books and articles about particular periods in particular countries; many of these works appear in due course in my notes, and I could not have proceeded without them. But because the divisions between academic disciplines make musicologists and literary scholars unlikely to read each other's work, I believe the task of synthesis and generalization I have performed here will prove useful; my fondest hope for this book is that it may educate an audience for future detailed studies of the historical and theoretical areas whose general topography it maps out. I have sought not only to make the important findings of some quite specialized scholarship more widely available, but to incorporate them into a narrative principally concerned with the many occasions on which a development in the theory or practice of one of these arts has decisively altered the course of the other. I have written neither a history of music nor a history of poetry but a history of the relations between the two: intimate, productive, sporadically marital relations, which have included episodes of jealousy, ironic misunderstandings, and attempts by practitioners of one art to control practitioners of the other. In different eras, there have been different points of contact between the arts, different perceptions of their possible relations; consequently, my book is in part a history of some basic components of poetic and musical creation—formal construction, emotional expression, and imitation in all its guises— and in part a history of the metaphors by which people have tried to explain the mystery of making.

No such book can claim to be all-inclusive: there are many possible paths through the material, and the one I have taken doubtless reflects my training as a teacher of eighteenth-century English literature, a student of poetry in other languages, ancient and modern, and a serious performer on the flute. Still, some further account of my principles of selection may be in order. I have been more interested in the technical and aesthetic relations between the two arts than in their social and psychological relations, and this interest in technique, this devotion to the poetic and musical skills I shall call "constructive," is reflected in my choice of examples and topics. As the varying chapter lengths show, I have given more space to developments from the Renaissance on, where the material is more familiar to most readers. In the early chapters, where the musical evidence is fragmentary, even scrappy, I have often had to speculate, but such speculation is less misleading than describing ancient and medieval poetry without reference to music, as has too often been done. About some parts of the early story, such as Roman music, virtually nothing is known; about others, such as Byzantine music and poetry, the scholarship is at such an early stage of deciphering that I have chosen to pass silently by. But from the Renaissance on, there are so many possible topics that any selection may seem arbitrary. Some of my omissions are strategic: I have concentrated on the Italian madrigal because the later English madrigal school has already attracted so much close study of the relations betweens its music and poetry; I have steered around a number of topics already covered by John Hollander; and I have not described some interesting German literary experiments with musical forms because they have been so ably treated by Steven Scher in his *Verbal Music in German Literature*. Other choices and emphases reflect polemical necessities: I have always been concerned to fit the relations between music and poetry into larger cultural patterns, but where this enterprise has led me to heterodox positions, most obviously in the account of the origins of Romanticism in Chapter V, I have had to give it more space. Smaller choices—this poem or that aria instead of some equally interesting alternative—doubtless reveal the same biases. It would be impossible and pointless to write this kind of history on a principle of scrupulous neutrality; selection and arrangement are themselves interpretive acts, and I have also engaged in more overt kinds of argument and speculation. Musical, poetic, and aesthetic theories are a central part of my story; a neutral presentation of the strongly colored opinions of an Addison or a Wagner, even if attainable, seems to me less useful than a presentation which addresses their arguments in an argumentative fashion. Nonetheless, I like to think my history will prove useful even to those who disagree with some or all of my aesthetic argument.

An account of developments in and intersections of musical and poetic technique cannot avoid technical terms, but I have sought to keep my discussions as free of needless difficulties as possible. Musical examples appear in modern clefs; quotations in prose appear in English, and poetic examples are accompanied by English translations, my own if not otherwise identified. I have made somewhat larger assumptions about my reader's knowledge of literature than about his knowledge of music, but the range of readers I hope to address is wide, and almost everyone will encounter some sections which cover familiar ground, and others for which he may require the assistance of a glossary or basic reference work; the index briefly defines some unfamiliar terms. The list of works cited is not meant to constitute an exhaustive bibliography, but it does include general or introductory works as well as more specialized studies; I have tried to use the notes as a way to describe and recommend further reading.

Acknowledgments

I have been preparing to write this book all my life, so any account of my debts must begin with my parents, who once bought a piano instead of a television, and who read and recited poetry to me from my earliest days. In my high school years, Mary Stewart Duerson, a Latin teacher whose mastery of Virgil extended to the niceties of his meter, kindled my interest in ancient poetry, while Francis Fuge initiated me into the mysteries of the flute. Among college teachers at Princeton whose stamp is on my work, let me name Henry Knight Miller, D. W. Robertson, David McGaughey, Robert Freeman, J. K. Randall, Milton Babbitt, and the late Arthur Mendel. Three close friends from college days—all musicians, all students of poetry—have read and commented on this manuscript; they are George P. Bassett IV, A. Michael Collins, and Robert A. Moreen.

In my years at Yale, which began with graduate school, I came under the particular care of Maynard Mack, whose detailed responses to this book as it took shape have been invaluable. My other major mentor, the late W. K. Wimsatt, did not live to see this book, but my study has been filled with his giant presence as I have tried to imagine him demanding clearer language, more precise distinctions; my frequent citations of his work are symptoms of a larger debt. The list of Yale colleagues who have read portions of the manuscript, answered questions, prevented errors, and provided support is large: Michael Cooke, Thomas Greene, John Hollander, George Lord, Hillis Miller, Ronald Paulson, Margaret Ferguson, Thomas Leitch, Ross Murfin, and Allen Shoaf in the English Department alone; John Herington, Kevin Crotty, and Greg Thalmann from Classics; David Large from History; Howard Garey from French; and from Music the late William G. Waite, who was still helping during what proved his final illness. The librarians of the Classics Library, the Jackson Music Library, the Beinecke Library, and the Sterling Memorial Library have been uniformly marvelous; let me single out Kathleen Moretto and Suzanne Selinger for devotion to this project well beyond referential assistance. Teri Edelstein of the British Art Center provided a public forum for a lecture based on Chapter V and funded the necessary musical performances.

My understanding of music doubtless owes something to every good musician with whom I have played; I learned lessons vital to this book from Ann Monoyios, Stephen Hart, Susan Almasi, and Charles Rudig. Samuel Baron, with whom I have studied the flute for the last ten years, has been particularly helpful and encouraging about this project. My composer friends, whom I have questioned incessantly about their methods, have provided

thoughtful responses; three who have been particularly concerned with this book are Mark Zuckerman, Robert Pollock,
and Arthur Paxton, who gave the entire manuscript a searching
reading.

My serious thinking about this specific project began during
a summer spent as a Mellon Fellow at the Aspen Institute, where
I met Michael Krausz of the Bryn Mawr Philosophy Department,
whose probing questions about aesthetic matters exposed my first
notions as naive and helped determine the direction of my research. A Morse Junior Faculty Fellowship from Yale provided a
much-needed year in which to do the actual writing. A generous
grant from the A. Whitney Griswold Fund made possible the
computer text-formatting of the final version; the indefatigable
operator was Lorraine Klump. The musical examples were ex-
pertly prepared by Kate Sanderson.

My greatest debts are to my family, who have had to live with
the project for more than two years. Some of their contributions
have been tangible; my brother-in-law, Kenneth Fox, an urban
historian and polymath, covered an early draft with helpful commentary; my daughter, Ellen, aged five, contributed her expert
skills in cutting and pasting to the final editing. Other contributions were less specific but not less important: my mother-in-law,
Diana Fox, helped me keep my work in perspective, as did my
son, Philip, aged three. My dedication is a bantering attempt to
acknowledge an unpayable debt to my wife.

May 1980

1

The Poet as Singer: The Ancient World

Introduction: Primitive Song

Music and poetry, as John Hollander has pointed out, "have become utterly different as human enterprises."[1] We now think of them as proceeding upon quite different principles and without dependence upon each other, coming together only in such "impure" collaborations as opera. But the origins and histories of the two arts make them more legitimate "sisters" or "spouses" than the more commonly paired painting and poetry. Music and poetry begin together, and the frequent separations in their history lead to equally frequent reconciliations.

The evidence we have about primitive song suggests that the first step toward poetry was the fitting of words to pre-existent melodies and dance rhythms. In his pioneering study of the songs of primitive cultures, C. M. Bowra argues that poetry "is in its beginnings intimately welded with music"; his hypothesis is that "song rises from rhythmical action," that dancing and wordless melody precede the rhythmic patterning of intelligible words. As evidence, he adduces the songs of the Yamana Indians of Tierra del Fuego, which consist of standard sequences of syllables having no meaning in their own language or any other; in Bowra's theory, such "senseless sounds" are "the most primitive kind of song. They anticipate later developments by making the human voice conform to a tune in a regular way, but the first step to poetry came when their place was taken by real words." Bowra posits five evolutionary stages: the meaningless line, the repeated intelligible line, the single stanza, the accumulation of stanzas into larger songs, and the accumulation of such songs into cycles.[2]

---

1. *The Untuning of the Sky*, p. 3.
2. *Primitive Song*, pp. 275, 29, 61; on the five-stage hypothesis, see p. 86.

1

This hypothesis reverses our modern sense of the order in which words and music come together to form a composite product. In our world, a composer usually writes music for a pre-existent lyric or libretto, and a poet who writes words "to the tune of" some well-known song is usually engaging in parody. The fitting of words to music as a definition of poetry has become a metaphor, but retains an important kind of truth: Ezra Pound, in 1912, could write of poets, "we all of us compose verse to some sort of tune."[3] Indeed, if we understand his words in Pound's way, what Bowra says about primitive song, literally made to music, might be said of any successful later poem:

> Once words have begun to be accommodated to music, they display qualities which might not be expected of them in their ordinary duties, and have not only lilt and balance, but tone and quality. . . . They are more carefully chosen than other words and have the compelling power which comes when words are loaded with evocative meaning.[4]

This book concerns the complex history of the claim made in those sentences: that the rhythmic and melodic qualities we associate with music are also present in poetry, accounting for some of its power and meaning.

The rhythmic affinities between music and poetry are more obvious to modern ears than the melodic ones, but ancient ears were finely attuned to the phenomenon we still call "vowel music." Late in the first century A.D. the rhetorician Demetrius reported a much more ancient Egyptian tradition which shows some interesting affinities with the "meaningless" songs of the Yamana: "In Egypt the priests, when singing hymns in praise of the gods, employ the seven vowels, which they utter in due succession; and the sound of these letters is so euphonious that men listen to it in preference to flute and lyre."[5] Such a sequence of "meaningless" vowels would not only be euphonious, but would have some qualities in common with a musical scale. Just as any scale arbitrarily selects a limited number of pitches from the infinite number of

---

3. "I Gather the Limbs of Osiris," following the text given in Pound's *Selected Prose* 1909-1965, ed. William Cookson, p. 37.
4. *Primitive Song*, p. 276.
5. *Demetrius on Style*, tr. W. Rhys Roberts, section 71, pp. 104-05.

pitches in any octave, so any sequence of vowels arbitrarily selects a limited number of stopping places along the *glissando*-like flow of vowel-sounds the human voice can utter. The different shaping of the mouth cavity and placement of the tongue necessary to produce different vowels actually give each vowel a distinct overtone which will be present whether the vowel is sung or spoken, whether the speaker is male or female. If you speak this sequence of words—beat, bit, bet, bat, boat, bought—you should hear those overtones descending in pitch; if you take away the sound of the vocal chords by whispering, the effect will be even clearer.[6] The Egyptian hymn of the seven vowels may have been a sung, pitched scale; the fact that Egyptian paintings show harps with seven strings suggests as much.[7] But even if the priests merely "uttered" the vowels "in due succession," without making a pitch difference with their vocal chords, Demetrius' account implies that men heard those vowels as a kind of music, that they appreciated their sounds in a physical and sensuous way. We may see in this ancient custom a confirmation of Bowra's hypothesis: for men who heard the music of vowels so clearly that they could prefer it to the music of instruments, there must have been little difference between the experiences we now call poetry and music.

Mousike *in Ancient Greece*

The ancient Greeks, about whose culture we have much fuller evidence, produced a highly musical poetry. The word describing the poet as a singer *(aoidos)* is older than the one describing him as a maker *(poietes),*[8] and while the exact process by which vocal sounds, pitched melody, real words, and regular rhythm came together to produce Greek poetry is shrouded in myth, and may not have followed the five neat stages of Bowra's hypothesis, there

6. Sir Charles Wheatstone first postulated this "fixed pitch" theory of vowels in 1837; it has been confirmed by the research of Helmholtz and of Dayton Miller. Whether a bass or a soprano speaks the syllable, "ah," scientific measurement will show the presence of a pitch of 824 cycles. See Philip Bate, *The Flute,* pp. 45, 50 (*n.* 20).

7. See Henry George Farmer, "The Music of Ancient Egypt," in *Ancient and Oriental Music,* ed. Egon Wellesz, vol. I of *The New Oxford History of Music,* p. 277.

8. See W. B. Stanford, *The Sound of Greek,* p. 27. Stanford's book, which includes a recording, has been questioned by other philologists, but is the best starting point for non-specialists.

can be no doubt that later Greeks considered the resulting combination a unified whole: they used a single word, *mousike,* to describe dance, melody, poetry, and elementary education. Even
those Greek thinkers who discuss differences between singing and
speaking describe them as differences of degree, not kind: Aristoxenos, a student of Aristotle who wrote about 320 B.C., makes a
distinction between the continuous or sliding motion of the voice
in speech and its lingering on more precise pitches in singing, but
he makes it clear that he is speaking of ordinary speech, not poetic
recitation; the later Neoplatonist Aristides Quintilianus describes
the pitch of the voice in poetic reading as falling between singing

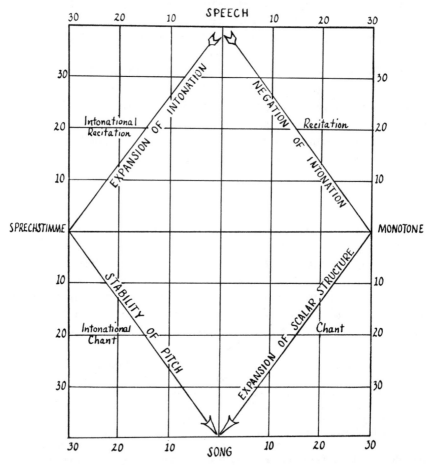

FIGURE 1. "Chart for Classifying Forms Intermediate to Speech and Song."
From "The Boundaries of Speech and Song," by George List, in *Ethnomusicology*
7 (1963): 9. Reproduced by permission.

and ordinary speech. These ancient distinctions are surprisingly similar to those made by modern ethnomusicologists; see for example George List's chart (figure 1). As the chart shows, Schönberg's *Sprechstimme,* which stipulates precise pitches from which the voice slides downward, is an artificial midpoint between ordinary speech and ordinary song; monotone, which negates the intonation we normally have in our speech, is its opposite. The sustained quality of singing, already noted by Aristoxenos, is here called "stability of pitch," and the somewhat musical reading of poetry described by Aristides Quintilianus appears here as "intonational recitation."[9]

But the distance between speech and song was smaller in ancient Greek than in any modern Western language. Ordinary speech had a pitch-accent, and music had vaguer, less stable pitches than those of our scalar music. Our understanding of the pitch-accent is imperfect, and our knowledge of ancient Greek music is even more fragmentary, but we know enough to recognize some detailed similarities between the linguistic and musical systems. Philological authorities now agree that the acute accent indicated a raised pitch, perhaps as much as a perfect fifth higher than the pitch of an unaccented syllable. The circumflex seems to have indicated a slide from a medium pitch up to the high pitch used for the acute and back again. About the grave accent, particularly the so-called "oxtone-grave," we are least certain, but W. B. Stanford supposes that it indicated a middle pitch.[10] So even in ordinary speech, there was a rudimentary melodic system involving two fixed pitches, a low one for unaccented syllables and a high one for syllables with an acute accent; between the fixed pitches lay a vaguer middle area from which the circumflex arose and toward which it fell, with the grave perhaps placed there as well. When this speech-melody was combined with the quantitative metrical system of Greek verse, whether in epic hexameters or the various lyric meters of dithyramb and tragedy, the result was a music already more complex than some primitive chants still sung in Africa and Australia. Considered as a musical unit, every line of Homer involves the interaction of at least three ele-

9. See Aristoxenos, *Elementa Harmonica,* ed. Rosetta da Rios, A, 8; pp. 12-13, and Aristides Quintilianus, *De Musica,* ed. R. P. Winnington-Ingram, I, 4; pp. 5-6.
10. See *The Sound of Greek,* especially p. 158, and cf. the more elaborate discussion of the problem in W. Sidney Allen, *Accent and Rhythm,* pp. 244-48.

ments: the rhythm of the dactylic meter with its rules and variants, the overtone pitches of a full range of vowels and diphthongs, and the vocal pitches prescribed by the accents. We can chart two of those three elements in a minimal notation by using fixed lines for the high and low pitches, a dotted line for the less-defined middle, and ordinary half-notes and quarter-notes to indicate the meter.[11] Here are the first two lines of the *Iliad:*

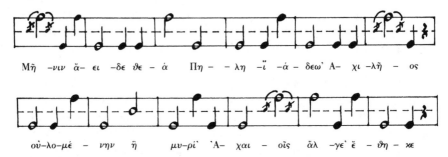

Mῆ –νιν ἄ– ει –δε θε – ά   Πη – – λη –ΐ –ά – δεω᾽ A– χι –λῆ – ος

οὐ–λο–μέ – νην ἤ   μυ–ρί᾽ Ἀ– χαι – οῖς ἄλ –γε᾽ ἔ – θη – κε

Rhythmically, there are only two possible feet, the dactyl (– ◡ ◡) and the spondee (– –). But the melody of pitches provides remarkable variety: in these two lines alone, there are five different kinds of dactyls and five different kinds of spondees; in the first ten lines, there are twelve different kinds of dactyls and nine different kinds of spondees. The requirement that the fifth foot be a dactyl, and the sixth a spondee, limits rhythmical variation to sixteen possible arrangements of dactyls and spondees in the first four feet, but the many posible melodic patterns for each foot so multiply possibilities that virtually every Homeric line has a unique melody! More important for the working oral poet, each of the verbal formulae from which the lines are constructed has a melodic identity, a fact which doubtless helped the bard retain it in his memory. Compare, for example, the line-ending formulae for "shining-helmed Hektor" and "great-hearted Achilles," rhythmically identical, but melodically distinct:

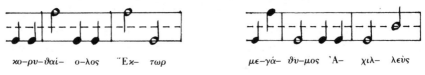

κο–ρυ–θαί– ο–λος   Ἕκ– τωρ   με–γά– θυ–μος ᾽A– χιλ– λεὺς

11. As will be apparent, I borrow this minimal staff from Isobel Henderson (see note 19 below). The use of half-notes and quarter-notes makes the usual assumption that one "long" syllable equals two "short" syllables. On this vexed question, see Allen, pp. 255-59.

As Eric Havelock points out in a discussion of the function of poetry in preserving knowledge for an oral culture, "the only possible verbal technology available to guarantee the preservation and fixity of transmission was that of the rhythmic word organised cunningly in verbal and metrical patterns which were unique enough to retain their shape."[12] Since the system of pitch provided an additional dimension, another way to differentiate rhythmically identical formulae, we may insist on its equal importance in oral composition and transmission.[13]

Indeed, studying Greek poetry with attention only to meter, assonance, and alliteration, without considering how all of these devices can be affected by pitch, is like attempting to analyze a painting from a black and white photograph. In fact, it is worse, since the photograph at least shows a range of dark and light shades corresponding in some respects to the colors of the original, while recitations of Greek verse without proper attention to the actual pitch-accents tend to produce the false impression that high pitch corresponds with metrical "length" or "weight." Julian Jaynes, for example, eager to demonstrate the "hypnotic" or "preconscious" qualities of the *Iliad*, alleges, despite his citations of Stanford's book, that every Homeric dactyl had the pitch-pattern "GCC."[14] This misrepresentation not only downgrades the impressive melodic variety of Homeric poetry, but combines and confuses its distinct systems of meter and pitch.

We call the ancient Greek meters "quantitative" because they can be transcribed with some accuracy by half-notes and quarter-notes; it would be better simply to call them "musical," since the patterns we call meters originated in music and dance, and then had words fitted to them.[15] The idea of a musical poetry with measurable lengths for its syllables is alien to us because the modern

12. *A Preface to Plato*, pp. 42-43. Havelock's statement depends upon the "oral hypothesis" of Milman Parry; for a systematic exposition, see Albert B. Lord, *The Singer of Tales*, ch. 2-5.

13. One musical scholar who has argued for the relevance of the "oral hypothesis" to the preservation of music is Leo Treitler; see "Homer and Gregory: The Transmission of Epic Poetry and Plainchant," *Musical Quarterly* 60 (1974): 333-72.

14. *The Origin of Consciousness in the Breakdown of the Bicameral Mind*, p. 364.

15. "There is now enough evidence to show that music regulated metre rather than *vice versa*," writes David Wulstan in an excellent recent discussion: "Introduction: Ancient Greece," which he revised from a draft by the late Isobel Henderson, and which appears as ch. 1 of *Music from the Middle Ages to the Renaissance*, ed. F. W. Sternfeld, p. 48. Subsequently cited as Wulstan.

English meters from which we naturally generalize when thinking about poetry are based on stress-accents, and allow so much variation of actual duration that musical transcriptions are arbitrary and subjective. It is not clear whether such accent by stress played any part in ancient Greek poetry. Ordinary spoken ancient Greek probably did not have dynamic stress, and scholars have often supposed that poetry also lacked stress, though Curt Sachs, arguing from the pervasive use of the terms *arsis* and *thesis* (upbeat and downbeat), and from the fact that the chorus-leader in tragedies wore a heavy, noise-making shoe, makes a strong case for the presence of an *ictus* or down-beat stress.[16] But whether or not the musical meter used such stress to clarify its patterns, the accents in post-Alexandrian texts notate a system of pitches which operated separately from the system of rhythms.

Philologists sometimes seem puzzled at the independence of the two systems. W. S. Allen's phrasing is typical: "there appears to be no attempt to achieve agreement between accent and metre in any part of the line in any spoken form."[17] The implication is that there should have been an "attempt," that "agreement" between the two systems, if "achieved," would constitute a technical advance. But such agreement would have made the music of Homer *less*, not more, complex: a music in which high pitches always coincided with downbeats (as in Jaynes' misrepresentation of Homer) would be hopelessly monotonous. Music thrives on the *interplay between* rhythms and pitches, and the complexity of this interplay in Homeric verse confirms its musicality.

Another more serious question also arises from the absence of "agreement" between pitch-accents and quantitative rhythms. We know that Homer's choice of words was constrained by his meter, that he had to have a rich vocabulary of synonyms in order to be able to fit words into appropriate rhythmic slots in his line. But it is more difficult to allege that considerations of pitch similarly constrained his choice of words; perhaps the varied melodies of his lines were arbitrary, almost accidental. Still, correspon-

---

16. *Rhythm and Tempo*, pp. 130-41. The controversy about the so-called *ictus* is old and complex. Another way out is John Caldwell's recent definition of the classical *ictus* as "a kind of regular *notional* stress analogous to the bar-line in music." *Medieval Music*, p. 15, emphasis mine.

17. *Accent and Rhythm*, p. 261.

dences between pitch-accents and assonance of vowels, operating in ways precisely analogous to correspondences between rhythmic position and assonance, suggest that Homer *was* consciously seeking melodic effects. In the very first line of the *Iliad*, another glance at the transcription will show that the assonance of the vowel *eta* (η) is emphasized by rhythm (three of four *etas* fall in downbeat position), while the assonance of the vowel *alpha* (α) is emphasized by pitch (three of four *alphas* are sounded at high pitch). Like many other questions about ancient poetry and music, the problem of melodic intent remains highly speculative; we simply do not know enough to resolve it. Beyond our ignorance, we are hampered by our modern tendency to think of some techniques as "musical" and others as "poetic," a distinction inapplicable to Homeric verse: even assonance, after all, involves overtone pitches. And if we retreat to what seems a safer distinction between sound, with all its various nuances, and narrative content, with its apparently separate concerns, the many famous and striking examples of imitative onomatopoeia in Homer confirm the ancient origin of another continuing topic of our study: the imitation of content by sound. The effects which make us hear the armor clattering upon all those dying Iliadic warriors, or feel the liquid seduction of the Sirens, are the products of meter, assonance, alliteration, and pitch. Our imperfect knowledge of the last of these factors, an inevitable result of the fact that pitch-accents were not indicated in Greek texts until centuries after Homer, does not necessarily mean that it was the least important of them: for Homer's hearers, the voice chanting in the firelight was the voice of a singer.

The surviving fragments of Greek musical notation, all much later than Homer, some from times when music and poetry had begun to diverge, nonetheless confirm the unified ancient origin of the two arts. With one exception, they are settings of poetic texts, and the poetic meter and musical rhythm are so much the same that most fragments have no rhythmic markings at all. When rhythmic indications are present, they clarify the placement of *arsis* and *thesis,* and sometimes indicate that a long syllable should have the duration of three short syllables, not two. For the relatively simple epic meter of Homer, a text, with its understood conventions about long and short vowels, could serve as an adequate rhythmic notation; for the more complex rhythms we call lyric meters, a text alone was not sufficient, at least not unambiguous. In late antiquity, the limitations of a text as a rhythmic notation led to the debates between the "metrists" and the "rhythmicists." The "metrists," from whom we draw our terminology about meter, analyzed the way lines, feet, and syllables looked in writing; the "rhythmicists," whose work is not so well known, were concerned with musical performance.[18] Our continuing uncertainties about Greek lyric meters derive from this debate, which was itself centuries removed from the practices it sought to describe, but in classical Greek practice, the poets obviously knew and followed the musical rhythms.

The melodies indicated in the fragments are monodic, with no separate part for the accompanying instrument, whose main function was surely to double the sung pitches.[19] The basic unit of musical grammar was the tetrachord, which had two fixed pitches a perfect fourth apart, the high one called *mese* and the low one called *hypate*. (We would normally translate *hypate* as "high," but it means a low pitch in modern terms; like most of our terms for discussing music, "high" and "low" are arbitrary metaphors.) Between *mese* and *hypate* there were two "movable notes," called *lichanos* and *parypate;* by the fourth century various placements of these movable notes had settled into three basic types of tetrachord, roughly described in the following diagram:

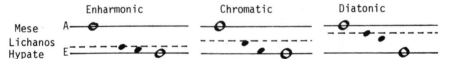

Two similar or dissimilar tetrachords could be stacked upon each other, either with a common tone in the middle (conjunct) or with a step between (disjunct):

18. See Wulstan, p. 48. Hephaestion was a typical metrist; Aristides Quintilianus was a rhythmicist.

19. The two notational systems, now mistakenly called "vocal" and "instrumental" notation, are in fact both instrumental, based upon the position of fingers on a string. There is some evidence that instrumentalists may have sounded different pitches from those sung, but "such accompaniments were heterophonic [i.e., moving at some parallel interval to the voice], not polyphonic or contrapuntal." Isobel Henderson, "Ancient Greek Music," in *The New Oxford History of Music,* vol. I, p. 339. Subsequently cited as Henderson.

Obviously, this procedure produced a wider range, but as Isobel Henderson warns,

> Greek music must never be conceived in terms of any continuous scale—least of all the harmonic series of our 'just intonation'. Its essential character lies in the logical priority of the fixed notes, which hold the melody between the iron girders of consonant progressions, over the contrasting flexible effects of the mobile notes, which bound various and irregular intervals, some hair-split, some widely gapped. . . . The unit of . . . analysis . . . is not the octave but the tetrachord.[20]

The similarities between this tetrachordal system and the system of pitch-accents in speech become even more striking when we learn that a more archaic style, employed in the stone inscriptions called the "Delphic hymns," had only one middle pitch between the fixed outer pitches.[21] Obviously such a three-pitch system bore an even closer relation to the system of pitch-accents; its expansion by subdivision of the notes from the movable middle area may even have some relation to the sliding of the voice in the spoken circumflex.

But the correspondence between ancient Greek music and poetry extends even beyond this essential similarity of system: the fragments of music we possess actually show close correspondence between the pitch-accents of the words and the notes used to set those words. In the most substantial of those fragments, the "Delphic hymns" and the "Seikilos epitaph,"[22] this correspondence is quite regular: most acutely-accented syllables are set with

20. Henderson, p. 345; both diagrams also from Henderson, pp. 387, 344.

21. See R. P. Winnington-Ingram, "Greek Music (Ancient)," in *Grove's Dictionary of Music and Musicians*, 5th ed., ed. Eric Blom, vol. III, p. 774.

22. For a facsimile of the Seikilos epitaph, with a transcription, see W. Sidney Allen, *Vox Graeca*, p. 110. For transcriptions of all the pieces of ancient Greek music known in 1960, including fragments, see Carlo del Grande, "I documenti musicali," in *Enciclopedia Classica*, sez. II, vol. V, tomo ii, pp. 435-76.

23. See Allen, *Accent and Rhythm*, p. 232. This phenomenon was noticed long ago; see, for example, R. L. Turner, "A Note on the Word Accent in Greek Music," *Classical Review* 29 (1915): 195-96.

pitches higher than those used for the other syllables in their words, and a similar regularity appears in the treatment of circumflex and grave accents.[23] It is tempting to leap directly from this evidence to an unqualified claim that music and poetry must have been essentially identical at some point in Greek prehistory, but there are many obstacles to such a leap: the Delphic hymns date from the late second century B.C., the Seikilos epitaph is no older and may be considerably later, and the one piece of earlier music we possess, a badly mutilated papyrus containing some lines from a chorus in Euripides' *Orestes,* appears not to display the correspondence between pitch-accent and melody so noticeable in the later pieces. Furthermore, the rhetorician Dionysius of Halicarnassus, writing in the late first century B.C., after describing pitch-accent quite precisely and even alleging that "the distinction between oratory and music is simply one of degree,"[24] goes on to make that distinction quite large, citing as evidence some other lines from *Orestes* in which the pitch-accent and the melody are apparently at odds. Many scholars have therefore concluded that the correspondences in the later fragments are peculiar to the Hellenistic period, or that the difficulties of composing a strophe and antistrophe which would agree not only in meter but in pitch-accent were so prohibitive that agreement between melody and pitch-accent, however ancient or desirable, was impossible in lyric poems and tragic choruses.[25]

Again, the fragmentary nature of the evidence makes speculation inevitable, but since recent studies of the Euripidean fragment have strengthened its claim to authenticity,[26] any theory

24. *Dionysius of Halicarnassus on Literary Composition,* tr. W. Rhys Roberts, ch. XI, pp. 124-29.

25. For a clear summary of the evidence favoring such skepticism, see Warren Anderson, "Word-Accent and Melody in Ancient Greek Musical Texts," *Yale Journal of Music Theory* 17 (1973): 186-203.

26. Douglas D. Feaver, in "The Musical Setting of Euripides' *Orestes,*" *American Journal of Philology* 81 (1960): 1-15, bases his argument for the age and authenticity of the fragment on the fact that its scale "is identical with an ancient scale quoted by Aristides in a commentary on the musical section of Plato's *Republic*" (p. 6), and unlike the scales listed by Aristoxenos. The recent discovery of a very similar papyrus fragment, also from Euripides *(Iphigenia in Aulis,* parts of lines 784-792), also with musical notation, would seem to support Feaver's claim. See the preliminary publication, with a photograph, by D. Jourdan-Hemmerdinger, in *Comptes Rendus de l'Académie des Inscriptions et Belles-Lettres* (1973): 292-302.

must try to account for Euripides' apparent violation of the putative rule requiring correspondence between melody and pitch-accent—both in the fragment and in the passage cited by Dionysius. In the latter case, as Douglas Feaver has established, Dionysius quotes an unreliable text; if we compare the melody he implies with the text as *we* have it, there are very few violations. And even in the problematic fragment, correspondences between melody and pitch-accent outnumber contradictions. Perhaps Euripides, who was criticized by Aristophanes and others for composing overly "modern" music, was simply treating an old rule rather loosely. But Feaver's research actually suggests a plausible reason for the inconsistencies: the passage we have on the papyrus comes from an antistrophe, and if we compare its melody to the words of the strophe of the same chorus, the results show a much closer correspondence. We know that an antistrophe always repeated the rhythm of the strophe; perhaps it repeated the melody as well. Ironically, Dionysius, whose comments on Euripides are one source of confusion, not only confirms this hypothesis, but describes melodic repetition *before* rhythmic repetition:

> The writers of lyric verse cannot vary the melodies [*melos*] of strophe and antistrophe, but whether they adopt enharmonic melodies, or chromatic, or diatonic, in all the strophes and antistrophes the same sequences must be observed. Nor, again, must the rhythms be changed in which the entire strophes and antistrophes are written, but these too must remain unaltered.[27]

Like later composers of strophic songs, Greek melodists were thus more likely to achieve a close fit between text and tune in the strophe or first verse than in the antistrophe, where new words might not conform so tightly to the repeated melody. For the tonal composers of our common experience, this problem has meant that a melodic or harmonic effect designed to imitate or express some particular word in the first stanza usually falls on a less appropriate word in subsequent stanzas. For Euripides, the problem was more technical, but no less constraining: imagine trying to write a chorus on the terrifying subject of matricide, with

27. ch. XIX; in Roberts, pp. 194-95.

your choice of words and syntax constrained not only by an obligation to repeat exactly in the antistrophe the complex rhythm of
the strophe, but by a similar melodic obligation as well! The tension between musical construction and dramatic expression,
which we shall see in many later periods, was already apparent in
classical Greece.

Even though the melodies of Greek lyric poetry are lost to us,
we can discover how closely the poets followed them by studying
what philologists call "accentual response," the degree of conformity in pitch-accent between a strophe and antistrophe. In a
general examination of this phenomenon, Erik Wahlström has
made statistical counts of the placement of accents in strophic
poems by Pindar and Sappho, in which "accents can be seen to
concentrate on certain points and avoid others."[28] He even constructs hypothetical melodies for some of these poems, melodies
whose shape conforms quite closely to the speech-melody of the
pitch-accent. It seems hard to avoid the conclusion that both
tragic and lyric poets worked within a system whose restraints included melodic considerations of some kind. Indeed, these formal constraints may help explain the grammatical ambiguities
and difficulties of their poetry. As modern readers of that poetry,
we can sense only a part of its effect, for the melodic part of its
composition and performance, obviously expressive and perhaps
sometimes mimetic, is lost to us. Though the entire subject will
always remain tantalizingly hypothetical, the tension between
word and tone displayed in the Euripidean fragment points us
ahead to more overt later struggles between musical and poetic
principles, while the continuing correspondence between poetic
and musical technique, even in this controversial "modern" work,
reminds us that those techniques were once, in Bowra's phrase,
"intimately welded."

Literacy and Theory

Illustrations of epic recitation suggest one very early stage in the
division of poetic and musical technique: the old oral poets, pic-

---

28. "Accentual Response in Greek strophic poetry," *Commentationes Humanarum Litterarum* 47 (1970): 21.

tured with lyres on vases and in the Homeric epics, gave way to the rhapsodes, pictured with long staves. Unlike the oral poet, who was always improvising to some extent and might have used his lyre to fill the intervals in which he collected his thoughts, the rhapsode was an actor delivering a polished performance of a memorized text.[29] The absence of an instrument suggests that rhapsodic performance was less musical than bardic perform-ance: using List's chart (see figure 1 above), we might think of this change as a motion from "intonational chant" toward "intona-tional recitation," a motion away from "stability of pitch." But the function of the rhapsode, like that of the bard before him, was still to preserve and pass on the customs and memories of a cul-ture; oral memorization of the Homeric epics was a fundamental part of education, reinforced by the public performances of the rhapsodes at religious festivals and by private recitations in schools and homes. So important was this process of memoriza-tion that its mastery led to power; as Havelock argues, boys in classical Greece memorized epic poetry because their ancestors, princes and chieftains in a fully oral culture, had delivered their orders and judgements in improvised poetry:

> The community's leadership lay with those who had a supe-rior ear and rhythmic aptitude, which would be demonstra-ble in epic hexameter. It would also however show itself in the ability to compose *rhemata*—effective sayings which used other devices besides the metrical, such as assonance and par-allelism. (p. 126)

The composition of such *rhemata* in prose represented a small motion away from meter, as the conventions of rhapsodic per-formance represented a small motion away from pitch. These changes had begun to occur even before the introduction of al-phabetic writing; as writing spread, and as its uses became more fully understood, it brought about much larger changes. Initially, however, writing was simply a compositional aid for an oral per-former. Havelock believes that all the Greek poets after Homer were able to write, but he points out that theirs was a "craft liter-acy," a skill used to make works which were still "composed for

---

29. On the rhapsodes, see G. S. Kirk, *The Songs of Homer*, p. 91, and plates 7a and 7b.

recital rather than reading" (p. 137). Oral considerations necessarily remained fundamental. Musical notation in our own time
may provide a crude parallel: a modern composer writes a score
which very few people can read, but which enables him (or another performer) to perform the work for an audience, many of
whom cannot read the simplest musical notation. In order to succeed, his work must reach that hearing audience; the written notation's understood function is to help the composer devise au-
rally effective patterns of sound. But the composer is doubtless
also tempted to include in his work expressions peculiar to the
written language, or at least more immediately obvious to a skilled
reader of the score than to someone hearing the work. Thus even
a "craft literacy" defines two audiences, and that effect took place
quite clearly in ancient Greek oratorical prose. Politicians who
used writing to prepare their speeches began by being concerned
with the audience that would *hear* their elegant and persuasive
patterns of parallelism and symmetry, but the alphabet gave such
speakers the opportunity to work out their patterns in advance on
wax tablets, and may explain their tendency to use increasingly
elaborate patterns—perhaps even patterns too complex for alert
Greek ears, though discernible to literate eyes. As in the case of
Greek music, our knowledge is imperfect, and causality is difficult
to establish, but the historian Diodorus Siculus reports the novel
impression made in Athens by the famous rhetorician Gorgias,
who "was the first to use the strikingly artificial figures of antithesis, isocolon, parison, [and] homoeoteleuton,"[30] and we can date
Gorgias' arrival precisely: it occurred in 427 B.C., at precisely the
moment when use of the alphabet was spreading to a significantly
larger part of the population.[31]

The alphabet, a visual mnemonic technology, gave the rhapsodes a written document from which to prepare their performances, and allowed the orators to lay out their parallel structures
in a visual format. By the fourth century, according to Havelock,
"its victory was nearly complete, meaning that the original func-

---

30. Diodorus Siculus, *Historical Library*, XII, 53, as translated in W. K. Wimsatt and
Cleanth Brooks, *Literary Criticism, A Short History*, p. 58.

31. The alphabet had been known long before, but it was not until the last part of the
fifth century that it was taught to young children. On the whole problem of dating the
introduction and spread of the alphabet in Greece, see Havelock's lengthy footnote, pp.
49-52, which summarizes the scholarship.

tional purpose of the poetic style was becoming obsolete" (p. 137). As we have seen, that style had deeply musical origins, and its melodic aspects had aided memorization; with the triumph of the alphabet, the melody of words necessarily became a less central aspect of some kinds of literature. But if melody was becoming less important in epic recitations and public speeches, it was still a part of lyric poetry, tragedy, and instrumental performance. Sappho, Pindar, and Euripides were evidently composer-poets, and their lyric forms, complex in meter and elaborate in euphonic pattern, demanded melodic ability. But the Euripidean fragment suggests a tension between melodic and poetic technique, and historical evidence confirms a growing separation: in the fifth century, with the development of dithyramb and tragedy, we begin to hear of performers on the *kithara* and *aulos* by name, and of their skills in the execution of instrumental pieces called *nomoi;* in the fourth century, monuments recording performances of tragedies begin to give the names of instrumentalists in addition to those of chorus-leaders and poets; and by the second half of the century, the name of the *aulos*-player frequently *precedes* that of the poet.[32] Music was becoming separate and specialized, appreciated on its own terms. Indeed, Aristophanes' *The Frogs* (405 B.C.), in which the competition between Aeschylus and Euripides contrasts their melodic styles as well as their verbal content, is one of the last depictions of the composer-poet, the artist who makes words and music together. When Athens fell, just one year later, a shared musical-poetic culture in which citizens were trained in singing and participated in tragic choruses gave way to a more specialized and professional culture. In the fourth century, as Henderson explains,

> A star kitharist might get for one concert a fee that would maintain a Greek trireme for a year, or more than the cost of a first-class dithyrambic chorus. . . . Sophisticated poets were growing incapable of making music, and musicians of writing sophisticated verse. (p. 400)

The virtuoso kitharist thus appears at the moment when the more humble mnemonic functions of his art have been usurped

---

32. See A. W. Pickard-Cambridge, *Dithyramb, Tragedy, and Comedy* (2nd ed., rev. T. B. L. Webster), p. 55.

by writing, newly free to pursue melody and rhythm for their own
sakes, not for the sake of aiding the memorization of a hallowed
text. And the alphabet had an even more immediate impact:
fourth-century musicians used its symbols to develop a "craft literacy" of their own. The older of the two Greek musical notations, the so-called "instrumental notation," is based on a very
early form of the alphabet, and the slightly later "vocal notation"
uses the letters of the Ionic alphabet, in their usual order, to represent descending pitches.[33] The development of a pitch notation,
like the use of the same arbitrary symbols to notate the sounds of
speech, must have involved losses as well as gains. In both cases
an older, more exact, more sensuous attention to the nuance of
pitch or vowel color was sacrificed in order to achieve encoding.
Poetic song, which had come to the ear of the listener from the
mouth of the poet-composer, or from the mouths of a chorus
trained by that poet-composer, could now be abstracted and written down and later decoded by someone else. Of course, the encoding was imperfect: it could not represent the subtleties of tuning of the "movable" pitches on the strings of a particular *kithara;*
it could not capture the particular quality of a chanting voice or
the phrasing and lilt of a complex meter. Indeed, some of the
most basic problems in musical and poetic interpretation are
grounded in the inadequacy of these and all later notational systems.

   The separation of musical and poetic notation, the fact that
the two systems assigned entirely different meanings to the same
characters and wrote them on physically separate lines, confirms
the separation that was occurring in the culture. What had once
come to the ear as *mousike,* an indivisible whole, was now visually
represented as a line of text with a line of pitches written above it.
Figure 2 is a representation of the Euripidean fragment, with a
restoration of the first line and an attempt to transcribe the music
into modern notation.[34]

   The alphabetic symbols, here used to write both text and music, also made possible the development of musical and literary

---

33. For an excellent summary, correcting a number of errors in standard reference
texts, see J. Murray Barbour, "The Principles of Greek Notation," *Journal of the American
Musicological Society* 13 (1960): 1-17.
   34. The half-sharp sign ($\not=$) indicates a pitch between A and B-flat.

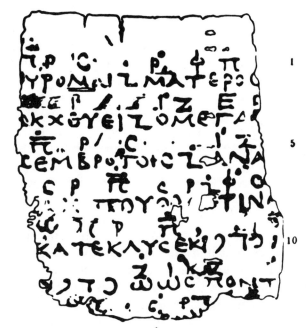

$$[\kappa\alpha \text{ - } \tau o \text{ - } \lambda o] \text{-} \varphi\upsilon \text{ - } \rho o \ \mu\alpha\iota \ \dot{\text{Z}} \ \mu\alpha \text{ - } \tau\acute{\epsilon} \text{ -} \rho o\varsigma \ [\alpha\tilde{\iota} \text{ -} \mu\alpha \ \sigma\tilde{\alpha}\varsigma]$$

FIGURE 2. The Euripidean fragment. From del Grande, pp. 438–39 (see note 22).

theory. In a fully oral culture, bardic technique, both verbal and melodic, had to be learned by repetition and imitation, by copying exactly and physically the singing and playing of a master. Our English idioms for this process—"learning by ear" and "learning by heart"—accurately emphasize its physical and emotional aspects, and anyone who has taken a music lesson from a master knows how much of the learning is not and could not be written down. But in a culture possessing the alphabet, it was possible to write down an oration, a poem, or even a melody and study it. Thus the early rhetoricians were able to describe, classify, and list as "figures of speech" some techniques of arrangement which had

evolved over centuries of oral practice, and which had been designed to have an aural impact. Reduced to writing, these techniques could be taught efficiently to those desiring persuasive
skill, though the encoding, as we have seen, was imperfect. But
with writing, as I have argued, comes the temptation to address
and impress others who know how to write: the increasingly artificial figures of Gorgias and his followers, brilliantly parodied by
Plato in the *Gorgias* and the *Symposium,* betray the use of tablet
and stylus, and the partial adoption of literary, rather than oral,
assumptions about audience. Such assumptions are even more obvious in later Greek poems addressed to the eye rather than the
ear: poems in the shape of various objects, or employing acrostics
and anagrams.

The early music theorists also used their notation to classify
the elements of what had once been an exclusively oral practice:
they defined the three types of tetrachord and worked out mathematical explanations of the discrepancies between various systems
of tuning. But while music was and is more stubbornly oral than
verbal art, its theory—mathematical from the beginning—has
stronger temptations toward abstraction. Ancient Greek musical
theory remains imperfectly understood, and its complex details
need not concern us here. But we may discern two strains in the
documents that have come down to us: a highly mathematical, at
times allegorical kind of theory, now usually called Pythagorean,
and a more practical kind of theory, more in touch with performance, mainly represented by Aristoxenos. The important point
for our purposes is that the Pythagorean strain was to prove
dominant, passing on its names for the "modes" and its mathematical mysticism to the entire later history of Western music.[35]
In working out abstract theoretical solutions to what had originally been practical problems of tuning and transposition, the Py-
thagoreans posited the existence of microtonal intervals smaller

35. No one understands perfectly what the various *harmoniai* and *tonoi* were, which of
them were actually played or sung, or why ancient theorists attached so much importance
to them. Medieval and Renaissance theorists, misunderstanding the ancient system, applied the names of the *tonoi* to various scales, but in ancient Greek music, which was not
scalar, the *tonoi* were actually *tunings,* various ways of preparing the *kithara* to be played. A
basic study is R. P. Winnington-Ingram, *Mode in Ancient Greek Music;* for a good short
discussion, see Gustave Reese, *Music in the Middle Ages,* ch. 2, now somewhat dated; Wulstan's account reflects recent scholarship.

than the human ear can detect. Despite their impressive intellectual sophistication, such theories were unlikely to aid actual performers, and these theorists did not set themselves up to instruct musicians as the rhetoricians had set themselves up to instruct orators. In fact, the invention of notation coincides with the waning of practical musical education in the schools and the rise of a class of instrumental virtuosi distinct from the music theorists and apparently ignorant of their work. For the Pythagorean theorists of the fourth century and later, argues Henderson, "harmonic science was superior to musical art precisely because it had no practical use" (p. 348).

So although both musical and rhetorical theory utilize the alphabet, their divergence is immediately apparent. Rhetorical theory, even in its most technical Alexandrian refinements, always claims to describe or prescribe how poets and orators have written or should write; citations of great authors occur frequently in ancient textbooks of rhetoric. Ancient textbooks of music theory, by contrast, do not quote actual pieces of music; instead, they give tables of hypothetical scales, most of which were probably never played or sung. Henderson blames this development on "the unbounded capacity of fourth-century thought . . . for generating abstract entities from words without facts" (p. 348), but the fourth-century theorists were not generating their musical abstractions from words. Starting with practical problems, they moved quickly into a region of mathematical and hypothetical speculation, just as many branches of mathematics (say, trigonometry) have moved away from the "applied" problems they initially set out to solve. The Greek music theorists, recognizing the element of mystery always present in abstraction, also attached mystic, even allegorical significance to their discoveries. Before we dismiss their work as frivolous, we should acknowledge that it involved the recognition of an important truth: that music, once separated from texts, was and is more abstract than poetry. Writing is less useful for explaining music than for explaining writing, so the music theorist, ancient or modern, resorts to numbers, charts, diagrams. Composers and performers, for whom a performance is superior to any analysis, have often insisted that the best comment on music is music, and in fifth-century Athens, where basic practical musical education was widespread, such a comment was still possible: Aristophanes, widely praised as the finest of Greek composers, built into his plays a criticism of contemporary music by means of musical parody, a criticism adequate without technical language.[36] But in Hellenistic times, when performance had become the province of a class of specialists, Pythagorean philosophers who could not play a note used alphabetic notation and mathematical formulae to erect a giant speculative construct called music theory. For all the imaginative beauty of its ratios, and for all the poetic resonance of its myths (including the "music of the spheres"), this theory neither described nor affected Hellenistic musical practice as we understand it, but its influence on later music, poetry, and theology was immense.[37]

The one important connection between musical theory and musical practice, and the one important resemblance between musical and rhetorical theory, was the doctrine of *ethos,* the claim that each of the various *harmoniai* or modes had a definite psychological effect on any hearer. Despite the claim that the various *ethea*—nobility, wildness, relaxation, and other moods—were inherent in the musical material of the *harmoniai,* John Hollander is surely correct in insisting that "the whole notion of musical effect [was] intimately involved with the notion of the sense of a text, and, ultimately, of the meaning of words" (pp. 35–36). Certain kinds of texts had traditionally been associated with certain *harmoniai,* so what strike us as unfounded psychological claims are actually extrapolations from convention. Thus Plato's famous exclusion of all *harmoniai* except the Dorian and Phrygian from his Republic is less a claim that these melodic idioms were nobly or manly *in themselves* than an acknowledgement that the Dorian and Phrygian *harmoniai* had traditionally been used in association with serious and patriotic texts; the *harmoniai* he excludes, such as the Mixolydian, had been associated with shrill dirges. Henderson correctly identifies the later belief that Plato was "attaching abstract ethical effects to the various *harmoniai*" as "a superstition,"

---

36. See Henderson, p. 394. Modern musical parodies, such as Hoffnung's wonderful avant-garde work by "Bruno-Heinz Jaja," assume a more limited and erudite audience. For an elegant discussion of the difficulty of talking about music, with an optimistic conclusion, see Jacques Barzun, *Music into Words.*

37. The continued life of these Pythagorean myths is the subject of Hollander's *The Untuning of the Sky.*

and notes that Aristoxenos, by far the most practical of the Greek theorists, repudiates it (p. 385), but that superstition had been fully incorporated into music theory by the time of Ptolemy's influential *Harmonics* (second century A.D.),[38] and would rise again to haunt the musicians and poets of the Renaissance.

The similar claims of the rhetoricians, based on rhythms instead of melodies, are more easily grasped because they supply examples. Dionysius of Halicarnassus, in his chapter classifying various metrical feet, attributes emotional effects to each one, but he also adduces examples from the poets in which it is apparent that the matter of the text contributes greatly to the effects attributed to the rhythm. He tells us that the *molossus,* a foot consisting of three long syllables, is "elevated and dignified, and has a mighty stride," but his example, a fragment addressing Castor and Pollux, surely owes some of its power to the *meaning* of its words:

− − −	− − −	− −	− − ˘
ὦ Ζηνὸς	καὶ Λήδας	κάλλιστοι	σωτῆρες

[O glorious saviours, Zeus' and Leda's sons.][39]

If the music theorists had adduced similar examples with musical notation and poetic texts in their discussions of *ethos,* and if we were confident of our transcriptions of the various *harmoniai,* the attribution of emotional effects to them might seem less fabulous.

Plato on Music and Rhetoric

The philosophical problems raised by the breakdown of *mousike* into music, poetry, rhetorical theory, and music theory appear quite dramatically in the works of Plato, whose statements about all these matters betray both urgency and ambivalence. As Havelock has shown, the banishing of poets from the Republic indi-

---

38. See especially the passage on modulation in the *Harmonics,* II, 7; in Ingemar Düring, ed., *Die Harmonielehre des Klaudios Ptolemaios,* p. 58.

39. ch. XVII; I quote the text and its translation from Roberts, pp. 172-73.

cates Plato's deep distrust of the oral, mnemonic, and irrational powers of *mousike*. Not that Plato wishes to replace oral education with a system based on writing; on the contrary, he shows equal suspicion of writing, describing it as a tool by which the rhetoricians preserve and extend the dangerous and potentially immoral techniques of persuasion developed in the oral culture. Plato's preferred form of communication is spontaneous spoken dialectic, in which each utterance has to defend itself, to win acceptance on the basis of its moral content, not its mnemonic structure. But the passage in the *Phaedrus* which makes these points is itself curiously rhetorical; Socrates speaks to Phaedrus:

> But he who thinks that in the written word, whatever its subject, there is necessarily much which is not serious, and that no discourse worthy of study has ever yet been written in poetry or prose, and that spoken ones are no better if, like the recitations of rhapsodes, they are delivered for the sake of persuasion, and not with any view to criticism or instruction; and who thinks that even the best of writings are but a memorandum for those who know, and that only in principles of justice and goodness and nobility taught and communicated orally for the sake of instruction and graven in the soul, which is the true way of writing, is there clearness and perfection and seriousness, and that such principles should be deemed a man's own and his legitimate offspring; being, in the first place, the word which he finds in his own bosom; secondly, the brethren and descendants and relations of his idea which have been duly implanted by him in the souls of others; — and who cares for them and no others—this is the right sort of man; and you and I, Phaedrus, would pray that we may become like him.[40]

The passage employs a gigantic framing device ("he who thinks . . . is the right sort of man"), which distances the opinions thus framed from us and from Socrates, who says at the end that he *would* pray to become *like* such a man. If what is really to be valued is clarity and dialectic, we may legitimately ask why the opinions are not more baldly declared, and why the description of "the

---

40. *Phaedrus,* 278a-b; in the translation of B. Jowett, III, p. 188.

true way of writing" immediately resorts to metaphor (good principles are the good man's "legitimate offspring," which he finds "in his own bosom"; they are part of a family of ideas "implanted by him in the souls of others"). In order to produce the impression of high morality ("justice and goodness and nobility"), Plato has had to resort to a rhetorical frame employing many nameable figures, and a metaphor tending in the direction of allegory. As Richard Lanham points out in a similar analysis of the rhetoric which surrounds the central assertion of the *Symposium,* "the soaring mystic forever falls back into the lap of ornament. He can soar beyond language only if we agree beforehand to overlook his language."[41]

A similar ambivalence appears in Plato's treatment of music. He proposes to reduce the number of years young boys spend learning music, excludes all *harmoniai* except the Dorian and the Phrygian from his Republic, and objects to fashionable new modulations. When confronted with the attempts of some theorists to hear physically the microtonal units they had theoretically posited, he paints a satiric portrait of foolish men bending over a *kithara,* listening for tiny variations in pitch.[42] But since Plato himself frequently employs language drawn from music theory, his objection must be to the physical procedure of listening for microtonal units, not to the theoretical procedure of positing them; not only does the Creation account in the *Timaeus* use Pythagorean imagery of music, but Ernest G. McLain has now identified the obscure description of eugenic marriages in the *Republic* itself as a musical allegory based on advanced study of the theory of tuning:

> From a musician's perspective, Plato's *Republic* embodies a treatise on equal temperament. ... With the adoption of equal temperament about the time of Bach we made into fact what for Plato had been merely theory. Musically the *Republic* was exactly two thousand years ahead of its time.[43]

Plato was evidently an expert in the numerical aspects of music theory; his objection to the theorists hunched over the *kithara* is

41. *The Motives of Eloquence,* p. 38.
42. *Republic,* 531a-c.
43. *The Pythagorean Plato,* p. 5. For the details of the marriage allegory, see ch. 2.

that they "put ears before the intelligence," but the passage continues by referring approvingly to the intellectual "consideration of which numbers are concordant and which not" as a "prelude to the song *[nomos]* itself . . . that dialectic performs."[44] As a metaphor for his ideal form of discourse, dialectic, Plato thus employs practical, performed music, not merely theory, and the word he uses, *nomos,* normally referred to an instrumental piece, as we have seen.

I have not collected these seeming inconsistencies in order to poke fun at Plato. His suspicion of all the offshoots of *mousike* was based upon a tough moral perception: he recognized that it was irrational to believe what a man said simply because he said it in perfect rhetorical patterns or sang it with the aid of meter and melody. But when Plato himself wished to express his beliefs about such topics as immortality, he was drawn toward poetic images and rhetorical techniques, the culturally available expressions of sublimity; these retained traces of their musical origin. And his dialogue on immortality, the *Phaedo,* shows Socrates composing, on the eve of his execution, a musical and poetic hymn to Apollo. Such moments are tacit admissions of the limitations of logic. If Plato the educational reformer had closed the front door to *mousike* in all her guises, Plato the maker of allegories needed to let her back in through the rear.

Roman Borrowings

Deprived of the unity and hegemony it had enjoyed under oral conditions, *mousike* was altered by the spread of the alphabet and threatened by the development of philosophy. But that very alphabet extended rhetorical technique and made music theory possible, and philosophers themselves took on problems in music theory and drew important imagery from musical performance. Even the least intellectual manifestations of *mousike,* acting and instrumental performance, retained their appeal in Hellenistic times, though the restriction of these activities to paid professionals gave them a different place in the culture than had been the case when every boy learned to sing and every father chanted

---

44. *Republic,* 531c-532a; in the translation of Allen Bloom, pp. 210-11.

Homer. But when we attempt to trace the relations between music and poetry in the Roman period, the lack of musical evidence is debilitating. Although we know from paintings of musicians and even some surviving contracts that Rome had no lack of musical performers, not one note of Roman music survives, with dire consequences for our knowledge of Latin poetic meters. As William Beare laments, discussing Roman drama:

> There was certainly a musical element present in the performance of plays; it seems fairly certain that the cantica were delivered to musical accompaniment, and that the iambic senarii were uttered without any accompaniment. Perhaps, then, the music, if only we knew more about it, would help us to understand the metre of the cantica.[45]

Similarly, more knowledge of the music might also help us with the vexing problem of the meter of the earliest Latin verses, called Saturnians, which have resisted all efforts to discover a consistent quantitative pattern, and were probably scanned by stress, though we do not know exactly how.[46] Lacking hard musical evidence, we must content ourselves with observing how the somewhat alien Greek meters which Latin poets adopted for their poetry came to occupy the same place in the creative process which musical considerations (both rhythmic and melodic) had occupied for the Greeks. As Hollander argues,

> It was when the speakers of an originally stressed Latin poetry took over Greek conventions that our traditional prosodic problems began to arise. The superimposition of schemata for the poetry of one language upon the hostile realities of another engender grave complexities; they may be seen in the effects of Romance prosodic conventions upon Old English, for example. But it was with the adaptation of Greek meters to Latin that poetry, originally inseparable from music, began to grow away from it. And it was then that poetry began to develop, in its meter, a seeming music of its own.[47]

45. *Latin Verse and European Song*, p. 151.
46. Beare's account of the Saturnian (ch. 11) is an amusing summary of the many failed attempts to scan it. For an even fuller discussion, see Thomas Cole, "The Saturnian Verse," *Yale Classical Studies* 21 (1969): 3-73.
47. *Vision and Resonance*, p. 11.

As I have argued, we may see signs of this separation earlier, in the graphic separation of verbal text from musical notation necessitated by writing, and in the wide divergence between rhetorical and musical theory. But in practical terms, Latin poetry represents a larger, more distinct step in the process of separation; its relations to music are arbitrarily imposed by convention, while the relations of Greek poetry to music, even after the functions of poet and composer became separate, remained organic and familial. The absence of a system of pitch and the use of a system of rhythm from another language were powerful forces separating Latin poetic practice from actual music. But in accepting the imposition of alien metrical rules, Latin poetry gained a contrapuntal richness, analogous to that resulting from the relations between Greek pitch-accent and meter, in the cross-rhythms resulting from the conflicts between its own word-accent and the requirements of the Greek meters. In both cases, two different patterns of organization, sometimes coinciding and sometimes conflicting, could be heard simultaneously in the same line.

Our knowledge of the performance of Roman poetry is fragmentary, but there is sufficient evidence to conclude that the poets were aware that they were manipulating two different systems of rhythm. W. S. Allen points to an interesting passage in which Horace gives directions to a choir of young boys and girls, as follows:

> Lesbium servate pedem meique
>   pollicis ictum, . . .

[Observe the Lesbian (i.e., Sapphic) measure and the beat of my thumb.]

As Allen points out, "the choir are specifically instructed to keep to the original Greek, Aeolic pattern, the stresses being determined by the music, and to ignore the accentual stress of the Latin words—with Horace as their leader keeping them in time."[48] Such sung performances of Latin lyric poetry were vivid reminders of its basis in Greek music, and the metrical rules of Latin poems in lyric meters are actually even more rigid than those of their Greek models. But the only performances of epic hexameter seem to

48. *Accent and Rhythm*, p. 349. The poem is *Ode* iv, 6.

have been readings, and it seems unlikely that such readings could have entirely suppressed the normal word accents in favor of the meter. As W. F. Jackson Knight and others have shown, there was a pronounced tendency to make the two systems coincide in the last two feet of the dactylic hexameter (99.8 percent of the time in Virgil, and over 90 percent even in the "primitive" Ennius).[49] This regular or "consonant" conclusion for most lines doubtless served a function not unlike that of rhyme in later European poetry; we may see its effects readily in the opening line of the *Aeneid:*

[normal word-accent]   / . / . . / . / . .   / . . / .

[Greek meter] |‒ ⏑ ⏑|‒ ⏑ ⏑|‒ ‒|‒ ‒ | ‒ ‒ ⏑ ⏑|‒ ‒

           Arma virumque cano Troiae qui   primus ab oris...

Such poetry has, in Hollander's phrase, "a seeming music of its own." It asks us to be aware of two different rhythms at once, just as music (even unaccompanied monody) asks us to be aware of both pitch and duration at once. The dependable "homodyned" end of each line, in which the two systems come together, provides the shaping and ordering that we associate with musical cadence. To be sure, the music of Roman verse is imaginary; it is not the genuine melody of Pindar, or even the pitched chant of Homer. But it has in common with Greek poetry the accommodation of a text to another set of aural requirements—arbitrary, abstract requirements which, for all their legendary emotional effects, must have required constant and rigorous attention to technique on the part of the poet. Dionysius has a wonderful verb, *philotechnein*, "to love technique," which he applies only to Homer and Demosthenes, his particular heroes. The necessity for poets to love and practice technique, even as poetry began to operate independently from music, may still be seen as their inheritance from those singers who were the first poets.

---

49. See W. F. Jackson Knight, *Accentual Symmetry in Vergil*, and Allen's summary, *Accent and Rhythm*, pp. 337-38.

2

The Word as the New Song:
Christian Developments

Introduction: Four Coordinates

Although traces of a unified primitive origin remained, the musical and literary heritage that Greek and Roman antiquity passed on to later Western culture was clearly divided. What had once been called *mousike* had now spawned four distinct developments, which we may think of as the coordinates of our discussion: (1) musical composition and performance, (2) literary composition and performance, (3) musical theory and philosophy, (4) rhetorical theory. Before we consider how Christian thought shifted and altered the relations among these coordinates, we should review the situation as it stood in late Roman times.

    1. Musical composition and performance, once wedded to poetic texts, had gained independence but lost prestige. Performances on the water-organ and other loud instruments were a part of public spectacles, and Roman trumpet-players even had a professional organization. Virtuoso kitharists, who did sing and therefore must have used poetic texts of some kind, had large followings and charged staggering fees, but the evidence suggests that the performer, not the song, was the center of attention in these performances. Perhaps Roman musicians were improvisers; such a hypothesis would account for the complete absence of surviving notation. But we may also speculate that the paucity of information about Roman music also reflects its low prestige relative to poetry.[1]

    2. Latin poetry—lyric, dramatic, and epic—retained in its me-

---

1. For a summary of our few scraps of knowledge about Roman music, see J. E. Scott, Roman Music," in vol. I of *The New Oxford History of Music,* pp. 404-20.

ters the vestiges of a close association with music, though the pitch system of Greek musical poetry had not passed into Latin. As we have seen, the "quantitative" meters, originating in Greek music and imposed upon Latin, often ran counter to the accents of ordinary speech. Such an artificial system could not last forever, especially in the absence of a real relationship to music, and the quantitative values assigned to Latin vowels to make them fit Greek meters eventually faded from the language, though word-accents remained. Beare believes that this change had occurred by the fourth century A.D., and that a larger change, the death of Latin itself as an ordinary spoken language, had begun to take place by A.D. 500. Between A.D. 500 and 1000, he argues, "the vernaculars which originated in Latin [became] distinct languages in France, Spain, Portugal, Italy and elsewhere."[2] None of these vernaculars, even in an early form, had a quantitative difference between vowels; all had word-accents. Therefore, the relations between music and poetry, in these languages and in the learned Latin of the Middle Ages, could not be continuous with those of antiquity. As we shall see, a new kind of melody, combined with a poetic rhythm based on word-accent, led to the development of new poetic forms.

3. Music theory, gathered from more ancient sources by Ptolemy, Aristides Quintilianus, Nicomachus, and (less competently) Alypius, retained its philosophical prestige, and passed into the medieval *quadrivium* along with arithmetic, geometry, and astronomy, to which it was closely related. But this branch of knowledge had little or nothing to do with composition and performance; it neither described ancient music nor prescribed methods for composing new pieces; it could not ameliorate the low prestige of performers. Theorists did continue to make the claim that hearers were emotionally or ethically affected by music; in that claim lay one of their few similarities to rhetoricians. Another similarity, or overlap, was that both musical and rhetorical theorists discussed the details of quantitative metrics: for the music theorists, metrical feet could be classified on the basis of ratios of short and long syllables, just as intervals could be generated by applying Pythagorean ratios to a sounding string; the more prac-

---

2. *Latin Verse and European Song*, p. 233; on the vowel change, see p. 215.

tical rhetoricians, while employing similar terminology, classified meters by their supposed effects.

4. The practicality of the rhetoricians is not surprising: they had always claimed to describe, appreciate, and criticize actual literature, and they served a practical function in society. The men who wrote the important Roman treatises on rhetoric were teachers of oratory, while the men who wrote the analogous treatises on music theory were philosophers, mathematicians, and astronomers, not instructors of vocal or instrumental performance. As Horace, Virgil, and Catullus became a part of the more distant past, and as even the rules of quantity came to be ignored or forgotten, rhetoricians took on not only a critical function, but a conservative one, proclaiming to an age they saw as corrupt and decadent the virtues of earlier literature. Thus, as W. K. Wimsatt explains, "what Horace [first century B.C.] was content to understand as a technical imitation of classical models becomes for Longinus [third century A.D.] something far more exciting, a powerful illumination and inspiration enjoyed through submission to the ancient masters."[3] In describing the use of "schemes of sound" by these ancient masters, Longinus is fully aware that some of the effects of such techniques are not logical, and uses an analogy to the effects of instrumental music to press his point:

> Harmonious arrangement is not only a natural source of persuasion and pleasure among men but also a wonderful instrument of lofty utterance and of passion. For does not the *aulos* instill certain emotions into its hearers and as it were make them beside themselves and full of frenzy, and supplying a rhythmical movement constrain the listener to move rhythmically in accordance therewith and to conform himself to the melody, although he may be utterly ignorant of music? Yes, and the notes of the *kithara*, although in themselves they signify nothing at all, often cast a wonderful spell . . . over an audience.[4]

3. *Literary Criticism, A Short History*, p. 100. In my frequent citations of this helpful work, I shall follow the authors' account of their several contributions: citations from ch. 1-24 will be identified as by Wimsatt; those from ch. 25-31 as by Brooks.

4. *Longinus on the Sublime*, tr. W. Rhys Roberts, ch. XXXIX, pp. 142-43. I have used *aulos* and *kithara*, Longinus' actual words, in place of the conventional mistranslations flute" and "harp," since the *aulos*, a raucous double reed, was by no means a flute, and

In the same chapter, Longinus goes on to praise a sentence from Demosthenes, in *prose*, which "owes its happy sound no less to the harmony than to the thought itself. For the thought is expressed throughout in dactylic rhythms, and these are most noble and productive of sublimity." Longinus slides around the problem of explaining *why* such effects arise from music and metrical speech: he believes that "it is folly to dispute concerning matters which are generally admitted, since experience is proof sufficient."[5] For all his interest in ecstasy, he remains a practical rhetorician in his appeal to experience. The music theorists, when explaining the same effects, had a more abstract or philosophical answer: they claimed that the power of ordinary, physically produced and perceived music arose from its being a faint worldly echo of the perfect mathematical music of the universe; Boethius would codify this doctrine in his distinction between *musica instrumentalis* and *musica mundana*. The similar separation between the practical rhetoricians and the speculative music theorists is reflected in the placement of rhetoric in the medieval *trivium* along with grammar and logic, while music theory took its place in the *quadrivium* of "higher" subjects. I have attempted to summarize these relations in Figure 3.

The impact of Christianity upon all four coordinates was immediate and powerful. Ancient pagan music, as we have seen, was normally associated with instruments and dancing, and featured the strong, regular rhythms preserved in "quantitative" poetry; Christian liturgical music, by contrast, was purely vocal, and reflected its Hebrew origin in a less precise kind of rhythm. In writing Latin words for these liturgical melodies, with their different principles of symmetry, Christian poets discovered new relations between words and music: the drift in Latin poetry away from quantitative verse toward accentual-syllabic verse, in which

---

since the *kithara* resembled the modern harp only in being strung. Quintilian uses the same analogy, in the *Institutia Oratoria*, tr. H. E. Butler, ch. IX, 9-10, pp. 510-11:"All the best scholars are convinced that the study of structure is of the utmost value, not merely for charming the ear, but for stirring the soul. For in the first place nothing can penetrate to the emotions that stumbles at the portals of the ear, and secondly man is naturally attracted by harmonious sounds. Otherwise it would not be the case that musical instruments, in spite of the fact that their sounds are inarticulate, still succeed in exciting a variety of different emotions in the hearer."

5. Longinus, ch. XXXIX; in Roberts, pp. 144-45.

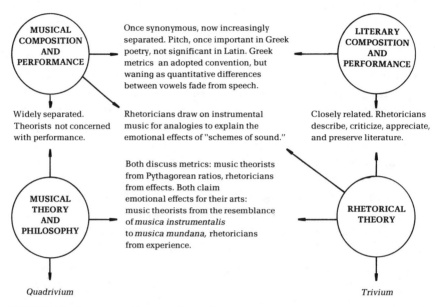

FIGURE 3. Four coordinates of *mousike*.

the hymns of Ambrose and Augustine are important documents, may be described as a drift away from writing Latin words to forgotten Greek tunes toward writing Latin words to new Christian tunes. But the fathers embraced the speculative music theory of the ancients as eagerly as they had scorned actual ancient music: they expanded the mystical and allegorical elements already present in such texts as Plato's *Timaeus,* adding Christian meanings to the ancient allegory of numbers. On the literary side, something quite opposite occurred: the fathers preserved ancient pagan poetry, especially Virgil, by the process of allegory; rhetorical theory, with its emphasis on persuasion, they regarded with suspicion, setting up the homely style of Christ's parables as a contrast. But rhetoric proved difficult to avoid, even for the fathers themselves; Augustine's interesting and ambivalent comments about music and rhetoric, a Christian recurrence of Plato's problems, dramatize the continuing appeal of those parts of *mousike* that Christianity sought to repress. In the ensuing centuries, the attempt to control these forces was played out in a more overtly political way: both church and state attempted to freeze liturgical chant, to arrest its development; but melodic ornamentation continued, and in writing words to the resulting melodies, monkish poets discovered such important new forms as the sequence and the trope. Finally, in the ninth and tenth centuries, improvements in notation and other practical contributions began to close the ancient gap between music theorists and performers.

Early Christian Music

The early Christian liturgy was evidently patterned on Jewish synagogue practice, and thus introduced into Western culture a different set of stylistic conventions about the relation of text to music.[6] Though quite different in detail from ancient Greek practice, Jewish liturgical song reflects a similarly oral origin, and therefore a similar closeness of text and tone. Obviously, Hebrew materials were significantly altered by translation and by contact with Hellenistic culture, though the lack of musical documents for the early centuries of Christianity makes this part of the story maddeningly difficult to trace, but scholars have generally agreed that there were three basic forms of singing, all essentially Hebrew in origin, each involving a different relationship between text and music:

1. In the cantillation or intoning of the Psalms, as Beare explains, "most of the verse was sung on a single note, with a rising introduction, or incipit, and a falling cadence."[7] Like all Hebrew poetry, the Psalms were accentual in form, but since neither the Greek nor the later Latin translations were in quantitative meters, the early Christian chants treated the Psalm texts as prose. The simply shaped, minimally chanted music merely served to animate the text.

2. If such cantillation sounded strange to Western ears, the elaborate, ecstatic melismata sung to the words *alleluia* and *amen* must have sounded even stranger, since we know of no ancient pagan music in which a single syllable of text was extended by many notes of melody, as was the case with these melismata, which were apparently constructed by combining various traditional melodic formulae. The fact that both Hebrew words have remained untranslated throughout the Christian tradition indicates

6. See Egon Wellesz, "Early Christian Music," in *Early Medieval Music*, ed. Dom Anselm Hughes, vol. II of *The New Oxford History of Music*, p. 3.

7. *Latin Verse and European Song*, pp. 220-21.

the primacy of music in this form, but the longer such melodies became, the stronger was the temptation to set new words to them, as we shall see.

3. The hymn involved a more equal partnership: its syllabic construction limited melismata, but its melody was more shapely than the crude arc of cantillation. The earliest decipherable Christian hymn we possess, the Oxyrhynchos papyrus (third century A.D.), sets each syllable of its text to one or at most two pitches; only the words *amen* and *theo* receive three pitches on a syllable, perhaps because both were frequently treated melismatically in other contexts.[8] Hymn texts were usually paraphrased from Scripture, and melodies were probably adopted from both Hebrew and Hellenistic sources. The resulting new compositions were designed for congregational singing and proselytism; adherents of various heresies and their orthodox opponents conducted much of their polemic through hymns, which were an effective way to popularize dogma. In composing texts to be sung, not by professional kitharists but by unlettered converts, the early Christian poets brought about significant changes in Latin poetry: they moved it decisively toward isosyllabic construction, end-

---

8. For a transcription, see del Grande, "I documenti musicali," p. 471. The notation follows ancient conventions, but scholars are divided as to the musical style. Paul Henry Lang, in *Music in Western Civilization*, p. 20, argues that "the piece still shows the characteristics of classical music intact. . . . While other literary sources indicate a merging of elements, this papyrus confirms the hypothesis that the original Hebrew songs as sung by the early Christians were displaced by examples of the highest type of antique musical practice soon after early Christendom came into contact with Greek civilization." Wellesz, by contrast, claims that "analysis of the structure of the music . . . shows that the melody is built up of a group of formulas. This principle is characteristic of Semitic melody construction, and is not to be found in ancient Greek music. As Christianity spread to the countries of the Mediterranean basin it carried with it this principle of composition, which is therefore to be found in both Eastern and Western chant, and which constitutes a proof of their ultimate Semitic origin" (pp. 4-5). General support for the latter position comes from John Caldwell, *Medieval Music*, p. 13:"By comparing the melodies of the West with those of isolated communities of Jews in the East it has been possible to show that a good many melodic elements which have survived into Latin chant are of ancient oriental origin." On the general question of the melodic sources of early Christian music, recent scholarship has tended to emphasize such connections with Jewish chant, but there is some evidence on the other side: Cölestin Vivell, in "Die direkte Entwicklung des römischen Kirchengesanges aus der vorchristlichen Musik," *Kirchenmusikalisches Jahrbuch* 24 (1911): 21-54, offers an impressive comparison between the Seikilos epitaph and the Gregorian antiphon *Hosanna filio David;* this example is conveniently reproduced in Reese, *Music in the Middle Ages,* p. 115.

rhyming, and accentual scansion. The simplicity of the resulting poetic forms, which involved less distortion of the Latin language as actually spoken than did the classical forms borrowed from Greek, was doubtless convenient for the purposes of evangelism and polemic.

Different as they were from each other, all three forms had in common a purely vocal performance, and some kind of responsorial or antiphonal singing was probably associated with each one. The early Church fathers frequently emphasized the importance of congregational participation, even by those without vocal talent or training. St. John Chrysostom is typical:

> Even though the meaning of the words be unknown to you, teach your mouth to utter them meanwhile. For the tongue is made holy by the words when they are uttered with a ready and eager mind. Once we have acquired this habit, neither through free will nor through carelessness shall we neglect our beautiful office; custom compelling us, even against our will, to carry out this worship daily. Nor will anyone, in such singing, be blamed if he be weakened by old age, or young, or have a harsh voice, or no knowledge at all of numbers [i.e., meter]. What is here sought for is a sober mind, an awakened intelligence, a contrite heart, sound reason, and clear conscience. If having these you have entered into God's sacred choir, you may stand beside David himself.[9]

For this communal and devotional singing, instruments were, as James McKinnon puts it, "stylistically irrelevant."

> The song of the Synagogue and early Church was . . . the only cult music of antiquity that did not use dancing, instruments, and regular meter, three elements that have always been closely related both in the music of antiquity and in later Western music. In being free from these elements, psalmody was as unique musically as the rites of the Synagogue and the early Church were unique liturgically from the normal ancient and primitive cultic types such as animal sacrifice and orgiastic dancing. This is not to say that psalmody was not

9. *Exposition of Psalm XLI*, as translated in Oliver Strunk's useful anthology, *Source Readings in Music History*, pp. 69-70.

influenced melodically by contemporary Roman and Hellenistic music; in fact it seems reasonable to assume that it shared a sort of tonal common denominator with all the music of the Mediterranean area. But its prose-like rhythm and its dissociation from dancing and instruments were sufficient to isolate it stylistically. There is also the testimony of the Fathers who unreflectingly referred to psalmody again and again as a distinct kind of music. It is revealing that the term "musica" was very rarely used with reference to Christian song; "psalms" and "hymns" were the normal terms.[10]

According to McKinnon, the vehemence of the patristic polemic against instruments reflects the need of the early Christians to set themselves apart from the surrounding culture, not an active struggle against advocates of instrumental music in church. But the relatively low status of music in late Roman times doubtless made instruments vulnerable to this attack: training in practical music-making was not an important part of education; professional musicians, however great their virtuosity and valuable their services, were still thought of in the same category with actors; and there was no systematic preservation of musical documents, despite the existence and apparent persistence of Greek letter-notation. Indeed, one of the most common patristic charges, that instruments suggested sexual immorality by their very shape, had been anticipated by those sturdy pagans Sallust, Lucian, and Livy.[11] By limiting music to forms with words, the Christian fathers further reduced its status; as Hermann Abert puts it, lamenting this development, "music as an independent art with an aesthetic effect on its hearer, in which function it had been understood by the ancients, found no honor in the eyes of these men."[12]

The absence of instruments posed a problem in scriptural interpretation: there were, of course, frequent references to instruments in the Psalms, so the fathers began to interpret such passages as allegories; Eusebios is typical:

> We sing God's praise with living psaltery. . . . For more pleasant and dear to God than any instrument is the harmony of

10. "The Meaning of the Patristic Polemic against Musical Instruments," *Current Musicology* 1 (1965): 78-79.

11. See McKinnon, p. 69.

12. In his classic work, *Die Musikanschauung des Mittelalters*, p. 83.

the whole Christian people. . . . Our cithara is the whole body,
by whose movement and action the soul sings a fitting hymn
to God, and our ten-stringed psaltery is the veneration of the
Holy Ghost by the five senses of the body and the five virtues
of the spirit.[13]

In this gloss, Eusebios employs an allegory of numbers, and such
appeals to the mystery in numbers had a wider application than
the Psalms: they enabled Christians to adopt much of the ancient
Pythagorean speculation about music for their own doctrinal purposes. As Abert points out, that ancient theory itself had grown
more and more mystical, so the Christians were not imposing an
allegorical interpretation upon it, as they frequently imposed
such interpretations upon pagan literature; they were simply developing elements already present in the ancient lore:

> The musical metaphysics of the Pythagoreans lived on in
> Christian musical aesthetics. Originally a product of pure
> mathematical speculation, music theory was already at the
> end of antiquity being drawn more and more into the sphere
> of the mystics. Already among the Neopythagoreans the
> physical side of the problem had given way to the metaphys-
> ical side, and in Christian teaching theological interests took
> over entirely. This mysterious, highly valued music of the
> universe, heard by no mortal, was a welcome means for the
> teachers of the church to preach to their congregations of
> believers the wisdom of heavenly Order. In principle this in-
> volved no alteration of the ancient teaching; it was simply
> necessary to fit it into the Christian doctrine of Creation. In
> this thoroughly Christian garb, this remarkable Greek theory
> held on throughout the clerical musical aesthetics of the en-
> tire Middle Ages, almost up to the threshold of modern
> times.[14]

We may observe this process at work in the treatises used to teach
music in the medieval *quadrivium;* the *De Institutione Musica* of
Boethius (c. 500), a gathering of materials from more ancient
writers, contains no overtly Christian language, but the treatises
of Cassiodorus (c. 550) and Isidore (c. 630) make their Boethian

13. *Exegesis of Psalm XCI,* as translated in Reese, *Music in the Middle Ages,* p. 62.
14. *Die Musikanschauung des Mittelalters,* pp. 82-83.

material explicitly Christian by means of allegory. This process widened still further the ancient gap between musical theory and practice: Boethius makes a crucial distinction between *musici* (theorists) and *cantores* (singers); the absence of instruments meant that singers were the only kind of musicians in the church; and the encouragement of participation, however incompetent, meant that the musical knowledge of such singers was unlikely to be imposing. But on the theoretical side, Christian allegorists provided mystical meaning for all the numbers of ancient music theory; in contrast to the ignorant *cantores*, these *musici* were learned clerics.

A simpler, earlier allegory identified Christ the *logos* or Word as the New Song. For Clement of Alexandria, in the second century, Christ is Word, Song, and Instrument:

> The Lord fashioned man a beautiful, breathing instrument, after His own image; and assuredly He Himself is an all-harmonious instrument of God, melodious and holy, the wisdom that is above this world, the heavenly Word. . . . Because the Word was from the first, He was and is the divine beginning of all things; but because He lately took a name,—the name consecrated of old and worthy of power, the Christ,—I have called Him a New Song.[15]

By this account, the Christ in whom there is neither Greek nor Jew is the Christ who is both Word and Song. To be sure, there is a persistent strain of argument in the fathers to the effect that melody is a necessary sweetening of doctrinal message; St. Basil, for example, says that "these harmonious melodies of the Psalms have been designed for us, [so] that those who are of boyish age or wholly youthful in their character, while in appearance they sing, may in reality be educating their souls."[16] But the continued singing of melismatic alleluias, which St. Augustine himself identifies as "songs of gladness without words,"[17] suggests that pure vocal melody, when its singers were thought of as "beautiful, breathing instrument[s]," could also be a legitimate and sanctified means of praise.

---

15. *Exhortation to the Greeks*, as translated in Strunk, p. 63.

16. *Homily on the First Psalm*, as translated in Strunk, p. 65.

17. "sonus . . . laetitiae sine verbis." *Exposition of the Ninety-ninth Psalm*, quoted in Wellesz, p. 5.

It would be centuries before these melismatic alleluias, by acquiring texts, could influence poetic form, and the cantillation of the Psalms, which remained essentially unchanged throughout the Middle Ages, was even less likely to have such an influence; in the strophic hymn, however, new relations between words and melody are strikingly apparent. Among the finest and most influential of early Christian hymns are those of St. Ambrose (340–397); we possess the texts of at least fourteen. Each consists of 32 lines in a meter the ancients called iambic dimeter, but which we would consider tetrameter: it consists of alternating spondees and iambs; an iamb may substitute for a spondee, but not *vice versa;* the normal pattern is $|- -|\smile -|- -|\smile -|$. F. J. A. Raby's description of the formal organization of these hymns clarifies their musical shape:

> After the second line in each strophe there is usually a 'sense pause', and, indeed, in the manuscripts the strophes are written as though composed of two long lines. There is, of course, a more emphatic pause at the end of each strophe, but, most important of all, after each two strophes there is a sense pause which can only be explained by the fact that the hymns were composed to be sung by alternate choirs.[18]

Not only does the organization suggest antiphonal singing, but the way the word-accents conform to the melodies suggests that Ambrose fitted his words to simple melodies with strong principles of symmetry and parallelism; among the poetic results are grammatical parallelism and occasional rhyme. Here are the first two strophes of his hymn on the martyrs, *"Aeterna Christi munera,"* with a transcription of the oldest extant setting, which has a fair claim to be the original:[19]

18. *A History of Christian-Latin Poetry,* p. 36.
19. Text from A. S. Walpole, *Early Latin Hymns,* pp. 105-108. I give the melody as it

[The eternal gifts of Christ / And victories of the martyrs, /
Bringing forth the praises we owe, / We sing with happy
minds. // The princes of the church, / Victorious chiefs in
war, / Soldiers of Heaven's court / And true lights of the
world.]

Several details of the poem's formal construction and meaning show more clearly when we consider the melody as well. On
the basis of the text alone, the rhymes *("uictorias"* and *"debitas"* in
the first strophe, *"principes," "duces,"* and *"milites"* in the second)
could be dismissed as accidental homoeoteleuton, rhymes resulting from inflected endings, but they gain added prominence from
the musical cadences on which they fall. The fact that the fourth
musical phrase is virtually identical with the first alerts our ears to
the close parallelism of lines 1 and 8:

Ae-ter -   na Chris-ti   mu - ne - ra . . .
et ve -   ra mun -di   lu - mi - na.

These lines are parallel in vowel pattern, grammatical construction, accentuation, and metaphoric function. To call the martyrs,
with neuter nouns, the "eternal gifts of Christ" or the "true lights
of the world" is to describe them at a different level of allegory
than that of the intervening masculine nouns calling them
princes, chiefs, and soldiers. The framing effect of this detailed
parallelism marks off the first eight lines as a discrete unit, and we
may imagine the second choir responding antiphonally at the be-

---

appears in Higini Anglès, "Latin Chant Before St. Gregory," *The New Oxford History of
Music,* II, pp. 68-69, where it is transcribed from the square notation of the *Liber Vesperalis,*
ed. Suñol, p. 444. The same tune, with the occurrences of B in the third phrase corrected
to B-flat, appears in *Monumenta Monodica Medii Aevi,* ed. Bruno Stäblein, I, 4, but with the
text of another hymn by Ambrose, "Jam surgit hora tertia." Stäblein identifies the tune as
belonging to the "earliest layer, the authentic Milanese hymn-style" (p. 502). The elaborate
earlier discussion of Ewald Jammers, "Rhythmische und tonale Studien zur Musik der
Antike und des Mittelalters," *Archiv für Musikforschung* 8 (1943): 27-45, also places this
melody among a small group of Ambrosian settings whose melodic structure suggests a
very early date. Jammers' attempt to minimize Jewish influence on early Christian music
and to argue for a direct development from classical culture, however, is doubtless more a
product of Nazism than of scholarship. Since the earliest readable manuscripts are from
the fourteenth century, any claims that these melodies are authentic, including mine, are
guesswork, but Suñol reports some undecipherable palimpsest fragments of the seventh
century which attest to the antiquity of the Ambrosian tradition.

ginning of line 9. Moreover, the technique is repeated in lines 25 and 32, the first and last lines of the final eight-line unit:

> in his paterna gloria, . . .
> in semipiterna saecula.

[In these the Father's glory, / . . . Into everlasting ages.]

Such patterns of repetition, perhaps too distant from each other for the ear to perceive in a read poem, are more easily heard when the similar phrases have melodic as well as verbal relations. Ambrose was discovering how the word could sing a new song; the new relations between words and melodies in his hymns stand at the beginning of the process by which Latin quantitative verse, itself an inheritance from an older wedding of word and tone, became obsolete. Ambrose himself never violates the rules of quantity, though his meter is a flexible one, but his hymns can also be scanned by an accentual system, and the melody strengthens the accents. So influential were these hymns that "Ambrosian" became a general term for a Latin hymn, and thousands of such texts were composed during the next six centuries. In some of these later texts, strict quantity is forgotten or violated, but the accentual scansion, grammatical parallelism, and strophic organization remain; rhyming becomes more frequent and regular. In the Ambrosian hymn, we see one result of the new melodic principles introduced by the early Church: a new kind of poetry, whose simple and explicit formal shape makes it an ideal didactic and devotional vehicle.

Augustine on Music and Rhetoric

Among those who reported being moved by the hymns of Ambrose was a teacher of rhetoric converted and baptized in Milan by Ambrose himself, St. Augustine. Augustine's writings touch all four coordinates of our discussion, and his opinions about music, poetry, music theory, and rhetoric had a decisive impact on the Middle Ages. His version of Christian aesthetics, which was to achieve the status of orthodoxy, consistently values the rational, allegorical, and intellectual over the passionate, literal, and emotional. The consequences of this position may be seen both in the selective version of classical art preserved by the Christian Middle Ages and in the art of that period itself.

Augustine was by no means ignorant of pagan secular music. He admits in the *Confessions* (III, 2) that he regularly attended the theatre in his youth, and in the *De Musica,* written just after his conversion, his downgrading of instrumentalists shows some familiarity with their technique. In order to separate the subject-matter of the *De Musica* from actual secular music, the *magister* or instructor in the dialogue defines music as *"scientia bene modulandi,"* the science of modulating well, and manipulates the *discipulus* or student into admitting that the methods of ordinary musicians in the theatre are not scientific. Here are the essentials of the argument:

> M. Finally we must consider why the word "science" is in the definition. Tell me then whether the nightingale seems to modulate its voice well in the spring.
>
> D. It certainly seems to.
>
> M. But it isn't trained in the liberal discipline, is it?
>
> D. No.
>
> M. Now tell me then, don't they all seem to be of a kind with the nightingale, all those who sing well under the guidance of a certain sense, although if questioned about these numbers or intervals of acute and grave tones they could not reply?
>
> D. I think they are very much alike.
>
> M. Those who play on flutes and lyres can't be compared to the nightingale, can they?
>
> D. I find a certain art in these instrumentalists, but only nature in the nightingale.
>
> M. That's true. But do you think it ought to be called an art even though they do it by a sort of imitation?
>
> D. Why not? For imitation seems to me to be so much a part of the arts, that if it is removed, nearly all of them are destroyed.
>
> M. But don't you think art is a sort of reason?
>
> D. It seems so.
>
> M. Therefore whoever cannot use reason, does not use art.
>
> D. I grant that too.

> *M.* Then either you would be forced to say magpies, parrots and crows are rational, or you have been pretty rash in calling imitation by the name of art. If all imitation is art, and all art reason, all imitation is reason. But an irrational animal does not use reason; therefore it does not possess an art. But it is capable of imitation; therefore art is not imitation.[20]

By stressing the word *scientia* in the definition, Augustine is able to distinguish true musicians who contemplate the verities of number from mere flute-players who perform by ear. This distinction, which may remind us of Plato's scorn for those who depended on their ears instead of their minds, became dogmatic for the Middle Ages; we have mentioned its prominence in Boethius' *De Musica.* But the force of Augustine's argument, the vigor with which he attacks the much-honored idea of imitation as a beastly skill observable in magpies, is more Pauline than Platonic. For Augustine, art is not imitation but reason, *ratio,* a word we might also translate as proportion. Its purpose is to express the eternal proportions of God's universe, high truths which transcend mere sense-impressions. Lower versions of art are not merely trivial, but sinful.

What emerges in the *De Musica* as sarcastic disdain for theatre musicians is not merely the class snobbery of a learned intellectual, not even merely the righteous scorn of a convinced Christian; it is an active fear of the temptations of sense, a fear so strong that Augustine actually worries about the sensual dangers of the music sung in churches. If we examine the imagery of the famous passage on this subject in the *Confessions,* we will find it quite similar to the imagery Augustine uses on the vital literary subject of scriptural interpretation. The passage begins by acknowledging the attractions of music:

> I used to be much more fascinated by the pleasures of sound than the pleasures of smell. I was enthralled by them, but you broke my bonds and set me free. I admit that I still find some enjoyment in the music of hymns, which are alive with your

---

20. *De Musica,* I, 5-11. I quote, with minor changes and frequent ellipses, the translation of R. Catesby Taliaferro, pp. 7-16.

praises, when I hear them sung by well-trained, melodious voices. But I do not enjoy it so much that I cannot tear myself away. I can leave it when I wish.[21]

The psychological drama here suggests the alcoholic who assures us that he can quit whenever he wants to, but as D. W. Robertson points out in an astute comment, "what is here stated 'autobiographically' might just as well be said in exposition impersonally, although it would then lose some of its effectiveness."[22] Augustine is dramatizing himself in order to emphasize a distinction he also uses in the *De Doctrina,* where he explains that readers of scripture must know the difference between things to be *enjoyed* and things to be *used:* "If we . . . wish to enjoy those things which should be used, . . . [we will be] shackled by an inferior love."[23] The image of shackling, here used to describe the bad effects of overly literal reading, is the same as that in the passage about music, where God breaks the "bonds" which have "enthralled" Augustine; the continuing fear is that Augustine will *enjoy* the music for its own sake, rather than *using* it to reach a higher truth.

The passage continues:

But if I am not to turn a deaf ear to music, which is the setting for the words which give it life, I must allow it a position of some honour in my heart, and I find it difficult to assign it to its proper place. For sometimes I feel that I treat it with more honour than it deserves.

Here the language recalls Paul's famous comment on the Law, "the letter kills, but the spirit gives life" (2 Cor. 3.6); but Augustine has made the music of the hymns, with its potential for misuse, analogous to the destructive letter of literal reading, while the words of the hymns are analogous to the spirit! As we shall see, later thinkers, especially in the Renaissance, would claim that music was able to give life to words, that through music one might reach a higher level, thus reversing Augustine's metaphor, itself a reversal of Paul's. In discussing the Pauline passage in the *De Doc-*

21. *Confessions,* X, 33, following the translation of R. S. Pine-Coffin, p. 238. All subsequent citations of the *Confessions* are from this translation.

22. *A Preface to Chaucer,* p. 64.

23. I, 4, following the translation of D. W. Robertson, p. 9. All subsequent citations of the *De Doctrina* are from this translation.

trina, Augustine returns to the image of captivity:"There is a miserable servitude of the spirit in this habit of taking signs for things, so that one is not able to raise the eye of the mind above things that are corporal" (III, 5; p. 84), and as the passage on music continues, he emphasizes the uses and dangers of the corporal senses:

> I realize that when they are sung these sacred words stir my mind to greater religious fervour and kindle in me a more ardent flame of piety than they would if they were not sung; and I also know that there are particular modes in song and in the voice, corresponding to my various emotions and able to stimulate them because of some mysterious relationship between the two. But I ought not to allow my mind to be paralysed by the gratification of my senses, which often leads it astray. For the senses are not content to take second place. Simply because I allow them their due, as adjuncts to reason, they attempt to take precedence and forge ahead of it, with the result that I sometimes sin in this way but am not aware of it until later.

The language about "kindl[ing] . . . a more ardent flame of piety" is exactly parallel to a passage on scriptural interpretation in one of Augustine's letters, where "things expressed figuratively" are described as "feeding and blowing upon the fire of love" more effectively than "naked" *(nuda)* or literal expressions.[24] By consistently using the same set of metaphors to describe figurative language in the Bible and vocal music in the church, Augustine reveals a more fundamental similarity: sung music, like such sensual scriptural texts as the Song of Songs, has a potential for proper use if correctly understood, and a danger for earthly enjoyment if the senses are allowed to take over.

In both cases, the arresting or sensual power of the medium, despite its dangers, is evidently effective in making converts and arousing the faithful. In acknowledging this power in music, Augustine draws on pagan traditions: the remark about "particular modes in song and in the voice, corresponding to my various emotions and able to stimulate them because of some mysterious

24. Letter LV, ch. XI, par. 21; ed. Goldbacher in *Corpus Scriptorum Ecclesiasticorum Latinorum,* vol. 34, pp. 191-92.

relationship between the two" is a compact statement of the ancient belief in *ethos*. Augustine differs from his pagan sources in his insistence that the senses and emotions, however stimulated, must maintain their place as "adjuncts to reason," but the power of music in the case of his own conversion prevents him from banishing it; a little later in the same chapter, the evangelist in Augustine overcomes the ascetic:

> Sometimes, too, from over-anxiety to avoid this particular trap I make the mistake of being too strict. When this happens, I have no wish but to exclude from my ears, and from the ears of the Church as well, all the melody of those lovely chants to which the Psalms of David are habitually sung; and it seems safer to me to follow the precepts which I remember often having heard ascribed to Athanasius, bishop of Alexandria, who used to oblige the lectors to recite the psalms with such slight modulation of the voice that they seemed to be speaking rather than chanting. But when I remember the tears that I shed on hearing the songs of the Church in the early days, soon after I had recovered my faith, [including, as other passages make clear, the hymns of Ambrose], and when I realize that nowadays it is not the singing that moves me but the meaning of the words when they are sung in a clear voice to the most appropriate tune, I again acknowledge the great value of this practice. So I waver between the danger that lies in gratifying the senses and the benefits which, as I know from experience, can accrue from singing. Without committing myself to an irrevocable opinion, I am inclined to approve of the custom of singing in church, in order that by indulging the ears weaker spirits may be inspired with feelings of devotion. Yet when I find that singing itself more moving than the truth which it conveys, I confess that this is a grievous sin, and at those times I would prefer not to hear the singer. (X, 33; pp. 238–39)

The closest analogue to this acknowledgement of the practical utility of music is Augustine's position about rhetorical eloquence. In Book IV of the *De Doctrina*, a revision of Ciceronian principles for Christian use, Augustine says that preachers should "use the ornaments of the moderate style . . . not ostentatiously but prudently, not content . . . that the audience be pleased, but rather using them in such a way that they assist that good we wish to convey by persuasion" (IV, 25; p. 162). The emphasis on ends, instead of means, and on a moderate style, runs parallel to the admiration for the precepts of Athanasius in the passage on music. The temptations to ostentation are also parallel: steeped in the tradition of classical rhetoric, Augustine may have tried to moderate his style after his conversion, but he never abandoned such oratorical figures as chiasmus. Consider this passage, on the central tenets of Christian doctrine:

> We were trapped by the wisdom of the serpent; we are freed by the foolishness of God. Just as that which was called wisdom was foolishness in those who condemned God, thus this which is called foolishness is wisdom in those who conquer the Devil. We ill used our immortality, so that we deserved to die; Christ used His mortality well to restore us. Our malady arose through the corrupted spirit of a woman; from the incorrupted flesh of a woman proceeded our salvation.[25]

Augustine would call our enjoyment of the splendid eloquence of this passage foolishness, insisting that a proper reading of his rhetoric, like a proper hearing of vocal music, should not focus on the intricate medium, but on the wisdom conveyed by that medium; and the passage does exemplify the impressive capacity of formal antithesis to convey the paradoxical doctrines of Christianity. But surely we may detect in Augustine not only the ambivalence he acknowledges about the temptations of church music, but a deeper and more personal ambivalence about language. Like Plato, Augustine endorses an ideal of simplicity which he cannot himself achieve; at crucial moments in his writing, rhetorical flourishes infect his style, even when they cannot be defended as effective means to communicate Christian wisdom. In the *Confessions,* for example, the image of Carthage as a "frying

25. *De Doctrina,* I, 14; p. 15. The chiasmus is strong enough to come across in translation, but of course even more impressive in the Latin: "Serpentis sapientiam decepti sumus, Dei stultitia liberamur. Quemadmodum autem illa Sapientia vocabatur, erat autem stultitia contemnentibus Deum; sic ista quae vocatur stultitia, Sapientia est vicentibus diabolum. Nos immortalitate male usi sumus, ut moreremur; Christus mortalitate bene usus est, ut viveremus. Corruptio animo feminae ingressus est morbus; integro corpore feminae processit salus" (Migne, *Patrologia Latina,* XXXIV, col. 24).

pan" of sensual temptations is based on the comic rhyme between *Carthago* (Carthage) and *sartago* (frying pan). In this case the sound of the words is not a medium for meaning but a determinant of meaning, as had been the case in the intricately musical poetry of ancient Greece. Despite Augustine's sincere desire to *use* the powers of *mousike* for doctrinal purposes, rather than enjoying them for their own sake, his rhetoric frequently exemplifies the capacity of *mousike* to survive as a creative principle, even in a hostile environment.

Despite such interesting lapses in his own work, Augustine's similar treatment of rhetoric and music, a comparison repeated by many later ecclesiastical writers, emphasizes the dangers inherent in both practices, not least their association with those elements of pagan culture the Christians hoped to discourage. The elaborate technical refinements of the rhetorician, like the virtuoso skills of the musician, were too likely to draw attention to themselves for their own sakes; a church seeking to spread its gospel, to make and keep converts in all classes of society, had to regard both rhetoric and music with caution. In both cases, Christians attempted to substitute elements brought into the cultural stream from Judaism, melodic and linguistic formulae free of association with paganism. We have already seen how melodies taken from the synagogue, though doubtless combined with Hellenistic material, gave early church music its own identity, with interesting poetic consequences. The special qualities of the Hebrew language, even in translation, had a similar effect on Latin style, as Raby argues in a discussion of Jerome's *Vulgate:*

> The mystical fervour of the prophets, the melancholy of the penitential psalms or of the *Lamentations* could not be rendered in Latin without giving that severe and logical language a strange flexibility, an emotional and symbolical quality which had been foreign to its nature. The whole literary imagination of the West was to be fed on the sonorous sentences of the Latin Bible, and Christian poetry, though true so long to its learned traditions, could not escape the spell or fail to learn the new language. (pp. 10–11)

Among the poets who learned that new language was Augustine. Despite his training in classical literature, and despite the extensive knowledge of quantitative verse he displays in the *De Musica,* Augustine's *Psalm against the Donatists,* as Raby notes, "is constructed in long strophes each of which begins with a letter of the alphabet; each line ends on the vowel *e* or *ae,* and there is a refrain which besides being linked to the strophe by its end-rhyme possesses also an internal rime.

> omnes qui gaudetis de pace, modo verum iudicate."

[All you who rejoice in peace, only judge the truth.] (pp. 20–21)

As that line shows, the verse form is not quantitative at all, but syllabic. The alphabetic arrangement, an effective mnemonic device, was surely borrowed from such Old Testament Psalms as 119, in which all the lines of each strophe begin with the same letter of the Hebrew alphabet, and the syllabic arrangement may have had a Semitic origin as well. The rhyme, more frequent in Latin rhetorical prose than in classical poetry, also serves a mnemonic function. And Augustine tells us specifically *(Retractions,* I, 19) that he wrote the psalm to be sung *(cantaretur)* by the congregation. While we have no precise idea what the music was like, the formal features of the text strongly suggest that Augustine wrote it to fit a simple syllabic setting which would itself have helped impress the polemical truths of the words on the minds of the singers.

But these small Hebrew influences on Latin prose and verse could hardly alter the continuing importance of classical literature, which remained a basic component of the educational curriculum. In music, as we have seen, the low status of performers and the absence of documents made a thorough Christian reform possible; but in poetry, there was no way to reduce the importance of Virgil. Even Augustine, despite his histrionic desire to "forget the wanderings of Aeneas and all that goes with them" *(Confessions,* I, 13; p. 34), shows the influence of Virgil in all his writings. Like the other fathers, Augustine approaches ancient literature as he approaches ancient music theory: he emphasizes those parts of its content which he finds consonant with Christian faith, and allegorizes the rest.

The simplest argument for the continued teaching of pagan

poetry in a Christian world was its valuable moral content; Augustine puts it succinctly:

> We should not think that we ought not to learn literature because Mercury is said to be its inventor, nor that because the pagans dedicated temples to Justice and Virtue, and adored in stones what should be performed in the heart, we should therefore avoid justice and virtue. Rather, every good and true Christian should understand that wherever he may find truth, it is his Lord's. *(De Doctrina* II, 18; p. 54)

Finding that truth may require discarding some elements of pagan literature, but the Christian will be able to distinguish between idolatrous superstition and valuable wisdom. Like the ancient Israelites, who carried off treasures when they made their exodus from Egypt, Christian converts will salvage whatever is valuable as they make their spiritual exodus from paganism:

> The teachings of the pagans contain not only simulated and superstitious imaginings and grave burdens of unnecessary labor, which each one of us leaving the society of pagans under the leadership of Christ ought to abominate and avoid, but also liberal disciplines more suited to the uses of truth, and some most useful precepts concerning morals. *(De Doctrina* II, 40; p. 75)

This willingness to find "Egyptian gold" in pagan literature was a more generous attitude than the Christians showed toward pagan music. But if one denies the old definition of art as imitation, as Augustine clearly does in the *De Musica,* one is denying music any explicit claim to have content. Literature, by contrast, can contain "useful precepts concerning morals," and can also be interpreted allegorically; such interpretation was another way to redeem classical poetry. The methods of scriptural interpretation outlined in the *De Doctrina* were widely applied to pagan texts by later thinkers: Odysseus and Aeneas became types for Christ, and Virgil, on the strength of an allegorical reading of the fourth *Eclogue,* was regarded as an inspired prophet.

But Augustine had a more abstract and mystical way to justify the preservation and study of classical poetry. Ancient music theorists, as we noted at the beginning of this chapter, had classified quantitative meters in a mathematical way, and Augustine's *De Musica* allegorizes this classification, locating a Christian truth in the numerical principles of quantitative meter, principles that were passing out of general use and knowledge as classical Latin degenerated. Not only did Augustine himself write poetry by the newer syllabic system, as we have seen in his *Psalm*, but he misunderstood some key terms in the old system, reversing *arsis* and *thesis*, for example. Still, the subject of the *De Musica* is neither the content of ancient poetry nor the metrical rules of its waning system; as Franco Amerio explains, "it is a true treatise on rhythm based upon the material most accessible to everyone, that is upon the word, which is not considered as such, but simply as a sound and motion."[26] For Augustine, the rules of quantitative poetry provided a clear example of *ratio*—numerical proportion and higher reason—which he was more than willing to separate from the other aspects of that poetry. In Book VI, the *magister* persuades the *discipulus* that his pleased response to well-proportioned rhythms is the result of an innate sense of order, analogous in its own way to the ordering of God's universe:

> And so that verse proposed by us, *"Deus creator omnium,"* [significantly, the beginning of another hymn by Ambrose], sounds with the harmony of numbers not only to the ears, but even more is most pleasing in truth and wholeness to the soul's sentiment. Unless perhaps you are moved by the stupidity, to speak mildly, of those who deny that anything can be made from nothing, even though God almighty be said to have made it. Can [bodies of plants and animals] be made of elements and these elements not have been made of nothing? For which among them is more ordinary and lowly than earth? Yet first it has the general form of a body where a unity and numbers and order are clearly shown to be. For any part of it, no matter how small, must be extended from an indivisible point in length, third takes on breadth, and fourth height, to fill the body. From where then is the measure of this progression of one to four? Where, I ask, do these things come from, if not from the highest and eternal rule of num-

---

26. *Il 'De Musica' di S. Agostino,* as translated in William G. Waite, *The Rhythm of Twelfth-Century Polyphony,* p. 30.

bers, likeness, equality, and order? And if you abstract these things from earth, it will be nothing. And therefore God almighty has made earth, and earth is made from nothing.[27]

By celebrating quantitative meter as a symbolic system of numbers, Augustine forged a connection between Christian musical allegory and pagan literature, redeeming poetry for the rhythm of its making. He also provided an explanation for the effects the rhetoricians had always claimed for various rhythms: the human body and soul, themselves created by a rational and orderly process, naturally respond to the similar "harmony of numbers" in poetry. Thanks to the preservation and influence of the *De Musica*,[28] this idea, variously understood at various times, justified the elaborate numerical methods of construction we shall be examining in medieval poetry and music. Such devices are usually referred to as "number symbolism," but many are so hidden as to raise the question of who might decipher the symbols. No matter: the makers of such works could believe with Augustine that the numbers sounding deep within them were a version of the numbers of Creation itself. R. P. Blackmur, a modern mystic, understood this doctrine perfectly:

> Number as an expression of pattern, though it is always available, seems always in the instance a fresh discovery, and never, after the event, seems an accident. Indeed, it is only matters of number that seem absolute law, an absolute coverage of ignorance. Better still, for Augustine, the patterns of number, in poetry and music, served as reminders of the skills of thought which have nothing to do with the language of words. For him the meanings of words were arbitrary, and by human authority, while the meanings of things, such as those which numbers moved, were true. . . . To Augustine the numbers made the form of the meaning according to laws which, with licenses of silence and elision allowed for, were absolute, were of interest in verse because of universal application, and were themselves a kind of limit to human knowl-

27. *De Musica*, VI, 57; in Taliaferro, pp. 196-97, again with minor changes and ellipses.
28. For an impressive account of the proliferation and influence of Augustine's treatise, see Waite, pp. 35-37.

edge. This is his way of claiming poetry as a form of knowledge, a form of being, or a form of revelation.[29]

Sequences and Tropes

For centuries after Augustine, the leaders of the church, following his lead, attempted to suppress the expressive claims of melody and rhetoric by insisting that their enjoyment was improper, while systematically allegorizing both music theory and pagan literature, the other pair of diagonal coordinates on our chart. But as Augustine's own example shows, rhetoric was difficult to suppress: despite the strictures of the fathers, and despite the disappearance of some important ancient treatises, the rhetorical figures of the ancients remained a source upon which poets could and did draw, especially during the so-called Carolingian Renaissance of the ninth century; the pervasive habit of allegory, developed as a method of scriptural interpretation and a way of Christianizing pagan literature, also had important effects on the content and imagery of medieval poetry. But in music, theory and practice remained separate. The elaborate musical allegories by which the fathers preserved a version of ancient theory, though repeated in treatise after treatise, had little measurable effect on the developing melodic technique of liturgical chant. The original theoretical lore of the ancients was garbled in transmission and increasingly misunderstood: when the "church modes" were devised as a way of classifying the huge, orally developed body of chants, they carried ancient Greek names, but those labels were incorrect because medieval theorists no longer realized that the Greeks had quoted their scales from top to bottom. And in practice, many chants did not conform to the supposed rules of these modes; the attempt to impose an insufficiently understood body of ancient theory upon an orally evolving musical practice was doomed to failure.[30]

29. "St. Augustine's *De Musica*. A Synopsis," in *Language as Gesture*, p. 367.

30. On the comic error by which the names of the modes were reversed, see Reese, pp. 153-56; Caldwell, pp. 39-41. On the extent to which the theory of modes fails to account for actual chant, see Hendrik van den Werf, *The Chansons of the Troubadours and Trouvères*, p. 58:"We have to conclude that there is a wide dichotomy between the writings about scales by the learned authors of the Middle Ages and the way in which scales occur . . . even in plain chant."

Gregory the Great, Pope from 590–604, may serve as an example of the anti-musical, anti-rhetorical attitudes which flourished in these years, against which there were nonetheless important developments in both areas. He is, as Raby has suggested, "the complete medievalist."

> Gregory is Augustine without the classical tinge. Augustine had once loved Cicero and the pathos of Virgil had moved him to tears; but Gregory upbraided a Gallic bishop for his interest in grammar and in a celebrated passage asserted a preference for a barbarous style to one which observed the rules of Donatus. . . . The general tendency of Gregory's mind was against the old culture, with its still recent association with the hateful memories of paganism. His favourite reading was the Vulgate, over which he pondered long and profoundly, drawing out with the aid of his sombre imagination the mysteries hidden in the sacred text. . . . His outlook on the world was to hold sway, at any rate until the twelfth century, and his shadow is over ecclesiastical literature until the days of Abelard. (pp. 122–23)

Gregory's shadow is still over ecclesiastical chant, which bears his name, and he was frequently painted with the Holy Ghost as a dove dictating melodies to him.[31] But the reality behind these legends is political, not musical. Far from expanding the role of music in the church, Gregory sought to control it: in 595, at the Concilium Romanum, he criticized the clergy for neglecting their pastoral responsibilities in order to improve their singing, and assigned the task of singing the service to those in the lower ranks; at the same time he reorganized the school in Rome which trained singers, and standardized the liturgy.[32] The process by which this standard liturgy and its chants became virtually uniform throughout the church probably began before Gregory and certainly continued after him; Charlemagne, two hundred years later, was burning Ambrosian liturgical books in the interest of church unity. The participation of both Pope and Emperor in this enterprise suggests its purpose: to discourage local or even national

31. For reproductions and analyses of several of these pictures, see Treitler, "Homer and Gregory," pp. 337-40.
32. See Lang, *Music in Western Civilization*, p. 64.

styles in church music by enforcing melodic uniformity, just as the Latin mass, until recent times, enforced linguistic uniformity. And the process was apparently successful: the oldest chant books we have, though they come from various countries, preserve what Jacques Handschin considers "a remarkable unity of melodic tradition."[33]

The extremely imprecise nature of the musical notation used in this period makes it remarkable that Gregory should have attempted such a reform, and even more remarkable that his followers should have achieved even a partial success. The Oxyrhynchos papyrus is the only Christian document we have that uses the precise ancient Greek letter-notation to indicate pitches; Boethius, in 500, describes that notation as an archaic device no longer in use.[34] In its place grew up a much less precise "neumatic" or "cheironomic" notation which reminded singers of familiar melodic *patterns,* not single pitches or precise intervals. Like the alphabet from which the Greeks adopted it, the old system of letter-notation sought to reduce sounds to single elements; the neumes of the new system were more like Chinese ideograms: most of them represented at least two notes, and they were frequently combined into more complex composite shapes. St. Augustine's remark about "intervals of acute and grave tones" in the passage from the *De Musica* quoted above is an important piece of evidence here, for it explains the origin of the neumes, and suggests the existence of some kind of proto-neumatic notation as early as the fourth century. According to Higini Anglès, "it is now agreed on all hands that the Greek accents gave birth to the Latin neumes in their primitive, embryonic state. The acute and grave accents are therefore regarded as the origin of the Latin neumes."[35] Once again, as it had centuries earlier in ancient Greece, music borrowed a linguistic sign as the basis for a notation. But there are curious ironies. In ancient times, when pitch-accents were a

33. See his useful chapter, "Trope, Sequence, and Conductus," in vol. II of *The New Oxford History of Music,* p. 141.

34. In *De Institutione Musica,* IV, 3; see Caldwell, *Medieval Music,* p. 27. Caldwell's concentration on matters of notation, which extends to brave attempts at transcription of manuscripts others label indecipherable, makes his book particularly valuable to the serious student.

35. In his article on "Gregorian Chant," in vol. II of *The New Oxford History of Music,* p. 106. Anglès cites both Augustine and his student Quodvultdeus; see p. 108.

part of normal speech and a principle of musical composition, they were not normally written down; the practice of using accents in manuscripts originated in Hellenistic Alexandria. But in the fifth century A.D., when some kind of primitive neumatic notation based on those same pitch accents was replacing letter-notation, spoken pitch-accent was long dead; the Greek of the early Christian era, like Latin, had a stress-accent. Yet somehow the old principle of melody construction by accent passed into Gregorian settings of Latin texts, even though accent there was a matter of stress: Gregorian melody is shaped to fit the word-accents of the Latin liturgy; high notes usually fall on stressed syllables.[36]

That correspondence of melodic shape and linguistic accent probably helped early Christian singers remember their chant melodies, as did the fact that early chant rarely employed intervals larger than a fifth, but as Gustave Reese explains, the imprecision of neumatic notation clearly necessitated a great deal of rote memorization:

> The neumes were written above the text and are spoken of as being *in campo aperto,* in an open field—that is, there are no staff-lines to show the precise intervals desired. How then, did the early singers read this notation? It must have been necessary for them first to memorize the whole liturgical repertory; then the notation became a guide, recalling the contours of this or that known melody. (pp. 133–34)

Another mnemonic principle, which we have already seen in both Homeric formulae and Ambrosian hymns, was doubtless central to this process of memorization as well: a phrase which has both a verbal and a melodic identity is easier to remember than either a phrase of wordless melody or a phrase of tuneless poetry. So it should not surprise us that the problem of memorization was most acute in the case of the wordless melismata sung to the final vowel of the word *alleluia.*

Nor should it surprise us that these melismata continued to develop and change after the Gregorian reform. Melodic creativity had to find some outlet, and an effectively wordless part of the liturgy was an obvious opportunity. In the eighth and ninth cen-

---

36. See Reese, p. 166, Anglès, p. 110.

turies, new, longer melismata were added; unlike the Gregorian chants to which they were appended, these melodies had a musical form, not a verbal one: they were constructed in shapely melodic phrases, each of which was repeated, often antiphonally. Despite this formal regularity, singers found the melismata difficult to remember; the eventual solution to this problem, a solution of great importance for the history of music and poetry, was of course to supply texts, and the writing of such texts provided an important outlet for literary creativity, which had been stifled by Gregory's hostility to rhetoric. The end result was the sequence, a composite musical and literary form in which two choirs sang together on an opening phrase, antiphonally on a series of parallel phrases with repeating melody and varied words, and together again on a closing phrase, producing the form: A BB′ CC′ DD′ . . . Z.[37]

We know of one important case in which the impetus for writing sequence texts was mnemonic: Notker Balbulus, a monk at the famous monastery of St. Gall and one of the greatest of sequence poets, wrote a *Proemium* to a collection of his sequences in which he describes his own difficulties in memorizing the melismata, which he calls the *longissimae melodiae*. One day, it seems, a monk from another monastery arrived, bringing a chant book with words written under the melismata. With some help from the abbot Yson, who had the idea of making the texts exactly syllabic, one syllable for each note, Notker wrote similar texts for the melodies used in his own monastery.[38] In his hands, the sequence became much more than a handy mnemonic device; it proved to be a genuinely new and highly expressive composite form. As Richard Crocker, a leading modern authority on the sequence, explains:

> There was no precedent (certainly not a classical one) for the particular shape of the 9th-century sequence, and the way the bicola [poetic couplets] were integrated into the musical couplet-structure.

37. I adapt this schematic account of the form from Dag Norberg, *Introduction a l'étude de la versification latine médiévale*, p. 171.

38. For the Latin text of Notker's *Proemium*, see Wolfram von den Steinen, *Notker der Dichter*, vol. II, pp. 8-11.

Crocker lists the following new modes of organization in the sequence form:

> ... syllable count, close duplication in the two lines of a couplet, uniform cadences, direct melodic progressions emphasizing a restricted tonal locus, clear layout of phrases in progressions from shorter to longer, lower to higher, motivic systems that bind a piece together by judicious repetition of short melodic patterns.[39]

The writers of sequence texts, since their work was neither quantitative poetry nor strophic accentual verse like that used for hymns, referred to their texts as prose; indeed, *prosa* was as frequent a label for this form as *sequentia*. But the musical structure, itself a great step forward from the loose, accentually determined melody of Gregorian chant, constrained a patterning of language sufficiently formal for us to recognize it as poetry—in Notker's case, poetry of a high order indeed. Because of its musically determined symmetries, the sequence proved a peculiarly appropriate vehicle for the densely allegorical content with which such writers as Notker loved to work.

We may see all these developments in Notker's sequence for the feast day of a martyr:[40]

[A]Quid tu,vir- go [1]ma-ter, plo-ras, Ra-chel for-mo-sa,[2] Cu-ius vul-tus Ja-cob de-lec-tat?
[What are you bewailing, virgin, mother, beautiful Rachel, whose face delights Jacob?]

[3] Ceu so-ro - ris a - ni-cu-lae
[4] Lip-pi-tu - do e - um ju-vet!
[As if the bleary eyes of your little old sister could please him!]

---

39. *The Early Medieval Sequence*. pp. 421-23.

40. The text and line-numbering scheme follow von den Steinen, vol. II, p. 86. The melody was first published by Anselm Schubiger, *Die Sängerschule St. Gallens*, example 15, but I follow here the much improved transcription of Crocker, p. 132, transposing it into a more familiar clef and writing out the two neumatic decorations. On the question of the B or B-flat in line 3, see Crocker, p. 122. The ensuing analysis is partially dependent on Crocker's account of the music.

[5] Ter-ge, ma -ter, flu-en -tes o - cu - los!
[6]Quam te de -cent ge -na -rum ri- mu - lae?
[Mother, dry your streaming eyes! How can fissures in your cheeks become you?]

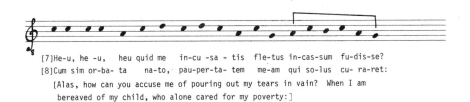

[7]He-u, he -u,   heu quid me   in-cu -sa - tis fle-tus in-cas-sum fu-dis-se?
[8]Cum sim or-ba- ta   na-to, pau-per-ta- tem   me-am qui so-lus cu- ra-ret:
[Alas, how can you accuse me of pouring out my tears in vain? When I am
bereaved of my child, who alone cared for my poverty:]

[9]Qui non hos-ti-bus ce-de-ret   an-gus-tos ter-mi-nos quos mihi Ja-cob ad-qui-si-vit:
[10] Qui-que sto-li-dus fratribus quos mul-tos,pro do-lor, ex-tu-li, es-set pro-fu-tu-rus.
[Who would not yield to the enemy those narrow bounds that Jacob won for me:
and who has gone before his dull brothers, the many ones I bore, oh pain.]

[ZI] Num-quid flendus est is-te [ZII] Qui reg -num pos-se -dit cae -les-te?
[But why must that one be bewailed, who has taken heavenly power?]

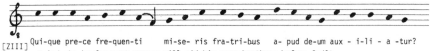

[ZIII] Qui-que pre-ce fre-quen-ti   mi-se- ris fra-tri-bus   a- pud de-um aux - i-li - a -tur?
[And who by frequent prayer will aid his poor brothers before God?]

The large divisions of Notker's text correspond precisely to
the large divisions of the melody. The opening lines (A, 1–2) are
mysterious, both textually and musically. In the first unison
phrase, as in the corresponding phrases of all of Notker's sequences, we hear a memory of the solemn intonation of the word

Al - le - lu-i - a

and in the first words, we seem to hear a memory of the question posed to Mary Magdalene by the risen Christ, the Vulgate text of which reads, *"Mulier, quid ploras"* (John 20. 15). But Notker uses the words *"virgo"* and *"mater,"* neither of which applies to Mary Magdalene, making that interpretation seem impossible. Mary the mother of Christ was both *"virgo"* and *"mater,"* but that interpretation also seems impossible when the speaker goes on to address instead the Rachel of the book of Genesis, emphasizing her physical beauty while asking her why she weeps. Musically, this phrase cadences on F, while all the others cadence on G; at the end of line 2, we are likely to be guessing incorrectly about both the mode of the music and the point of the text. In the rest of the first large section, the melody finds its way to the G mode and the text concentrates on Rachel. Lines 3 and 4, with wider leaps and an almost teasing melody, suggest that Rachel is weeping because she is jealous of her weak-eyed older sister Leah; lines 5 and 6, with a lower range and a smoother contour, tenderly urge Rachel to dry her own eyes and regain her beauty.

The second large section, lines 7–10, has a consistently higher range, mainly involving the pitches  . The unsettled melody of the first section and the very low range of line 6 make the higher pitches and melodic clarity of this section a dramatic shift. Notker takes advantage of this clear musical break to change speakers; now Rachel answers, giving a strong reason for her tears: she has lost her son. These expressive phrases are longer and more closely connected than those in the first section; the melody of line 9 (and 10) is an expanded version of the melody of line 7 (and 8), and the phrases have identical cadences (indicated here by the bracket). In the text, the levels of allegory expand greatly in this section. We are still aware of the Rachel of Genesis, whose son Joseph went ahead (*"esset profuturus"*) into Egypt because of the machinations of his brothers (*"stolidis fratribus"*). But the Rachel of Genesis, who died in childbirth, never wept for the loss of a son; it was the prophet Jeremiah, lamenting the exile of the *tribes* of Joseph and Benjamin, who first cast her in that allegorical role: "A voice is heard in Ramah, lamentation and bitter weeping. Rachel is weeping for her children;

she refuses to be comforted for her children, because they are not" (Jeremiah 31.15). And the evangelist Matthew, describing Herod's slaughter of the Innocents, quoted these lines as a prophecy fulfilled (2. 18). The military terms of Notker's text (*"hostibus . . . angustos terminos"*) recall the grim events of Jeremiah, and the occasion, the feast of a martyr, reminds us that the Innocents were sometimes referred to as the first martyrs. In a larger allegory, Rachel is a type for the church, the true bride of Christ, in contrast to Leah, a type for the weak-eyed and uncomprehending Synagogue.[41] Following this interpretation, any martyr is a true son of the Church, helping her defend the narrow boundaries won for her by Christ, here represented by his type Jacob. Indeed, the emphasis on the loss of a single son, rather than children, suggests that our earlier guess about the Virgin is possible after all. The central section of Notker's sequence touches upon all these allegories and is at the same time a sustained expressive cry of grief.

Finally, with a downward shift of range, the choirs join again in two phrases which rhyme both in music and in words (Z I and Z II; the double bracket shows the pairing of *"Num*quid" and "reg*num*," as well as the more obvious rhyme of *"iste"* and *"caeleste"*). These lines recall and fulfill the opening lines: the same speaker again discourages Rachel (and Mary and the Church) from weeping, but this time for the more serious reason that she need not weep for Him who reigns not merely in some earthly boundaries but in the celestial kingdom. As line Z III makes clear, the Church should rejoice in its martyrs (and, by typological extension, its Saviour); by their intercession salvation comes to the *"miseris fratribus."* The melody of that last line recalls the shape of the middle section, as does the repetition of the word *"fratribus"* from line 10. In this new context, we may reinterpret the words *"esset profuturus"* (line 10): they apply not only to Joseph going into Egypt, but to the risen Christ, who is described in Mark's gospel as "going before" his disciples into Galilee (16.7), and who tells Mary Magdalene, in the same conversation with which Notker apparently began, "go to my brethren (*ad fratres*) and say to them, I am ascending to my Father" (John 20.17). The musical

41. This is the allegory emphasized in von den Steinen's interpretation; see p. 399.

and poetic length of line Z III (22 syllables) is identical to that of lines A, 1, and 2 taken together; beginning and ending are linked formally as well as doctrinally.

To modern minds, there may appear to be far too many allegories here, and the evident conflicts between them may seem irreconcilable. But as D. W. Robertson has taught us, we must "contrast a dominant medieval convention, the tendency to think in terms of symmetrical patterns, characteristically arranged with reference to an abstract hierarchy, with a dominant modern convention, the tendency to think in terms of opposites whose dynamic interaction leads to a synthesis."[42] For Notker, there is no need to synthesize the various Biblical references to Rachel used here, or even the implied equations of Rachel with the Church, the Virgin, and Mary Magdalene. The confusion of sons and husbands produced by the use of both Jacob and Joseph as types for Christ is also left unresolved. All these allegories are parallel versions of the same truth, just as the different poetic phrases used for each melodic phrase are formally parallel. Indeed, Notker wrote another complete text to this melody, for the Sunday after Easter; evidently, he did not believe that a melody had to have only one kind of meaning, any more than he believed that a reference to Rachel had to mean only the character as she appears in Genesis. Just as many different texts might be fitted to a melody whose original meaning had been *alleluia*, so many different allegories might be used to express a truth, one of whose names was the New Song. At the most basic level, the fitting of several texts to one melody provides a model of allegorical thought, in which the music may be thought of as the unchanging but infinitely variable truth of God's order, while the texts represent various more specific versions of that truth, all ultimately one universal hymn of praise.

In the new relations between music and poetry worked out in such sequences lay the seeds of much future development for both arts. The notion of parallel lines of differing length, necessitated by the musical repetition, led not only to end rhyme but to all kinds of internal chiming. Lines 9 and 10 are particularly striking in this regard; I have marked the more obvious concords:

42. *A Preface to Chaucer*, p. 6.

Qui non hosti bus ceder et an gustos terminos quos mi hi Jacob ad qui sivit:
Qui que stolidus fratri bus, quos multos pro dolor, extu li, ess et profuturus.

As we shall see, the troubadours and trouvères of the next several centuries would be fascinated by such subtle patterns of repetition in sound, and would make from them a profoundly musical poetry. Musically, the formal principles of the sequence—repetition and parallelism, particularly at cadences—would remain basic principles in the making of melodies until the death of the tonal system 1000 years later.

In the early years at least, the order of composition of the sequence was the order we have described in Notker's practice: a poet fitted words to an extant melody. The other new form which arose in this period, the trope, involved new music and new words, made at the same time. As Paul Evans explains, in a fine recent study:

> Not only is the music of the trope newly composed, but it and the text are simultaneously conceived. . . . A trope is not constructed by adding words to a preexisting melody. . . . On the contrary, it is a true musical composition in which new words are set to music, and the whole serves to embellish the liturgical chant.[43]

A trope could be placed before a part of the liturgy as a new preface to it, or interpolated within almost any liturgical text. A *Kyrie* with additions between the words "*Kyrie*" and "*eleison*," for example, was called a troped *Kyrie* or (more picturesquely) a "*Kyrie cum farsura*," a *Kyrie* with stuffing. Here is part of such a text:

> *Kyrie*, rex, genitor
> Ingenite,
> Vera essentia,
> *Eleison*.

---

43. *The Early Trope Repertory of Saint Martial de Limoges*, pp. 8-9. Evans' work, which includes transcriptions of all the Proper tropes and some of the Ordinary tropes from one of the St. Martial manuscripts, is a valuable corrective to the looser terminology of some standard reference works.

Kyrie, qui nos tuae
    Imaginis
    Signasti specie
    Eleison.

Kyrie, luminis fons
    Et rerum conditor
    Eleison.

[*Lord*, king, begetter / Unbegotten / True essence, / *Have mercy.* //
Lord, who has marked us / With the form / Of thy image /
Have mercy. // *Lord*, fountain of light / And maker of the
world, / *Have mercy.*][44]

To trope a *Kyrie* or any other prayer was to stuff it with additional meanings, and the metaphor of stuffing must have come
readily to people whose accounts of scriptural meaning so often
used such metaphors as grain and chaff. When the text to be
troped came from the Old Testament, the troping interpolations
frequently clarified a typological connection to the New Testament, the same allegorical method we have seen in Notker's sequence. Thus, for example, an introit using the text of Psalm 118,
in which the speaker describes being persecuted by his enemies,
was troped for use on the feast day of St. Stephen with interpolations which made the Psalm into an explicit prediction of Stephen's fate.[45]

As the sequence, with its formal parallelism, provided an appropriate vehicle for a literature which argued that Old Testament events were typologically parallel to New Testament events,
the trope, with its possibilities for interpolation, provided a form
which could be opened up to accommodate new allegories, new
glosses, new melodic extensions. Indeed, tropes were often
troped again; a form that allowed such activity was particularly
convenient for the kind of poetry that arose from medieval religious thought, with its accretions of meaning.

The relations between text and music in the trope, however,
proceeded in the opposite direction from those in the sequence.
In the sequence, as we have seen, the process of fitting a text to

44. Quoted in Norberg, p. 178.
45. Evans gives this text (p. 7) and translates it (p. 57).

an extant melody influenced the form of the text. In the trope, the earliest texts were probably prose, but Carolingian poetry in the old quantitative meters, now sometimes ignorantly scanned by accent rather than by real quantity, was used as well, and hexameters actually became the dominant form in the tropes Evans has transcribed. The musical settings of these poems, says Evans, "ignore vowel quantity and rely only on the stress accent of each word as the basic principle of text declamation. In addition, text elision is ignored in the musical settings." Evans concludes from these facts that "it is unlikely that the functions of poet and composer were generally exercised by the same man," but he recognizes a more general way in which the form of the text influenced the form of the melody:"the length and uniformity of the hexameter trope lines give a conciseness of phrase to the melodies, and frequently there is a sense of symmetrical organization controlling the relationship between the individual trope lines within the framework of the chant" (pp. 70–73). Poetic form, even an archaic form imperfectly understood by the composer, nonetheless affected musical form.

Thus formal influences in this period moved in both directions: in the sequence, musical repetition encouraged new kinds of poetic parallelism; in the trope, poetic uniformity encouraged melodic concision. Many other works had forms which fell between categories; for these, the term *versus* was used as a catchall label, and as Crocker has recently shown, these forms also involved influences between the two arts:

> Much of the new poetry . . . had . . . complex structures, lying in between hymns and the irregular couplets of prose [sequences]. . . . Whatever the poetic shape, it was translated directly into musical terms through the close relationship of text and melody. . . . Just as the poet now exercised increasing control over the interior of the poetic line, making his stresses fall regularly every two or three syllables—even using extensive internal rhyme—so the composer made the interior of his melodic line increasingly related to the overall structure.[46]

46. *A History of Musical Style*, p. 48; Crocker analyzes a *versus* from St. Martial which verifies these generalizations, pp. 49-50. All future citations of Crocker refer to this useful textbook.

Under the influence of the trope and the *versus* forms, writers of sequences moved toward a much more regular poetry now called the "second sequence style"; rather than writing texts for extant melodies, they began to compose both words and music for new sequences. In this style, typified by the works of Adam of St. Victor (c. 1150), we may recognize the accentual-syllabic, rhyming, strophic forms which would become standard in later European poetry. The opening lines of one of Adam's sequences will suffice as an example:

> Salve, mater salvatoris
> vas electum, vas honoris
> vas caelestis gratiae,
>
> Ab aeterno vas provisum,
> vas insigne, vas excisum
> manu sapientiae.

[Hail, mother of the Saviour / chosen vessel, vessel of honor / vessel of heavenly grace, // Vessel provided from eternity, / vessel marked out, vessel carved out / by the hand of Wisdom.][47]

This will strike most of us as "normal" poetry, and as we have seen, the story of its development is as much the story of musical form as of poetic form. Not only is it impossible to explain the development of Christian liturgical music without considering how its composers responded to the task of setting various kinds of texts; it is equally impossible to account for the development of medieval Latin poetry without considering how its poets responded to the task of supplying texts for the various kinds of music they heard around them.[48] When the new poetic forms

47. Following the text of Handschin, who gives the complete sequence with a transcription of its music, pp. 162-64.

48. For an admirable account, with many interesting details not included here, see Norberg, ch. VII, "La Versification rhythmique et la Musique." As we have seen, music was one of the ways poets moved from quantitative verse to accentual verse. But ironically, in at least one instance, music probably helped to preserve something like classical meter. Speaking of Old Irish hymns, Norberg makes this ingenious argument:"One may perhaps suppose that this poetry was created in the following fashion: someone wrote a text for an already extant melody following syllabic principles and without paying attention to the quantitative poetic form which had actually been there from the start and for which the

came to be classified, in later medieval treatises on Latin rhythm, the terminology employed was a hodgepodge of labels, some properly classical and quantitative, others newly coined. But virtually all such treatises acknowledge the role of music in determining poetic form.[49] Despite patristic claims of precedence for the text, and despite the paralyzing effects of the Gregorian attempt to standardize liturgical melodies, the sequence and the trope may stand as evidence of the creative symbiosis of music and poetry in this period. Neither art led the way continuously in the development of these forms; as our examples have shown, some new poetic styles arose in response to changes in musical form, and some new patterns of musical phrasing arose in response to poetic form. This flexibility and cooperation, this willingness of poets and composers to learn from and adapt to the practices of one another, led to richer and more rapid developments in both arts than might have occurred had the arts been thought of as separate.

One well-known example of this symbiosis is the way the form of the trope led to the first timid attempts at church drama. The famous *Quem quaeritis* trope, added to the Introit of the Easter Mass, exploits the dramatic possibilities inherent in the antiphonal form; it is a sung dialogue between the three Marys at the tomb and the angel. We know that it was actually performed as a drama at least as early as 980, and that the next two centuries saw a great many more such dramas, including, not surprisingly, a dramatization of the slaughter of the Innocents incorporating the highly dramatic sequence of Notker.[50] Historians of the drama have long recognized the importance of these plays, which signal the rebirth of drama in the West after a sleep of centuries, and which stand at the beginning of paths that lead to the national dramas of Europe. It is less frequently pointed out that these plays began as tropes, and that, like other tropes, they are therefore a product of creative interaction between music and text.

---

melody had probably been composed" (pp. 136-37). On the whole, however, as Norberg makes especially clear in his conclusion (pp. 184-190), music was the means by which poetry liberated itself from the ancient rules of quantity.

49. The standard collection of such treatises is that edited by Giovanni Mari, *I Trattati Medievali di Ritmica Latina.*

50. See W. L. Smoldon, "Liturgical Drama," in vol. II of *The New Oxford History of Music,* pp. 180, 203-04.

Practical Developments in Theory

The composition of new music as a result of the popularity of sequences, tropes, and church dramas meant that the mnemonic problem Notker had set out to solve, the necessity for singers to memorize a large repertory, remained urgent. Around the year 1000, it was finally solved in its own terms by a combination of various earlier improvements upon neumatic notation. For centuries, some scribes had "heightened" the neumes as a vague spatial indication of their relative pitch; increasingly, they came to use a "dry point" line, drawn without ink, as a point of reference for this heightening. Evidently this practice proved useful; later manuscripts show the line in colored ink. Later came two lines; still later a staff, which could show relative pitches more precisely. Medieval treatises, in their enumeration of modes, had employed various systems of letter-notation, though these had never been used to train singers. When a clef, originally a letter, was set at the beginning of a staff, giving one of the lines a fixed pitch, our modern notational system was essentially in place.[51]

Traditionally, the credit for consolidating these systems, doubtless a process contributed to by many hands, has gone to Guido d'Arezzo (c. 980–1050), who also invented a system of scalar syllables *(ut, re, mi, fa, sol, la)* based on the familiar hymn *"Ut queant laxis,"* the lines of which began on those syllables and also happened to begin on rising stepwise pitches. Guido may also have devised a visual mnemonic called the "Guidonian hand," and he caused a sensation by teaching Pope John XIX how to sing a new melody at sight from a part written in staff-notation; as we have seen, such sight-singing was not possible from neumes.[52] Guido's practical use of theory distinguishes him from earlier philosophical theorists, as he himself sometimes recognized:"I have simplified my treatment for the sake of the young, in this not following Boethius, whose treatise is useful to philosophers, but not to singers."[53] He may serve as one example of the new practicality which came into some treatises on music during these years, the consequences of which included not only improved no-

---

51. See Caldwell, *Medieval Music*, pp. 27-29.
52. For a good account, with a picture of the Guidonian hand, see Reese, pp. 149-51.
53. *Epistola de ignoto cantu*, as translated in Strunk, p. 125.

tational and instructional systems, but principles of composition based on actual musical experience, not merely on ancient mystical lore. Aurelian of Réomé, whose treatise *Musica Disciplina* is considerably earlier (c. 843), is a transitional figure in this process: he copies whole chapters from Boethius and Cassiodorus, but he draws his musical examples from the current Gregorian repertoire, shows an active concern for the practical training of singers, and even provides details about fitting together musical and poetic rhythm.[54] The anonymous author of the *Dialogus de Musica* (c. 1000) gives an account of melodic construction strongly dependent on practical considerations, and a general principle of composition which emphasizes the ear: "in any case it is to be observed that we follow these rules only so far as we do not offend against euphony, since it seems to be the whole intent of this art to serve that."[55] Plato, with his abstract interest in mathematical rules, might not have agreed, nor would Augustine have endorsed euphony as a principle; but this monkish author, by endorsing the notion of bending rules to produce pleasing sounds, was feeling his way toward a more expressive aesthetic.

Along with a number of other theorists, these men stand at the beginning of the process by which the ancient gap between *musici* (theorists) and *cantores* (singers) began to close. As we shall see, this process took centuries, and involved many combinations of and compromises between constructive principles derived from classical speculation or Christian allegory and expressive principles discovered in the making of actual music. Even the leaders were hesitant: Guido began one of his treatises by echoing the old Boethian distinction:

> Musicorum et cantorum magna est distantia
> Isti dicunt, illi sciunt, quae componit Musica.
> Nam qui facit, quod non sapit, diffinitur bestia.

[There is a great distance between theorists and singers, / These say, those know, of what music is composed. / For

---

54. See Reese, p. 125. Aurelian's treatise has now been translated by Joseph Ponte.

55. In M. Gerbert, ed., *Scriptores ecclesiastici de musica sacra*, I, 278a. See the discussion of this treatise in Abert, pp. 253-57. Until recently, the *Dialogus* was attributed to Odo of Cluny, but M. Huglo has shown that it is the work of an Italian monk, c. 1000; see *Revue de Musicologie* 55 (1969): 119-71.

whoever does what he does not understand, may be defined as a beast.][56]

But the effect of his career, as we have seen, was to reduce that distance dramatically: he freed even boy singers from rote memorization by selecting from ancient wisdom those principles that could actually help them, and by inventing new pedagogical and notational principles of his own. As Nan Cooke Carpenter explains, his treatises and others from the ninth, tenth, and eleventh centuries

> . . . make it abundantly clear that although instruction in music in the medieval schools followed two trends—*musica theoretica* and *musica practica*—the two were generally quite closely connected. Many of the great teachers distinguished for their work in musical speculation were also prolific in the *ars musica*, famous as singers, poets, and composers.[57]

Indeed, the very lines just quoted from Guido show his skill as a poet and exemplify the combination of ancient wisdom and modern form: they state a truism as old as the Greeks, but their poetic form is rhymed, accentual verse.

In rhetoric, where the gap between theory and practice had always been smaller, there was nonetheless a similar motion toward helping the practitioner in the performance of his daily tasks. James J. Murphy describes this process in the *De Institutione Clericorum* (c. 819) of Rabanus Maurus, who

> . . . offers advice to the preacher gleaned sometimes from Augustine, sometimes from Cicero, and sometimes from *dialectica* or even from personal experience. . . . He is the first of many medieval writers to make a pragmatic choice of only those ideas which are useful to him without swallowing the whole system which gave birth to the ideas.[58]

In short, Rabanus' purpose was to help the average preacher, much as Guido's purpose was to help the average singer; for both men, that purpose meant that practical experience could be at least as important as erudition in ancient lore. By trusting their

56. In Gerbert, *Scriptores*, II, 25.
57. *Music in the Medieval and Renaissance Universities*, p. 30.
58. *Rhetoric in the Middle Ages*, pp. 82-83.

own ears and responses, such thinkers began to break the tyranny of the ancient treatises. But in neither art was this motion toward practical craft decisive. As we shall discover in the next chapter, classical and Christian ideas, especially allegory, retained enormous prestige and importance, and played central parts in new developments in both music and poetry.

3

Polyphonists and Troubadours: Construction and Expression in the Later Middle Ages

Introduction

Two important new developments, polyphonic music in the church and stanzaic secular poetry in the vernacular languages, came into prominence in the eleventh and twelfth centuries, though both had older roots. The Winchester Troper, containing music composed before the Norman Conquest, is the earliest manuscript showing actual performed polyphonic music,[1] and Guillaume of Acquitaine (1071–1127) is the oldest troubadour whose name we know; but theoretical treatises as early as the late ninth century mention *organum*, the practice of singing in parallel fourths, fifths, and octaves, and the earliest troubadour poems we have reveal a highly stylized art, doubtless the result of centuries of unrecorded tradition. The sequence and the trope, in which text and melody had been closely related, may be connected with the origins of both sacred polyphony and vernacular poetry, but the two arts developed in contrasting and somewhat independent ways.

The troubadours adapted the elaborately rhymed stanzaic forms of the "second sequence style" to the vernaculars. Fascinated by the sounds of their syllables, they prided themselves more on inventing new rhyme-schemes than on innovations in content, which tended to be conventionally frozen. In their art, for the first time, poetic form is more complex than musical form, absorbing into itself what had been relations between words and music in earlier times. Though Dante defines poetry as combining

1. See John Caldwell, *Medieval Music*, p. 116.

music and rhetoric, "music" has now become somewhat meta-phorical; poetic form itself has become sufficiently demanding to occupy the attention once devoted to making words fit a pre-ex-isting tune or a musically determined rhythmic scheme. We begin to hear of tunes composed *after* words, and in the later period the tunes, always simpler in their form than the poems, begin to drop away.

Meanwhile musicians made their single most stunning ad-vance: they invented polyphony. I believe they got the idea of combining two or more melodies from the literary notion of alle-gory, realizing that the mystical simultaneity of an Old Testament story and its New Testament analogue could become, in music, actual simultaneity; the earliest evidence we have confirms this hypothesis. Quite quickly, however, the new harmonic and rhyth-mic problems involved in composing polyphony began to occupy the attention of composers. One result, oddly parallel to the drop-ping away of music from the troubadour tradition, was that texts became less important in polyphonic vocal music than they had been in monodic music. Composers cut them up, stretched them out, and redistributed their rhythms in ways that entirely de-stroyed the original poetic form, obscured the rhyme scheme, and made the content impossible to hear, especially in pieces where several texts were sung simultaneously.

Nonetheless, composers continued to borrow ideas and tech-niques from poets:"modal rhythm," the first precise rhythmic no-tation in centuries, was based on a somewhat misunderstood ver-sion of ancient quantitative scansion, and later developments in rhythm, phrasing, and melodic style were influenced by the use of vernacular texts in the upper parts. In the motet, the form which came to dominate both sacred and secular music in the years 1250–1375, the relations between text and melody exem-plify the most important common principle in later medieval po-etry and music: elaborate numerical construction. Influenced by Christian versions of ancient Greek numerological music theory, both poets and composers constructed their works by complex, mystical, mathematical formulae. French isorhythmic motets, tricky crab canons in which one line is the other sung backwards, anagrammatic poems concealing the names of mistresses—all elaborate forms whose constructive principles cannot be heard in performance—flourished as representations of the numerical mystery of the universe, or (for adepts in both arts) as secret displays of technical ingenuity. The poet-composer Philippe de Vitry, whose treatise *Ars Nova* gave its name to a musical style, provides striking examples. But in the works of Guillaume de Machaut, the leading poet-composer of the next generation, we may hear a tension between this kind of constructive virtuosity and a simpler, more hearable and dramatic kind of expression, a tension also apparent in Chaucer's poetry, or in the resistance of Italian music to French innovations. Construction and expression, principles whose interaction and combination will help us understand much later poetry and music, appear quite distinctly in both arts in the later Middle Ages.

The Troubadours and Trouvères:
  Music as a Metaphor for Poetic Technique

First, then, the secular singers. They have been greatly romanticized, a process which began with the drawing of colorful miniatures in the manuscripts that preserve their songs, and which has led to their being "considered as perpetually enamoured young men who performed songs for beautiful young women on balconies, while accompanying themselves on a lute or other esoteric instrument."[2] As Hendrik van den Werf, the author of that caricature, points out, there is little evidence for this fiction, indeed little evidence that these songs were instrumentally accompanied at all, or that the writers of the songs necessarily performed them. But there is a strong tradition that both the troubadours (who wrote in Old Provençal) and the trouvères (who wrote in Old French) were poet-composers, that they normally produced both words and music. The extent of the accuracy of that tradition is difficult to assess; if it does represent a norm, we can recognize that some of these men were more successful at one part of the process than at the other: the tradition includes some brilliant poems set to indifferent melodies, and some beautiful tunes wasted on dull verse. This is hardly surprising, even if the tradition of unified rather than collaborative composition is accurate,

2. Hendrik van den Werf, *The chansons of the troubadours and trouvères*, p. 13.

but the intricate, subtle, nuanced relations between music and text we might expect from a single maker are infrequent in these secular songs; indeed, such relations are more common in the earlier tropes and sequences, where two separate makers were often involved.

Some patterns of rhyming and other kinds of repetition in the secular poems bear a family resemblance to such patterns in sequences and *versus* forms, but it is not possible to show a precise evolutionary development of the troubadour and trouvère forms out of earlier combinations of Latin poetry and music. The music of secular Latin songs might provide some hints, but too little of it is accessible to us: even the well-known thirteenth-century codex called *Carmina Burana* shows the music in indecipherable unheightened neumes, so we are able to reconstruct only a few melodies from later sources. Surveying this meager harvest, J. A. Westrup concludes that "no valid distinction can be made between the religious and secular Latin songs of this period; the same types of melody, the same forms occur in both."[3] The vernacular songs provide a much larger body of material for study: of about 2600 troubadour songs, 273 have melodies, and of about 2400 trouvère songs, some 1700 have melodies.[4] In their tonality and structure, these melodies show the influence of Gregorian chant, but this influence manifests itself in general shapes, not in specific borrowings. Opening lines of the songs frequently resemble the recitation patterns of liturgical psalmody, but again the relation is a general one. It is simply not possible, given the evidence, to trace a direct line of development from any liturgical form to the music of the troubadours and trouvères; it is even less possible to find specific musical models for the stanzaic patterns of their poetry.[5]

One way to account for the newness of the art of the troubadours and trouvères has been to insist on the importance of its secular erotic subject matter; C. S. Lewis's influential assertion that courtly love "appears quite suddenly at the end of the eleventh century in Languedoc"[6] is a version of this thesis. But Peter Dronke's work on earlier medieval lyrics has discredited this view:

---

3. "Medieval Song," in vol. II of *The New Oxford History of Music*, p. 222.
4. See Friedrich Gennrich, *Troubadours, Trouvères, Minne- und Meistergesang*, p. 5.
5. See Westrup, p. 229, and van den Werf, pp. 47-49.
6. *The Allegory of Love*, p. 2.

far from being novel, the subject matter and typical expressions of troubadour and trouvère poems have clear antecedents in centuries of earlier verse in various languages; the fact that theirs in the first substantial body of secular vernacular verse to be preserved is more a function of patronage and the exigencies of manuscript making than of the novel or "revolutionary" character of their writing. D. W. Robertson, also attacking the myth of the troubadours as "rebels . . . , impatient with the restrictions of the Church," points out that "a surprisingly large percentage of them spent their last days in perfectly orthodox monasteries."[7] These poets would not have understood our dualistic and dialectic concept of the sacred and the secular. The language they used to address the ladies elevated in their poems is closely related to the language earlier poets had used to address the Virgin Mary or the personified Sapientia. Dronke puts it tellingly:

> A wealth not merely of love-language, but of precisely that kind of love-language which is most consonant with *amour courtois,* had accumulated over the centuries in the mystical and theological tradition itself. . . . The more deeply religious the language, the closer it is to the language of *courtoisie.* The virtues acquired by the soul illuminated by divine grace are exactly those which the lover acquires when his soul is irradiated by his lady's grace: they are truly a courtly lover's virtues.[8]

So much for secularity. The attempt to attach special or defining significance to the fact that the troubadours and trouvères wrote in the vernacular is similarly dubious, since Dronke has assembled an impressive collection of Latin love-lyrics from the ninth century on which anticipate later vernacular poetry in both content and form. Indeed, "anticipate" may be the wrong word; it may be more accurate to speak of a unified tradition of love-lyric which understandably results in *written* texts earlier in Latin than it does in the vernacular. Nor can the claim be made that the use of the vernacular is particularly personal, local, or popular, because the language used is in fact highly literary, even artificial.

7. *A Preface to Chaucer,* pp. 10-11.
8. *Medieval Latin and the Rise of European Love-Lyrics,* vol. I, p. 62.

Although prose documents show great dialectal variation by region, the troubadours did not write in local dialects, but in a common poetic language whose generosity about alternate forms has been neatly explained by H. J. Chaytor, who suggests that "the intricacy of the rime-schemes employed . . . inclined poets to liberality and even to license in the admission of variant word-forms to the poetic vocabulary."[9] Indeed, it may have been precisely the availability of rhymes in the vernacular that most induced these poets to choose it as a medium; the flexibility of the vernacular languages for poets seeking to develop ever more intricate forms was a clear advantage over Latin. This formal consideration probably outweighed any democratic desire for popular appeal as a motive for writing in the vernacular. The troubadours and trouvères were not addressing peasants; their frequent allusions to Ovid and the Song of Songs suggest an educated, courtly audience.

It is hard to escape the conclusion that formal intricacy itself was a more important defining characteristic of the art of the troubadours and trouvères than either the use of the vernacular or the treatment of secular subjects. As a recent music history argues, "the striking contrast between the variety of forms and the sameness of themes in troubadour poetry clearly shows that what mattered was not the subject itself but the manner of its presentation."[10] For the most part, the fertile invention of forms took place within certain conventional restrictions, usefully laid out by van den Werf:

> The conventionality is most apparent in the strong preference shown for a stereotyped form in which the stanza is divided into two parts. The first part, called *frons*, is itself subdivided into two identical sections, called *pedes*, usually of two lines each. The second part, called *cauda*, varies in most aspects from poem to poem, but usually it is from three to six lines long. . . . The total rhyme pattern of this conventional

9. *From Script to Print*, pp. 37-38.
10. Richard H. Hoppin, *Medieval Music*, pp. 274-75. There are exceptions to Hoppin's useful generalization: van den Werf prints and translates a poem by Thibaud de Navarre, *"Dex est ausi comme li pellicans"* (God is like the pelican), whose serious content is elaborately theological and allegorical. Most of the chansons, however, are highly conventional love-poems.

stanza may be given graphically as *ab ab x* or *ab ba x,* in which the first four letters represent the rhyme of the frons, and the letter *x* the freely composed cauda. (p.60)

But within these conventions, there was remarkable variety: Istvàn Frank lists 1000 Provençal chansons of the general type *ab ba x,* but these 1000 chansons employ 200 different specific rhyme-schemes, and nearly 500 different metrical schemes.[11] Unlike ancient Greek poets, who fitted their words to musical forms, unlike Roman poets, who followed those same forms after their intimate connection with music was forgotten, and unlike Christian hymn and sequence writers, who fitted their words to the shape of extant melodies, the troubadours and trouvères invented poetic forms whose structural sophistication exceeded that of the music to which they were set. It is hardly surprising that they devoted so much energy to formal innovations and derived so much pride from them; the terms *troubadour* and *trouvère* derive from a verbal root meaning "to find" or "to discover," and the chief discovery of the men who bore those names was that poetry could achieve within itself a richness of pattern worthy to be called music.

As a compact example, we may consider the opening stanza of Jaufre Rudel's justly famous chanson, *"Lanquan li jorn son lonc en may,"* with its highly conventional content and its intricately crafted form:

> Lanquan li jorn son lonc en may
> M'es belhs dous chans d'auzelhs de lonh,
> E quan mi suy partitz de lay
> Remembra·m d'un amor de lonh:
> Vau de talan embroncx e clis
> Se que chans ni flors d'albespis
> No·m platz plus que l'yverns gelatz.

[When the days are long in May, / The sweet song of birds in the distance is beautiful to me. / And when I have left there, / I remember a distant love. / I go on with head bowed with

11. See van den Werf, p. 63, summarizing the findings of Frank's *Répertoire métrique de la poésie des troubadours.*

desire, / So that a song and the flower of the hawthorn /
Please me no more than the icy winter.][12]

The six succeeding stanzas follow this rhyme scheme *(ab ab ccd)*,
using the same rhyming sounds: the key word *lonh* concludes lines
2 and 4 of every stanza; the *a, c,* and *d* rhymes are exactly repeated
with varying words (for example, in the case of the *d* rhyme, *gelatz,
remiratz, solatz, platz, clamatz, palatz,* and *amatz.)* The same melody
is used for each of the stanzas, and this economy of rhyming
sounds enforces a similar repetitive quality in the poetry. But as is
frequently the case, the three different melodies for this chanson
preserved in the manuscripts correspond to the poetic form only
in the *frons,* where melodic repetition matches rhyme scheme. In
all three, the third line repeats the entire melody of the first line,
and the fourth repeats the second, producing the form: AB AB.
But in the *cauda,* two melodies have the form CDB, differing from
the poetic rhymes, and the third melody has no phrasal repetition
at all.

This lack of correspondence between poetic and musical
form in the *cauda* is typical, however much we might expect or
wish it otherwise.[13] As van den Werf explains,

> The manuscripts make it abundantly clear that the form of
> the poem must have been of far greater interest to everybody
> involved than the form of the melody. . . . Within the cauda
> of the text there is always rhyme and often a recurrence of
> rhyme sounds from the frons, whereas in the cauda of the
> melody there is rarely repetition of earlier-heard melodies
> either from the frons or from within the cauda. . . . For every
> chanson with . . . carefully designed formal unity [of text and

12. I quote the text as printed in van den Werf, p. 88, with the translation provided
there, by F. R. P. Akehurst. Van den Werf also gives transcriptions of the three known
musical settings, pp. 86-88.

13. Musical scholars have sometimes treated this problem with wishful thinking.
Friedrich Gennrich, for example, in *Grundriss einer Formenlehre des mittelalterlichen Liedes,* p.
18, alleges that "the creator's will toward form . . . manifests itself most clearly in the combination of musical structure and the form of the text" (van den Werf's translation, p. 68).
But Carl Appel, one year later, concluded from specific evidence that the rhyme schemes
and musical forms of most troubadour chansons have little to do with each other; see "Zur
Formenlehre des provenzalischen Minnesangs," *Zeitschrift für romanische Philologie* 53
(1933): 151-71.

melody] we find at least a hundred chansons that have little or no agreement between the two forms beyond the frons. (pp. 63, 65, 67)

We can confirm the centrality of poetic technique in the troubadour tradition by more than statistics about basic forms. If we look at the *internal* chiming in Rudel's stanza, we will discover an attention to detail, a subtle repetition and variation of vowel and consonant sounds for which the corresponding music has no equivalent. Lines which rhyme at the end also have internal relations of the kind we noticed in Notker; in lines 1 and 3, these are particularly obvious:

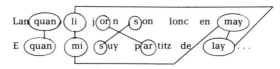

The key word *lonh*, besides being repeated twice in every stanza, echoes internally throughout the poem. Its initial consonant is the most persistent alliteration: in the first stanza alone, there are 7 initial *l*'s and 9 medial ones. The *on* sound, the part of *lonh* sustained in singing, pervades the poem, with its vowel sound continually varied; it comes five times in the first line alone:

> *L*anqu*an* li j*or*n *s*on l*on*c *en* may . . .

Internal rhyme *(belhs . . . auzehls),* alliteration *(platz plus),* and all kinds of other intersecting patterns of sound occur in every stanza. The repeated words and rhymes insure a framing unity, but the internal patterns of sound naturally differ from stanza to stanza; a strophic musical setting could not hope to achieve correspondence or even equivalent complexity.

Discrepancies among the manuscripts confirm our impression that the poem matters more than the melody. When a given song appears in a number of manuscripts, there is far more textual unanimity than melodic unanimity, a fact which suggests greater care in the preservation and transmission of the words. When two versions of a melody are preserved, the agreement between them often deteriorates after the *frons,* where there was usually a rough equivalence of form between text and music; in the *cauda,* where text and music diverge in form, manuscripts are less likely to preserve identical or even similar melodies. Van den Werf has a hypothesis which goes a long way toward explaining these phenomena:

> The poems are sophisticated creations in carefully designed forms and it seems conceivable that some authors made their poems with the help of 'pen and ink'. Consequently it must have been relatively easy for the performers to retain the basic form of the poem and for the scribes to correct whatever errors may have occurred. The melodies, on the contrary, sound to us like remembered improvisations in a very traditional and simple fashion and it seems unlikely that notation was used in the process of making them. . . . Understandably, the flow of the melody was smooth, straightforward, and in conjunct motion, but it was difficult for the performers to retain it precisely as made up by the composer and, because of the lack of design, it was impossible for the notators to reconstruct the original. (pp. 70–71)

If van den Werf is correct, the elaborate "design" of this poetry is another case of the consequences of a "craft literacy," while the lack of design in the melodies suggests the improvised expressive qualities we associate with oral composition. The absence of repeating patterns in the melodies, especially in the troubadour part of the tradition, extends to a number of examples we might call "through-composed," melodies with no repeating phrasal structure. Dante's *De Vulgari Eloquentia*, which contains detailed accounts of many of the poetic forms in the tradition, recognizes the existence of such settings, describing them as "a single melody continuing right up to the end, without any melodic repetition and without a division in the middle."[14]

The troubadours who set their intricate lyrics to such simple melodies were not musical poets in the way that the makers of earlier and closer combinations of words and tones had been. But since their formal virtuosity is something we now respond to more readily in music than in poetry, we may gain a better understand-

14. "Una oda continua usque ad ultimum progressiue, hoc est sine interatione modulationis cuiusquam et sine diesi," *De Vulgari Eloquentia*, II, 10; in the edition of Ludwig Bertalot, p. 59. I quote Westrup's translation (p. 236 of his article in *The New Oxford History of Music*).

ing of the troubadours by considering their art along musical coordinates. Arnaut Daniel, the inventor of the complex form called
the *sestina* and the *"miglior fabbro"* of Dante's *Purgatorio* (xxvi, 117),
provides one example. As Linda Paterson explains,

> Arnaut absorbs all the styles of the troubadours, from Mar-
> cabru onwards, into the love lyric. It is probably irrelevant to
> question his "sincerity" or "originality" in the actual content
> of his poems; he takes over the commonplaces of a century-
> old tradition as the basic material for his art, in which ideas
> are probably intended to be expressed not in personal but in
> universal terms.[15]

The aesthetic standards this comment urges us to apply to Arnaut
are not ones that modern readers normally apply to poets; "sincerity" of self-revelation and "originality" of content are precisely
what we require of our poets, as the most cursory glance at journalistic criticism of modern poetry will confirm. Our assumptions
about music are closer to the aesthetic within which an Arnaut
labored and by which his efforts ought to be judged: we rarely
discuss the "sincerity" of a composer, and we have a different definition for his "originality." To say of a Mozart that he "takes over
the commonplaces of a . . . tradition as the basic material for his
art" is not to deny his astounding gifts, merely to acknowledge
that he made use of earlier harmonic and melodic conventions,
building from those conventional materials structures with extraordinary symmetry, balance, and precision, just as Arnaut, by
accepting a stable set of commonplaces about courtly love, was
able to concentrate his creative powers on building from those
ideas and phrases the structures whose formal sophistication was
so impressive to Dante and Pound. In this sense, we may call him
a musical poet, if that metaphor helps us understand and properly judge his devotion to formal technique.

But the metaphor is anachronistic; we are comparing the formal intricacy of Arnaut's poetry to that of some much later music.
In Arnaut's own lifetime, the increased sophistication of poetry
was making music a servant to texts. Even in the church, where

---

15. *Troubadours and Eloquence*, p. 205. For similar comments, see Chaytor, pp. 69-70,
and the *Anthology of the Provençal Troubadours*, ed. Raymond Thompson Hill and Thomas
Goddard Bergin, p. 74.

words had followed melody in the early sequence, the increased metrical regularity and more elaborate rhyming of the second sequence style reversed the order of composition of words and music and weakened the interest of the melodies. In these later sequences, according to Jacques Handschin, "the melodies were composed with a particular text in view—or at least a particular structure, [and] in general the melodies are more 'trivial' in character than the older ones."[16] The ultimate piece of evidence, in the development of secular verse, is that the music slowly dropped away. No written melodies accompany the fourteenth-century poems which carry on the style of the troubadours and trouvères,[17] and in Italy, where similar poems were written from about 1230 on, poets did not compose melodies for them.[18] The Italians, while evidently learning such forms as the *canzone*, the *ballata*, and the sonnet from the troubadours, did not take over the musical part of the tradition.

Why, then, does Dante define poetry as "*fictio rethorica musicaque poita*, a product of imagination expressed with the aid of rhetoric and music"?[19] To read this definition literally will not accord with the facts, but a passage a few pages later can help us understand more fully what Dante meant:

> For no trumpeter or organist or lutenist calls his melody a song, except insofar as it is married to some [verbal] song; but those who make melody of words call their works songs: and even such words as are written down on papers without a reciter we call songs.[20]

Dante recognizes here two of the essential ways in which poetry may resemble music even when an actual combination with music is absent. Poets, especially poets making the complex stanzaic forms of which Dante himself was a master, need to consider not

16. "Trope, Sequence, and Conductus," pp. 161-62.

17. See van den Werf, p. 46.

18. See K. Foster and P. Boyde, eds., *Dante's Lyric Poetry*, Introduction, vol. I, p. xlv.

19. *De Vulgari Eloquentia*, II, 4; in Bertalot, p. 46; translation from Foster and Boyde, vol. I, p. xvii.

20. "Nullus enim tibicen, uel organista, uel citharedus melodiam suam cantionem uocat, nisi in quantum nupta est alicui cantioni; sed armonizantes uerba opera sua cantiones uocant; et etiam talia uerba in cartulis absque prolator iacentia cantiones uocamus," *De Vulgari Eloquentia*, II, 8; in Bertalot, p. 57.

only their content and their syntactical rhetoric, but their form: the search for rhymes is a search for appropriate sounds; the balancing and counting of syllables is an exercise of the ear; the maintaining of a consistent style, whether *"dolce"* or *"aspro,"* sweet or harsh, is as much a function of the *sound* of the words selected as of their meaning. In a period when poets were remembered for their rhyme-schemes, Dante's definition, *"armonizantes uerba,"* those who make melody of words, acknowledges the centrality of such abstract, aural, "musical" craft in the poet's vocation. In his comment about our willingness to call even a written, not-yet-recited poetic text a song, he recognizes that such a text is a potential script for performance. It will be organized by formal techniques whose sound will be pleasing to a hearer, and by rhetorical techniques whose persuasive function also presupposes oral delivery. And if we confront such a poem on paper rather than in a recitation or a musical performance, we either read it out loud or hear its sounds in our minds;[21] even in such a personal or imagined realization, it remains a *"fictio rethorica musicaque poita,"* a work of art defined by the ways it organizes sounds.

We have aready considered the "imaginary music" of Latin classical poetry, in which the functions of melody in other kinds of song were fulfilled by the arbitrary rules of Greek quantitative scansion. In writing his *Rime,* Dante made his words fit a form defined by syllable counting and rhyming, not by melodic shape or musical rhythm.[22] Nonetheless, as his definition of poetry

21. On reading aloud as the normal mode of reading in the Middle Ages, see Chaytor, p. 10.

22. The question of the relation of poetic meter to musical rhythm in secular monody has been much debated. Early in this century, having discovered a few manuscripts which gave melodies for trouvère songs in "modal rhythm" (see below, pp. 91-94), some scholars concluded that all the songs in this tradition were in regular rhythm. Others, notably Gustave Reese, have argued for some correspondence between the word-accents of Old French and the rhythm of the melodies. But Hendrik van den Werf marshals impressive evidence "for rejecting the usual unproven and ineffective theory that all chansons of the troubadours and trouvères were meant to be performed in some form of fixed and regular meter," and finds "an abundance of reasons for assuming that the vast majority of the chansons were performed in what may be called a *free rhythm* largely dictated by the flow and meaning of the text. Somewhat more specific might be the term '*declamatory rhythm*' indicating that these songs were sung, or *recited,* in the rhythm in which one might "*declaim* the poem without the music" (p. 44). Curt Sachs, in *Rhythm and Tempo,* concurs: "As to vocal music, should we not realize that in the secular monody of the French, the words were more important than the tune? And would not the next step be to realize that French

shows, he still considered this kind of writing a musical process. To be sure, some of his lyrics were actually set to music: Boccaccio tells us that Dante was fond of music, knew the leading musicians of his time, and was eager to have his lyrics set;[23] Dante himself introduces his friend the singer Pietro Casella in *Purgatorio* ii, where Casella sings his setting of one of Dante's love songs. But these settings, none of which survive, were made after Dante had already accommodated his words to a set of formal requirements which might themselves be called musical. Like Euripides contriving an antistrophe whose pitch-accents would conform to the melody of his strophe, like Notker contriving a text whose syllable-count and dramatic divisions would fit an extant melody, Dante worked within the constraints of a set of technical requirements, as he acknowledges at the end of the *Purgatorio* in a phrase about "*lo fren dell' arte,*" the curb of art (xxxiii, 141). If it is not possible to show, for Dante or for the troubadours and trouvères before him, an explicit development of poetic form from musical form, it is certainly possible to argue that the elaborate stanzaic forms of these poets came to serve a function in the creative process which on other occasions and in other traditions had been filled by actual music.

Polyphony and Polysemy

Dante's metaphorical assertion of the musicality of the poetic process is obviously different from the earlier explicit combinations of music and poetry to which I have compared it. But in the rest of our story, moments when a poet thinks of himself as doing something musical, or when a composer thinks of himself as doing something literary, will be as important as moments when explicit combinations of musical and literary creation occur. For example, I believe that polyphony, arguably the most important invention in Western musical history, was initially a metaphor, an

---

versification is neither metric nor accentual, but simply numerical? And that, as a consequence, we must not impose upon these melodies patterns of either meters or accents? . . . Monophonic music, far from being subject to the *modi*, had the privilege of free rhythm" (p. 176).

23. *Vita di Dante*, ch. 8, cited by Leonard Ellinwood in "The Fourteenth Century in Italy," in *Ars Nova and the Renaissance* , ed. Dom Anselm Hughes and Gerald Abraham, vol. III of *The New Oxford History of Music,* p. 40.

attempt to create a musical equivalent for the literary and theological technique of allegory. Those who claim that polyphony
originated in some accident of practical music-making, from imitating the sound of the organ or attempting to replicate overtones
heard in monodic singing, are postulating a more independent
and "instrumental" conception of music than I believe existed in
the liturgical world of the monasteries, where we know polyphony
began. The musicologist Alfred Einstein, in an essay on "Fictions
That Have Shaped Musical History," suggests that the invention
was conscious:

> I am convinced that medieval polyphony is the product of a
> fiction. It is not correct to say that the so-called "latent feeling
> for harmonic relationships" led to writing for many voices.
> Polyphony and harmony have originally nothing to do with
> each other. What occurred was that in certain monastery
> schools there was an attempt, not to find a new melody ap-
> propriate to one already known, but to combine existing mel-
> odies. Religious and mystic concepts most certainly played a
> role in this. Polyphony did not come from the people or the
> folk tradition, but was invented.[24]

We can be more precise about what the "fiction" was, for we have
already seen in action the "religious and mystical concepts" which
led to this pivotal invention: we have seen how the process of troping, with its constant alternation of old chant and newly composed
music, Old Testament text and New Testament commentary, implied the mystic simultaneity of events from different times; we
have seen how Notker, in typical medieval fashion, made a poetic
counterpoint from the Biblical references to Rachel and other
weeping women. In the text of a sequence or trope, the poet
could suggest the effect of simultaneity, as Notker does, by frequent alternation between various component strands of meaning. I suspect polyphony was invented when someone recognized
that *actual* simultaneity could be achieved in music. To locate the
origin of "free *organum*," in which the motion of the parts is not
strictly parallel, in an attempt "to combine existing melodies" is
simply to assert that medieval men began at some point to make

24. *Essays on Music,* p. 7.

music by processes of combination they had long employed in making literature.

Even parallel *organum*, motion in strict parallel intervals, may have a symbolic or metaphorical origin. Dom Anselm Hughes directs our attention to some sequence manuscripts in which musical phrases are repeated not at the unison, as we should expect, but a fifth higher. As Hughes argues, it was a short step from singing these phrases in sequence to singing them simultaneously in parallel fifths, and our earliest theoretical records of polyphony, such as the Irish treatise called *Musica Enchiriadis,* describe such motion in parallel fifths.[25] If we remember that sequences usually had allegorical texts, we may think of parallel *organum* as a musical emblem of the basic allegorical claim made in those texts, that events in the Old Testament run parallel to those in the New Testament.

The fact that music could achieve actual simultaneity, that it could have vertical as well as horizontal events, was a revolutionary discovery. I have argued that this discovery occurred in an attempt to imitate a literary technique, the idea of polysemous writing elaborately developed in the medieval theory of fourfold allegory. But that theory, even as expounded in Dante's famous letter to Can Grande, was inevitably an imaginative or interpretive theory. In literature, one could claim that a line of poetry had four layers of meaning, but in music one could actually write four simultaneous parts. It is one of the many ironies of our story that polyphony, a successful attempt to find a musical equivalent for a literary technique, led to a dramatic separation of musical and literary technique. Until this point in history, both the recitation of a poem and the singing or playing of a piece of music had reached the ear as a single series of sounds in time; now music had a new kind of interest, the accidental or contrived vertical combination of two or more pitches. Harmonic considerations began to play a part in composition, as composers sensed the different effects on the ear of different simultaneously-sounded intervals.

Inevitably, there was some conflict between the intellectual

---

25. See "The Birth of Polyphony," in vol. II of *The New Oxford History of Music,* p. 276, and Caldwell, *Medieval Music,* pp. 114-16.

principles out of which polyphony had arisen and the harmonic principles that were evolving in its practice. Einstein's essay continues:

> Only after the principle of polyphony had been invented and the crude combination of melodies had been accomplished with increasing success, did a feeling develop for the harmonic relationships between these melodies. One could represent the whole history of [later] medieval music as the history of the weakening, reduction, and repression of the polyphonic principle in favor of the harmonic. It is a battle between intellectual, mystic, abstract polyphony and sensuous harmonic sonority. (p. 7)

Our earliest examples of practical, performed polyphony (as opposed to samples in treatises) confirm this account. The Winchester Troper describes its polyphonic pieces as "*melliflua*," honey-sweet, and John Caldwell's recent attempt to transcribe one of its sequences shows us a music with a great deal of contrary motion, a variety of intervals between the two parts, and a clear feeling for cadence.[26] A fragment from Chartres, also from the eleventh century, now destroyed but fortunately transcribed by H. M. Bannister in 1911, shows similar attention to harmonic considerations and a surprising fondness for intervals of a third.[27] In both these fragments, one part is a plainsong of which we have other records; the other part, which crosses the plainsong frequently, seems to have been composed according to what Einstein would call the "harmonic principle." Still, even if this music results from the composition of a new part to fit with an old melody, rather than the combination of two old melodies, the compositional process remains essentially the process of troping, now made simultaneous rather than sequential. A more substantial collection of polyphonic pieces from the monastery at St. Martial also confirms this hypothesis, as Richard Crocker explains:

26. See *Medieval Music*, pp. 117-19.

27. For a transcription, see Hughes, "The Birth of Polyphony," pp. 282-84. Since the manuscript uses a four-line staff, we can be more certain of the intervals of this piece than in the case of the Winchester Troper, which is in neumes. Of 241 readable intervals, 67 are thirds, 48 are fourths, and only 15 are fifths.

In a typical case, *Noster cetus,* the text consists of a series of couplets, set to what looks like chant. But the melody over the second line of each couplet is entirely different from the melody over the first linemnot unheard of, but suspicious. In another source, the same two lines of melody appear with the same couplet, but now written as a piece of two-part polyphony, sung to the first line of the couplet and then repeated for the second line. . . . Characteristic of these cases is strong contrary motion, and note-against-note motion in the two parts. (p. 62)

But the same manuscript also contains pieces in what was to become a new and dominant style, in which the upper part has as many as fifteen or twenty notes against each note in the lower part, the *cantus firmus* or original plainsong. Here a literary analogue might be the process of glossing, in which a single word of scripture could accumulate a vast marginal commentary.

In this newer style, the problem of coordinating the voices, doubtless already severe in note-against-note writing, must have become truly pressing, and the way composers set about solving that problem suggests that Einstein's account of this period as a "battle" between an intellectual or mystic concept of music and a sensuous or practical one needs some qualification. We have already seen how practical treatises of this period drew on ancient theory as well as modern discoveries, and the development of the notation now called "modal rhythm" by Leonin of Paris is a striking example of the process. The problem was eminently practical: how were the singers to stay together? But the solution to the problem, as William G. Waite has shown, came from a source squarely within the intellectual and mystic tradition, St. Augustine himself:

As far as one can ascertain, none of the polyphonic music prior to Leonin's work shows any evidence of a coherent rhythmical system. It was Leonin's incomparable achievement to introduce a rational system of rhythm into polyphonic music for the first time and, equally important, to create a method of notation expressive of this rhythm. . . . In his search for a rhythmic basis for his music Leonin turned directly or indirectly to the treatise on rhythm by St. Augustine, *De musica libri sex*. From this work he derived, with but slight modifications, the fundamental doctrines of rhythm that came to be known as the rhythmic modes, i.e., rhythmic patterns derived from metrical feet.[28]

The derivation of the rhythmic modes from ancient poetic feet and the "slight modifications" of Leonin's system may be seen in the following chart:

Ancient foot	Metrical pattern	Mode	Rhythmic pattern [in modern note-values]
trochee	▬ ‿	Mode I	♩ ♪
iamb	‿ ▬	Mode II	♪ ♩
dactyl	▬ ‿ ‿	Mode III	♩. ♪ ♩
anapest	‿ ‿ ▬	Mode IV	♪ ♩ ♩.
spondee	▬ ▬	Mode V	♩. ♩.
tribrach	‿ ‿ ‿	Mode VI	♪ ♪ ♪

The first, second, and sixth modes transcribe the trochee, iamb, and tribrach correctly, producing triple rhythms. Correct transcriptions of the dactyl, anapest, and spondee, however, would have produced duple rhythms, so the third, fourth, and fifth modes have been modified to make a practical fit; like the others, their rhythms have been made divisible by three. Medieval treatises are united in describing such rhythms as "perfect," and in connecting their perfection with the doctrine of the Trinity, though modern accounts of musical history generally dismiss these explanations as symbolism after the fact. But as Gustave Reese points out, "extraneous considerations, such as affected

28. *The Rhythm of Twelfth-Century Polyphony*, p. 8. Waite's thesis has been controversial, but I find his evidence for the widespread influence of Augustine compelling, and his transcriptions make musical sense to my ears.

medieval music in other connections, may very well have exerted their influence here too. Medieval speculation regarded the number three as a symbol of perfection long before the development of the modal system" (pp. 274–75). And as Waite has shown, Leonin derived his solution to the practical problem of rhythmic coordination from Augustine, the details of whose treatise were by now surely "extraneous" to the practical development of medieval music. Once having done so, he faced the practical problem of making the modes compatible; it hardly matters whether the symbolism of the number three was a reason for perverting the old shape of the dactyl and anapest or a convenient defense for having done so. In either case, the system of modal rhythm represents a combination of the practical and the mystical.

Thus quantitative scansion, originally a musical system in ancient Greece, then for centuries an abstract formal principle for poetry, provided the basis for a new system of musical rhythm in twelfth-century Paris. Ironically, this rebirth of the ancient metrical feet in music occurred at a time when poetry—sacred and secular, Latin and vernacular—was being written largely by syllable-counting, rhyme, and accent. Cast out of its place in poetry by these newer systems, some of which had developed in response to musical forms, quantitative scansion lived again as a purely rhythmic principle for music.

Many of the texts Leonin and his follower Perotin set were not poetry at all, but brief prose phrases from the Vulgate Bible. In the music, each syllable of text stretches over one or more long notes in the lower part or tenor, above which the upper part sings its melismatic, modally measured, and presumably textless melody. Even when phrases from the sequence repertoire, including lines once measured by syllable-counting and rhyming, were set polyphonically, they were treated in the same way, as if they were prose. Waite stresses the resulting break between poetic and musical rhythm:

> Although the modal system is derived from [ancient] metrics, it is not in any way dependent upon the prosody of the text being set to music. The musical rhythm is an independent one and thus the Notre Dame composers [Leonin and Perotin] initiated the long development of purely musical rhythm which enabled music to free itself from its subservience to

poetical rhythm and to develop rhythmic subtleties unknown to poetry. (p. 53)

As we shall see, the rhythmic independence gained by music in the Middle Ages became a point of contention in the Renaissance, when there was a serious attempt to render musical rhythm once again subservient to poetic rhythm. The Renaissance musical humanists, who favored this reform, were sensitive to a phenomenon already apparent in twelfth-century polyphony: not only was poetic rhythm distorted by the "rhythmic subtleties" of the new modal system; the importance of the *meaning* of the text was greatly reduced. In the works of Leonin and Perotin, the words are so spread out, so broken up, that they cannot be perceived as a meaningful text. When a single syllable occupies as many as 65 measures, we hear a vowel sound, not a unit of meaning; a phoneme, not a morpheme.[29] The harmonic relations between the two voices and the modal rhythm of the top line are sufficiently interesting to absorb a listener's attention, especially since there is no obvious effort at text-setting in the sense of making the music "express" the text in form or effect. As Einstein explains in an essay on "Words and Music":

> With the rise of polyphony the word is forced to lose its supremacy. A looser union of music and text is a patent result of the emancipation of music. For with the growth of polyphony the constructive element gained such an ascendancy that the word as such could no longer be respected and, in fact, had to be violated in many cases. . . . Music is no longer fitted so snugly to the word as before; it is now draped more loosely around the text, which, in fact, usually disappears under the smothering new garb. (p. 102)

The evidence supports these generalizations: in the thirteenth century the relative unimportance of the text is confirmed by the frequent use of instruments to strengthen or even carry polyphonic parts. But while words had lost their "supremacy," they

---

29. See Hans Nathan, "The Function of Text in French 13th-century Motets," *Musical Quarterly* 28 (1942), especially p. 445: "Although in all emotional styles vowels play an important role, they stand out in Perotin's music to such an extent that their vocal quality outweighs their logical connotation. . . . Within the powerful tone-streams emanating from the *cantus firmus*, the word ceased to be a literary unit."

remained a factor in the compositional process, and as we shall see, the presence of a text continued to affect the shape and importance of a musical line.

We might usefully compare the waning importance of the text in polyphony with the disappearance of musical settings from manuscripts of vernacular poetry at about the same time. For poets, as I have argued, the task of finding the rhymes for an elaborate stanzaic form came to occupy the place in the creative process once taken by fitting words to a melody; for composers, the task of adding a new melodic line to an extant chant came to absorb the interest once devoted to adding a melody to a poetic text, while the devising of a modal pattern with rhythmic interest of its own replaced the attempt to match poetic rhythm musically. But even as actual music faded away from vernacular poetry, and as the texts of polyphonic pieces became harder to hear, the techniques of each art retained elements of the other: Dante's definition of poetry testifies to his awareness that satisfying the requirements of those complex rhyme schemes and metrical forms was a musical task; Leonin's invention of modal rhythm drew upon a rhythmic system long associated with poetry; and the basic process by which the earliest polyphonists added new melodies to Gregorian chant was deeply analogous to, even borrowed from, the literary process of troping.

Toward the Motet

This troping or accretive technique remained fundamental even as polyphony developed other forms. Our earliest examples of three-part music show a third part added in a different hand, just as literary tropes had often been troped again by another poet. And even when composers began to write all the parts of a polyphonic piece from scratch, they did not compose the parts together by some vertical principle of harmony, but wrote a fresh tenor which then occupied the place previously taken by the liturgical tenor. Franco of Cologne, one of the most important theorists of this period, explains this process in his *Ars cantus mensurabilis* (c. 1260):

> Observe that in all [polyphonic forms] except the *conductus* there is first taken some *cantus prius factus* [a song made be-

fore] (called tenor, since it supports the discant and has its place from it). In the *conductus,* however, this is not the case, for cantus and discant are written by the same person. The word "discant," however, is used in two senses—first, as meaning something sung by several persons; second, as meaning something based on a cantus. . . . He who wishes to write a *conductus* ought first to invent as beautiful a melody as he can, then, as previously explained, use it as a tenor is used in writing discant.[30]

The *conductus,* which became clearly separated from other forms in the thirteenth century, was unlike the melismatic *organa* of Leonin and Perotin; not only did it have a newly composed tenor, but its upper parts moved in rhythmic unison with that tenor, which was not in long notes like those used for *organum.* The tenor of such a piece, although it lacked the ancient authority and slow-moving grandeur of the Gregorian tenors, was still the most important part; the upper parts, written to accompany the tenor, remained subordinate.[31]

As will already be apparent from Franco's two definitions of discant, composers and theorists of this period were far from unified or precise in their use of the various terms which grew up to describe the forms and subforms of polyphonic music. *Discant, organum, conductus,* and other labels were used differently in different countries and at different times. The important point for our purposes is that in all these forms, the music was of more interest than the text: in forms with sustained tenors, as we have seen, the text was so spread out as to be reduced to its vowels; in the *conductus,* with its more rhythmic tenor, the upper parts were probably wordless, and internal evidence suggests that those parts were sometimes performed on instruments.[32] In a section cataloguing various ways of combining texts and melodies, Franco describes the *conductus* as written "with and without words," an odd phrase which may mean that one part has a text, while others do

---

30. I follow, with minor ellipses and alterations, the translation in Strunk, pp. 153, 155.

31. For details, see Dom Anselm Hughes, "Music in Fixed Rhythm," in vol. II of *The New Oxford History of Music,* p. 317.

32. Hughes, p. 326; for examples of "instrumental suggestion," see pp. 327-28.

not.[33] That passage may also serve as our introduction to the motet, in which different parts have different texts:

> Discant is written either with words or with and without words. If with words, there are two possibilities—with a single text or with several texts. Discant is written with a single text in the cantilena, in the rondellus, and in any ecclesiastical chant. It is written with several texts in motets which have a triplum or a tenor, for the tenor is the equivalent of some text. It is written with and without words in the *conductus* and in the ecclesiastical discant improperly called organum.[34]

As this passage makes clear, and as the derivation of its name from French *mot* (word) suggests, the motet is a musical form defined by the way it uses texts. I have argued that the origins of polyphony lie in the literary process of troping; in the case of the motet, the evidence is explicit; here is Caldwell's account:

> Two-part motets initially had a Latin text in the *duplum* [upper voice] which alluded in some way to the [liturgical] text in the tenor: thus the text was a kind of trope. Just as the sequence in its melismatic form—a 'successive' trope—later acquired a syllabic text, so the *clausula*—a 'simultaneous' troping of plainsong—became a motet by the same process. Three-part motets at first shared the same text in the upper parts; later, a third part might have another Latin text or else a French one; and there are early examples of a single French text in a two-part work and of two French texts in three-part works. Normally a text in French would be profane in character, and it is not uncommon for a Marian text in Latin to be combined with a French text on the subject of profane love.
> (p. 149)

The resulting simultaneous performance of a Latin text in praise of the Virgin and a vernacular text in praise of some earthly woman, however ludicrous it may seem to us, is further evidence for the accuracy of Dronke's argument about the similarity of the language of religion and the language of *courtoisie*. Indeed, even the existence of a thoroughly obscene Provençal text for the up-

33. For a different interpretation, see Reese, p. 307.
34. In Strunk, p. 153.

per part of a motet whose Latin text praises St. Katherine ought not to be surprising to readers of Boccaccio and Chaucer.[35] Our surprise at such combinations arises from our tendency to see a conflict between spirit and flesh, where medieval thinkers tended to see a hierarchical continuum. Motets which combine Latin and vernacular texts are simply extreme examples of the inclusiveness of medieval thought, its willingness to see fleshly love as an emblem or version of spiritual love. In any case, the bilingual motet was a short-lived phenomenon, perhaps because the Church denounced it as improper,[36] but doubtless also because it must have been nearly impossible for any hearer to follow both texts.

In both the brief period of the bilingual motet and the more continuous tradition of the entirely vernacular motet, texts from the secular poetic tradition found new musical homes, but with an important difference of status: in the songs of the troubadours and trouvères, the form of the text had been the central focus of interest; in the motet, from the beginning, the rhythmic form of the music involved predetermined mathematical relations between the phrase-lengths of the various parts. Verses made to fit such phrases could not be regular, and when a regular text was pressed into service in a motet, its poetic form was necessarily distorted.[37] Each text also had to compete for interest with the texts and melodies of the other parts, not to mention the vertical interest of the harmonic events. As the simple spreading out of the text in melismatic *organum* reduced its potential for meaning, so the multiplication of texts in the motet reduced the comprehensibility of the resulting composite. Of course, this change was not instantaneous: some early French texts use interjections and other odd forms in order to end their phrases on the same vowels as the old Latin text of the tenor, and the predominant vowels of the original Latin *cantus firmus* often dominate the new troping texts as well.[38] These techniques may be seen as attempts to retain

35. For a text and translation, see Gordon Athol Anderson, *The Latin Compositions in Fascicules VII and VIII of the Notre Dame Manuscript Wolfenbüttel Helmstadt* 1099 (1206), vol. I, pp. 7-8, 12.

36. See Dom Anselm Hughes, "The Motet and Allied Forms," in vol. II of *The New Oxford History of Music*, p. 373.

37. See Ernest H. Sanders, "Polyphony and Secular Monophony," in Sternfeld, *Music from the Middle Ages to the Renaissance*, p. 114.

38. See Nathan, "The Function of Text . . . ," pp. 454-58, for a number of examples. See also Yvonne Rokseth, *Polyphonies du XIII ᵉ Siècle*, vol. IV, ch. vii.

some of the homogeneity which had characterized *organa,* but the trend was toward more independent parts, and toward greater interest in the uppermost part. Hughes explains this change by emphasizing the prominence which high pitch gave to the upper line:

> In the upper parts of the motet, which are independent horizontal lines in a way that the voices of the conductus are not, the topmost voice stood out more prominently because of its clearer and more penetrating tones: so that it [began] to be regarded as the most important voice—an idea as radical in its own day as it is a commonplace with us.[39]

But surely the addition of *texts* to upper parts which had been either wordless or sung on sustained vowels also helped give those upper parts their new prominence. With three texts and three musically distinct lines, a listener had to choose a part to follow, at least a part on which to concentrate, and the part most likely to attract his attention would be the part with the most rapidly-moving, most comprehensible, most often vernacular text: the *triplum* or top part.

To argue that the presence of a text gave the top part a new prominence is not to deny that the motet remained primarily a musical form, in which the text was but one of a number of elements; it is merely to notice that the text, reduced in importance and obscured by multiplication, was nonetheless capable of having an effect on melodic style, as Hans Nathan explains:

> In organa, small melodic steps had been pressed together into a continuous chain by the horizontal driving power of their melismatic line. In the motet, however, these small intervals became separate, disconnected units, through the presence of words.[40]

The lowest part, which had been dominant in *organum* by virtue of its Gregorian authority, and had retained its melodic prominence in the earlier *conductus,* became in the motet a kind of bass line, now usually written without words and apparently often performed instrumentally. Once again the presence of a text, even a text whose form may have been distorted and whose words may

39. "The Motet and Allied Forms," p. 383.
40. "The Function of Text . . . ," pp. 448-49.

have been garbled by the other lines, had brought about a significant shift in musical style.

This shift necessitated further changes in notation. The modal notation of Leonin had used ligatures, groups of notes written together as units, to indicate which rhythmic mode, which characteristic pattern of long and short values, was to be used in a given piece; the ligatures (♮ ♩ ♮) for example, indicated the rhythm (𝄢). But the syllabic underlay of a text, as Nathan points out, broke up those ligatures; the solution, another major advance in precision, was the use of a particular sign (❚ , the *virga* of plainsong) for a long note, and a different sign (■ , the *punctum*) for a short note called a *breve*. Hughes' account also connects this change to the presence of texts, and describes its musical results:

> The ligatures remain, with certain modifications . . . , but their use is mostly confined to the tenors, which do not require syllabic treatment because they are textless or melismatic: whereas the upper parts with their verbal texts run mostly in single notes. . . . The composer, having these single notes before him, material representing definite duration, begins to find it attractive, easy, and effective to subdivide his notes, to break up the breve into two and three parts, and to ornament his upper melodies with various time-patterns.[41]

The new "mensural" notation, codified by Franco of Cologne, was at least as significant an advance as the "modal" notation invented by Leonin; it gave composers an even better way to indicate their rhythms, which were now obviously much more complex than poetic rhythm had ever been. Ancient quantitative poetry, for all its variety of feet, had had only two time-values, long and short, and the newer syllabic poetry lacked even that distinction. Modal rhythm, by modifying some of these ancient feet to keep its entire system ternary, had produced three different time-values (♪ , ♩ , and ♩. in modern notation), but the notation remained ambiguous, insufficiently precise to indicate the exact proportions between these values. Mensural notation was a giant step toward mathematically accurate and divisible note-values,

41. "The Motet and Allied Forms," p. 380.

and an obvious step toward an even more independent musical rhythm. Just as the troubadours, by inventing formal shapes for poetry which were more sophisticated than the shapes of the melodic settings, had effectively made poetic technique far more independent of music than it had been for Notker, the mensuralists, by inventing rhythmic patterns for music which were more sophisticated than the patterns of the texts being set, made musical rhythm more independent of poetic rhythm than it had ever been before. But without the presence of syllabic texts in the upper voices of motets, rendering the modal ligatures inadequate, there would surely have been less immediate pressure for this change.

The development of the motet style during the next century, however, had very little to do with texts. The coining of new, smaller note-values continued: Franco's treatise (c. 1260) already recognized the semibreve (◆), and the motets of Petrus de Cruce (fl. c. 1290) included as many as seven semibreves in the space of one breve; the obvious next step was the minim (♩), followed a few years later by the semiminim (♪). At least as important as the introduction of these ever-smaller rhythmic units was the return of duple rhythm: Philippe de Vitry—poet, composer, bishop, and correspondent of Petrarch—developed a notational system allowing both the old ternary rhythmic modes, still known as "perfect," and the basic duple patterns, labeled "imperfect" but now employed both by themselves and in combination with triple rhythms. These innovations are the most important contribution of his treatise *Ars Nova* (c. 1320), which has given its name to an entire century of European music.[42]

Anagrams and Cancrizans

It is a commonplace of music history to claim that the *ars nova* is "the first full manifestation of pure musical art, freed from the service of religion or poetry and constructed according to its own laws,"[43] but this claim needs at least two important qualifications.

42. The standard edition of Vitry's treatise, which exists only in obviously imperfect copies, is that edited by Gilbert Reaney, André Gilles, and Jean Maillard, volume viii of the series *Corpus Scriptorum de Musica*. The letters from Petrarch to Vitry appear in volume II of *Le Familiari*, ed. Vittorio Rossi, Book IX, no. 13, Book XI, no. 14; pp. 246-56, 354-55.

43. Heinrich Besseler, *Die Musik des Mittelalters und der Renaissance*, p. 129, as translated in the Introduction to vol. III of *The New Oxford History of Music*, p. xvii.

It is indeed true that the motets of Vitry and of Guillaume de Machaut are constructed according to elaborate mathematical proportions which strike modern minds as abstract (hence "pure musical art"); so powerful was this constructive principle that composers treated both melodic material from the liturgical tradition and textual material in Latin and French as a tailor treats cloth: the integrity of a melody or a poem was clearly less important than the grand proportional design of an entire motet. But for Vitry and Machaut, both of whom were clerics, these mathematical proportions were by no means abstract; they held the same mystical truth expounded by Augustine almost 1000 years earlier. If mortals could not hear these higher harmonies in the music (and they certainly could not), neither could mortals hear the music of the spheres, and in both cases the belief remained that the music of mathematical proportion expressed and pleased God. So much for "pure musical art" and "freedom from religion." As regards freedom from poetry, we have already seen how the text was becoming less and less important in the motet tradition, distorted in its form and obscured in its meaning. But motets were not the only kind of music being written, as Einstein's essay on "Words and Music" reminds us:

> In the fourteenth century new forms, based on the art of the troubadours and trouvères, begin to share the stage with the motet. The composer first invents the top voice, while the other voices are reduced to a more lowly function; they are accompaniment, mere support for the melody. In France, these new forms are the *ballade* (with three stanzas), the *rondeau,* the *chanson,* and the *virelai* (or *chanson balladée),* Guillaume de Machaut being the most important composer; in Italy, where Florence stands out as the center of creative activity, they are the madrigal and the *ballata.* (p. 110)

Rather than one kind of composition, "freed from the service of poetry," there were clearly two kinds: a motet style, written from the bottom up, in which constructive principles of mathematical proportion were dominant, and a *chanson* style, written from the top down, in which expressive principles of melodic text-setting were dominant. We need not exaggerate the differences; Machaut, after all, composed highly successful pieces in both styles. But the relations between what I have called constructive and expressive principles may be a useful rubric under which to study both music and literature in this period: Machaut's poetic career, at least as influential as his musical career, shows evidence of the same two forces at work, and they may also be seen in the writings of Geoffrey Chaucer.

In the motet, the bias toward constructive principles appears most radically in a technique called *isorhythm,* in which one or more voices repeat a static rhythmic pattern over and over again. This pattern came to be called a *talea,* or "cutting," and its effect was to cut up melodic material which, in the case of the tenors, had already been cut out of the Gregorian chant repertoire. When a melody was repeated, each repetition was called a *color,* a word borrowed from rhetoric, where it served as a general term for repetition. Obviously, there were a variety of possible mathematical relations between *colores* and *taleae.* The next page shows the tenor of a motet entitled *"Inter amoenitatis,"* from the *Roman de Fauvel* (1316), in which 8 *taleae* = 3 *colores,* transcribed schematically in order to make those proportions apparent.[44]

As will be obvious from this diagram, the fact that the number of *taleae* is not evenly divisible by the number of *colores* produces an overlapping of repetitions such that each *talea* is melodically distinct and each *color* is rhythmically distinct. Such overlapping was not restricted to tenors. In the upper parts of such a motet, the phrase-lengths might correspond exactly to the *taleae* of the tenor, or they might be related to those *taleae* by another set of proportions. Nor were the repetitions always exact. A longer *talea* might be repeated in diminution, with its note-values halved. In a fully isorhythmic motet, in which each part has its own *talea,* the resulting total rhythm is often so complex as to suggest twentieth-century procedures.[45]

44. *Le Roman de Fauvel,* a substantial satiric poem in two parts by Gervais du Bus, appeared in 1314; a version with musical interpolations apparently collected by Raoul Chaillou is extant in a beautiful manuscript datable to 1316, published in facsimile by Pierre Aubry. The music is transcribed in vol. I of Leo Schrade, *Polyphonic Music of the Fourteenth Century.* The motet quoted here appears on folio 21 v of the manuscript, and on p. 42 of Schrade.

45. For a number of examples, and a chart showing the proportions between *colores* and *taleae* in the motets attributed to Vitry, see Gilbert Reaney, "Ars Nova in France," in vol. III of *The New Oxford History of Music,* pp. 9-11. For one typical modern response, see Pierre Boulez, *Notes of an Apprenticeship,* pp. 143-44, where isorhythm is called "the most rational attitude toward rhythm in our occidental music."

Original liturgical melody (*color*)

Repeating rhythmic figure (*talea*)

(= 56 notes = 8× 7 = 3× 19 [−1 final repetition of G the last time])

When constructive principles of this kind dominate composition, melodic interest tends to be weakened. In our example, the different rhythmic guises in which the liturgical melody appears make it difficult to discern the repetitions of the *color* as repetitions. Surely no one listening to the whole motet, with its rhythmically busy, textually interesting upper part, would have heard the recurrences of the *color* in the tenor. Although the manuscript dutifully labels the tenor by its liturgical name, *"Revertenti,"* its identity must have been lost in this arbitrary treatment. Complaining about just such techniques in a famous decree issued in 1322, Pope John XXII argued that the "disciples of the new school, much occupying themselves with the measured dividing of the *tempora*, . . . must be losing sight of the fundamental sources of our melodies in the Antiphoner and Gradual, and may thus forget what that is upon which their superstructure is raised."[46] The whole decree is a last-ditch attempt to assert what was surely by now a fiction: the idea that liturgical polyphony was an elaboration or decoration of the ancient chant. The composer of our example might have replied to the accusations of "wantonness" in this document by pointing out that he had erected his superstructure upon numbers with solid allegorical meaning: three, the number of the Trinity; and eight, the number of the octave, of Sunday, of Pentecost, and of the eight-sided baptismal font.[47] If men and Popes could not hear the higher music of those relations, God could. But such a defense of constructive principles by appeal to allegory, applicable in varying degrees to the isorhythmic motets of Vitry and Machaut, could not and cannot undo the fact that such constructive principles resulted in an altogether arbitrary treatment of melody. And it is hard to escape the conclusion that the composers also hoped their ingenuity in constructing these motets would be noticed by performers and others who studied the music, that they hoped to appeal to a *coterie* who would discover and appreciate their recondite achievements. As Nanie Bridgman points out, the subtleties of isorhythm

46. Following the translation given along with the original Latin in H. E. Wooldridge, *The Polyphonic Period*, vol. II of the old *Oxford History of Music*, pp. 89-90.

47. These numbers could also be easily related to each other. Three is the sum of the integers 1 and 2; the ratio 1:2 produces the musical octave, the eighth scale tone. See D. W. Robertson, *A Preface to Chaucer*, pp. 122-24.

"were not perceptible to the average listener and only revealed their secrets to informed musicians; thus this technique, which takes such pains in order to satisfy the intellect, reflects the medieval predilection for a symbolical art addressed only to a restricted group of the initiated, and at the same time constituting the supreme test of the composer's skill."[48]

The virtuosity of these motets is by no means the open display of a Paganini; it is a recondite virtuosity, discernible only after difficult study, unlikely to be heard in performance. In speaking of studying the music, I should make it clear that part of the difficulty of these pieces lies in the fact that they were not written in score, with parts arranged vertically. Instead, the normal arrangement was for the upper parts to be written out separately in mensural notation, one on the left side of the page and the other on the right, while the tenor, which obviously took up less space, was squeezed in at the bottom in modal ligatures.[49] Thus the performers had to work out the coordination of their parts without common bar-lines—indeed, without any bar-lines at all. These basic difficulties of deciphering apply to all motets of this period, but there were also pieces in which the composer deliberately made his notation a puzzle, such as crab canons or *cancrizans*, in which the second part sang the notes of the first part backwards, or mirror canons, in which one singer read his notes with the book upside down. Augmentation, in which one part doubled the rhythmic values of another while using the same pitches, and diminution, a similar technique in which rhythmic values were halved, were also common, though frequently not explicitly notated. Thus, in a piece where the tenor was to be repeated in diminution, the performers presumably had to discover that fact by trial and error. The most famous such enigmatic piece is Machaut's *"Ma fin est mon commencement et mon commencement ma fin"* (My end is my beginning, and my beginning my end), which appears in the manuscripts as a few brief lines of music, with a text oddly disposed about them: some words are larger than others; some are written upside down. From this cryptic notation, which contains no instructions besides the label "countertenor"

---

48. "France and Burgundy: 1300-1500," in Sternfeld, *Music from the Middle Ages to the Renaissance*, p. 153.

49. See, for example, any of the motets in the *Roman de Fauvel* in Aubry's facsimile.

affixed to the bottom line, the performers were supposed to deduce a three-part setting by discovering, for example, that the texted line played backwards would harmonize with the forward version.[50]

The texts of isorhythmic motets often contained similar enigmas, similar concealed symmetries. As we have seen, the musical rhythm, increasingly subdivided on the small scale and controlled by principles of proportion on the large scale, normally violated the poetic rhythm of the texts. Since the texts were written out beneath the musical notation, there was no indication of their original lineation, which had to be deduced from the rhymes. In terms of what a listener could hear, the treatment of the texts was at least as arbitrary as the treatment of borrowed melodic material: both were cut up to fit predetermined patterns. But in terms of what someone studying the manuscript might discover, the composition and combination of the texts involved the same recondite virtuosity as the composition and combination of the musical parts. When the composer was also the poet, as was the case with both Vitry and Machaut, the fitting together of musical and poetic shapes involved kinds of ingenuity before which even modern scholarship must stand amazed.[51]

We may take as one example the motet *"Garrit Gallus—In nova fert—Neuma,"* ascribed with reasonable certainty to Philippe de Vitry, quoted as an example in his *Ars Nova*, and appearing in full in the *Roman de Fauvel*.[52] Here the most important proportion is 3:2. By means of red notes, as explained in the *Ars Nova*, Vitry changes what we now would call the time signature from triple to duple rhythm and back. The first *talea* of the tenor is as follows:[53]

---

50. For a transcription, see Reese, pp. 351-52. For a copy of the original notation, see Johannes Wolf, *Geschichte der Mensuralnotation von 1250-1460*, vol. II, p. 40.

51. For an impressive account of these relations in Machaut's motets, with helpful transcriptions, charts, and formulas, see Georg Reichert, "Das Verhältnis von musikalische und textlicher Struktur in den Motetten Machauts," *Archiv für Musikwissenschaft* 13 (1956): 197-216.

52. Vitry's allusion comes on p. 28 of the treatise in the edition of Reaney et al.; the motet occupies folio 44 of the *Fauvel* manuscript; for a complete transcription, see Schrade, vol. I, pp. 68-70.

53. I follow the rhythmic notation of Schrade's transcription. A more recent transcription in Crocker's *History of Musical Style*, pp. 108-10, uses even longer note-values, but it is incomplete and its text is less reliable.

[These notes originally red.]

This *talea* is repeated 6 (i.e., 3 × 2) times; it states only 6 different pitches, and the entire *color*, which equals 3 *taleae* and is thus repeated 2 times, is restricted to those same 6 pitches. The *talea* contains 5 (i.e., 3 + 2) bars each of 3/4 and 2/4 time, in the sequence 2 bars, 5 bars, 3 bars. These facts are commonly noted in analyses of this piece, but no one seems to have noticed that the texts of the *triplum* and *motetus* are also constructed to exemplify this numerical proportion. Here are the texts:

Triplum
Garrit Gallus flendo dolorose,
luget quippe Gallorum concio,
que satrape traditur dolose,
excubitus sedens officio.
Atque vulpes, tamquam vispilio
in Belial vigens astucia,
de leonis consensu proprio
monarchisat, atat angaria.
rursus, ecce, Jacob familia
Pharaone altero fugatur;
non ut olim Iude vestigia
sub intrare potens, lacrimatur.
in deserto fame flagellatur,
adiutoris carens armatura,
quamquam clamat, tamen spo-
    liatur,
continuo forsan moritura,
miserorum exulum vox dura!
o Gallorum garritus doloris,
cum leonis cecitas obscura
fraudi paret vulpis proditoris.
eius fastus sustinens erroris
insurgito: alias labitur
et labetur quod habes honoris,
quod mox in facinus tardis ul-
    toribus itur.

Motetus
In nova fert animus mutatas di-
    cere formas
draco nequam quem olim pe-
    nitus
mirabili crucis potencia
debellabit Michael inclitus,
mox Absalon munitus gracia,
mox Ulixis gaudens facundia,
mox lupinis dentibus armatus,
sub Tersitis miles milicia
rursus vivit in vulpem mutatus,
fraudi cuius, lumine privatus
leo, vulpe imperante, paret.
oves suggit pullis saciatus.
heu! suggere non cessat et aret
ad nupcias carnibus non caret,
ve pullis mox, ve ceco leoni!
coram Christo tandem ve dra-
    coni.

[*Triplum:* The rooster chatters, weeping in anguish; indeed, the whole flock of roosters mourns, for it is deceitfully betrayed to the satrap while sitting vigilantly at its post. And the fox, like a grave-robber, flourishing with the shrewdness of Belial, rules with the particular approval of the lion—what distress! Lo, once again the family of Jacob flees another Pharaoh; not able as before to enter the promised land by following the path of the Jews, they weep. In the desert they are beaten by hunger, lacking the supplies of an ally; however much they wail, they are still robbed; if this keeps up they will likely die—the painful cry of the miserable exiles! The pitiful chatter of the roosters while the deep blindness of the lion yields to the fraud of the treacherous fox. Rise up, you who bear the arrogance of his crime: otherwise what you have left of honor is falling and will fall, for when the avenger is late, it soon turns into guilt.

Motetus: The mind demands to speak of forms changed into new things. The wicked dragon that glorious Michael will one day entirely defeat by the power of the marvelous cross, now furnished with the charm of Absalom, now rejoicing in the persuasiveness of Ulysses, now armed with wolflike teeth like a soldier in Thersites' army, lives again, turned into a fox whose fraud, hidden from light, the lion, controlled by the fox, allows. Gorged with chickens, he sucks the sheep. Alas! He does not stop sucking, thirsts for nourishment, and does not lack for meat—woe to the chickens, woe to the blind lion! But finally woe to the dragon in the face of Christ.][54]

The first line of the *motetus* ("the mind demands to speak of forms changed into new things") is a highly appropriate motto for this piece—both for the music, which exhibits the new technique of alternating triple and duple rhythm, and for the poetry, in which this line of classical dactylic hexameter (lifted, of course, from the first line of Ovid's *Metamorphoses*) immediately yields to

---

54. Following the Latin text given in Schrade. As Schrade explains in the *Commentary* volume accompanying volume I of his collection, the fox represents Enguerran de Marigni, chief counselor to Philippe the Fair, the "blind lion" who protected him. Not long after the accession to the throne of Louis X, Enguerran was hanged. Two other *Fauvel* motets, both also attributed to Vitry, develop the same political story with similar recourse to the traditional beast fable. See Schrade's *Commentary,* pp. 30-33. One might compare, among others, the various fables about cocks, foxes, and lions in Aesop (or Phaedrus), and the *Nonnes Preestes Tale* of Chaucer.

a newer form: the accentual, rhyming, decasyllabic line in which the rest of the *motetus* is written. In a piece of poetic symmetry reminiscent of *cancrizans* technique, Vitry ends the other text, the *triplum*, with another hexameter line, this one apparently of his own composition, since it connects in syntax and in rhyme with the rest of that text. If we count each of these hexameters as one line, the *triplum* has 24 lines, and the *motetus* has 16, a proportion of 3:2. And although a dactylic hexameter line may have as few as 13 or as many as 17 syllables, the line Vitry borrowed from Ovid has exactly 15 syllables, and is thus related to the other 10-syllable lines in the proportion of 3:2. Allowing for some overlap, the 6 four-line strophes of the *triplum* correspond roughly to the 6 *taleae* of the tenor; the *motetus*, whose 16 lines cannot be evenly divided by 6, is distributed in the pattern 2 lines, 3 lines, 3 lines, 3 lines, 3 lines, 2 lines. Given these remarkable replications of the basic proportional scheme of the music, we may surely apply the musical label *isorhythmic* to the text as well. In addition to writing a witty, learned political allegory in two related versions, Vitry was clearly also composing a text whose principles of construction, though entirely concealed in performance, were fully analogous to the principles upon which he was composing the music.

In the motets of Vitry and Machaut, such isorhythmic proportions provide constructive principles for the whole and for many much smaller details of music and text. Some fourteenth-century poems not written for music employ similar kinds of construction. The most obvious example is Dante's *Commedia,* with its three *cantice* replicated on the smallest scale by the persistent three-line pattern of the *terza rima,* whose overlapping rhyming suggests the patterns of overlap we have noticed in isorhythmic music. Even the way Dante adds an "extra" canto to the *Inferno* so that the total of cantos in the poem will be 100, the number of perfection, ought to remind us of similar adjustments at the end of "*Inter amoenitatis.*" And although Chaucer was once thought ignorant of music theory, David Chamberlain has recently shown that the *Parlement of Foules,* which alludes explicitly to the music of the spheres, ought to be printed with 700 lines; its total of lines is thus a product of that same number of perfection (100) and the number 7, which is the traditional number of tones in the music of the spheres, the sum of the cardinal and theological virtues

(4 + 3), and the number of lines in each of Chaucer's stanzas![55]

One aesthetic rationale for such procedures, and for the similar procedures of the isorhythmic motet, was the ancient claim, at least as old as Augustine's discussion of scriptural interpretation, that "the intelligible—the 'grain' which nourishes the interior understanding—is synonymous with the beautiful."[56] This extraordinarily tenacious theory, restated by Boccaccio, Petrarch, and Jean de Meun,[57] was based upon the practice of exegesis, careful, word-by-word study of a text, and was thus not fully applicable to the conditions under which most people heard music and poetry in the fourteenth century. An English courtier hearing Chaucer recite the *Parlement* could not possible have been aware of its constructive principles, nor could a French courtier hearing a performance of Vitry's "*Garrit gallus*" have heard all the ways it manifested its central proportion. Even the expectation that those very few who studied manuscripts would discover these proportions seems an act of faith: Chaucer's manuscripts have no line numbers; Vitry's have no bars. Perhaps the makers of such works believed that even if no one *ever* discovered all of the "intelligible" principles upon which they were constructed, it was nonetheless better to follow such principles than merely to aim for sensuous appeal on the surface.

If we imagine a continuum of poetic techniques in which such easily-heard surface patterns as alliteration occupy one pole, and such imperceptible constructive principles as the total number of lines occupy the other, we might provisionally bisect that continuum by separating techniques which appeal to the ear from techniques which appeal to the eye. And despite the fact that printing was still a century away, there are a number of techniques in fourteenth-century poetry which have to be classified as visual

55. See "The Music of the Spheres and *The Parlement of Foules*," *Chaucer Quarterly* 5 (1970): 32-56. For the older view, see Claire C. Olson, "Chaucer and Music of the Fourteenth Century," *Speculum* 16 (1941): 64-91, which minimizes Chaucer's familiarity with musical theories and techniques, and John Stevens, *Music and Poetry in the Early Tudor Court*, which claims that Chaucer's "references to music are general and untechnical; he shows little acquaintance with it either as a science or a craft" (p. 36). Chamberlain's essay disproves these assertions, as does the similar work of Russell A. Peck, "Theme and Number in Chaucer's *Book of the Duchess*," in Alastair Fowler and Douglas Brooks, *Silent Poetry*, pp. 73-115.

56. Robertson, *A Preface to Chaucer*, p. 58.

57. For samples of their restatements, see Robertson, pp. 60-64.

rather than aural.[58] The clearest example is anagram, and its use was frequent. Gervais du Bus, author of the *Roman de Fauvel*, hid his name in an anagram near the end of that work, and the name *Fauvel* is itself constructed as an anagram from the first letters of *Flatterie, Avarice, Vilenie, Variété, Envie,* and *Lacheté*.[59] These puzzles are both relatively easy, but it was only in 1970 that James Wimsatt discovered an acrostic in Machaut's Sixth Complaint which apparently reveals the identity of the much-addressed Marguerite as a woman admired by Pierre de Lusignan, King of Cyprus, whose name follows hers in the acrostic.[60] As an extreme example, we might consider this *Ballade Triple* by Pierre de Compiègne, which sounds like one poem to the ear, but reveals two other concealed poems and an acrostic to the eye:

Bien doit amant	qui vuet amours servir
Joyeusement	par maniere ordonée
Au temps plaisant	avoir doulz souvenir
Vray sentement	faut qu'il ait c'est l'entrée
Tenir en soy	largesce et courtoisie
Et esbanoy	si convient sans boidie
Car bien dire os	se il vuet remanoir
La ou enclos	par amoureux vouloir
A sens bonté	son cuer comme soubgis
Rens par compos	en la fin puet avoir.
Trait souffisant	bonne amour sans faillir
Et tresor gent	honnour clarté louée
Huy a servant	donne par vray desir
Ou il apent	d'amour enamourée
Notable aroy	pris los et siegnourie
Nul mal ce croy	a l'amant quoy qu'on die
En nul propos	en fait ny en sçavoir
Voir n'y puet sos	nul ne puet son pouoir
Raison pesé	amenryr ce m'est vis
Riens n'est au los	qu'il n'ait s'il fait devoir.

58. For some interesting details about fourteenth-century manuscript production, see Sarah Jane Williams, "An Author's Role in Fourteenth-century Book Production: Guillaume de Machaut's 'Livre ou je met toutes mes choses,'" *Romania* 90 (1969): 433-54.

59. As explained in the Introduction to the modern edition of *Le Roman de Fauvel*, ed. Arthur Langfors, p. iv. The anagram giving the author's name comes at line 3277 (p. 118 in Langfors).

Il soit parlent	amant doit requerir
Celéement	qu'il ait grace affermée
Humblement quant	en aler en venir
Esprins se sent	d'amoureuse pensée
Soy gengle poy	de sa dame agencie
Soy tienge quoy	disant: Flour et amie
En lieu desclos	mon cuer taindés en noir
Et par doulz flos	et au main et au soir
Tout son aé	a l'amoureux pourpris
Prenra repos	u on puet percevoir.
Rimes en mos	Princes sans non chaloir
Ycy enté	sens bien en vous a mis
Sont dont je los	chil qui puet esmouvoir.[61]

This poem may be read in ordinary fashion, all the way across each line, but the short lines alone also make a poem, as do the long lines alone, and the first letters of each line spell out the phrase *"Biauté, Clarté, Honneur, Richesse, et Pris."* Like every other line in the poem, the "line" produced by the acrostic is a ten-syllable line divisible into a four-syllable line and a six-syllable line; its rhymes are exactly those of lines 9, 19, 29, and 32 in the poem itself. Like the musical works it so clearly resembles, this poem has a kind of unity in its multiplicity: all three poems—all four, if we count the acrostic—describe the ideal qualities of a lover.

I have not provided a translation because all three poems, especially the composite poem produced by reading all the way across, depend on grammatical devices which cannot be replicated in another language. In the very first line, for example, *qui* must mean "whoever" in the long-line poem, which it begins, but simply "who" in the composite poem, where it modifies *amant*, "the lover." Compiègne also exploits the ambiguities of preposi-

---

60. See *The Marguerite Poetry of Guillaume de Machaut*, especially pp. 40-45.

61. This poem appears as an example in an anonymous treatise entitled *Les Règles de la Seconde Rhétorique*, datable to the earliest years of the fifteenth century; so far as I have been able to discover, it is the only known poem by Compiègne. The treatise appears, with a number of others, in a splendid collection edited by E. Langlois, *Recueil d'Arts de la Seconde Rhétorique;* see pp. 100-01. My friend and colleague, Professor Howard Garey of the Yale French Department, spent an afternoon demonstrating to me the futility of attempting a translation.

tions: in the third stanza of the long-line poem, we learn that "the lover should ask that he have plighted grace, in going and coming, with the loving thoughts of his ennobled lady." The last phrase, *"de sa dame agencie,"* looks like a subjective genitive: the lady is thinking the loving thoughts. But in the composite poem, the same phrase must be read differently; the lover "should prattle little about his ennobled lady." In other phrases, the strain of producing three simultaneous poems is more obvious: the frequency of parenthetical filler *("sans faillir," "Qu'on die,"* "without fail," "as they say," and the like) and the tortured syntax of participles are symptoms of that strain. As the makers of isorhythmic motets had distorted poems and melodies in order to make them fit a predetermined structure, Compiègne distorts and weakens his meaning in order to maintain his predetermined form.

Indeed, the adjustments Compiègne has to make in order to produce phrases which can either stand alone or fit into larger syntactic units are precisely analogous to the adjustments motet composers had to make in order to produce musical phrases which could be played against each other in canon or diminution. Because of the relative neutrality of musical materials, a quality we shall encounter again, these adjustments were easier for composers than for poets; the sacrifices Compiègne has to make in order to achieve something like polyphonic poetry are crippling. But in his willingness to make such sacrifices, to elevate construction as a principle for poetry, Compiègne is absolutely typical of his period. To modern minds, a defense of such techniques by recourse to mysticism may seem absurd, particularly in the case of secular works, but we ought to remember that a medieval man who considered a cathedral, motet, or other proportional artwork the ideal offering to his God would naturally apply the same aesthetic principles to works made for an earthly woman. We have already seen how the vocabulary of *courtoisie* depends upon the vocabulary of religious devotion; in the same way, the constructive techniques of the well-made love poem or love song draw on the symbolic proportions of the well-made religious poem or motet. Our modern sense that secular occasions demand a more spontaneous utterance is an attitude we must suspend in order to enter the aesthetic world of the fourteenth century.

But even if we can accept the notion that high artifice was

equally appropriate to religious and secular subjects, the display of artifice in crab canons and triple ballades remains a problem. Surely such works owe some of their intricacy not to the reverent replication of heavenly proportion but to the ingenuity of their human makers, and to the desire of those makers to have their skill appreciated. Again, the distinction between the eye and the ear points up the problem. The audiences for whom these works were made, even the courtly audiences to whom they were primarily directed, usually *heard* them performed: we know the dates and places of public readings by Chaucer and of musical performances of Machaut's works. But some of these works, as we have seen, involve techniques which may only be detected by the eye: no one can retain the first letters of each line of a poem in his head so as to construct an acrostic while listening to a recitation; no one can separate the musical lines he is hearing sung sufficiently to identify a mirror canon. In both cases, these techniques must be aimed at a *coterie* with access to manuscripts and the technical training to understand notations, both musical and poetic, which were at times deliberate puzzles.

Yet neither in music nor in poetry is it the case that *all* constructive techniques are beyond hearing. Crab and mirror canons may be "eye music," but ordinary canons, with each voice making an independent entry, are one of the most "hearable" kinds of musical construction, and they were understandably popular in the fourteenth century. The *chace* in France and the *caccia* in Italy were also usually supplied with texts about hunting, so that the idea of pursuit exemplified in the canon form was made explicit in the text—a strong indication that this constructive principle was also expressive. In poetry, even the simplest *rondeaux* use their formal repetitions for rhetorical purposes: if the lines to be repeated are, for example, a noun phrase, they may be the subject of a verb in their first appearance, the object of another verb in their second. By constructing his poem from blocks of material which can be inserted into different kinds of syntactic slots, the poet turns repetition into variation—with comic or ironic results for any alert listener.[62] Chaucer even uses the musical technique

62. See Howard B. Garey, "The Variable Structure of the Fifteenth-century Rondeau," in *The Sixth LACUS Forum* (1979), now in press.

of diminution with a hearable and expressive effect, in these lines from the *Parlement:*

. . . And over the gate, with lettres large iwroughte,	
There were vers iwriten, as me thoughte,	[4 lines narrative]
On eyther half, of ful gret difference,	
Of which I shal now seyn the pleyn sentence:	
"Thorgh me men gon into that blysful place	
Of hertes hele and dedly woundes cure:	
Thorgh me men gon unto the well of grace,	
There grene and lusty May shal evere endure.	[1 stanza
This is the wey to al good aventure.	gold inscription]
Be glad, thow redere, and thy sorwe of-caste;	
Al open am I—passe in, and sped thee faste!"	
"Thorgh me men gone," than spak that other side,	
Unto the mortal strokes of the spere	
Of which Disdayn and Daunger is the gyde,	
That nevere tre shal fruyt ne leves bere.	[1 stanza black
This strem yow ledeth to the sorweful were	inscription]
There as the fish in prysoun is al drye;	
Th' eschewing is only the remedye!"	
These vers of gold and blak iwriten were,	
Of which I gan astoned to beholde,	[2 lines narrative]
For with that oon encresede ay me fere,	[black]
And with that other gan myn herte bolde;	[gold]
That oon me hette, that other dide me colde:	[gold / black]
No wit hadde I, for errour, for to chese,	[1 line narrative]
To entre or flen, or me to save or lese.[63]	[gold / black / gold / black]

I am not claiming that a listener would necessarily have noticed that each section of intervening narrative is half as long as its predecessor, or that the exact sizes of the alternating references to the two inscriptions are first a stanza, then a line, then a half line, than a quarter line. But surely any attentive listener would have heard the general effect: an increasing speed of alternation, dramatically representing the speaker's indecision as he turns his head from one inscription to the other.

And here we have reached an important point, for it is just when constructive techniques have a perceptible and dramatic ef-

---

63. Lines 123-47, following the text of F. N. Robinson, *The Works of Geoffrey Chaucer,* p. 312.

fect that the attempt to separate them from expressive techniques fails. We may safely assign the fact that the *Parlement* has 700 lines to the classification of constructive techniques, and conclude that the meaning of that fact, for anyone who discovers it, is "intelligible," mystical, allegorical. We may say, indeed have said, similar things about the constructive techniques of any isorhythmic motet. We may dismiss *cancrizans* and anagrams, mirror canons and palindromes as constructive techniques without such mystic resonance, serving instead to demonstrate the ingenuity of their makers. But when we confront this elegantly constructed *and* psychologically affecting piece of diminution in Chaucer, or the equally symmetrical, equally dramatic hunting canon of Avignon, in which the three voices actually chase each other,[64] the notion of any absolute division between constructive and expressive principles must be abandoned. Both are always present in any work of music or literature worth calling art, and it is a part of the artistry of such works to blur the line between them.

Still, as I suggested earlier, the varying admixture of constructive and expressive techniques may help us make a crude distinction between the motet style and the *chanson* style. In Machaut's *corpus*, for example, the twenty-three motets, all written before 1356, include twenty employing some form of isorhythm and ten employing diminution in the tenor. While it is a legitimate claim for these pieces that "their musical sensitivity always cleverly conceals the strictness of the carefully calculated structure,"[65] they remain polyphonic, isorhythmic, and polytextual. By contrast, the pieces Machaut called by names as old as the trouvère tradition—*ballades, virelais, lais,* and *rondeaux*—will immediately strike any listener as much more "hearable" than the motets.[66] The most im-

---

64. For a transcription of this extraordinary piece, which is found in the Ivrea manuscript, see *Archiv für Musikwissenschaft* 7 (1925): 251-52, where the canon appears in two parts. Actually, we now know that it works in three parts; see Reaney, "Ars Nova in France," pp. 16-18.

65. Bridgman, "France and Burgundy," p. 159, summarizing the findings of Ursula Gunther, "The Fourteenth-century Motet and its Development," *Musica Disciplina* 12 (1958): 27-58, an admirable essay.

66. Gilbert Reaney has published extensively on the development of these forms in poetry and music. Three important articles are "A Chronology of the Ballades, Rondeaux and Virelais set to Music by Guillaume de Machaut," *Musica Disciplina* 6 (1952): 33-38, which includes an analytical table of forms; "Guillaume de Machaut: Lyric Poet," *Music and*

mediate evidence for the centrality of melodic expression in this style is the surprising persistence of monody: most of the *lais* and *virelais* are monodic, despite the evident general triumph of polyphony throughout the western world by this date. And even when there are supporting musical parts, the melody takes clear precedence, and there is only one text. Though capable of extraordinary feats of construction, Machaut evidently placed great trust in the expressive power of naked melody, as, in their quite different ways, would many later composers.

An even cruder distinction between national styles may be made along the same lines. In Italy, where the troubadour influence remained strong, and where there was also a popular tradition of monodic religious songs called *laude,* polyphony was usually restricted to two parts and followed the pattern of the old *conductus,* with both parts sharing a text and usually singing the same word at the same time. Even though French innovations in notation were known and partially adopted in Italy, isorhythmic intricacies were much less common. "In the work of Italian composers," says Federico Ghisi, "there was a pronounced striving to safeguard the expressive values of their own tradition, based on the linear quality of the melody, whose monodic character is enlivened by a vocalization full of freedom and fancy."[67] Italian composers also showed a stronger respect for poetic form and a reluctance to violate its shape as the French motet writers had done. So different was this Italian music from the French motet style that Leo Schrade has argued against the wholesale adoption of *ars nova* as a label for fourteenth-century music: "Despite active communication between Italy and France, the Italians never used the term *Ars nova* for their fourteenth-century music, nor was it ever used in countries such as England and Germany."[68] It would probably be more precise to follow Schrade and restrict the specific term *ars nova* to the isorhythm and allied techniques of the French school, but it would be a serious misconception to imagine that

Letters 39 (1958): 38-51; and "The Development of the Rondeau, Virelai, and Ballade Forms from Adam de la Hale to Guillaume de Machaut," in *Festschrift Karl Gustav Fellerer,* pp. 241-47.

67. "Italy: 1300-1600" in Sternfeld, *Music from the Middle Ages to the Renaissance,* p. 241.

68. In the *Commentary* to Volume I, p. 5.

the more general importance of constructive techniques in this period could be limited to any one country or any one group of composers or poets. The contrapuntal subtleties of some four-teenth-century music, like the grand numerical designs of some fourteenth-century poems, are their inheritance from Pythago-rean music theory and patristic allegory. In every country and in every art, these hierarchical habits of mind, founded upon classi-cal and Christian wisdom, strengthened by the *quadrivium,* and nurtured by the aural and visual habits of a manuscript culture, held their own tenaciously.

But in poetry, a change was coming; John Fleming calls it "a movement from broad intellectual abstraction to concrete ex-ample and, hence, to verisimilitude."[69] The moral impact of Chau-cer's *Canterbury Tales* for example, is as much a product of their tough, perceptive depiction of human greed and pride as of their formal and allegorical sophistication. And I believe that Chaucer came to recognize that artistic pride could be a powerful motive for employing ingenious constructive techniques of the kind we have noticed in his *Parlement;* that work, described as "the book of Seint Valentynes day of the Parlement of Briddes" is among the "translacions and enditynges of worldly vanitees" which Chaucer revokes in his retractions at the end of the *Parson's Tale.* [70] He had never been as fond of recondite virtuosity as Machaut, and the motion of his later career is away from formal and musical display and toward explicit moral urgency: his last work, the *Parson's Tale,* is a prose sermon on penitence.

Many accounts of the later career of Machaut make a similar argument, describing him as turning away from "artifice" not to-ward Chaucer's kind of moral force but toward a Romantic and "authentic" expression of self. Much has been made of a pas-sage in the *Remède de Fortune* in which Machaut declares that he composes

>   . . . chansons et lais,
>   Balades, rondiaus, virelais
>   Et chans, selonc mon sentement,
>   Amoureus et non autrement;

69. The *"Roman de la Rose": A Study in Allegory and Iconography,* p. 30.
70. Lines 1084-86; in Robinson, p. 265.

> Car qui de sentement ne fait,
> Son ouevre et son chant contrefait.

[*chansons* and *lais*, / *ballades, rondeaux, virelais* / and melodies, following my feeling, / loving, not hypocritical; / for whoever does not compose from feeling / is counterfeiting his text and tune.][71]

The omission of motets from the list of forms is significant, as is the fact that this passage precedes the interpolation into the poem of a monodic *lai*, but we should be prevented from over-reading these lines by considering some of the actual techniques of Machaut's love poems and love songs, those supposedly written from *sentement*. The *Livre du Voir-dit,* Machaut's account of his aged dalliance with a young woman named Peronne, contains, among other anagrams, this line:

> Pour li changier nule autre dame;
> Madame . . . ,

[To exchange for her no other lady / Milady . . .]

which yields the names "Perone d'Armantière" and "Guillaume de Machau."[72] And the text of the refrain from one of the musical *rondeaux* in the *Voir-dit* is a number anagram which yields Peronne's name:

> Dix et sept, cinq, trese
> quatorse et quinse . . .

[17 (= R), 5 (= E), 13 (= N), / 14 (= O), and 15 (= P).][73]

Not only do these numbers conceal Peronne's name, but their total is 64 (17 + 5 + 13 + 14 + 15); the text has 12 syllables, and both the texted part in the music and the countertenor contain 52 notes. 52 + 12 = 64! So much for our notion of *sentement* as some

---

71. Following the French text of *Oeuvres de Guillaume de Machaut,* ed. Ernest Hoepffner, vol. II, 403-08.

72. *Le Livre du Voir-dit,* ed. Paulin Paris, p. 370.

73. I follow the text and transcription of the refrain given by Gilbert Reaney (*The New Oxford History of Music,* vol. III, pp. 25-26), including the editorial tie in bar 11. For the whole piece, see Schrade, vol. III, pp. 160-61.

kind of spontaneous overflow: even the extravagant *ballade* of Compiègne, after all, includes "Vray sentement" among its list of ideal qualifications for the lover. Evidently fourteenth-century sentiment could express itself in recondite artifice, and the *Voir-dit* claims that Peronne is delighted with anagrams and makes one herself. Rather than accepting a dialectical account of the later career of Machaut as incipient Romanticism, we should see his work as effecting a combination of constructive and expressive principles. His secular songs, beautiful and affecting as they are, often involve techniques learned in the making of isorhythmic motets; his letters and poems to Peronne, touching as they may be, display the full range of his rhetorical virtuosity.

A more balanced account of Machaut will have to see him as at once the heir of the trouvères, with their similarly conventional claims of sentiment and their similarly intricate poetic forms, and the heir of the early polyphonists, with their mystical reverence for number and their literary fondness for troping. In the relations between constructive and expressive techniques, of which Machaut's music and poetry present paradigm cases, the two arts found renewed opportunities for mutual influence. Machaut himself left no treatise on either art, but his student Eustache Deschamps, in *L'Art de Dictier* (1392), describes the relations between *musique naturelle* (poetry) and *musique artificielle* (performed music) as *"comme un mariage,"* like a marriage,[74] employing the same metaphor Dante had used in *De Vulgari Eloquentia* . The sweeping changes in musical and literary technique during the four centuries preceding Deschamps' treatise, barely sketched in this chapter, had doubtless frequently tested that marriage, but somehow it remained a viable partnership.[75] Like human spouses, music and poetry had so influenced each other, so pervasively borrowed from one another, that it seemed impossible to divide their properties.

---

74. In *Oeuvres Complètes de Eustache Deschamps,* ed. Gaston Raynaud, vol. VII, p. 271.

75. The absence of musical analysis weakens the attempt to separate music and rhetoric in Douglas Kelly, *Medieval Imagination: Rhetoric and the Poetry of Courtly Love.* See especially pp. xiii, 7-12, 239-56, valuable for collecting many contemporary comments on the functions of music and rhetoric in medieval French poetry; my conclusions are somewhat unlike Kelly's.

4

The Rhetorical Renaissance

Introduction: Ears and Eyes

In September, 1416, during a recess in the deliberations of the Council of Constance, a temporarily unemployed apostolic secretary named Poggio Bracciolini visited the monastery of St. Gall, where Notker Balbulus had lived and worked centuries before. Poggio, however, had never heard of Notker, and the documents for which he was searching were not musical but literary. In the dungeon of St. Gall, he found a book that had been lost to the learned world for nearly 600 years: a complete copy of Quintilian's *Institutio oratoria*.[1] The enthusiasm with which other learned men greeted both this find and the similar recovery of a complete text of Cicero's *De oratore* in 1421 was intense, and may seem puzzling to us. After all, the pseudo-Ciceronian *Ad Herennium* and other technical handbooks from antiquity had been well-known throughout the Middle Ages, as such medieval treatises as the *Poetria Nova* of Geoffrey of Vinsauf amply demonstrate. But both the classical treatises preserved by the Middle Ages and the medieval treatises themselves tend to describe rhetorical technique in constructive terms, without explaining *why* orators should use it or how audiences could benefit from it. Quintilian, by contrast, endorses rhetoric as a system of education and a way of life; the recovery of his treatise helped such humanists as Poggio define themselves against the scholastic Middle Ages, where rhetoric had been a set of prescriptions or ornaments for preaching. For the humanists, rhetoric was aesthetic and moral, essential to a secular and civic way of life. To authenticate their preference

1. See Murphy, *Rhetoric in the Middle Ages*, pp. 357-58.

for an expressive, persuasive, kinetic rhetoric, they reached back to Quintilian, Cicero, Longinus, and ultimately to Aristotle, cherishing particularly those passages describing the power of rhetoric to move its hearers. Hanna Gray summarizes their attitude:

> They believed . . . that men could be moulded most effectively, and perhaps only, through the art of eloquence, which endowed the precept with life, immediacy, persuasive effect, and which stimulated a man's will as well as informing his reason. In attacking scholastic logic and scholastic Latin, the humanists were condemning at once an attitude toward knowledge which appeared to stress the abstract and intellectual, to have no true utility or direct relevance for human life, and criticizing what they regarded as the failure of the scholastics to communicate important truths with persuasive effect.[2]

The humanists embraced an expressive theory of rhetoric, and their rediscovery of such texts as Quintilian enabled them to appeal to classical authority in support of a drift toward expressive practices which was already evident in both poetry and music well before Poggio's visit to St. Gall.

It has been customary since Burckhardt to stress the rise of individualism in the Renaissance, but many of the resulting studies of "self-consciousness" and "self-expression" reveal more about modern preoccupations with psychology than about Renaissance ways of making art. We might more usefully approach the question from the other side, by examining how Renaissance poets and composers thought of their audiences, how they hoped to persuade or impress them. As we have seen, the disparities between what one can learn about a medieval poem or composition by examining a manuscript and what one can deduce from hearing it read or sung are so significant as to suggest that medieval poets and composers thought of themselves as addressing three different audiences; the relative importance of those audiences changed in the Renaissance.

1. First of all, regardless of whether the work was nominally sacred or secular, the medieval artist was addressing God. The

---

2. "Renaissance Humanism: The Pursuit of Eloquence," in *Renaissance Essays*, ed. Kristeller and Wiener, pp. 202-03. Compare the more elaborate work of Nancy S. Struever, *The Language of History in the Renaissance*.

ultimate truths expressed by literary allegory or isorhythmic polyphony were truths about God, indeed, versions of the hierarchy
by which God had wisely ordered His world. Secular love poetry
and song could draw upon these constructive techniques because
their makers sought to honor earthly women by offering them
artifacts made with th same techniques, and expressing the same
distance and awe, as artifacts explicitly made for God. These techniques, addressed to the intellect and rooted in Augustine's mystical aesthetic of number, were modified and attenuated in the
Renaissance as both Protestant and Catholic piety moved toward
a more personal expression of devotion, and as such myths as the
"music of the spheres" ceased to command actual belief and became instead, as John Hollander has shown, "decorative metaphors and mere turns of wit."[3] Once supported by the enormous
prestige of ancient wisdom as Christianized by the Fathers, large-
scale mathematical methods of organization in both poetry and
music, never audible to human ears, had ceased by the end of the
Renaissance to claim such mystical meaning. They survived into
the eighteenth century, on a more human scale, as exercises in
artistic technique.

2. Medieval manuscripts reveal another class of constructive
techniques which had always displayed ingenuity rather than
piety: anagrams, acrostics, palindromes, mirror canons, *cancrizans*. These techniques, also usually imperceptible to the ear, define another audience: those able to discover and appreciate such
artifice upon examining a given manuscript. For music, this audience would particularly include musicians, who would need to
solve notational puzzles in order to achieve performances, and
would thus necessarily notice elements of compositional technique which their performance of the music would nonetheless
be unable to make audible. For poetry, this audience would have
to include scribes, who would have a chance to notice anagrams,
acrostics, and similar niceties in the slow physical process of copying a text. In both cases, membership in such an audience qualified one as an adept—a member, if only an apprentice, of the
same craft as the composer or poet who had made the first version
of the work. In their quest for persuasive expression and their

3. *The Untuning of the Sky,* p. 19; Hollander's title is a metaphor for this process.

enthusiasm for classical models, the humanists sometimes attacked these devices as "Gothic barbarisms," but the printing press, by distributing more widely the technical knowledge about polyphonic composition and poetic form which medieval artists had painstakingly worked out, enlarged the pool of adepts in both arts. Consequently, a dogmatic humanist position, which would define rhetoric exclusively as moral or emotional persuasion, restrict imitation to classical models, and purge music of "artifice" in order to restore its fabled moral "effects," could not be sustained, although some theorists of each art argued passionately along those lines. In practice, poets and composers remained fascinated by technique as an end in itself and eager to display their technical skills, even as their interest in a more expressive or "hearable" art increased.

3. Finally, more obviously in Italy than in France, poets and composers from the thirteenth century on were developing their vocabularies of expressive devices, techniques particularly directed toward what was always the largest audience for any poem or musical work: those who would hear it performed. In medieval culture, the suspicion of "surfaces" brought about by Augustine's distinction between things to be used and things to be enjoyed, and by the similar distinction between letter and spirit in allegorical interpretation, had deprived poets and composers of moral or even aesthetic authority for pursuing thrilling melodies or affective language, though no one who has heard a live rendering of a canto of Dante or a *chanson* of Machaut can deny that these men, like most great medieval artists, paid close attention to the "surface" of their works, those aspects one could hear. But the philosophical grounding provided for such concern by the rediscovery of Quintilian and (later) of Aristoxenos and other ancient writers on music was important; it provided the needed authority for an art that was increasingly seeking to move its hearers.

The lines between these techniques, and between the audiences they implied, were not absolute. Mystical techniques shaded into ingenious techniques, and as we have seen, such methods of construction as simple canon and rhyme could be heard in a performance as well as studied in a manuscript. But in terms of Walter J. Ong's "sensorium," which arranges human senses as follows,

touch—taste—smell—hearing—sight,

the basic motion of the early Renaissance, greatly aided and increased by the humanist revival of rhetoric, was toward the left, the direction of "concreteness, matter, potency, indistinctness, . . . subjectivity."[4] Employing physical verbs of touching, Petrarch could claim that Cicero, Seneca, and Horace

> . . . stamp and drive deep into the heart the sharpest and most ardent stings of speech, by which the lazy are startled, the ailing are kindled, and the sleepy aroused, the sick healed, and the prostrate raised, and those who stick to the ground lifted up to the highest thoughts and to honest desire.[5]

This language is astonishingly close to the claims urged for ancient music by the later "musical humanists," who fixed on Biblical and classical legends—David healing Saul with his harp, Timotheus arousing and calming Alexander with his lyre—and urged composers to restore such miraculous and kinetic effects to music. As a "medieval" constrast, here is a tercet from the *Inferno* in which Dante insists on visual metaphors as a way of urging us to understand his allegory:

> O voi ch'avete li 'ntelletti sani,
>   mirate la dottrina che s'asconde
>   sotto 'l velame de li versi strani.

> [Oh you who have sound intellect, gaze upon the doctrine which conceals itself beneath the veil of these strange verses.] (IX, 61–63)

These metaphors capture the constrast between an ideal reader whose intellectual eyes can penetrate the veil of poetry to reach an allegorical meaning and an ideal hearer so moved by what he hears that the words touch and sting him.

But the contrast was not actually so sharp. Dante's *Commedia*, however allegorical and intellectual, has a highly expressive surface and a moral fervor not unlike that we noticed in the later

---

4. *Interfaces of the Word*, p. 136.

5. *De sui ipsius et multorum ignorantia*, tr. H. Nachod in *The Renaissance Philosophy of Man*, ed. Cassirer et al., p. 104.

Chaucer; Petrarch's poetry, however expressive and sonorous, also employs techniques learned from the recondite virtuosity of the Middle Ages, including anagrammatic distortions of Laura's name. The sensorium is a continuum, not a dialectic, and the general motion toward the sense of hearing did not require abandoning entirely those aspects of art connected with sight, the formalism and abstraction which had been a part of music and poetry throughout the later Middle Ages. Rather than breaking sharply with those older techniques, Renaissance poets and composers found new uses for them; techniques which had originated as means of construction acquired more precise expressive values. As composers began to judge their works by more obviously expressive criteria, they began to attach more specific expressive meaning to their vertical harmonies, developing a fuller "harmonic vocabulary." In the sixteenth-century Italian madrigal, harmony became a means of text-setting: the contrasts between major and minor triads, consonant and dissonant harmonies were used to emphasize contrasts between sweet words and painful words. Even polyphonic counterpoint was drawn into the orbit of expression; it proved a highly successful method for dramatizing the division of the speaker in Petrarchan poetry. Poets made similar expressive demands of their constructive materials. The formal divisions of Petrarch's sonnets, for example, are often structural examples of oxymoron; the form reflects the conflicts within the speaker, and it was this aspect of Petrarch, the investing of a previously constructive element with expressive significance, to which Ronsard, Sidney, and a host of later Renaissance poets responded so vigorously. Even rhyme, which had originated as a constructive device, became for these poets, preeminently for Shakespeare, a way to extend and complicate poetic meaning.

The humanist disciples of the ancient rhetoricians may have begun this process by making large persuasive claims for formal devices, including the claim that the sound of the word as a sound could have moral force. But the printing press, by multiplying the availability of medieval scholastic rhetorics, and by exposing more people to the visual appearance on the page of artificial formal devices, kept alive a more technical and constructive view of language; the *Doctrinale* of Alexander of Villedieu, a rhetorical manual written in leonine hexameters in 1199, ran through 267 editions between the invention of printing and 1558.[6] Literary treatises of the Renaissance found ways to combine such medieval and constructive lore with the classical and expressive concerns of the humanist movement, despite potential conflicts. Puttenham's *Arte of English Poesie* (1589), for example, elaborates the ways various figures of speech can persuade, but also devotes an entire book to poetic "proportion," a term borrowed (along with many others) from music theory. But in music theory itself, there was a more explicit and polemical struggle between the champions of construction and expression. Of our four coordinates (see figure 3, in ch. 2), music theory had been the most abstract, idealist, and constructive in the Middle Ages, though the late centuries, as we have seen, produced more treatises from the hands of practicing musicians. But in the sixteenth century, older music theory, and older music, came under a concerted attack from "musical humanism," a poetic and expressive movement fueled by the rediscovery of ancient writings on music and dedicated to a more arresting and persuasive modern music. The most extreme musical humanists opposed polyphony and other constructive devices, arguing that they obscured the expression of the text; they were of course unable to eliminate those practices, but they did alter the course of musical history by inventing the recitative and championing the cause of early opera. A little later, and for similar reasons, some English poets began to attack rhyme; they were similarly unable to eliminate rhyme from lyric poetry, for rhyme, like counterpoint, had become a valuable expressive technique, not merely an abstract means of formal construction. But in the dramatic and heroic forms which were becoming more important as the influence of Aristotelianism filtered slowly into England, blank verse was dominant: Marlowe's *Tamburlaine* (1588) declares its independence from "jigging veins of rhyming mother wits," and the line of development from Marlowe's blank verse through Shakespeare's to Milton's is a clear one. All these writers were first-class rhymers who chose to do without rhyme in certain works, just as Monteverdi, a brilliant madrigalist and contrapuntal com-

---

6. See Baxter Hathaway's introduction to the facsimile edition of George Puttenham's *Arte of English Poesie*, pp. viii-ix. All citations of Puttenham follow this text.

poser, chose to modify some of his constructive techniques when he turned to the composition of operas. In neither case did the adoption of a more flexible form necessarily entail the dogmatic rejection of past techniques.

Despite the general Renaissance motion toward expressive form, in practice and in theory, some poets and composers continued to cultivate more abstract and constructive forms as tests of skill. The rise of instrumental music, which is less obviously expressive than music with a text, and the continued use of poetic techniques designed to dazzle us by their complexity constitute clear evidence of the irrepressible appeal of virtuosity. Spenser's numerical games in the *Epithalamion* and John Bull's hexachordal keyboard fantasies are two English examples of such techniques taken to recondite and intellectual extremes. Among theoretical works, Joachim Burmeister's *Musica Poetica* (1606), a musical rhetoric that applies names long used for various rhetorical devices to compositional techniques, with examples drawn from Orlando di Lasso and other polyphonic composers, makes its analogies between literary and musical practice along strictly constructive lines. And even in such overtly expressive and dramatic masterworks as the plays of Shakespeare and the operas of Monteverdi, there are methods of organization, patterns of symmetry, exuberances of rhyme and canon for which no one can claim a precise persuasive effect; they are present as demonstrations of the skills of their makers, a motive Richard Lanham captures perfectly when he describes *Venus and Adonis* and *The Rape of Lucrece* as "masterpieces in the old sense of the word—pieces made by an artist to prove he is a master."[7]

Music from Machaut to Josquin: Expressive Developments

Now for some details. According to a whimsical account of the arts in France in Martin le Franc's *Le Champion des dames*, a long poem dedicated to Philip the Good, the leading composers of the generation after Machaut—Tapissier, Carmen, and Césaris—were quickly forgotten when people heard the superior works of Gilles Binchois and Guillaume Dufay, both born about 1400. Binchois and Dufay, says le Franc,

7. *The Motives of Eloquence*, p. 82.

> . . . ont prins de la contenance
> Angloise et ensuy Dunstable
> Pour quoy merveilleuse plaisance
> Rend leur chant joyeux et notable.

[. . . have taken on the English countenance, and followed Dunstable, which is why a marvelous pleasantness makes their music happy and distinguished.][8]

We do not know exactly what le Franc meant by *"la contenance Angloise,"* but the notion that French composers could wear English faces is a striking metaphor, one which suggests that Binchois and Dufay took from Dunstable a fresh sound, not merely an intellectual technique. Richard Crocker argues that the influence was harmonic, that Dufay "contrived a new way to produce rich sounds, parallel thirds and sixths; these were apparently what struck [his] ears and what [he] felt to be responsible for the English success" (p. 146). International influences in the late Middle Ages had been primarily technical; French innovations in notation, for example, had spread with minor modifications to Italy and England. But this influence, coming back into France, was sensuous: it was Dunstable's sonorities that Dufay was anxious to emulate. *Le Champion des dames* also mentions the beautiful playing of two blind violists from Spain; when they played, according to the poet, one could see

> Dufay despite et frogne
> Qu'il n'a melodie si belle

[. . . Dufay angry and frowning, because he does not have so lovely a tune.][9]

It does not matter whether this account is fiction or truth; the fact that le Franc could portray the leading composer in France as jealous of someone else's melody indicates the extent to which expressive and aural criteria had gained importance.

Some of the most obvious developments in fifteenth-century music—the more frequent use of a four-part texture, the richer

8. Following the French text given in Gustave Reese, *Music in the Renaissance*, p. 13. All citations of Reese in this chapter refer to this book.

9. In Reese, p. 51.

choral sound produced by using more than one singer on a part, the wider total vocal range, the composition of leaping counter-tenor lines which filled in harmonies, even the "parody" tech-nique in which a mass was built on the melody of a secular song—may be seen as results of the increased importance of expressive criteria. But these expressive innovations, while they brought about changes in the techniques we have been calling construc-tive, could not and did not replace those techniques. In fact, ca-nonic and retrograde treatment of melodic material flourished in the second half of the fifteenth century, as Crocker explains:

> The techniques characteristic of the big motet in the early 1400s—cantus-firmus tenor and strictly periodic rhythm—were rarely combined after 1450 to produce an isorhythmic motet, and then only for ceremonial purposes. But separately these techniques lived on. . . . Deep within the sounding tex-ture the cantus firmus was sung backward or upside down, its notes and rhythms selected and combined in ever-changing orders at the fancy of the composer. Such elaborate constructions occurred after 1450 with unprecedented fre-quency . . . [and] helped guide the composer through the maze of rich, varied harmonies out of which he would build his work. (p. 155)

Dufay's *Missa Se la face ay pale* provides a paradigm case of the skill with which fifteenth-century composers assimilated the expressive and hearable to the constructive and intellectual. The mass is based on a secular *ballade* Dufay had composed earlier, a melody with syncopated rhythms and frequent wide leaps; in the mass, this tune becomes a tenor and takes on a constructive function, appearing in different parts of the mass in different, mathemati-cally determined proportions. The titles of the masses of Johan-nes Ockeghem (c. 1420–1495), Dufay's younger rival, indicate his similar interest in both kinds of technique: the *Missa Ma Maistresse* and the *Missa Au travail suis* take their titles from secular songs used in composing them, while the *Missa cuiusvis toni* and the *Missa prolationum* take their titles from technical features of their construction—in the first, the fact that the music may be per-formed in any of four modes by merely changing the clef; in the second, the fact that each of the four voices employs one of the four basic rhythmic patterns described as "prolations" in Vitry's *Ars Nova*.[10]

Despite the persistence of these older techniques, the fifteenth century saw a significant change in the fundamental methods of composition. Composers like Machaut, whether writing a motet from the bottom up or a *chanson* from the top down, had begun with a melodic line, either pre-existent or newly composed, and had added other lines to that part one at a time; their method is usually called "successive" composition. Dufay's emulation of the harmonic sonorities of Dunstable, and his frequent employment of the technique called *"fauxbourdon,"* which produces chains of parallel six-three chords (triads in first inversion), may stand as examples of "simultaneous" composition. Composers were acquiring the ability to think in chordal terms. This process, which was by no means instantaneous, would eventually lead to the breakdown of the modal system and the evolution of the tonal system.

Some theorists recognized the importance of this change quite early. Johannes Tinctoris (c. 1435–1511), in the third of his twelve treatises, explains that the idea of modes applies only to a single line, and recognizes that polyphony demands a different theoretical language, one capable of describing harmonies.[11] Pietro Aron, in *De institutione harmonica* (1516) announces that composers have abandoned successive composition for simultaneous composition. Whether these early examples of attention to simultaneity, practical and theoretical, constitute an incipient awareness of the harmonic grammar we now call the tonal system is a matter of considerable scholarly debate. But we need not resolve that debate to recognize in fifteenth-century music what Gustave Reese judiciously calls "a heightened feeling for chordal sonority and especially for tonal centers."[12]

10. For technical details about the Dufay mass, see Reese, p. 70. where the *ballade* melody is quoted. For discussions of the various Ockeghem pieces, see pp. 129-34. Some recent recordings of parody masses based on secular *chansons* include performances of the *chansons;* two distinguished examples are the Nonesuch recording of Ockeghem's *Missa Ma maistresse* and *Missa Au travail suis* by Pomerium Musices, directed by Alexander Blachly, featuring Ann Monoyios, and the Titanic recording of Josquin's *Missa Fortuna desperata* by the Boston Camerata, directed by Joel Cohen, featuring Rufus Hallmark.

11. See Reese, p. 141.

12. p. 287. At one extreme in the musicological debate stands Edward Lowinsky, who

Among indices of their increased attention to these harmonic matters is the way some composers began to use chords to set texts. In the first half of the fifteenth century, Arnold de Lantins, Binchois, and Dufay all introduced sections of block chords with fermatas as a powerful way to declaim important words. Here is such a passage from de Lantins, a setting of the phrase "daughters of Jerusalem"; the text of the motet comes from the Song of Songs:[13]

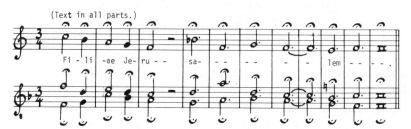

(Text in all parts.)

Fi - li -ae Je- ru - - sa- - - - - - - - - lem - - -- -

---

has asserted, in *Tonality and Atonality in Sixteenth-century Music*, p. 1, that "the written image of polyphonic music of the Middle Ages and the Renaissance conceals the inroads of a nascent feeling of tonality upon the modal structure." In his earlier essay, "Music in the Culture of the Renaissance," *Journal of the History of Ideas* 15 (1954), p. 530, he applies this idea to Dufay, claiming that "tonal harmony . . . in a series of three-part *chansons* by Dufay . . . shows the beginnings of the feeling for tonic-dominant relationships." Even more extravagant is Lowinsky's hypothesis that motets of the Netherlands school in the sixteenth century, apparently more conservative and modal than contemporaneous Italian compositions, actually conceal a "secret chromatic art," an idea developed in his most controversial book, *Secret Chromatic Art in the Netherlands Motet*. Those opposing Lowinsky stress the continued importance of modal considerations throughout the sixteenth century: William Byrd, writing 150 years later than Dufay in conservative England, can be rigorously modal, as R. O. Morris argues in *Contrapuntal Technique in the Sixteenth Century*. Richard Crocker, in a severe review of Lowinsky's *Tonality and Atonality*, appearing in the *Journal of Music Theory* 6 (1962): 142-53, and in an essay of his own, "Discant, Counterpoint, and Harmony," in the *Journal of the American Musicological Society* 15 (1962): 1-21, attacks even the common distinction between "successive" and "simultaneous" composition as "a false dichotomy." Crocker believes that medieval composition "is not more successive than our own. The really important difference is that the medieval system uses a basic unit consisting of two notes, whereas we use a unit of three notes" (pp. 12-13). Claude Palisca, also reviewing Lowinsky in the *Journal of the American Musicological Society* 16 (1963): 82-86, is more inclined to accept Lowinsky's major hypothesis. It is easy to see why this debate is so difficult to resolve: the processes it seeks to describe, the development of the capacity to think in harmonies and the accommodation of that capacity to existing methods of composition, were sure to proceed in different ways and at different speeds in different countries, and to involve experimental failures as well as successes.

13. I follow the transcription given in Reese, p. 40.

Dufay used such chords to emphasize the names of Eugene IV and Sigismund in a motet celebrating a treaty they signed in 1433; Binchois used them for a pious address to the wood of the holy cross. This technique draws on the power of chords as chords, not as passing consequences of melodic motion (which is minimal) or of rhythmic motion (which is suspended by the fermatas); it also insures the audibility of the text, which counterpoint, as we have seen, tends to obscure.

Even in more normal melodic and rhythmic contexts, where consonances (now usually defined as including thirds and sixths) tended to fall on strong beats, dissonances on weak beats, unusual harmonic series were frequently associated with painful or emotional moments in the texts. One striking example is a motet on the story of David and Absalom by Josquin des Prez (c. 1445–1521), the greatest composer of his generation. In this piece, Josquin uses a striking series of harmonies to set the phrase, "*sed descendam in infernum plorans*" (but I will go down weeping into hell), shown on p. 135.[14] This is not the only unusual passage; Reese directs our attention to an earlier sonority in the same piece, "a suspension on a major seventh, which would obviously sound quite harsh inserted in the typical sound-context of the period, [but which] helps to establish a mood of lamentation" (p. 257).

In using these dissonances as a means of text-setting, Josquin was making a major discovery: he was exploring the expressive capacities of harmony. The use of chordal sonorities to express the emotions of a text was fundamentally different from earlier text-setting techniques: by making an arresting or unsettling series of harmonies coincide with a particularly painful phrase in the text, composers clearly intended to create a unified and sensuous effect; they were striving for immediacy and drama, seeking to enhance the pathos of the text rather than its poetic form or allegorical meaning. But the ability to use harmonies for such purposes came out of the experience gained in manipulating them in more obviously constructive ways. The same Josquin pro-

14. Following the version given in the Supplement volume of *Werken van Josquin Des Prez*, ed. A. Smijers, p. 25. The key-signature of this passage has been variously printed, and editors have made different guesses about the application of *musica ficta;* compare the different version given by Lowinsky in *Secret Chromatic Art*, example 23.

duced a quadruple canon with twenty-four separate voice parts, and even composed some melodies by arbitrarily deriving pitches from the vowels of verbal phrases (for example, the *cantus firmus* of a Mass for the Duke of Ferrara, where *Hercules Dux Ferrariae* yields *re ut re ut re fa mi re*).[15] Not only were the skills Josquin displayed in these works important for the making of expressive harmonies, but the general constructive developments that had taken place since the invention of polyphony were necessary as well; only when a grammar of normal chord sequences had been

15. See Reese, p. 236. The 24-part canon is a setting of Psalm 90; see p. 250.

developed could such passages as the chord series in *Absalon fili mi*
strike the ear as meaningful deviations.

The praise accorded Josquin by his contemporaries reflects
the success of his work as measured by both constructive and expressive criteria. Some comments stress his contrapuntal sophistication; others, his lyrical melody, ravishing harmony, or skillful
attention to the text. As a modern history points out, Josquin deserved both kinds of praise:

> Josquin's achievement was to weld the musical advances of his
> predecessors into a perfectly integrated style, one in which
> the voices of a polyphonic composition are completely related
> through the systematic use of imitation. This technique he
> fused with a melodic idiom in which the music is wedded to
> the text through an identity of rhythm and phrasing. . . . The
> importance of the text in the concept of musical imitation
> cannot be overemphasized. It is the line or the phrase of the
> text which determines the length and usually the rhythm of
> the musical phrase.[16]

We need only contrast the arbitrary arrangement of texts, radical
independence of voice parts, and relative incoherence of harmony in the isorhythmic motet to recognize how impressive Josquin's achievement was. In the isorhythmic motet, as we have
seen, relations between the various elements were intellectual,
mystical, constructive, and often inaudible. In Josquin's work,
which retains many aspects of the high artifice of the late Middle
Ages, the relations between the various elements—text, melody,
harmony, rhythm—have been rendered more audible by the use
of syllabic declamation, contrapuntal imitation, and a more regular harmonic grammar.

From Frottola to Madrigal: Text-Setting and Musical Style

The sophisticated techniques of Josquin were greatly admired in
Italy, where most of the French and Netherlandish composers of
the fifteenth century found employment, either in the papal choir
or in various aristocratic chapels. But it took a change in *literary*

16. Beekman C. Cannon, Alvin H. Johnson, and William G. Waite, *The Art of Music*,
pp. 165, 168.

taste to force Italians to apply these techniques to the setting of secular texts. As the fifteenth century drew to a close, the dominant style in Italian secular music was that of the *frottola,* which combined a tuneful, chordally-organized music with a similarly relaxed poetic style. Most of the texts were written by aristocratic poets affecting such simple, four-square forms as the *strambotto,* the *barzelletta,* and the *frottola* (a specific form which gave its name to the whole *genre*); in keeping with these popular forms, the poets employed a humble, pseudo-plebeian diction. The composers who set the texts, even professionals like Bartolomeo Tromboncino, used top lines with a limited range and frequent repetition; the other parts, rarely contrapuntal or imitative, provided strong triadic harmony and were laid out in phrases corresponding to the lines of the poem. There was no attempt at harmonic expression or staggered declamation of the kind we have noticed in Josquin. The studied artlessness and rigid form of these settings make them seem crude in comparison to the Netherlandish music Italians were able to hear in their chapels, or in comparison to the French secular songs available from Ottaviano Petrucci, the first important printer of music, who published a collection of one hundred such songs, largely by Northern composers, in 1501. Nevertheless, the *frottole* remained popular: Petrucci published eleven books of them between 1504 and 1514. But the *frottola* style was conservative, even reactionary, and attempts to reform and improve it led to a much more important and influential combination of secular poetry and music: the madrigal.

Here the impulse for change came from the poets, not from the musicians. Under the powerful influence of Pietro Bembo, later a cardinal, Italian poets began to abandon the popular forms in favor of the sonnet, the *canzone,* and other older forms that had been practiced by Petrarch two centuries earlier, forms whose complexity could accommodate a more elevated diction, a more seriously passionate tone, and a more subtle rhetoric. Bembo's edition of Petrarch (1501) was an important early step in this process; his *Prose della volgar lingua* (1525), which dogmatically establishes Petrarch as the sole model for Italian lyric poetry, is a declaration of victory. Bembo admired in Petrarch the very process we have been noticing in Renaissance music: the development of expressive values for constructive techniques. In Petrarch, rhyme and stanzaic form, constructive devices for the troubadours, become highly expressive; rhetoric becomes structural, not merely ornamental, as William Kennedy has shown in a recent study:

> The Petrarchan speaker's rhetorical strategy of alternating and suspending contrarieties within his own *ethos* in fact generates structural transformations in each poem. His expression of joy and lament, hope and despair, certitude and doubt characteristically balances thesis against antithesis, statement against counterstatement, and reversal against counter-reversal, allowing a dialectical unity to evolve out of multiplicity through patterns of shading and contrast, challenge and fulfillment, assertion and negation. The result of such a rhetorical patterning is a careful structural proportioning of the poetic utterance into antithetically balanced words, phrases, lines, couplets, tercets, and quatrains, all combining to form antithetically balanced sestets and octaves.[17]

Thus oxymoron, the distinguishing rhetorical habit of Petrarchan poetry, could become more than local ornament; it could be, and often was, a principle of structure.

The impact on music of the adoption of Petrarchan models for poetry may be traced in the steady increase in examples of the older forms in Petrucci's collections; Walter Rubsamen's careful study provides statistics:

> If the inclusion of a sonnet or *canzone* in early prints or manuscripts of *frottole* had been of rare occurrence, the exception became a rule in collections compiled during the second and third decades of the *cinquecento*. . . . In Petrucci's eleventh book of *frottole*, published in 1514, poems for the populace were for the first time in the minority, there being only twenty-one *barzellette* and six *strambotti* in comparison with forty-one examples of more literary types: *canzoni*, sonnets, and *capitoli*. . . . The growing popularity of the musical *canzone* in particular is an evidence of reaction to the all-too-great formal regularity of popular verse schemes. A strophe of the *canzone* is characterized by free alternation between endeca- and septisyllabic lines, the number of which is op-

17. *Rhetorical Norms in Renaissance Literature*, p. 20.

tional and the rhyming irregular, except that the last two lines
are usually matched. When such a pattern is harmonized,
greater rhythmic variety results, since the musical accentuation is no longer bound to the ever-recurring trochaic octo-
syllabic or iambic endecasyllabic line.[18]

The "greater rhythmic variety" produced by composers setting
canzoni was the first step toward the greater harmonic variety and
linear independence of the madrigal. But poetic form was only
one part of the process. The content of the typical Petrarchan
canzone and the rhetoric of its expression were at least as important: the frequency of such figures as oxymoron encouraged composers to seek for a musical equivalent, a similarly compressed
grammar of contrast which ultimately found expression in harmonic and contrapuntal terms.

In short, the motion toward a more formally flexible, more
rhetorically expressive poetic style exposed the limitations of the
musical conventions of the *frottola*. The search for a musical style
more appropriate for Petrarchan poetry led to the adoption of
the text-setting techniques that characterize the madrigal: chromatic harmonies, highly decorated vocal lines, contrapuntal imitation, and witty rhetorical "word-painting." In the *frottola,* there
had been a close, even rigorous connection between poetic form
and musical form, but an absolute contradiction between the content of the text and the style of the music.[19] It is not impossible
that there was sometimes conscious irony in that contradiction;
the basic gambit of these poems, the adoption of plebeian forms
and diction by aristocratic poets, may be described as the exploitation of an ironic *persona,* and a deliberately inappropriate musical setting could enhance this irony: a lover's complaint set to a
rhythmically symmetrical tune moving through cheerful major
triads certainly avoids the charge of sentimentalism. But the Petrarchan texts encouraged by Bembo, more flexible in their form,
more elevated in their diction, more serious in their rhetoric, demanded a musical setting which would fit the poetry in content as

18. Walter H. Rubsamen, *Literary Sources of Secular Music in Italy,* pp. 6-7. My account
of the *frottola* is generally dependent on this excellent study, which includes transcriptions
of eleven representative pieces; like all students of this period, I have also profited from
Alfred Einstein's detailed study, *The Italian Madrigal.* On the *frottola,* see vol. I, pp. 34-115.

19. See Einstein, vol. I, p. 79.

well as in form. As Alfred Einstein explains, this demand ultimately destroyed the rhythmic and harmonic characteristics of
the *frottola:*

> The madrigal style originated in a disintegration of the
> frottola, more exactly, a disintegration for the sake of expres-
> sion. Into the frottola there intrude polyphonic or quasi-
> polyphonic passages which spread healing or even poisonous
> enzymes, penetrating and transforming the whole tissue, the
> entire structure, of the composition. It is above all the defi-
> nite songlike and often even dancelike rhythm of the frottola
> which gives way to a rhythmic suppleness. The relative defi-
> niteness of tonality is destroyed. . . . Within the frame of the
> chosen key, whether major or minor, every harmonic liberty
> is permitted if it serves the ends of individual expression.
> Compared with the frottola, the harmonies of the madrigal
> begin to assume a fluctuating and labile character.
> (vol. I, p. 119)

As we have seen, polyphonic equality of parts, "rhythmic sup-
pleness," and advanced harmony were all characteristics of the
Netherlandish composers working in Italy at this time. Considered as musical techniques, all three had traceable constructive
origins; Josquin had begun to find ways to make them expressive—both for the dramatic Latin Psalm texts he favored in his
motets and for the lighter French and (occasionally) Italian texts
of his secular *chansons.* So it should not surprise us that two of the
first three composers of madrigals, Verdelot and Arcadelt, were
actually Northerners, while the third, Costanzo Festa, was a native
Italian known for his skill at the "Netherlandish" kind of church
music. In responding to the challenge of setting the rhetorically
sophisticated poetry of Petrarch and his imitators, these composers significantly furthered the process begun by Josquin: the assigning of expressive values to previously constructive techniques.

Construction as Expression:
Four Analogues between Poetic and Musical Technique

In the madrigal, we may see composers responding to Petrarchan
poetry by working out precise musical analogues for poetic techniques. Simplifying a much more complicated situation, we may

divide these techniques, poetic and musical, into four groups: (1) rhythmic, (2) melodic, (3) harmonic, (4) contrapuntal.

1. The most obvious analogues between poetic and musical technique lie in the area of rhythm. We have already seen some parts of the history of these relations, including the separation of poetic and musical rhythm in the late Middle Ages. In the madrigal, composers borrowed from poets the idea of using rhythm mimetically. Classical poets, most obviously Ovid and Virgil, had already made rhythmic technique expressive, writing fast, slow, choppy, or smooth lines not merely for formal variation but to enhance the meaning of their words; Petrarch and his Renaissance followers were enthusiastic imitators of these procedures, though the different metrical systems of their poetry required them to modify or adapt some classical techniques.

In a passage dealing with rapid motion, an accentual-syllabic poet may add extra syllables to a line to invite a faster reading; Petrarchan poetry frequently replaces iambs with anapests for that purpose. In a passage emphasizing slower motion, fatigue, or despair, the poet may employ consonant clusters to slow down the recitation. Thus the headlong rush of Petrarch's line describing a woman escaping from Cupid:

> E de' lacci d'Amor leggiera e sciolta . . .

[Out of the snares of Love light and nimble . . .]

And the contrasting impeded motion of these lines describing a suffering lover:

> Se la mia vita da l'aspro tormento
> Si può tanto schermire e da gli affani . . .

[If my life can withstand the harsh torment and the breathlessness . . .][20]

In a passage where the poet wishes to emphasize a strong break in the syntax, he may employ a distinct medial *caesura;* again, examples abound in Petrarch. But the difference between the fastest line Petrarch can construct and the slowest is not quantitatively great, nor can the strongest medial *caesura* last very long; even in

20. Following the text of *Francesco Petrarca: Le Rime,* ed. Giosue Carducci and Severino Ferrari; Sonnet VI, line 3, p. 8; Sonnet XII, lines 1-2, p. 14.

the most extreme cases, these techniques can only *encourage* certain rhythmic features of a recitation. Musical notation, by contrast, can absolutely *control* rhythmic performance, and its range of variation is at once greater and more precise. Thus the musical versions of imitative rhythm—rapid runs of short notes for words dealing with running or flying, long-held notes for words describing stasis, oddly placed rests when the speaker of the poem breaks off his syntax in despair—are more obvious, more dramatic, and more exact than the corresponding poetic versions. Since their resources in this area were so much richer, madrigal composers were able to extend rhythmic imitation far beyond the simple effects possible in poetry, but they learned to pursue such imitative effects from the poetry they were asked to set.

2. There is a more distant analogue between poetic and musical technique in the area of pitch. Because of the apparent pitch-difference between front and back vowels (see p. 3 above), poetic manipulations of what is usually called "vowel color" may suggest musical manipulations of register. A line restricted to a narrow range of vowel sounds is likely, in Petrarch, to describe a calmer emotional state than a line with more extreme contrasts of vowel sounds. Thus the beginning of one of the sonnets playing on the resemblance of Laura's name to *l'aura* (the air) and *lauro* (the olive tree) uses those two words to frame a line otherwise restricted to the vowel *e:*

> L'aura celeste che 'n quel verde lauro . . .

> [The heavenly air in that green laurel tree . . .]

But the beginning of the first sonnet after Laura's death juxtaposes many different vowel sounds, appropriately suggesting the violence of the speaker's response:

> Oimè il bel viso, oimè il soave sguardo!

> [Alas that lovely face, alas that sweet glance!][21]

Again, musical resources are richer. Madrigal composers could use wide leaps of register to set texts about sudden changes; they could give a large expressive interval to one part or move the com-

21. Sonnet CXCVII, line 1, p. 283; Sonnet CCLXVII, line 1, p. 369.

posite texture down by dropping out the upper voices and scoring some despairing phrase for low male voices alone. In their general suggestive quality, these manipulations of pitch to achieve tone-color were somewhat analogous to a poet's choice of vowels, but the melodic imitative techniques which became virtually mandatory in madrigal writing were more obvious and literal-minded: high notes to set such words as *"ciel"* (heaven), low notes to set such words as *"sepulcro"* (grave), stepwise passages in the appropriate direction for words describing motion up or down.

Limited in his choices of vowels by considerations of meaning as well as of sound, a poet could usually only suggest a mood, and his contrasts of vowels, dependent on overtone pitches, were much more vague and illusory than the obvious contrasts of fundamental pitch in music. Nonetheless, John Milton, centuries later but still spiritually in the Renaissance, did achieve a melodic, scalar, imitative use of vowels: in the apocalyptic lines on Satan's fall in *Paradise Lost,* the sequence of vowels from *Ethereal* to *bottomless* suggests a jagged, precipitous fall:

> Him the Almighty Power
> Hurl'd headlong flaming from th'Ethereal Sky
> With hideous ruin and combustion down
> To bottomless perdition, . . . (I, 44–47)[22]

But what for Milton was a virtuoso feat was, for a madrigal composer, as easy as writing a scale. As the term "word-painting" implies, composers could be quite precise in matching pitches to words, sometimes so precise as to bring expression back toward recondite construction: such punning practices as the use of the scale pitches *la, sol,* and *mi* to set the Italian words which happen to be their homophones were evidently designed to appeal to the singers of madrigals, not their hearers, as were the frequent examples of "eye music," in which black notes were employed to set texts referring to darkness or death.

3. But if composers had more precise means of expression in the areas of rhythm and pitch, poets had a similar advantage in describing emotional conflict. Not only did their words have understood meanings in a way that no note or chord could, but

22. This and all citations of Milton are from *John Milton: Complete Poems and Major Prose,* ed. Merritt Y. Hughes.

they were able to use rhetorical figures, puns and oxymorons, to express ironies, paradoxes, antitheses. For these techniques, as for rhetoric generally, composers lacked an obvious melodic or rhythmic equivalent; even with unusual rhythms or dissonant intervals, it was difficult for a single vocal line to express ambiguity. But the increasing harmonic sophistication we have seen in Josquin held more promising possibilities. Many of the phrases William Kennedy uses to describe rhetorical technique as a structural device in the passage already quoted could easily be applied to Renaissance harmonic technique. The harmonic shape of many an Italian madrigal could also be described as a "strategy of alternating and suspending contrarieties," and the power of harmonic organization to mark off portions of a piece as related to one another gave composers more subtle ways to shape their pieces than the simple matching of the evenly-measured and repetitive phrases of the *frottola*. The "expression of joy and lament, hope and despair" became positively identified in this period with the alternation of major and minor harmonies; "a dialectical unity evolv[ing] out of multiplicity" is practically a Renaissance definition of harmony; and the greatly increased use of chromaticism in this period resulted from a search for "patterns of shading and contrast." The harmonic innovations of the Italian madrigal composers, some of them wild experimental failures, some of them successes so decisive as to affect the whole later history of tonal music, began as attempts to find musical equivalents for the persuasive power of Petrarchan rhetoric.

But chords are not words, and the meaning of a Petrarchan oxymoron ("freezing fire" or "living death"), however problematic, is more specific than the meaning of two juxtaposed contrasting chords. The association of major chords with cheerful sentiments, minor chords with sadness, and dissonances with tortuous or difficult matters was quite well established by the middle of the sixteenth century, but we ought to recognize that these associations, like the Greek teaching about *ethos,* were utterly arbitrary. Major and minor are different, and the exploitation of that difference was a crucial step in the development of tonality, but there was no reason for assigning major harmonies to joy and minor ones to sorrow on purely musical grounds. My own suspicion is that the mystical or symbolic association of certain kinds of texts with certain church modes in the Middle Ages led slowly, as the modal system was modified by the advent of polyphony, to the simpler and more general associations that major and minor still carry for Western ears. Gioseffe Zarlino, the greatest theorist of the Renaissance, gives precise instructions for harmonic techniques of text-setting in his *Instituzioni armoniche* (1558), defining "sad harmony as one which combines slow movement with the use of syncopated dissonances and minor chords, whereas gay harmony prefers major chords in light and fast rhythms."[23] But he prefaces this discussion by quoting Horace and Ovid on the use of appropriate meters for tragedy and comedy, making it clear that his rules for composers proceed on the analogy of literary practice: "if the poet is not permitted to write a comedy in tragic verse, the musician will also not be permitted to combine unsuitably these two things, namely, harmony and words."[24] Earlier in the same treatise, in a general discussion of the uses of dissonance, Zarlino falls naturally into a series of Petrarchan phrases:

> A dissonance causes the consonance which immediately follow it to seem more acceptable. Thus it is perceived and recognized with greater pleasure by the ear, just as after darkness light is more acceptable and delightful to the eye, and after the bitter the sweet is more luscious and palatable.[25]

In this metaphorical way, harmony could achieve antithesis, both as a local phenomenon and as a structural one. But its two basic contrasts—major versus minor and consonance versus dissonance—obviously constituted a more limited vocabulary than that available to poets. The composers who sought most restlessly for new harmonic effects and distant tonal territories—Adrian Willaert, his pupil Cipriano de Rore, and (at the end of the century) the astounding Don Carlo Gesualdo—were seeking to develop a wider and more precise harmonic vocabulary. But unlike poets, who could expect their readers to know the dictionary

---

23. I quote the summary given by Lowinsky in his article,"Music in the Culture of the Renaissance," p. 537. The entire passage is translated in Strunk, pp. 256-57.

24. Chapter 32, following the translation given in Strunk, p. 256.

25. Chapter 27; in Strunk, p. 232. A forthcoming book by the Israeli musicologist Dom Harran, entitled *From Hebrews to Humanists: The Poetics of Music in the Renaissance*, will show that Zarlino's learning extended to Hebrew accents and the relations between words and tones in psalmody.

meanings of the words they then combined in oxymoronic patterns, composers, once they ventured beyond the understood,
culturally conditioned meanings of major and minor, consonant
and dissonant, could not communicate so precisely. Gustave Reese
says of Gesualdo that his "approach to the text [was] too individual to give rise to an enduring school" (p. 432), and it was perhaps inevitable that Gesualdo's development of harmonic technique along expressive lines would end, as Einstein puts it, "in a
blind alley" (vol. II, p. 715). My point is that Gesualdo arrived at
his justly famous harmonic extravagance by extending earlier
attempts to express oxymoron and other rhetorical devices in
chordal terms. If his pieces do not communicate with the preci-

sion of Petrarchan poetry, they remain one fascinating example
of what can happen to music when it aspires to the condition of
rhetoric. Stravinsky's fondness for Gesualdo, as we shall see, was
a recognition of kinship.

4. But it is misleading to separate harmonic technique from
contrapuntal technique, and in the manipulation of their overlapping and interlocking voices the Italian madrigal composers
found other ways to imitate and extend rhetorical technique.
Below is a passage from Willaert's setting of a Petrarch sonnet in
which the speaker asks a group of ladies where his own beloved
is, referring to her, in a characteristic oxymoron, as "my life, my
death."[26]

26. I follow the version given in Einstein, vol. III, pp. 63-64, changing the clefs and
using tied notes rather than dots across bar-lines. The piece was printed in 1559.

Harmonically, Willaert has used the conventional language: *"vita"* is set with major triads, *"morte"* with minor ones. But the staggered declamation makes the oxymoron more subtle. The declamation of the word *"vita,"* beginning with the lower voices, takes us from D major to G major to C major, a strong regular sequence of triads. But while the C in the bass on the weak fourth beat of the third bar of our excerpt does provide brief root support for the upper parts, it is also the beginning of the phrase leading to *"morte."* On the next beat, the bass motion to A alters the harmony to A minor; by the time the top part has reached the second syllable of *"vita,"* the F on which it arrives is the third of a D-minor triad, and the bass has already reached the climactic word *"morte."* This overlapping technique, which continues throughout our excerpt and may be found in hundreds of similar passages, was a successful way for composers to express and surpass literary oxymoron. When Petrarch calls Laura "my life, my death," he urges us to hold those contradictory epithets in suspension, to consider how one woman could be both things. But he must use his words sequentially; literary technique may only suggest simultaneity. By assigning those same words to overlapping voices, Willaert achieves actual simultaneity: not only are there chords, with their sensuous power and their conventional significance, but one voice can be emphasizing *"vita"* while another has already begun to emphasize *"morte."* The compositional techniques of canon and free imitation, upon which these effects depend, had of course originated as means of construction; in searching for ways to dramatize Petrarch's oxymoronic rhetoric, the madrigal composers found a way to give these contrapuntal techniques expressive significance.

In a study I have already quoted, William Kennedy explains how the pervasive use of oxymoron in Petrarchan poetry implies a divided speaker, at once infatuated and aware of the foolishness of his infatuation. Richard Lanham, in his engaging discussion of rhetoric in the Renaissance, argues that all rhetorical writers seek to avoid a stable, central, serious identity. The basic conventions of contrapuntal text-setting in the Italian madrigal present just such a division of the speaker, in contrast to earlier conventions. In ancient and medieval monody, text and melody were fitted together in a one-to-one relation. In the polytextual motet, each voice part had its own text, sometimes its own language, with the effect of a combination of or a contest between distinct speakers. In the *frottola,* whether sung in four parts or by one singer accompanied by instruments,[27] the top line of music, the only line under which the entire text was normally printed, played the role of the speaker. But in the madrigal, in which all parts have the same text, but sing it at different times on different pitches with different rhythms, no part has a special claim to represent the "real" setting of the text. What poetry had to suggest by oxymoron, irony, conflicts between form and content, and other forms of "multiple ordering,"[28] music could present by offering different simultaneous or overlapping settings of the same text. In the hands of the Italian madrigal composers, the techniques of polyphonic counterpoint developed in the centuries from Leonin to Josquin became ways to dramatize, with irony and wit, the multiple *personae* of the Petrarchan speaker.

Virtuoso Rhyming in Shakespeare

In poetry not written for music, there was a similar appropriation of constructive techniques for expressive and rhetorical uses; rhyme provides the clearest example. For the troubadours and trouvères, as I have argued, the invention and perfection of rhyme-schemes had been an end in itself, a musical and technical discipline whose main concerns were balance, order, and symmetry. In Renaissance lyric poetry, which continued to employ many forms and rhyme-schemes developed by the troubadours, there was a more conscious effort to use rhyme rhetorically, either to point up and strengthen the assertions made by the syntax or to "impose upon the logical pattern of expressed argument a kind of fixative counterpattern of alogical implication," a function of rhyme identified by W. K. Wimsatt.[29] In the latter case, the "fixative counterpattern" implied by the rhyming words functioned as a kind of imaginary counterpoint, an expression of aspects of the

27. There is some debate on this question, as Rubsamen and Einstein make clear.

28. I borrow this phrase from Stephen Booth, *An Essay on Shakespeare's Sonnets,* p. 1 and *passim.*

29. In his important essay, "One Relation to Rhyme to Reason," in *The Verbal Icon,* p. 153.

divided speaker not stated by the syntax as syntax. When, for example, the two disparate members of an oxymoron could be made to rhyme, the implication of similarity enforced by the rhyming pushed the two words together as surely as their meanings pulled them apart. This procedure was the best equivalent poets had for the more obvious harmonic and contrapuntal simultaneity available to composers. The "English Petrarch," Sir Philip Sidney, employs this device in *Astrophel and Stella* (1582, printed 1591), where the rhyme-pair "joy-annoy" closes Sonnets 44, 100, and 108; as Stella is Astrophel's joy, she is also, as the sequence amply demonstrates, his annoy, his grief.[30] William Shakespeare, never one to blink at borrowing useful material, picked up that same rhyme-pair in Sonnet 8 ("Music to hear"). His uses of rhyme are the most varied and interesting in English Renaissance poetry: he took over techniques which had been formal conveniences for other poets and made them supple means of expression.

Shakespeare's first published poem, *Venus and Adonis* (1593), has a relatively high proportion of feminine rhymes, a fact which suggests the influence of Marlowe's witty Ovidian couplet-poem, *Hero and Leander*.[31] Both poets often produced these rhymes by ending lines with pronouns. Thus Marlowe:

> Chaste Hero to herself thus softly said:
> "Were I the saint he worships, I would hear him,"
> And as she spake these words, came somewhat near
>   him.[32]

And Shakespeare:

> Then mightst thou pause, for then were I not for thee;
> But having no defects, why dost abhor me? (137–38)[33]

---

30. Cf. the related rhymes "toys-annoys" (Sonnet 18), "joy-enjoy" (Sonnets 68, 70), and "enjoyeth-destroyeth" (Song 5).

31. I accept M. C. Bradbrook's argument that "there are sufficient likenesses between the two to make it probable that Shakespeare knew Marlowe's poem before he composed his own." *Shakespeare and Elizabethan Poetry*, p. 65.

32. *Hero and Leander*, I, 178-80, following the text given in *Christopher Marlowe: The Complete Poems and Translations*, ed. Stephen Orgel.

33. This and all citations from *Venus and Adonis* follow the text of *The Poems*, ed. F. T. Prince, in the Arden Edition.

But Shakespeare produces a more striking effect by combining one such line-ending with a polysyllable that happens to rhyme, thus moving beyond parallelism, here with a comic result:

> Now is she in the very lists of love,
> Her champion mounted for the hot encounter.
> All is imaginary she doth prove;
> He will not manage her, although he mount her.
>   (595–98)

Here the contrast between the rhyming words is not an oxymoron of meaning, as in "joy-annoy," but a striking disparity of diction and syntax: polysyllabic noun rhymes with monosyllabic verb and pronoun. In the word "encounter," we hear the sophisticated voice of the wry, detached narrator who has also rhymed such highfalutin words as "satiety" and "variety" (19–21). But in the frank phrase "mount her," we hear the voice of the country boy from Stratford who knows what happens in barnyards, and who has been manipulating a contrast between people and horses throughout this poem. The discovery that words suggesting such different narrative attitudes could be made to rhyme was like the discovery that contrapuntally distinct melodic lines could be made to form expressive consonances.

The stanza form of *Venus and Adonis (ababcc)* allows more different kinds of rhyming than the continuous couplets of *Hero and Leander*; Shakespeare is able to put particular pressure on the last two lines of each stanza, using their rhyming words to summarize the meaning of the entire stanzaic unit:

> Now quick desire hath caught the yielding prey,
> And glutton-like she feeds, yet never filleth,
> Her lips are conquerors, his lips obey,
> Paying what ransom the insulter willeth;
>   Whose vulture thought doth pitch the price so high
>   That she will draw his lips' rich treasure dry. (547–52)

The first four lines offer two distinct metaphors for Venus: she is a gluttonous bird of prey, insatiably devouring her catch, or a military conqueror, demanding an exorbitant ransom. The couplet forces a combination of these metaphors: "vulture" and "pitch," a technical term for a bird's flight, jostle with "price" in the first line;

"draw . . . dry" frames "treasure" in the second. The double operation of his rhymes enables Shakespeare to effect this contrapuntal combination of metaphors: the word "high" fits conveniently into both metaphors (vultures fly high; prices may be set high), while the less versatile word "dry" is forced by position to apply to treasure as well as blood.

Perhaps it is no accident that "pitch" and "high" suggest an additional musical metaphor: common as they are, Shakespeare's rhyming words here work equally well in two different metaphorical contexts, just as a constant bass note, in Gesualdo, can work equally well in two or three successive chords. Here is an example:[34]

The C-sharp in the bass is first the root of a C-sharp major triad, then the fifth of F-sharp minor; the D is first the third of B minor, then the fifth of G major, then the root of D minor; the E is first the fifth of A minor, then the root of E major. By holding the bass note constant while all other parts change, Gesualdo emphasizes the one pitch each of these sequences of chords has in common. When the bass notes change, another part is holding (the F-sharp in the top line between bars 2 and 3, the A in the alto between bars 3 and 4). The doubly-functioning held notes link the chords exactly as Shakespeare's doubly-functioning rhymes link his metaphors.

Repetition of important rhymes gives a narrative poet an economical way to unify a longer poem, as repetition of a familiar tonic cadence can help a composer unify a longer tonal piece. In English poetry, this technique may be found as far back as Chaucer, whose *Troilus and Criseyde* frequently repeats such important thematic rhymes as "desyre-fyre," "fantasie-die," "pace-grace," and "serve-sterve." But Shakespeare tends to repeat such rhymes

34. As transcribed by Einstein, vol. II, p. 714.

with slight alterations, producing a more complex and ironic effect. In *Venus and Adonis,* he uses "desire-fire" five times, in quite different grammatical contexts but with the same essential thematic force; then, just at the end of the poem, he rhymes both those words with "sire," producing a richer pattern of cross-reference:

> [Love] shall be cause of war and dire events,
> And set dissension 'twixt the son and sire;
> Subject and servile to all discontents,
> As dry combustious matter is to fire. (1159–62)

> "Poor flower," quoth she, "this was thy father's guise,—
> Sweet issue of a more sweet-smelling sire,—
> For every little grief to wet his eyes;
> To grow unto himself was his desire." (1177–80)

There are powerful ironies here: the destructiveness of fire (a typical Ovidian motif), the narcissism of Adonis ("to grow unto himself"), the failure of Adonis to sire human offspring, made pathetic by Venus' attempt to describe the flower as his child or "issue." My point is that these ironies are more powerful here because the conventional rhyme-pair "desire-fire" has occurred so frequently earlier in the poem. The effectiveness of the final alteration, the expanding outward of the frame of reference of the rhyme to include "sire" and (internally in line 1159) "dire," depends upon that earlier repetition.

In the sonnets, whether considered as separate poems or as parts of a connected sequence, rhyme is one of Shakespeare's most important techniques for achieving the "multiple ordering" to which Stephen Booth has directed our attention. Sonnets 16 and 17, for example, are connected by the shared rhyme-pair "Time-rime," which also connects Sonnets 106 and 107. But the speaker's attitude in the two sets of poems is quite different. In Sonnet 16, the speaker urges the young man addressed to marry ("a mightier way / Make war upon this bloody tyrant, Time"); otherwise, the loved one will live only in the poet's "barren rime."[35] In the companion piece, Sonnet 17, the poet further belittles his writing, though the couplet suggests one way it may survive:

35. This and all citations of the sonnets follow the edition of Douglas Bush.

> But were some child of yours alive that time,
> You should live twice—in it and in my rime.

Sonnet 106 ("When in the chronicle of wasted time") looks backward rather than forward: the speaker suggests that not even the ancient poets would have had sufficient "skill"[36] to praise his loved one. But in Sonnet 107, the poet is suddenly conscious of his own mortality, and defies death with a very different use of the same rhyme-pair:

> Now with the drops of this most balmy time
> My love looks fresh, and Death to me subscribes,
> Since, spite of him, I'll live in this poor rime,
> While he insults o'er dull and speechless tribes.

The two intervening sonnets employing this rhyme-pair, 32 and 55, show a similar contrast. In Sonnet 32, the poet belittles his "poor rude lines," which the loved one is asked to preserve "for my love, not for their rime." But in Sonnet 55, the speaker is again proud and defiant about the power of his verse:

> Not marble nor the gilded monuments
> Of princes shall outlive this pow'rful rime,
> But you shall shine more bright in these contents
> Than unswept stone, besmeared with sluttish time.

For the sonnets themselves, this assessment of the power of rhyme seems accurate indeed. As in *Venus and Adonis,* each recurrence of a rhyme-pair is enriched by previous occurrences, so that even when the poet implicitly or explicitly denies what he has said before with the same rhyming words, our memory—fresh if the sonnets are paired, subliminal if they are distant—keeps us aware that there are always, in these rich poems, multiple orderings, multiple meanings.

In these examples, Shakespeare demonstrates how much syntactic and thematic variation can be achieved around the same pair of rhymes; an even more impressive effect occurs when a repeated rhyme-pair is itself varied. Sonnets 21, 38, 71, and 81, for example, employ the rhyme pair "verse-rehearse," and in each case, "rehearse" has the sense of repetition or recitation, a natural

---

36. The 1609 text has "still," i.e., style.

use with "verse." But in the emotionally powerful Sonnet 86, "verse" is followed by an unexpected rhyme, with a devastating effect:

> Was it the proud full sail of his great verse,
> Bound for the prize of all-too-precious you,
> That did my ripe thoughts in my brain inhearse,
> Making their tomb the womb wherein they grew?

Other repetitions contribute to the power of these lines, to be sure: the imagery of gestation and fertility, central to the early sonnets, is here used metaphorically for the poet's invention, and the internal rhyme "tomb-womb" has been used at line-ends in Sonnet 3. But the real explosion in this quatrain occurs with "inhearse," not merely because it is a self-contained metaphor, but because when we hear "verse" in the first line, we probably expect "rehearse."[37]

Again, the madrigal style provides an analogue: the shock and surprise we feel on hearing the innovative harmonies of some of the madrigalists are not exclusively results of the tonal expectations we all anachronistically bring to our listening; often the earlier course of the piece itself has deliberately led us to expect more normal motion. In Luca Marenzio's setting of a sestina by Jacopo Sannazaro, for example, the first two cadences, coinciding with the ends of poetic lines, are on G minor, the tonic. But then the second line of the text, *"E tu fortuna muta il crudo stile"* (and you, oh Fortune, change that awkward manner), is repeated with different music, reaching a brief cadence on B-flat minor which leads, with another repetition of the words *"il crudo stile,"* to a strong, root position arrival in D-flat major, a tritone away from the tonic.[38] The colorful harmonic motion toward the flat keys is more effective because Marenzio has first set that tempting line of text in a more normal fashion—just as Shakespeare's "inhearse" gains shock value from the earlier repetitions of "rehearse."

Such variations in Shakespeare's rhyming extend to a chain-reaction technique. The first rhyme-pair of the Sonnets, "increase-decease," captures the imperative for procreation and the reason

37. Cf. Spenser's rhyme of "happy herse" and "joyful verse" in the November eclogue.

38. For a transcription, see Einstein, vol. III, pp. 252-56.

for its urgency; variations using each of the words with other new rhymes begin early and suggest further complications: Sonnet 11 has "increase-cease"; Sonnet 13, "decease-lease"; Sonnet 15, "increase-decrease." Each of the words participating in this widening group is enriched by the others, and may be heard as a variation on the original pair. And when Shakespeare repeats the original pair in Sonnet 97 ("How like a winter hath my absence been"), that pair has gained such suggestive force that the passage functions as a compressed echo of the entire procreation group:

> And yet this time removed was summer's time,
> The teeming autumn, big with rich increase,
> Bearing the wanton burden of the prime,
> Like widowed wombs after their lords' decease.

For many earlier poets, repetition of rhymes had been a convenience or at best a thematic shorthand. For Shakespeare, as these examples should suggest, it was something much more expressive, a means to achieve irony, to make a word carry with it the echoes of its earlier occurrences in the sequence, including the echoes of other words with which it had been rhymed. His discovery and exploitation of these expressive possibilities for rhyming ought to remind us of such similar musical developments as the newly expressive use of contrapuntal imitation in the Italian madrigal.

Rhetorical Theory: The "Auricular" and the "Sensible"

As we have seen, both composers and poets in the Renaissance learned to appropriate as means of expression techniques which the Middle Ages had developed as means of construction. The connection between this development and the concept of rediscovery and imitation implicit in the word Renaissance is complex. As I suggested in the opening pages of this chapter, the passion of the early humanists for eloquence, their willingness to make large claims for rhetoric, was confirmed by some important rediscoveries and led to fresh readings of ancient texts never lost by the Middle Ages. Imitation of these texts, for Petrarch and his followers, was not mechanical but sensuous, as Hermann Gmelin has suggested:

What provided the impulse [for Petrarch's fresh approach] was that in that land of the troubadours [Avignon, where Petrarch grew up after his father's exile], his ear was trained in the melodies of their songs, and that he now conceived the notion of reading the Latin authors for the first time as well with that musical sense of the troubadours, and making himself drunk on the sounding beauty of the Ciceronian language. How this seized him, even as a boy, as a kind of musical intoxication, he reported himself in one of his letters written in old age: "at that age I could understand nothing, only the sweetness and sonority of the words held my attention, and anything else, whether I read it or heard it, seemed raucous and dissonant to me for a long time" (Sen. 15, 1). This musical feeling and precise ear determined his entire approach to classical literature and . . . also the character of his imitation.[39]

Of course, it is impossible to prove as fact that the melodies of the troubadours or any other specific music made Petrarch's ear for Latin poetry as sensitive as it was. Still, Gmelin's intuition accords well with that Renaissance inclination toward the ear and its mode of perception which we have been noticing in sonnets and madrigals. Medieval commentators had looked at Virgil as a text to be allegorized, interpreted, understood intellectually; the sensuous appeal of the sound of the Latin poetry, if acknowledged at all, was described as leading toward a higher understanding. Petrarch, as the letter Gmelin quotes makes clear, was freshly alive to the music of Virgil and the power of Cicero, willing to allege that the sound of their language was its primary means for moving an audience. We have seen some of the ways this perception affected his own poetry; it also affected his influential pronouncements on literary theory.

Petrarch and his followers came to believe that their emphasis on the sonorous qualities of classical poetry constituted a recovery

39. "Das Prinzip der Imitatio in den romanischen Literaturen der Renaissance," *Romanische Forschungen* 46 (1932): 98-99, translation mine. My attention was drawn to this article by Nancy Struever, who quotes this passage, in German and Latin, on p. 48 of *The Language of History in the Renaissance*. Unfortunately, the Latin phrase from Petrarch's letter is seriously misprinted there, with eight words omitted and the last verb *(videretur)* appearing as *rideretur*.

of the aesthetic principles upon which that poetry had originally been written; they committed themselves to an imitation of classical poetry based on those principles, and entered into imaginary dialogues with the ancient poets. By allying themselves with the ancients, they rendered problematic their relations to their more immediate predecessors, the poets and rhetoricians of the Middle Ages. We may discern three basic solutions to that problem:

1. The most extreme position was outright polemical rejection of all things medieval. This dogmatic purism was the doctrine of the Ciceronians, who scorned the medieval Latin of the "schoolmen" as "barbarous," refused to use any Latin words or constructions not found in Cicero's works, and were thus constrained to employ ludicrous circumlocutions in order to discuss Christian theology. The debate they sparked was intense, but the more moderate position represented by Erasmus ultimately prevailed.[40]

2. Other theorists succeeded in preserving useful medieval techniques by simply claiming that they were ancient. George Puttenham, in his *Arte of English Poesie* (1589), uses this tactic as a way of defending rhyme; he claims, without any specific evidence, that "the Hebrues and Chaldees who were more ancient than the Greekes, did not only vse a metricall Poesie, but also with the same a maner of rime, as hath bene of late obserued by learned men . . . , which proues also that our maner of vulgar Poesie is more ancient then the artificiall of the Greeks and Latines . . . [and] no lesse to be allowed and commended then theirs" (I, v; p. 26). A few pages later, Puttenham adduces a rhyming distich from Ovid with similar intent. This argument had the advantage of allowing poets to claim allegiance to the principle of imitating the ancients while actually combining ancient and medieval techniques; it had the disadvantage of resting upon claims which were historically false.

3. But in practice, particularly the practice of vernacular lyric poetry, the successful techniques of the Middle Ages could neither be purged by decree nor falsely legitimized as ancient. Restriction of imitation to the classics was orthodox dogma only for

---

40. For Erasmus' dialogue *Ciceronianus*, see *Desiderii Erasmi Roterdami Opera Omnia*, ed. John Le Clerc, col. 973-1026.

the Ciceronians; the majority of Renaissance poets and theorists made practical combinations of ancient and medieval techniques. Petrarch himself, as the Elizabethan critic Samuel Daniel pointed out, gained more fame with his rhymed Italian lyrics than with his Latin epic *Africa*.[41] For critics like Daniel and Puttenham, who wished to salvage effective techniques, whatever their origin, the humanist and "ancient" emphasis on the capacity of the spoken word to inflame or improve its hearers could be satisfied by claiming expressive force for rhetorical devices which medieval treatises had considered and classified more abstractly. Thus Daniel can claim that rhyme gives "both to the Eare an Eccho of a delightfull report & to the Memorie a deeper impression of what is deliuered therein" (pp. 7–8).

The fact that both medieval and Renaissance theorists used the same Greek and Latin names for most rhetorical devices made polemical hostility unlikely. After all, much of the knowledge involved was the same, even if the emphases were different: a sixteenth-century theorist would define chiasmus exactly as a twelfth-century (or first-century) rhetorician would have, though he might make a larger persuasive claim for such a figure than his medieval counterpart. And with the advent of the printing press, knowledge of such rhetorical terms, once the private property of a few learned men, became far more widespread; the manuals of rhetoric which spread this knowledge were reprints of medieval manuscripts.[42] The printing of these manuals, which made technical knowledge about writing available for the price of a book, coincided with the new moral claims for rhetoric being made by the humanist movement, so that knowledge about devices of rhetorical construction was spreading significantly in the very years in which the humanists were making their case for rhetorical expression. The inevitable combination of ideas from ancient and medieval sources in Renaissance treatises often involved sidestepping real conflicts in aesthetic doctrine: few Renaissance treatises qualify as examples of consistency. But the rhetorical exuberance

41. See Daniel's *Defence of Ryme* (1603), bound together with Campion's *Observations in the Art of English Poesie* (1602), which it refutes, ed. G. B. Harrison for the Bodley Head series, p. 20. Later citations of Campion are from this edition.

42. See Elizabeth Eisenstein, "The Advent of Printing and the Problem of the Renaissance," *Past and Present* 45 (1969): 67-68.

of Renaissance literature profited from the same inclusive and combining spirit which these treatises represent.

Puttenham, who has already provided us with an example of pseudo-scholarship, is as genial and undogmatic as any Renaissance theorist: his treatise exemplifies the confluence of constructive and expressive theories of language. In a chapter ostensibly explaining *"How ornament Poeticall is of two sortes according to the double vertue and efficacie of figures,"* Puttenham at first appears to distinguish between abstract techniques of construction and calculated techniques of persuasion, but then immediately recognizes that some techniques serve both purposes:

> This ornament then is of two sortes, one to satisfie and delight th'eare onely by a goodly outward shew set vpon the matter with wordes, and speaches smothly and tunably running: another by certaine intendments or sence of such words and speaches inwardly working a stirre to the mynde: that first qualitie the Greeks called *Enargia,* of this word *argos,* because it geueth a glorious lustre and light. This latter they called *Energia* of *ergon,* because it wrought with a strong and vertuous operation; and figure breedeth them both, some seruing to giue glosse onely to a language, some to geue it efficacie by sense, and so by that meanes some of them serue th'eare onely, some serue the conceit onely and not th'eare: there be of them also that serue both turnes as common seruitors appointed for th'one and th'other purpose. (III, iii; p. 155).

The mixture of metaphors concerning sight ("goodly outward shew," "glorious lustre and light," "glosse") with those concerning hearing ("speaches smothly and tunably running," "inwardly working a stirre to the mynde"), like the punning etymology of *Enargia* and *Energia,* tends to muddle the distinction between what Puttenham later calls "auricular" and "sensible" figures. So it should not surprise us to discover such devices as zeugma classified among "auricular" figures, but discussed in ways that show Puttenham's awareness of their effect on the sense of a passage:

> . . . Thus much for the congruitie, now for the sence. One wrote thus of a young man, who slew a villaine that had killed his father, and rauished his mother.

Thus valiantly and with a manly minde,
And by one feate of euerlasting fame,
This lustie lad fully requited kinde,
His fathers death, and eke his mothers shame.

Where ye see this word *[requite]* serue a double sence: that is to say, to reuenge, and to satisfie. For the parents iniurie was reuenged, and the duetie of nature performed or satisfied by the childe. (III, xii; p. 177)

In the terms we have been employing, this passage is an analysis of the expressive effect of a constructive device. Not only does Puttenham thus combine constructive and expressive concerns, but he seems unaware of any potential conflict between the claims of proportion and those of persuasion. In Book II, "Of Proportion Poetical," he discusses the tricky poetic forms, including anagrams and geometrically shaped stanzas, which we have seen flourishing in the constructive Middle Ages; here he employs musical vocabulary at every turn, entitling one chapter *"Of Proportion in Concord, called Symphonie or rime"* (IV, v). In the first chapter of that book, he links poetry and music in phrases that will remind us of Dante and Deschamps:

... Poesie is a skill to speake and write harmonically: and verses or rime be a kind of Musicall vtterance, by reason of certaine congruitie in sounds pleasing the eare, though not perchance so exquisitely as the harmonicall concents of the artificial Musicke, consisting in strained tunes, as is the vocall Musicke, or that of melodious instruments, as Lutes, Harpes, Regals, Records and such like. (II, i; p. 79)

But in his later discussion of the persuasive uses of allegory, he sounds more like Castiglione:

The vse of this figure is so large, and his vertue of so great efficacie as it is supposed no man can pleasantly vtter and perswade without it, but in effect is sure neuer or very seldome to thriue and prosper in the world, that cannot skillfully put in vre [sic], in somuch as not onely euery common Courtier, but also the grauest Counsellor, yea and the most noble and wisest Prince of them all are many times enforced to vse it. (III, xviii; p. 196)

And when he comes to the explicit discussion of those figures which are both "auricular" and "sensible," he calls them "rhetoricall," having reserved that powerful word for this special use. Puttenham's explanation of the way such figures enter and influence the mind through the ear may serve as a concluding exhibit; in the metaphors of this paragraph, we may see the humanist definition of rhetoric as moral persuasion embracing the medieval definition of rhetoric as ornamental construction:

> And your figures rhetoricall, besides their remembred ordinarie vertues, that is, sententiousnes, and copious amplification, or enlargement of language, doe also conteine a certaine sweet and melodious manner of speech, in which respect, they may, after a sort, be said *auricular:* because the eare is no lesse rauished with their currant tune, than the mind is with their sententiousnes. For the eare is properly but an instrument of conueyance for the minde, to apprehend the sence by the sound. And our speech is made melodious or harmonicall, not onely by strayned tunes, as those of *Musick,* but also by choice of smoothe words: and thus, or thus, marshalling them in their comeliest construction and order, and as well by sometimes sparing, sometimes spending them more or lesse liberally, and carrying or transporting them farther off or neerer, setting them with sundry relations, and variable formes, in the ministery and vse of words, doe breede no little alteration in man. For to say truely, what els is man but his minde? which, whosoeuer haue skil to compasse, and make yeelding and flexible, what may not he commaund the body to perfourme? He therefore that hath vanquished the minde of man, hath made the greatest and most glorious conquest. But the minde is not assailable vnlesse it be by sensible approches, whereof the audible is of greatest force for instruction or discipline: the visible, for apprehension of exterior knowledges as the Philosopher saith. Therefore the well tuning of your words and clauses to the delight of the eare, maketh your information no lesse plausible to the minde than to the eare: no though you filled them with neuer so much sence and sententiousnes. (III, xix; pp. 206–07)

Some of the metaphors here make the orator a kind of general, "marshaling [his words] in their comeliest construction and order" so as to "vanquish the minde of man." Others make him a kind of seducer, using "sensible approches" and "smoothe words" to "rauish" the ear and "breede no little alteration in man." The combination of those contrasting patterns of imagery, sometimes in the same sentence, recalls the conventional Petrarchan personification of the loved one as a fort or castle to be taken by military force; more importantly for our purposes, it suggests the willingness of Puttenham and other Renaissance literary theorists to embrace construction as a means of persuasion.

The Musical Humanists

The musical theorists now usually called the "musical humanists" also confronted the problem of how their art might imitate that of the ancients. But because the information available about ancient Greek and Roman music was much scrappier than the analogous information about ancient literature, the musical humanists came to the problem later, argued it more intensely, and resolved it somewhat differently than did their literary counterparts. Medieval music theory had depended upon Boethius as a transmitter of knowledge about ancient music and had extended the habit of allegorizing already inherent in Boethius; it had also extended Boethius' prejudice in favor of Pythagorean, mathematical, speculative thinking about music and against Aristoxenian, practical, and emotional theories. For Zarlino and some other theorists of the sixteenth century, the musical mysticism of Plato's *Timaeus* was the important inheritance from the ancient world, but in the later years of that century, under the influence of the learned philologist Girolamo Mei, humanist writers on music placed greater emphasis on the doctrine of *ethos*, the teachings of Aristoxenos, and the generally mimetic and emotional concerns typified by Aristotle's *Poetics*. Zarlino had been content to commission a translation into Latin of Ptolemy's *Harmonics*, but Mei read all the available documents in the original Greek, and transmitted his learning to the eager polemical writer Vincenzo Galilei, father of the astronomer, a member of the remarkable Florentine *Camerata* that gathered around Count Giovanni De' Bardi.[43] In that

43. I summarize the findings of Claude Palisca, most easily available in the introduction to his edition of Mei's *Letters on Ancient and Modern Music*, addressed to Galilei and Bardi. For an even fuller account, touching on earlier figures, see Palisca's Harvard Ph.D.

group, and in the slightly later Parisian *Académie de Poésie et de Musique* led by Jean-Antoine de Baïf, there was vigorous study of ancient musical lore: Plato, Aristotle, and Plutarch were ransacked for information; the scraps of ancient notation preserved by Boethius and other medieval treatises were newly studied; and there was great excitement about the myths of Orpheus and Timotheus, which appeared to support the notion that ancient music had explicit and powerful emotional effects on its hearers.

This excitement was analogous to that felt by the literary humanists who rediscovered Quintilian, but the problems involved in applying this knowledge to the existing musical tradition were more imposing than those involved in reforming rhetoric. As we have seen, medieval rhetoric, while it may have been reduced to a smaller role than the Renaissance humanists would claim for it, nonetheless preserved the techniques and terminology of ancient rhetoric. But the polyphonic and canonic music developed in the Middle Ages was entirely unlike the lyric monody of the ancient world. While the principle of imitating the ancients could be applied to rhetoric and poetry without entirely rejecting the immediate past, applying that principle to music, a radical change advocated by Mei, would have meant abandoning the polyphonic sophistication music had been developing since the eleventh century, the rhythmic independence it had been pursuing at least since the *ars nova,* and the harmonic syntax it was beginning to work out in the sixteenth century. To advocate so sweeping a reform on the basis of fragmentary and ill-understood documents was difficult, and as more documents came to light, the humanists quarreled about the nature of ancient music, the feasibility of imitating it, and the desirability of eliminating such modern innovations as harmony. In his influential account of the musical humanists, D. P. Walker divides them rather roughly into three groups, basing his division on their different opinions about reforming modern music:

> Gafori, Artusi, Salinas and Cerone had a purely scholarly interest in ancient music; they were satisfied with the music of their time and did not consider reforming it. Tyard, Galilei,

---

dissertation, "The Beginnings of Baroque Music; Its Roots in Sixteenth Century Theory and Polemics."

Mei and Doni had an exactly opposite point of view; they believed that modern music was very inferior to ancient music, which they wished to revive as completely as possible. Glareanus, Vicentino, Zarlino and Mersenne are midway between the other two groups. They held that in certain respects only was ancient music superior to modern, and that, though some reforms were desirable, yet in many ways modern music had advanced far beyond ancient.[44]

The members of that last group, those wishing to bring about some kind of combination of ancient and medieval principles, will remind us of Puttenham, not only in their use of metaphors to muddle distinctions, but in their defense of constructive principles on expressive grounds. Here is Heinrich Glareanus—poet, composer, and friend of Erasmus—praising his hero Josquin by attributing expressive effects to his various compositional techniques, and by comparing him to Virgil in an obvious attempt to make him seem "ancient":

> No one has more effectively expressed the passions of the soul in music than this symphonist, no one has more felicitously begun, no one has been able to compete in grace and facility on an equal footing with him, just as there is no Latin poet superior in epic to Vergil. For just as Vergil, with his natural facility, was accustomed to adapt his poem to his subject so as to set weighty matters before the eyes of his readers with close-packed spondees, fleeting ones with unmixed dactyls, to use words suited to his very subject, in short, to undertake nothing inappropriately, as Horace says of Homer, so our Josquin, where his matter requires it, now advances with impetuous and precipitate notes, now intones his subject in long-drawn tones, and, to sum up, has brought forth nothing that was not delightful to the ear and approved as ingenious by the learned.[45]

44. "Musical Humanism in the Sixteenth and Early Seventeenth Centuries," *The Music Review* 2 (1941), p. 5. Like all students of this subject, I am generally indebted to Walker's article, published in installments in volumes 2 and 3 of *The Music Review*. Some of his subsequent essays are collected in *Studies in Musical Science*.

45. *Dodecachordon* (1547), Book III, ch. 24; I quote, with minor alterations, the translation appearing in Strunk, pp. 220–21.

It is especially revealing that the ending of this passage pairs as equals the expressive and aural criterion of delight and the constructive and visual criterion of ingenuity. Later and more extreme musical humanists would attack both these criteria: not only were they bitterly opposed to the polyphonic ingenuity of the Netherlandish school, but even the long-held notion that music should give pleasure disturbed those among them who sought, in Walker's words, to "resuscitate the ethical qualities of music," to make it "an art which should arouse and control passions, inculcate and preserve virtue, even cure disease and ensure the stability of the state" (vol. 2, p. 9).

Glareanus praised Josquin (and Virgil) for knowing how to "*express* the passions of the soul," but the Italian and French academies sought to restore to music its fabled power to "*arouse* and *control*" the passions of its hearers. In order to achieve these ends, to substitute these ethical effects for the delight and ingenuity sought by earlier composers, the academicians needed to decide what the technical qualities of ancient music had been. But the fragmentary nature of the evidence led inevitably to guesswork and controversy, as Frances Yates explains in her study of the French Academy:

> In the case of the arts of sculpture or architecture [or literature!] the Renaissance enthusiast endeavouring to return to the antique had surviving examples of classical art to imitate. But the musician who wished to revive ancient music was trying to imitate an art of which practically no examples survived, and of which the theory cannot, even now, be reconstructed with any degree of certainty. The musical humanists were obliged to theorise as to what ancient music was like, and how its "effects" were obtained, and their theories differed.[46]

Furthermore, as Claude Palisca points out, both the academic attempts to recover ancient rhythm and the even earlier attempts to recover ancient microtonal tuning were "attempts to realize the effects of ancient music by copying one of its external features." The speculation was directed toward "the shell rather than the

---

46. *The French Académies of the Sixteenth Century*, p. 46.

core of Greek art."[47] Only when the quarrels about these external features had been laid aside could the really important impact of ancient musical thought be felt, in the baroque revolution of the so-called *"seconda practica"* of Monteverdi, in which the rules of counterpoint are bent and stretched in the name of emotional expression.

Nonetheless, the humanist controversies about compositional technique are revealing, and will remind us of analogous controversies in poetic theory. We may consider them briefly as they concern four different elements of musical style: (1) linear pitch (scales versus modes versus Greek *genera);* (2) rhythm (musical and poetic); (3) polyphony (versus monody or homophony); and (4) the proper techniques of text-setting.

1. The most extreme position about linear pitch, represented in Italy by Nicolo Vicentino and in France by Pontus de Tyard, held that the miraculous "effects" of ancient music could only be restored by the revival of the Greek chromatic and enharmonic *genera* (see ch. 1 above). Even these distinguished scholars were surely guessing about the exact pitches involved in the ancient tetrachords, but their ignorance did not stop them from attempting to write and perform music replicating what they took to be the sounds of ancient Greek music. Vicentino wrote a famous treatise called *L'antica musica ridotta alla moderna practica* (1555), composed vocal pieces in which dots over certain notes were supposed to indicate microtonal sharpening, and built a six-manual harpsichord called an *archicembalo,* which divided every whole step into five microtonal parts, so that each octave contained 31 separate pitches.[48] The pieces Vicentino and others wrote for the *archicembalo* were never published, and the reforms they advocated were obviously too extreme to gain general acceptance, but *archicembali* were still being built throughout the seventeenth century, and some of the experiments in the Italian madrigal with chromaticism as we define it were related to the interest in Greek microtonal chomaticism stirred up by Vicentino and Galilei.[49]

47. In his introduction to Mei's *Letters,* pp. 1-2.

48. See Lowinsky, "Music in the Culture of the Renaissance," p. 553; for information about the vocal pieces, with a brief example, see Reese, pp. 328-29.

49. Walker suggests that the popularity of such chromatic pieces as the famous *Prophetiae Sibyllarum* of Orlando di Lasso "may well have been due ultimately to the influence

The situation in modal theory was even more ludicrous. Plato and Aristotle, as all the humanists knew, had attached various *ethea* to various *harmoniai,* and medieval theorists had attached the Greek names for those *harmoniai* to their quite different church modes. But attempts to reconcile medieval terminology with re-discovered ancient terminology produced impossible conflicts, and by the middle of the sixteenth century, as Yates explains, "there were . . . three rival systems in existence for the naming of the modes and the composer who wished to write a tune in the Phrygian mode would have first of all to decide which theory he accepted as to which *was* the Phrygian mode" (p. 48). This hope-less confusion of terminology weakened the attempt to revive the theory of *ethos,* since one man's sober Dorian might be another's passionate Phrygian. And as we have seen, the medieval modal system itself was breaking down as compositional practice moved closer to the scalar and chordal grammar of tonality. However earnestly the humanists wished to restore ancient practice in this area, they were ultimately influenced by the music of their own time. As Walker concludes, "the treatment of the modes in *musique mesurée,* or in [the] early Italian monody [of Bardi's circle], is in practice, whatever the theories of the composers may have been, indistinguishable from that of any other contemporary music" (vol. 2, p. 226).

But if we move beyond the shell to the core, to repeat Palisca's useful metaphor, we can discover in the melodic lines of Monte-verdi's operas a fulfillment of humanist aims. Though never mi-crotonal, his melodies employ expressively dissonant relations, both within the line itself and between the line and its accompani-ment, now usually notated in a new chordal shorthand called *basso continuo* or figured bass.[50] Laid out thus in linear fashion, the harmonic devices developed by madrigal composers (including Monteverdi himself) can function as dramatic expressions of emotional states, not merely as rhetorical colorations of single words.

---

of humanism" (vol. 2, p. 120). Transcriptions of the opening section of Lasso's piece appear in Crocker, pp. 211-12, and in Lowinsky, *Tonality and Atonality in Sixteenth-century Music,* p. 40.

50. For an example from Monteverdi's *Orfeo* (1607), with an excellent analysis, see Joseph Kerman, *Opera as Drama,* pp. 30-32.

2. There was a wider consensus about rhythm. Most of the humanists believed that poetic and musical rhythm in the ancient world had been identical: even though Gafori had already published a fragment of ancient rhythmic notation, Galilei's influential *Dialogo della musica antica e della moderna* (1581) contains a passage in which Count Bardi explains to Strozzi that the ancient Greeks needed no rhythmic notation because the long and short syllables of their poetry dictated the rhythm.[51] The humanists were also familiar with the many passages in which ancient rhetoricians attributed various effects to various rhythms (see, for example, the claims of Dionysius in ch. 1 above). Hoping to recover these effects, both the Italian and French academies adopted as an essential principle the absolute subjection of musical rhythm to poetic rhythm. Glareanus had attributed expressive effects to Virgil's poetic rhythm in order to compare the effects of Josquin's quite different musical rhythm, but some later academicians were not content with such analogies; they preferred an exact technical equivalance. Glareanus himself may have experimented along these lines: he admits making musical settings of Horace in his youth, but these are lost and we cannot be sure of their rhythmic method. We do know that Petrus Tritonius published some musical settings of Latin poetry as early as 1507, well before the founding of the Italian and French academies, in which the musical rhythm is exactly that of the quantitative Latin poetry, and in which the parts move in homophonic chords.[52] This style, although it obviously did not represent a return to actual ancient practice, was the expedient eventually settled upon by the French academy, whose *"vers et musique mesures á l'antique"* usually took the form of four-part homophony with a rhythm determined by artificially imposing upon French a version of ancient rules of quantity.

This sweeping program for rhythmic reform necessarily opposed the contrapuntal rhythms of motets and madrigals, in which different parts employed different rhythms, and the musi-

---

51. For details, see Walker, vol. 2, pp. 298-99. Walker also explains how Zarlino and Artusi, misled by the two different systems of Greek notation ("vocal" and "instrumental"), imagined that one of them was a rhythmic notation.

52. For details, see Reese, p. 705, and Lowinsky, "Music in the Culture of the Renaissance," p. 525.

cal humanists attacked those practices vigorously, alleging that contrapuntal rhythms cancelled each other out and destroyed all hope of expression. Count Bardi's humorous polemic in his *Discourse on Ancient Music and Good Singing* is typical; in the madrigal, according to Bardi,

> ... Messer Bass, soberly dressed in semibreves and minims, stalks through the ground-floor rooms of his palace while Soprano, decked out in minims and semiminims, walks hurriedly about the terrace at a rapid pace and Messers Tenor and Alto, with various ornaments and in habits different from the others, stray through the rooms of the intervening floors. For in truth it would seem a sin to the contrapuntists of today (may they be pardoned these mixtures of several melodies and several modes!)—it would seem, I say, a mortal sin if all the parts were heard to beat at the same time with the same notes, with the same syllables of the verse, and with the same longs and shorts; the more they make the parts move, the more artful they think they are.[53]

The homophony which the contrapuntists would consider a "mortal sin" is, of course, precisely the rhythmic procedure Bardi advocates. Not only did this reform program propose to undo the whole rhythmic development of composition since the *ars nova*; it also deprived composers of the rhythmic advantages they had over poets. We have seen how madrigal composers, with their varied rhythms and precise notation, could use rhythms to express mimetically the meaning of words in a poetic text. Despite their proclaimed commitment to expression, the academic humanists were effectively limiting composers to the much smaller range of rhythmic variation already available to poets.

When the texts to be set were actual quantitative Latin verse, the task of setting down the rhythm became, for the academicians, an absolutely mechanical one. But French and Italian poetry had never been quantitative, a fact which necessitated another compromise between the desire to imitate the ancients and the difficulty of eradicating the practices of the intervening centuries. One solution, adopted by Alberti and Tolomei in Italy, by Sidney and Campion in England, and by Baïf in France, was to

53. As translated in Strunk, pp. 293-94.

attempt to write quantitative verse in the vernacular, either by arbitrarily declaring certain vowels long and others short, or by
treating as quantitatively "long" syllables that were normally
stressed.[54] To this end, Baïf even invented a system of phonetic
spelling; his efforts and those of his counterparts in other countries involved an impressive expenditure of energy and ingenuity,
but they were clearly doomed, as Yates explains:

> Just as all attempts to imitate the modes of ancient music are
> rendered nugatory by a radical impossibility—the impossibil-
> ity of knowing what the ancient modes were like—so the at-
> tempts to impose classical quantity on the French language
> collapse into ambiguity, owing to the radical impossibility of
> writing quantitative verse in a language in which quantity, in
> the classical sense, does not exist. (p. 53)

This "radical impossibility" may be perfectly clear to us, but the
ambiguous use of ancient poetic terms to describe modern poetic
practices made it less clear to the humanists, who used the terms
"long" and "short" to describe accented and unaccented syllables,
and who fervently hoped that their languages could be made to
behave as Latin and Greek had. As late as 1685, Dryden, who
should have known better, was alleging in print that there was "as
great a certainty of quantity in our syllables as either in the *Greek*
or *Latin*."[55] The dream of restoring classical measures and their
fabled effects died hard.

But if the musical humanists were destined to fail in their
attempt to make modern languages conform to classical rhythm,
they were more than a little successful in making musical rhythm
follow the rhythm of modern dramatic speech, whether poetry or
prose. Indeed, the most obvious continuing legacy of Bardi's
Academy is the operatic recitative, in which a free rhythm without
a rigid beat replicates the personal and expressive rhythms of
speech. No Italian academician was a really professional composer: even Bardi's own works were privately performed and

54. For an excellent short account of the problems involved in attempting to write
quantitative verse in English, see W. H. Auden's Preface and John Hollander's Introduction to their beautiful edition of *Selected Songs of Thomas Campion.*

55. Preface to *Albion and Albanius,* in the California edition of *The Works of John Dryden,*
ed. Hooker, Swedenberg, et al., Vol. XV, p. 9. All citations of Dryden are from this edition
unless otherwise noted.

never printed; and while Jacopo Peri and Giulio Caccini, two younger members, caused a sensation with their dramatic mono-dies, also privately performed at the Academy, and with their more elaborate court dramas, now usually identified as the first operas (*Dafne,* 1597; *Euridice,* 1600), neither was a competent con-trapuntist. Nonetheless, when professional composers, including Monteverdi, began to compose operas, they followed the model of the Florentine amateurs, adopting the *stilo recitativo,* in which a solo voice sings a highly dramatic text, usually a soliloquy, above a figured bass.[56] The rhythm of these recitatives—simple in its no-tation, free in its performance, closely replicating the rhythm of excited speech, and destined to survive in opera and oratorio for centuries—is our heritage from the musical humanists.

But the *stilo recitativo,* despite the claim that it was a revival of ancient Greek monody, was not an entirely antiquarian invention. As D. T. Mace has suggested, a new development in Italian poetry may have been as important an influence as the increased atten-tion to ancient practices:

> The end of the madrigal, like its beginning, was associated with the appearance of a new poetic style to which music had to adjust itself . . . , the new pathetic style of Tasso which, instead of intellectualizing feeling in witty rhetorical figures, expresses it directly in what Tasso himself called *vigore d'accenti*. . . . [For such poetry] the regular *tactus* of the mad-rigal stood heavily in the way of satisfactory musical treat-ment of the words. Nothing but very free monody would do in which the singer might proceed *senza battuta* [without a rigid beat]. . . . However elaborate the polemics of the Flor-entine Camerata were in favour of restoring Greek music, that group was essentially at pains to create a musical style which would bring rhythm and sound in music into rapport with the new kind of 'pathetic' diction stemming from Tasso.[57]

Of course, Tasso himself had a considerable commitment to clas-sical imitation: *Gerusalemme liberata* conforms far more closely to

56. For a good short account of the beginning of opera, see Crocker, pp. 225-32.

57. "Musical Humanism, The Doctrine of Rhythmus, and the Saint Cecilia odes of Dryden," *Journal of the Warburg and Courtauld Institute* 27 (1964): 254-55.

Aristotelian rules for epic than the episodic poems of Boiardo and Ariosto, and its most famous "pathetic" passage, frequently set to music and widely imitated in recitative texts, is Armida's outburst on being abandoned by Rinaldo, which owes its passion and its choppy rhythm to a similar speech by Virgil's Dido, a passage which was itself frequently set to music in the sixteenth and seventeenth centures.[58] The scholars of the *Camerata* and the early opera composers were not merely using classical imitation as a pretext to write music properly suited to Tasso's style; both they and Tasso were exploiting a particular aspect of classical poetry, the capacity of its rhythms to express emotion. The stylistic shift from madrigal to monody was analogous to the shift from the rhetorical, divided Petrarchan speaker to the dramatic, isolated speaker like Armida; in invoking the classical past as precedent for these changes, musicians and poets naturally emphasized some aspects of that past at the expense of others.

The resulting emphasis on expressive rhythm, in theory and in practice, worked against mathematical and proportional conceptions of rhythm: not only were the proportional intricacies of isorhythm forgotten, but the simpler mathematical equivalences of a rhythm based on classical quantity eventually yielded to a freer recitative which clearly took modern accent into account. Issac Vossius's *De poematum cantu et viribus rhythmi* (1673) is, as Mace points out,

> . . . the final logical step in the humanist discussion of poetic rhythm in the seventeenth century: the mathematical aspect of the classical feet is entirely ignored and they are discussed only as "forms" and "images" having affective significance. Vossius' ancient authority is not St. Augustine with his emphasis on the mathematical proportions of the feet but Dionysius of Halicarnassus and Quintilian who treat the feet more nearly as "images." (p. 288)

The claim that rhythmic patterns could have specific emotional effects, whether made by Dionysius or Vossius, may strike us as metaphysical, but we should realize that there was a simple, prac-

---

58. The passages are *Gerusalemme liberata* XVI, 47, and *Aeneid* IV, 591-629.

tical way in which the rhythmic reforms of the humanists did make music more expressive: a simple, homophonic rhythm obviously increased the audibility of the text.

As the humanists were fond of pointing out, the staggered declamation of the text in motets and madrigals made the resulting composite difficult if not impossible to hear. The rhetorical sophistication of the text-setting in these pieces was doubtless enjoyable to the singers, but much of it must have been lost on anyone merely listening. Indeed, madrigals seem to have been primarily intended for an audience of performers: anecdotal accounts of madrigal singing in Italy and England stress participation; a gentleman was supposed to be able to manage his part, not to sit passively listening. The *musique mesurée* of Baïf's *Académie,* by contrast, was performed by salaried professionals for an audience whose behavior was rigorously controlled by regulations: members were not allowed to converse during the singing, and latecomers had to wait until a piece had ended before being seated.[59] And the audience served an experimental function as well: everyone wanted to know whether they would exhibit signs of the fabled "effects." The composers of early Italian operas also sought to impress an audience, usually a courtly assembly in Florence or Rome. In both cases, audibility of the text was critical in a way it had not been for the madrigal composers, who were presumably content to have a single singer recognize a rhythmic or melodic nicety in his part which might be far from obvious in the composite texture.

3. The humanists' objection to staggered or proportional rhythm was also, in effect, an objection to polyphony. The most extreme humanists, especially Galilei, wanted to eliminate every aspect of current compositional technique, to return to the naked monody which had been the Greek norm. Predictably, there were dissenters: Doni and Salinas seized on a passage in Plutarch to argue that ancient music had actually been polyphonic, while Zarlino claimed, without evidence, that Greek melodies had been accompanied by a three-note drone.[60] Others, notably Claude Le Jeune, did not resort to scholarly obfuscation; they admitted that

59. See the Statutes of the *Académie,* printed in full in Appendix I of Yates.
60. See Walker, vol. 2, pp. 57-59.

ancient music had been monodic, but were not therefore willing
to abandon harmony, which they recognized as an important re-
source. Their hybrid solution, chordal settings of verse in which
all parts sang the same words at the same time in identical, poeti-
cally determined rhythms, became the norm in the Paris *Académie*.[61]
Italian practice, as we have seen, was more frequently monodic,
but the tradition that Greek solo song had been instrumentally
accompanied allowed the preservation of a chordal underpinning
in figured-bass form. Neither of these solutions was in fact a return to Greek practice, but both represented major deviations
from contrapuntal polyphony.

The early Italian operas gained variety by using both forms:
the lengthy recitatives which carried most of the text alternated
with choral songs in a strophic, homophonic style. As compared
to the contrapuntal madrigal, both these forms insured the audibility of the text, an important goal for the humanists and a practical necessity for drama. But because of the figured bass, both
forms also insured a steady stream of triadic harmonies; despite
the humanist polemic, working composers were naturally unwill-
ing to abandon the sonority which had become a normal component of all music in the preceding centuries. Contrapuntal polyphony, now less dominant in vocal music, lived on in the increasingly important instrumental music of the late Renaissance. In the
very passage in which he condemns vocal polyphony, Bardi himself concedes that such construction

> . . . is the concern of the stringed instruments, for, there
> being no voice in these, it is fitting that the player, in playing
> airs not suited to singing or dancing—it is fitting, I say, that
> the player should make the parts move and that he should
> contrive canons, double counterpoints, and other novelties to
> avoid wearying his hearers. (p. 294)

Bardi goes on to identify such pieces as "the species of music so
much condemned by . . . Aristotle in the Eighth Book of his *Politics*, where he calls it artificial and wholly useless," but his recognition that instrumental homophony could be "wearying" is an

---

61. See Le Jeune's Preface to *Le Printemps*, translated in Yates, pp. 56-57, and the
examples of music written on these principles by Le Jeune and Mauduit in Yates, Appendix VIII.

important concession. Even the much-heralded vocal recitative could be musically boring: as early as 1620, according to Richard Crocker, "we hear the word 'tedious' applied to the recitative, [doubtless because] all recitative tends to sound alike—the paradoxical result of letting the music exactly express the text" (p. 231). It was perhaps for this reason that some of the more liberal humanists were more generous toward counterpoint, so long as the text was not overwhelmed. As in other areas, ideological purity had to be tempered by practical experience, and practical considerations revealed the advantages of existing compositional procedures.

4. A final area of humanist controversy concerned methods of text-setting. The extremists scorned the word-painting of the madrigalists, believing instead that if a composer chose the correct mode and followed the poetic rhythm, he would be doing all he could to express the text. The composers most directly influenced by the academies followed this procedure: Mauduit and Le Jeune in France, like Peri and Caccini in Italy, ascetically avoid imitative devices. But like counterpoint, the mimetic devices of the madrigalists were too effective to be purged, and some important composers within the humanist orbit, such as Lasso and Monteverdi, continued to use them. If we think of the text-setting techniques of the madrigalists as rhetorical, and those advocated by the humanists as dramatic, we can recognize that a dogmatic separation was unlikely to last: it was no more possible to eliminate rhetorical text-setting from vocal music than it would have been to eliminate rhetorical speeches from the drama itself. Shakespeare's characters may be more psychologically rounded than their ancestors in the plays of Lyly and Kyd, but their speeches have hardly been stripped of rhetoric; Monteverdi's operatic recitatives may be more "pathetic" than comparable vocal lines in the madrigal school, but some of their effect derives from rhetorical madrigalisms.

There are many ironies in the curious history of the musical humanists. Despite their desire to recover the marvelous "effects" of the ancients, the most rabid among them advocated reforms that would have deprived composers of some of their most effective means of expression. Like their literary counterparts, they sometimes used the notion of returning to the ancients as a pretext, willfully misinterpreting ancient evidence in order to support what were really modern aesthetic prejudices. The greatest irony, and the most interesting for our study, is that under the cover of restoring the ancient union between music and poetry, many of the musical humanists were actually trying to assert the superiority of poetry over music, to curtail music's growing independence, to bring it under the control of texts. Marsilio Ficino, in a burst of neo-Platonic enthusiasm, could claim that the fifteenth century had, "like a golden age, restored to light the liberal arts that were nearly extinct: grammar, poetry, rhetoric, painting, sculpture, architecture, music, [and] the ancient performance of songs with the Orphic lyre." But in his treatise *De divino furore*, he makes a distinction between the arts which confirms the suspicion we might have had from the order of that list: he alleges that "poetry is superior to music, since through the words it speaks not only to the ear but also directly to the mind."[62] Ficino makes explicit a prejudice we may detect in the later musical humanists. For all their talk about the miraculous effects of ancient modes and rhythms, the humanists sidestepped the implications of those ancient documents which claimed such effects for instrumental music.[63] Stripped of its scholarly trappings, their reform program was an attempt to reduce music to the role of merely intensifying effects already present in a poetic text; their proposed reunion of music and poetry assumed and legislated the primacy of poetry.

The arguments marshalled by the humanists against "modern" music—that it aimed merely at delighting the sense, that it could not be "significant" in the way that words could be, that it could only be judged by musicians, that its simultaneously-sounded polyphonic lines cancelled each other out—were destined to become, in the hands of later thinkers anxious to assert

62. The first passage comes from a letter to Paulus Middelburgensis, as translated in Paul Oskar Kristeller, *The Philosophy of Marsilio Ficino*, p. 22. The second is Kristeller's paraphrase (p. 300) of a passage in which Ficino interprets Plato as having also believed that poetry was superior to music. See Ficino's *Opera omnia*, p. 614.

63. These included Aristotle's *Problems*, then considered genuine, and passages in the *Poetics* and *Politics*. As Walker points out, "both Galilei and Mersenne mention the affective power of purely instrumental music, and both even refer to Aristotle in support of it. But the former, having done so, manages to forget all about it in the rest of his book, and the latter ingeniously, if not very convincingly, claims that these effects are due to instrumental music being reminiscent of, or similar to some song" (vol. 2, pp. 226-27).

the absolute superiority of poetry, arguments against music in general. In what D. T. Mace has called "the curious seventeenth-century war between word and tone," Boileau and Saint Evremond criticized opera itself, the result of the humanist movement, as confused and inarticulate. As Mace points out, "it is ironic that these late-seventeenth-century critics condemned the opera with arguments used by its inventors to flay polyphony" (p. 258). That irony reveals the deep literary bias of the humanist movement. In identifying this bias, I do not mean to impugn the sincerity of the humanists' desire to recover the effects of ancient music. But I do believe that in advocating a return to ancient practices, the humanists were reacting, with various degrees of consciousness, against the independence which music had been gaining in the late Middle Ages and early Renaissance. They directed their attack against those musical techniques that had outstripped poetic techniques: if musical rhythm, with precise notation and the multiplying possibilities of counterpoint, had become vastly more complex than poetic rhythm, they proposed to reduce it to the narrower means available to poets; if polyphonic simultaneity had demonstrated its ability to represent allegory and oxymoron, kinds of simultaneity which poetry could only suggest, they proposed monody; if music was capable of abstract and artificial kinds of structure, complexities of design well beyond the reach of poetry, they attacked such ingenuity as meaningless. They claimed to advocate musical reform, but their arguments, as the next century proved, were well suited to a more frontal attack on music. In wishing to make music more like speech, simpler and more precise in its significance, they were denying all the ways in which music was *not* like speech, and the capacity of speech itself for an abstract formality like that of music.

One final anecdote may serve to demonstrate how the desire to reduce music to speech lay behind the proclaimed desire to return to the practices of the ancients. Vicentino's *archicembalo*, that extravagant and unwieldy invention, was ostensibly built in order to recover the sounds of the ancient Greek chromatic and enharmonic *genera*. But Vicentino's treatise reveals other possibilities for its use:

> The inflections and intervals that all nations of the world use in their native speech do not proceed only in whole and half

tones, but also in quarter tones and even smaller intervals, so that with the division of our harpsichord we can accommodate all the nations of the world.[64]

The *archichembalo*, as its inventor goes on to boast, could thus replicate the sounds of speech in German, French, Spanish, Hungarian, and Turkish. Considered in this light, it was not only a fantastic proto-modern musical instrument, but an all-purpose linguistic reproducing machine. Behind the antiquarian impulse to recover Greek music lay the literary impulse to make music as much like language as possible.

The Survival of Construction

But music would not be so reduced. The timid academic exercises of Mauduit were stillborn, and if Claudio Monteverdi, the giant whose compositions were to determine the future of European music, showed the influence of Peri and Caccini in adopting the recitative, he maintained and extended many of the compositional techniques that the most extreme musical humanists had attacked. To these elements he added some important techniques of harmonic and formal organization learned from the *villanella* and *canzonetta,* popular Italian forms whose folklike style and parodistic texts provided a contrast to the learned madrigal on the one hand and the academic monody on the other.[65] Monteverdi's sensitivity to literature is evident in his careful selection of texts by Tasso, Guarini, and Rinuccini, and in his restless search for fresh, less stylized ways to express those texts musically. But he was no more willing to submit to the literary dictatorship of poetry advocated by the *Camerata* than he was to remain within the limits of the rules of counterpoint formulated by Zarlino. As Leo Schrade explains in his biography:

> For Monteverdi, music, not theory, was the beginning and the end . . . , and the violence with which the Florentines set themselves against the techniques of counterpoint might re-

64. *L'antica musica* . . . , Book IV, ch. xxix, as translated by Lowinsky in "Music in the Culture of the Renaissance," p. 553. Walker gives the Italian (vol. 2, p. 305).

65. See the excellent chapter on the *canzonetta* in Leo Schrade, *Monteverdi, Creator of Modern Music*, pp. 106-23.

sult in the sacrifice of many artistic skills. . . . To him, the problems of the new composition never involved the question of how to destroy counterpoint. The Florentines had shown how easy that was. The question was how to create a new counterpoint. Not until he had found an answer to this question did he turn to the style of pure monody, and when he did so he made use of the elaborate techniques he had worked out for the new style as a whole. (p. 189)

The operas of Monteverdi, undoubtedly the most significant compositions of the early seventeenth century, are only in the narrowest sense the results of musical humanism. In the strength of their musical invention, they actually constitute a refutation of Florentine and Parisian strictures, a vigorous example of the impossibility of subordinating music to literature.

This process continues in the Venetian operas of Cavalli and Cesti, in which we may hear the beginnings of the rhythmically regular, formally shaped aria which was to become a showcase for the talents of the virtuoso singers who spread opera to the capitals of Europe in the second half of the seventeenth century. As Joseph Kerman points out, the aria had legitimate dramatic possibilities: "composers now could take a momentary sentiment and project it as a realized emotion rather than as an impulsive flash of passion in the manner of Monteverdi" (p. 39). But it was also easy for the words, and the emotion, to be overwhelmed by the musical virtuosity of either the composer or the singer; the *coloratura* aria, even though a solo, was open to some of the same charges as the madrigal. The fact that audiences in Vienna or Dresden were hearing operas in Italian doubtless contributed to the emphasis on vocal feats; in Paris, where the Italian Giovanni Battista Lulli became Jean-Baptiste Lully and composed his operas to French texts, a style dominated by the recitative held on. In the development of opera, despite its literary origins and dramatic possibilities, purely musical considerations were often central; in the *opera seria* of the eighteenth century, they became dominant.

In literature itself, the survival of rhyme provides a small-scale parallel. Giangiorgio Trissino (1478–1550), author of the ghastly epic *L'Italia liberata dai Gotti,* liberated his poem from the Gothic ornament of rhyme, writing blank hendecasyllabics which he defended as the equivalent of ancient hexameters.[66] But as we have seen in our survey of musical humanism, imitation of the ancients was more likely to succeed when it coincided with the modern desire for dramatic expression, and Trissino's poem, far from providing drama, degenerates into endless lists. In England, later in the century, the Elizabethan dramatists turned to blank verse as a way to achieve a more flexible, less stylized medium. The prologue to Marlowe's *Tamburlaine* (1558), a proud declaration of independence from rhyme, claims that the new form will contribute to dramatic illusion, that the audience will be more intimately involved, more imaginatively present in the scenes of the play than they would have been in a popular interlude cast in rhymed fourteeners:

> From jigging veins of rhyming mother wits,
> And such conceits as clownage keeps in pay,
> We'll lead you to the stately tent of war,
> Where you shall hear the Scythian Tamburlaine
> Threat'ning the world with high astounding terms
> And scourging kingdoms with his conquering sword.
> View but his picture in this tragic glass
> And then applaud his fortunes as you please.[67]

The play was immensely popular, and its importance in establishing blank verse as a staple medium cannot be overstated. But rhyme was not to be so easily killed. The half-rhyme ("glass-please") that closes Marlowe's prologue suggests an impulse toward cloture which becomes explicit later in the play. The king of Arabia expires with a conventional speech-ending rhyme, telling Zenocrate:

> Deprived of care, my heart with comfort dies,
> Since thy desired hand shall close mine eyes.
>   (V, ii, 368–69)

And Tamburlaine takes possession of his bride and ends the play in the same fashion:

---

66. For a translation of Trissino's theoretical arguments against rhyme, in Division V of his *Poetica*, see Allan H. Gilbert, *Literary Criticism: Plato to Dryden*, pp. 214-15.

67. This and subsequent citations of Marlowe's plays follow the text of *The Complete Plays of Christopher Marlowe*, ed. Irving Ribner.

> Then, after all these solemn exequies,
> We will our rites of marriage solemnise. (V, ii, 470–71)

Even in Marlowe's later plays, where the blank verse becomes more supple, less heavily end-stopped, rhyme still appears as a way to close scenes and speeches.[68] Like the recitative, blank verse was a simpler, freer form than those that preceded it, and it clearly contributed to dramatic immediacy; but just as the early opera composers discovered that they had to break up the recitative by interpolating choral songs, with their richer harmony and more regular rhythm, Marlowe and Shakespeare discovered the effectiveness of breaking up the blank verse by interpolating occasional passages in rhyme. The final, tortured, blank-verse soliloquy of Marlowe's Faustus, for example, gains effectiveness because it is preceded by a stylized, rhyming duet between Faustus and his Bad Angel.[69] As Monteverdi brought to the composition of opera techniques developed in the composition of madrigals, Marlowe and Shakespeare brought to the writing of plays techniques developed in the writing of lyric poetry.

Neither Marlowe nor Shakespeare made any dogmatic disavowal of rhyme of a theoretical kind, but Thomas Campion, who had been a writer of lovely rhymed lyrics and a distinguished composer, mounted a full-scale attack in his *Observations in the Art of English Poesie* (1602). The passion of its polemic will remind us of Bardi or Galilei:

> There is growne a kind of prescription in the vse of Rime, to forestall the right of true numbers [i.e., quantitative verse], as also the consent of many nations, against all which it may seeme a thing almost impossible, and vaine to contend. All this and more can not yet deterre me from a lawful defence of perfection, or make me any whit the sooner adheare to that which is lame and vnbeseeming. . . . Old customes, if they are better, why should they not be recald, as the yet flourishing custome of numerous poetry vsed among the *Romanes* and *Grecians:* But the vnaptness of our toongs, and the difficultie of imitation dishartens vs; againe the facilitie &

68. See Tucker Brooke, "Marlowe's Versification and Style," *Studies in Philology* 19 (1922): 186-205.

69. See *Doctor Faustus*, V, ii, 120 ff.

popularitie of Rime creates as many Poets, as a hot sommer flies. (pp. 3–4)

To prove his point by demonstration, Campion includes exemplary exercises in various classical meters. Here is "a short Poeme in *Licentiate Iambicks,* which may giue more light to them that shall hereafter imitate these numbers."

> Goe numbers boldly passe, stay not for ayde
> Of shifting rime, that easie flatterer
> Whose witchcraft can the ruder eares beguile;
> Let your smooth feet enur'd to purer arte
> True measures tread; what if your pace be slow? (p. 12)

Even in this awkward and self-conscious effort, which is surely closer to blank verse than to any genuine classical model, Campion's own impulse to rhyme is not well concealed. The internal chimings ("stay—ayde, shifting—witchcraft, ruder—your—smooth—enur'd—purer") betray the poet as a rhymer fighting his impulses as if he had suddenly decided they were sinful. We have already seen analogues to this phenomenon among the musical humanists: the way such proscribed techniques as word-painting, musically independent rhythm, and contrapuntal motion of parts crept into pieces written by composers who had attacked them in theory. Successful recitative was enriched by versions of these techniques, just as successful blank verse, from Marlowe to Shakespeare to Milton, was enriched by the experience its poets had had with rhyme, and by their consequent ability to employ the repetitive patterns of consonants and vowels, alliteration and assonance, which make their blank verse something far grander than "measured prose."

Indeed, in the case of Milton, it is possible to argue that the shift in musical style had a more explicit influence. Milton's father was a composer of polyphonic madrigals, and such madrigal composers as Marenzio and Gesualdo are among those whose works the poet purchased in Italy. But he also purchased books of Monteverdi's music, and he may well have seen one of Monteverdi's operas while abroad.[70] His poems reflect intimate knowledge of

70. For detailed information, see Mortimer H. Frank, "Milton's Knowledge of Music: Some Speculations," in *Milton and the Art of Sacred Song,* ed. Patrick and Sundell, pp. 83-98.

various kinds of musical ideas: "At a Solemn Music," celebrating
the "mixt power" of the "Sphere-born harmonious Sisters, Voice
and Verse," makes use of Pythagorean lore, specifically the myth
of musical creation; the sonnet "To My Friend, Mr. Henry Lawes,
on his Airs," falls more within the humanist orbit, praising Lawes
for his rhythmic accuracy in setting English verse. The scholarly
debate about whether the "Monody" *Lycidas* is more like a recitative or a madrigal actually reflects the success of that work in
achieving both dramatic immediacy and intricate construction.[71]
Again, rhyming is the clearest illustration; Milton came to treat it
much as Monteverdi had treated counterpoint: he mastered it
early, then bent its rules (with short lines, slant rhymes, and the
like), and finally, in *Paradise Lost,* apparently abandoned it.[72] But
in both cases, the artist absorbed into the new technique the essential strengths of the old: Monteverdi's recitatives dwarf those of
Peri and Caccini because the harmonic sophistication he had developed in writing madrigals allows him to achieve a more dramatic melodic line; Milton's blank verse draws strength from the
flexible English dramatic tradition in that medium, but also prof-
its from his training in rhymed lyric. The dismissal of rhyme in
the headnote to *Paradise Lost* as "trivial and of no true musical
delight" ought not to make us insensitive to the way the musical
delights of that poem, defined there as "apt Numbers, fit quantity
of Syllables, and the sense variously drawn out from one Verse to
another" constitute an embracing of the binding effects of rhyme
without its cadential jingle.

One example will have to suffice, the conclusion of the description of Eden:

> The Birds thir choir apply; airs, vernal airs,
> Breathing the smell of field and grove, attune
> The trembling leaves, while Universal *Pan*
> Knit with the *Graces* and the *Hours* in dance

---

71. See Gretchen L. Finney, "A Musical Background for 'Lycidas,'" *Huntington Library
Quarterly* 15 (1952): 325-50, and Ants Oras, "Milton's Early Rhyme Schemes and the Structure of *Lycidas,*" *Modern Philology* 52 (1954): 14-22.

72. For more useful information, and a more extreme position than that taken here,
see J. Max Patrick, "Milton's Revolution against Rime, and Some of Its Implications," in
Milton and the Art of Sacred Song, pp. 99-117. Patrick believes that the successes in Milton's
early verse "were achieved despite, not because of, the rhyme" (p. 108).

> Led on th' Eternal Spring. Not that fair field
> Of *Enna,* where *Proserpin* gath'ring flow'rs
> Herself a fairer Flow'r by gloomy *Dis*
> Was gather'd, which cost *Ceres* all that pain
> To seek her through the world; nor that sweet Grove
> Of *Daphne* by *Orontes,* and th' inspir'd
> *Castalian* Spring might with this Paradise
> Of *Eden* strive. (IV, 254–75)

The pervasive assonance of murmuring *er* sounds (B*ir*ds—v*er*-nal—Univ*er*sal—Et*er*nal—Pros*er*pin—H*er*self—fair*er*—gath*er'*d—h*er*—w*or*ld) comes very close to rhyme in the parallel placement of "vernal" and "Universal."[73] At the ends of lines, "attune," "*Pan,*" "dance," and "pain" match some of their sounds, as do "airs" and"flow'rs," both of which are internally repeated, as are variants of "fair" and "gather." And the shuffling of *r, s,* and long *i* sounds in "inspir'd," "Paradise," and"strive" gives the end of the passage its cadential force. The frequent enjambment, here as elsewhere, suggests those many recitatives in which dissonant tension is achieved by having the voice appear to run ahead of its harmony; a phrase like "attune The trembling leaves," which could have served as a short line in *Lycidas,* is here stretched across a line-break, so as to participate simultaneously in several rhythmic patterns.

The constructive patterns of this passage have been absorbed into its flexible and lyrical movement, but *Paradise Lost* also contains passages where construction is more overt and mechanical, such as Eve's *carmen perpetuum* (IV, 641–56), which has the shape of concentric circles, its first nine lines repeated in condensed form in the next seven lines, its first and last words identical. Constructive techniques, despite the arguments of the Galileis and the Campions, despite the disclaimers of Milton, proved difficult to purge. Not only did they creep covertly into the works of the very men who had attacked them in theory, but they flourished openly in instrumental music and lyric poetry. Keyboard toccatas and fantasias, "for the virginals" in England, for various sorts of organ in Germany, drew heavily on the canonic polyphony and propor-

---

73. This pattern begins earlier; lines 259-63 have "p*ur*ple—Lux*ur*iant—m*ur*m*ur*ing—disp*er*st—m*yr*tle—m*irr*or."

tional rhythm of the early Renaissance masters. Virtuoso pieces
for the lute, whether improvised or notated, usually involved diminution and other mathematical forms of rhythmic variation. The
favored forms of lyric poetry, despite the attempts to introduce
quantitative verse and eliminate rhyme, remained the rhyming
stanzas inherited from the troubadours and perfected by the Pe-
trarchans: sonnets, villanelles, even sestinas. Whether overtly displayed or secretly tested, artistic skill was a central issue: poets
and composers who set themselves difficult technical tasks were
trying and confirming their professional abilities. Two extreme
examples, both English, both dating from the end of the sixteenth
century, are the *Epithalamion* of Edmund Spenser and the fantasia, *Ut, re, mi, fa, sol, la* of John Bull.

There is a good deal of musical imagery in the *Epithalamion*.
In the opening stanza, the poet praises his muses for their ability
to sing songs of praise, or when appropriate, to turn their strings
"to sadder tenor." Asking their aid, he compares himself to Orpheus. Later in the poem, we hear the "merry Musick" of some
peasant minstrels playing "the pipe, the tabor, and the trembling
Croud." In the church, we hear "roring Organs," "Choristers"
with "hollow throates," and an alleluia sung by angels. But the
most revealing musical passage is the morning song of the birds,
with its curiously medieval terminology:

> Hark how the cheerefull birds do chaunt theyr laies
> And carroll of loues praise.
> The merry Larke hir mattins sings aloft,
> The thrush replyes, the Mauis descant playes,
> The Ouzell shrills, the Ruddock warbles soft,
> So goodly all agree with sweet consent,
> To this dayes merriment.
> Ah my deere loue why doe ye sleepe thus long,
> When meeter were that ye should now awake,
> T'awayt the comming of your ioyous make,
> And hearken to the birds louelearned song,
> The deawy leaues among.
> For they of ioy and pleasance to you sing,
> That all the woods them answer and theyr eccho ring.[74]

---

74. *Epithalamion*, 78-91, following the text given in *Spenser: Poetical Works*, ed. J. C.
Smith and E. de Selincourt.

The music described here is contrapuntal: each bird's independent part contributes to a harmonious polyphony, a "louelearned
song," and Spenser may well have meant that last phrase to serve
also as a description of his poem, which expresses love for Elizabeth Boyle by means of a technique so learned, so rigorous, and
so covert that it remained undiscovered for over three centuries.
As we have known since the publication of A. Kent Hieatt's remarkable findings in 1960, the *Epithalamion* contains 24 stanzas
(the number of hours in a day), 365 long lines (the number of
days in a year), and 68 short lines (a number which may represent
a total of the seasons, months, and weeks [4 + 12 + 52 = 68]).[75]
The precedents for this kind of recondite virtuosity will be clear
to readers of this book: the learned, mathematical, isorhythmic
procedures of the Middle Ages, against which the Renaissance
humanists had waged their polemical war. To be sure, England
was artistically conservative, and Spenser, as his archaisms suggest, was conservative even for England, but the survival of these
medieval techniques, and the values they represent, in a poem
published in 1595 is striking. At a moment in history when aural
and expressive devices were attracting theoretical attention and
determining musical and poetic fashion, at a moment in his life
when he had a great personal joy to celebrate, in the act of writing
a poem whose lyric and expressive beauty would win praise in
centuries unaware of its secret, Spenser still saw value in adhering
to the mystical, hierarchial, and technical values we have noticed
in Augustine, Dante, Vitry, and Machaut. He must have believed,
like those men and like R. P. Blackmur, that"patterns of number,
in poetry and music, [are] reminders of the skills of thought
which have nothing to do with the language of words."[76] Considered as a whole, the rhetorical Renaissance was less interested in
those skills than earlier periods; the musical humanists, in their
attempt to make music more like the language of words, represent an extreme case of that bias. They ultimately failed, and
Spenser succeeded, because those abstract, constructive "skills of
thought" are as important for the making of poetic and musical
art as the expressive and persuasive skills which so fascinated the
humanists. Even Milton, in his sonnet "On the Late Massacre in

75. See *Short Time's Endless Monument.*
76. *Language as Gesture,* p. 367.

Piedmont," made "hundredfold" the hundredth word.[77]

Another stubborn Englishman, John Bull, provides a musical example of the survival of those same skills. His fantasia *Ut, re, mi, fa, sol, la* takes as its *cantus firmus* the hexachord spelled out by those pitches:[78]

After stating this theme beginning on G, harmonizing it in rigorous, four-part modal counterpoint, Bull repeats it, beginning on A and then on B. To write out the fourth repetition beginning on C-sharp would require an E-sharp, so Bull alters the notation by means of an enharmonic equivalence (C-sharp/D-flat), and writes that hexachord in flats, with a hair-raising harmonic effect; I quote the conclusion of the third repetition and the beginning of the fourth (the theme in the alto voice):

The repetitions continue to move up by whole steps (the fifth is on E-flat, the sixth on F), but rather than end the piece by returning to G, Bull contrives to begin the seventh repetition on A-flat, by means of another startling modulation, then continues by whole steps until he reaches the twelfth repetition, on F-sharp, which finally leads to the thirteenth, on G. The remainder of the piece, four more repetitions of the *cantus firmus*, remains in G, but each of the repetitions displays rhythmic variation. The fifteenth variation is fully isorhythmic; p. 189 shows its beginning.

This passage could have come directly out of Vitry, and Bull's piece is archaic in some respects, but its modulation through all

77. See Patrick, "Milton's Revolution against Rime," p. 111.
78. All citations of this piece follow the version given in *Musica Britannica*, vol. XIV, ed. John Steele and Francis Cameron, pp. 53-55.

twelve keys looks ahead to the *Well-Tempered Clavier,* not back to
the Middle Ages. If Spenser's virtuosity was so recondite as to remain unknown for centuries, Bull's was so advanced as to remain
unplayable. Keyboard players in Bull's time used "mean-tone"
temperament to tune their instruments; triads in the "normal"
keys were well in tune, but the distant areas reached in Bull's un-
compromising scheme would have sounded extremely dissonant.
Equal temperament, the modern compromise which permits
chromatic modulation, did not come into use until the eighteenth
century. In extending a constructive and mathematical rigor directly descended from medieval practices, Bull wrote a piece
whose realization had to await the tuning practices of the time of
Bach.[79] Development in the arts, despite Romantic theories, is not
inevitably the result of restless self-expression breaking through
the restraints of rules; it can also be achieved by intellectual extension of the consequences of the rules themselves.

There were even theorists of music and poetry who broke
new ground by thinking in constructive terms. Joachim Burmeister published in 1606 a treatise entitled *Musica Poetica,* in which
he attempted to apply rhetorical terms to compositional procedures. It is no accident that most of Burmeister's examples come
from Orlando di Lasso, Giaches de Wert, and other Northern polyphonists; their motets, whose construction I have already described as rhetorical, did employ techniques of ordering and
repetition which were legitimately analogous to figures of rhetoric. One example must suffice. Anaphora, in poetry, is defined by
Puttenham as occuring "when we make one word begin, and as
they are wont to say, lead the daunce to many verses in sute, as
thus.

---

79. Even Gustav Leonhardt, on a Telefunken recording of English virginal music
otherwise employing mean-tone temperament, uses equal temperament for this piece.

> To thinke on death it is a miserie,
> To thinke on life it is a vanitie:
> To thinke on the world verily it is,
> To thinke that heare man hath no perfit blisse." (III, ix; p. 208)

Burmeister's definition is as follows:

> Anaphora is that ornament, which repeats similar sounds in various other voices of the harmony, though not all, in the manner of a fugue, but which is not actually a fugue.[80]

For an example, he directs our attention to a motet by Lasso, "*Surrexit pastor bonus*," in which he discovers anaphora in this passage:[81]

The bass line, to which Burmeister specifically refers, begins the phrase with three identical pitches, as do the tenor part and the first soprano. Thereafter, the three parts with similar beginnings proceed differently; there is no strict canon and certainly not a

---

80. *Musica Poetica*, p. 65. On Burmeister's life and work, see Martin Ruhnke, *Joachim Burmeister*. On the larger connections between rhetoric and music, see Wilibald Gurlitt, "Musik und Rhetorik—Hinweise auf ihre geschichtliche Grundlageneinheit," *Helicon* 5 (1944): 67-86, and Hans-Heinrich Unger, *Die Beziehungen zwischen Musik und Rhetorik im 16.-18. Jahrhundert.*

81. I follow the version given in Lasso's *Sämtliche Werke*, v, iii, p. 57, changing the clefs of the lower three parts.

fugue. To call this anaphora is not to make a very challenging discovery, and some of Burmeister's definitions are even less interesting. What is important for our purposes is that Burmeister's analogies treat repetition, in music and poetry, as a matter of abstract design. In a discussion of these matters which mentions Burmeister, John Hollander argues that "the strained attempt in the seventeenth century to equate musical devices with rhetorical patterns seem[s] to be based upon a desire to identify the persuasive powers of the first and the second,"[82] and that desire was doubtless a strong one, given the emphasis on persuasion everywhere in the culture and the particular challenge represented by musical humanism. Burmeister's opening pages talk about using music to make arguments, to move the affections, and to influence the heart. But when we reach the examples, this desire, however earnest, finds no expression. Instead, Burmeister patiently equates each rhetorical figure with its musical equivalent as if both were geometric designs.

Nor was such attention to design exclusively the province of pedantic German theorists. A recurring topic in Shakespeare criticism, and properly so, has been the extraordinary balancing of short scenes and long scenes, soliloquies and dialogues, poetry and prose in his mature plays. Not only are the lengths, shapes, and styles of the various components of each play carefully tailored for dramatic effect, but a larger view will often reveal structures whose abstract design is pleasing. In Monteverdi's masterpiece, the *Incoronazione di Poppea* (1642), Leo Schrade perceives a similar attention to symmetry:

> The monologues of Ottone and Ottavia, which are not only very long but also of the greatest dramatic intensity, are almost always divided into well-defined parts, so that the recitative never serves a purely narrative purpose but is always reserved for dramatic passages. The first monologue of Ottone illustrates this technique. Seven strophic entities are to be distinguished within the musical form. Twice the aria, and twice the recitative organize the whole complex, in perfect proportions. (p. 361)

82. *The Untuning of the Sky*, pp. 198-99.

And we have already seen how smaller details in the work of both these artists involve display of technique as an end in itself.

As any performer knows, establishing one's skill requires doing something which others can recognize as technically difficult. To be sure, a musician can show us important qualities when he plays a slow movement: beautiful tone, eloquent phrasing, expressive *rubato*. But few musicians would stake their chances in an important competition on such a movement; dazzling technique proves something. The survival in the Renaissance of the musical and poetic techniques I have been calling constructive was, in part, a result of the continuing need of poets and composers to demonstrate their skills, to prove they were masters by producing masterpieces. But that perfectly legitimate motive is not the only reason for the survival of tricky rhyme schemes and rigorous counterpoint. It cannot account for the secret sacrifices made at the altar of technique by Spenser and Bull, who must have believed in technique as a profound and enthralling mystery, a high calling in itself. The poets and composers of the Middle Ages had not hesitated to call that mystery holy, but some of their Renaissance successors, inspired by the ancient stories of persuasive rhetoric and moving music, sought to make all technique serve the end of human communication, to make every element of every poem or piece enforce a meaning, arouse an emotion, influence an action. As a theory, this reform program arose quite naturally from the spirit in which the Renaissance read and interpreted ancient literature. But in practice, it could not be dogmatically enforced, especially in music, where formal techniques ultimately descended from medieval mathematical speculation had evolved into a supple and coherent, if not unequivocal language. Renaissance thinkers perceived and extended the ways in which this language was analogous to the language of words: the madrigal style develops those analogies along a rhetorical axis, while the recitative style develops them along a dramatic or emotional axis. But there are, to quote Blackmur once more, "skills of thought which have nothing to do with the language of words," and those skills are evident not only in the constructive analogies between rhetoric and counterpoint listed by Burmeister, not only in the secret sacrifices of Spenser and Bull, but in the works of such giants as Shakespeare and Monteverdi, both of whom recognized that attention to dramatic effect need not preclude attention to proportion, symmetry, and design.

5

Imitations

Introduction

"Music is just as much an imitation or representation as poetry, tragedy, or painting, as I have said elsewhere, because it makes with sounds, or with the articulate voice, what the poet makes with verse, the actor with gestures, and the painter with light, shadow, and colors."[1] So wrote the wide-ranging Jesuit investigator Marin Mersenne in his *Harmonie Universelle* (1636), an immense encyclopedic treatise which sums up a great deal of Renaissance thought about music, and which (as Dean Mace has shown) strikingly anticipates many eighteenth-century attitudes and controversies.[2] Although Mersenne was familiar with and dependent upon the work of the musical humanists,[3] he did not ultimately endorse their attempt to subjugate music to poetry; on the contrary, the cumulative effect of his inclusive and inconsistent work is to make larger claims for music as an independent art than were dreamed of in earlier Renaissance thought. The sentence I have quoted may serve as a small example: it suggests the central issues of this chapter.

Imitation, the crucial word in Mersenne's sentence and the basis on which he compares music not only to poetry but to painting and acting, acquired so many conflicting meanings in the two

1. Marin Mersenne, *Harmonie Universelle,* Vol. II, p. 93.
2. Dean T. Mace, "Marin Mersenne on Language and Music," *Yale Journal of Music Theory* 14 (1970): 2-31. Like Mace's splendid article on Dryden, this essay should be required reading for anyone trying to sort through the maze of opinion about music and literature in the seventeenth century. Citations of Mace in this chapter refer to the article on Mersenne.
3. D. P. Walker includes Mersenne among the musical humanists; see, for example, the passage quoted above, p. 165.

centuries following his work that it cannot be considered a unified concept at all. For writers, imitation initially meant modeling one's work on the classics, a familiar Renaissance practice which took a particularly rigorous form in seventeenth-century France, where the emphasis was on rules supposedly derived from the ancients. Such rules also had considerable force in eighteenth-century England, but were qualified there by a Longinian emphasis on "natural genius," one argument for which was a misleading analogy to music, which was supposed to have *"nameless Graces* which no Methods teach." But among composers, whose actual ancient models were too fragmentary and primitive to serve the function served by the analogous ancient literary materials, there was intense interest in rules and methods: the *stile antico* of church music, derived in part from the practice of Palestrina and codified most importantly in Fux's influential textbook *Gradus ad Parnassum* (1725), became, despite its increasing distance from the *stile moderno,* a fundamental training ground for composers, as it still is today. Among the techniques taught in this rigorous modal school of composition was a method of part-writing that Fux called imitation, the general principle behind the various canonic devices which reached their apogee in the fugal compositions of J. S. Bach, where they were used to manipulate melodic material with strong tonal implications. The combination of the linear, imitative techniques preserved from the Renaissance by Fux with the tonal harmonic thinking of which Rameau was the most passionate advocate made it possible for Bach and other late baroque composers to pack an unprecedented amount of musical content into their instrumental compositions: even a single line could now carry a surprisingly large quantity of musical information. Fux's musical imitation, an abstract principle of melodic construction, thus gained new force because the harmonic grammar of dominant progressions gave melodic lines more clearly defined goals. Far from being a basis for comparing music and literature, this kind of imitation actually drove them apart by giving pure music a rich, complex meaning of its own.

But in music with texts, baroque composers added to the musical kinds of meaning obtainable from polyphonic imitation and tonal harmony other kinds of meaning resulting from a different kind of imitation: the "word-painting" techniques they had inherited from the Renaissance. Using their more limited resources in this area, poets also pursued punning versions of such techniques. Musical examples, usually attempts to find equivalents for words dealing with motion, abound in the vocal compositions of Bach and Handel; poetic examples, also usually based on motion, include the familiar lines demonstrating how sound should echo sense in Pope's *Essay on Criticism*. But in both arts, this kind of imitation tended to be a local effect: in music, a particularly clever imitation of the meaning of some word or phrase was likely to work against the integrity of the whole piece by drawing undue attention to itself or by interrupting some larger musical shape; in poetry, lines in which the writer had achieved some lucky matching of sound and sense also tended to detach themselves from the poem as a whole. Composers, because of the plasticity of their materials, were sometimes able to solve this problem by using musical ideas generated from attempts to imitate words as basic structural elements, not merely as local effects. For obvious reasons, poets found it much more difficult to employ this kind of imitation as a large structural principle, though Dryden's "Song for St. Cecilia's Day, 1687" is a remarkably successful attempt. Like many works of Bach in which locally imitative ideas become principles of construction, Dryden's poem makes extensive use of numerical patterns of ordering which we may recognize as descendants of the recondite techniques of medieval music and poetry. Ironically, then, local matchings of sound and sense in both arts, charming to the ear and dangerous to the larger structure because of their immediate perceptibility, tend to become abstract and imperceptible when employed as principles of structure. Music, more abstract by nature, suffered less than poetry from this impasse.

Interest in the art of painting led some literary theorists to stress a more direct kind of imitation: the representation of external objects, the holding of a mirror up to Nature. The influence of this definition of imitation is evident in the frequent use of the Horatian tag *ut pictura poesis* and in the "visually centered sensationalist aesthetic"[4] promulgated in Addison's famous series of *Spectator* essays on the "Pleasures of the Imagination." But those

---

4. Wimsatt, *Literary Criticism, A Short History,* p. 263.

essays, like Dryden's earlier poem to the painter Kneller, qualify the visual norms they apparently embrace, arguing that painters and poets must select and beautify the objects they imitate. Addison also suggests that objects touched by and therefore arousing emotion are especially beautiful; this was the form necessarily taken by such imitation in music, where the difficulties of imitating Nature, except for birdcalls and other trivial details, were obvious. Composers claimed to hold their mirrors up to *human* nature, drawing upon the rhetorical tradition of the Renaissance to create a system of composition called the *Affektenlehre*, according to which "mental states, that is, the feelings or 'affections' of man, [could] be represented in music by certain tonalities and meters as well as by distinct melodic, rhythmic, and harmonic turns and figures."[5] Such eighteenth-century treatises on musical composition as Mattheson's *Vollkommene Capellmeister* (1739) offer detailed instructions.

But Mattheson, for all his methodical Fuxian rule-giving, for all his orderly Cartesian classification of the emotions, recognizes the importance of natural genius in the invention of melodies, and acknowledges the *disorderly* power of emotions as a source on which composers may draw. He even recommends at one point that composers "sink themselves" into various passions, taking on emotional roles in order to invent melodic expressions for them. Mersenne's emphasis on the gestures of the actor in the quotation with which we began suggests one source of this almost Stanislavskian recommendation: the theatre itself, where the stylized and rhetorical acting of the Renaissance was being somewhat modified in the direction of psychological realism, as Steele's essays on Betterton suggest. There was even a parallel motion in poetry: Alexander Pope, while drawing on the rhetorical conventions of various poetic genres at least as heavily as baroque composers drew on the rhetorical conventions of the *Affektenlehre*, also admitted drawing on his own emotional experiences, sinking himself into various poetic roles in much the way advocated by Mattheson for composers. In these developments, we may see the Renaissance notion that music and poetry should arouse the passions of their

5. Paul Henry Lang, "The Enlightenment and Music," *Eighteenth-Century Studies* 1 (1967): 96.

hearers (by essentially rhetorical means) blurring into the related but significantly different notion that they should express the passions of role-playing poets and composers.

As a result of many factors, not least the slow displacement of a Cartesian model of the mind by a Lockean and associative one, the gestural, nuanced, actorish expression of emotion advocated by Mattheson and practiced by Pope as a minor modification of an essentially imitative and rhetorical aesthetic gained such strength that literary and philosophical voices (though not, for a long time, musical ones) began to make a more radical claim: that poetry and music should express the *actual* emotions of their makers. In this fundamental and wrenching change, which took place gradually over at least two centuries, various kinds of speculation about the relations between music and poetry played a central role. Comparisons between the arts, which had previously been made on formal or technical grounds, or on the basis of their capacity to communicate with precision or rhetorical force, were now made on the more shifting and metaphorical criterion of their capacity to express feelings. Mersenne, as Mace argues, was an early and uncertain anticipator of this movement:

> Mersenne began by thinking that all art must be founded on reason; he ended by believing—at least at intervals—that it should be founded on feelings, on the passions. He began by examining—with all desire to approve—the reigning Renaissance opinion that the word, as the image of reason, is the most perfect interpreter of human experience, and he ended by allowing music this honor, and for reasons which were not unlike those brought forward later by the eighteenth century. He allows us to see the curious inner history of the movement which gave prestige to music at the expense of poetry.
> (pp. 4–5)

This change in prestige occurred without an alteration in the definition of music: Renaissance thinkers had considered music inferior to poetry because its meaning was vague; later thinkers preferred music for that very vagueness. Thus the Abbé du Bos, writing some eighty-three years after Mersenne, "found that musical sound was no less than the voice of nature itself, whereas articulate language consisted of mere arbitrary and artificial symbols."[6] A century after du Bos, Schopenhauer would define a composer as one who "expresses the deepest wisdom in a language which his reason does not understand; as a person under the influence of mesmerism tells things of which he has no conception when he awakes."[7]

This Romantic definition of musical creation as a process independent of intellection comes, we should hasten to note, from a philosopher, not from a composer, and the philosophical drift toward an aesthetic of feeling, of which this statement represents an endpoint, was not the only reason for the growing respect with which music and musicians were treated. As I have already indicated, the happy confluence of polyphonic imitation and harmonic grammar gave late baroque music a richness of design, logic, and coherence of a purely musical kind; other leading developments in the years 1650–1750 had the same effect. Large-scale forms, for example the trio sonata and the concerto, took their shape from purely musical principles, and the opera itself saw the increased use of forms whose shape was musical, not poetic, especially the *da capo* aria. Technical advances, most importantly the discovery and adoption of equal temperament for keyboard instruments, which enabled composers to build larger, more complex pieces by modulating to more distant keys, helped incorporate into the syntax of music chromatic alterations which had been merely expressive or colorful in the Renaissance. Such successes surely had less to do with the incipient triumph of an aesthetic of feeling than with the ongoing importance of the concept of virtuosity, about which Hugo Leichtentritt has written:

> The seventeenth and eighteenth centuries make virtuosity a legitimate and indispensable element of artistic writing and cultivate it with great zeal and enthusiasm, not only in singing but also in purely instrumental music. There were, of course,

6. Mace, p. 2, paraphrasing du Bos, *Reflexions critiques sur la poésie et sur la peinture,* Vol. I, ch. xlvi *("De la Musique proprement dite"):* "Tout ces sons, comme nous l'avons déjà exposé, ont une force merveilleuse pour nous émouvoir; parce qu'ils sont les signes des passions institués par la nature dont ils ont reçu leur énergie, au lieu que les mots articulés ne sont que des signes arbitraires des passions." I give the text of the "Nouvelle Edition revuë and corrigée" (Utrecht, 1732), p. 364. The first edition was in 1719.

7. *The World as Will and Idea,* Book III, para. 52; in the translation of R. B. Haldane and J. Kemp, vol. I, p. 336. The original German publication was in 1818.

many degrees of virtuosity, from empty display to a highly accomplished mastery of structural complexities. We must never forget that the greater part of Bach's work is virtuoso music of the purest and highest type, demanding for its writing an extraordinary technical skill in polyphony, harmony, and construction, and for its rendering an equally remarkable skill in singing, conducting, and playing.[8]

The exercise of this kind of skill, not some mesmerized automatic communication of emotion, was the real reason why music gained prestige at the expense of poetry in these years. In opera, the most obvious field for collaboration, there was a clear shift in the relative power of composers and poets: Monteverdi had presumably been taking a politically calculated position when he declared that the text should be the master of the music, but Mozart, 175 years later, was secure enough in his power to claim openly that the poetry in an opera should be the obedient daughter of the music.[9]

But in conservative England, whose greatest native composer, Henry Purcell, died in 1695, the response of literary men to the growing power of music was to attack music along essentially Renaissance lines, to stress its "foreign," "effeminate," "empty" inferiority to poetry, and to praise it only for successes which could still be called imitative. Dryden grumbled about having to "cramp" his verses for the music of Purcell and Grabu, and by the time Handel began composing oratorios, collaborating with a composer had become a "Degradation, to which Men of Genius would not easily submit," so that "he was forced to apply to Versifiers instead of Poets."[10] Addison and Pope, both of whom wrote St. Cecilia odes, also both criticized the absurdities of the Italian opera, recogniz-

8. *Music, History, and Ideas*, pp. 123-24.

9. Lang links these two quotations in "The Enlightenment and Music," p. 107. Monteverdi's remark ("Orazione sia padrone della musica") appears in the preface to the fifth book of madrigals (1605); Mozart's ("bey einer opera muss schlechterdings die Poesie der Musick gehorsame Tochter seyn") occurs in a letter to his father dated 13 October 1781. Of course, Mozart proved fortunate in his librettists: Lorenzo da Ponte had a deserved literary reputation, and if Emanuel Schikaneder (the original Papageno) was no poet, he was a consummate man of the theatre.

10. John Brown, *A Dissertation on the Rise, Union, and Power, the Progressions, Separations, and Corruptions of Poetry and Music*, p. 208.

ing that its shape was more and more dictated by purely musical considerations, despite its origins in the literary atmosphere of the Florentine *Camerata*. Swift wrote a marvelous burlesque cantata whose fundamental message was that words written for music would inevitably degenerate into nonsense. And Samuel Johnson, when the great music historian Charles Burney mentioned a concert by Johann Christian Bach, responded with a compact and irascible version of the same prejudice: "And pray, sir, who is Bach? Is he a piper?"[11] Like all prejudices, this English distrust of music, especially instrumental music, was grounded in ignorance; unlike their Renaissance forbears, these literary opponents of music lacked first-hand experience with musical technique. In the poem from which this book takes its title, Addison refers to the "unsuspected eloquence" of music, by which he means its supposed power over the passions, its capacity to "manage all the man with secret art."[12] But what had really happened was that music had gained, through technical, logical, and formal means, an eloquence which Addison himself did not understand.

The authors of the numerous treatises on music and poetry published in England in the second half of the eighteenth century—John Brown (1763), Daniel Webb (1769), Anselm Bayly (1789), and many others—were not always as ignorant of music as the poets, but they shared similar views. On the continent, word-painting, the *Affektenlehre,* and the whole view of music as an imitative art were growing less important as composers devoted more and more of their output to instrumental music, but these English writers clung to imitative theories, expressing deep distrust of instrumental music and proposing various schemes for the reunion of music and poetry. Despite such conservative declarations, these treatises, in their fascination with the emotive power of music, point the way toward the developing Romantic attitude: when they praise music, they tend to speak approvingly of its "primitive sentiment." Webb's hedging formula, "music acts in the double character of an art of impression as well as of imitation,"[13] betrays

---

11. See Boswell's *Life of Johnson*, ed. G. B. Hill, rev. L. F. Powell, vol. II, p. 364*n* .

12. "A Song for St. Cecilia's Day, 1694, at Oxford," line 31; in Addison's *Miscellaneous Works*, ed. A. C. Guthkelch, p. 22.

13. *Observations on the Correspondence between Poetry and Music*, p. 28.

the weakening of the notion of imitation, even in the works of its self-appointed preservers.

It was a short step from "impression" and "sentiment" to "expression," and by the last decade of the eighteenth century, explicitly Romantic voices in Germany and England were enthusiastically applauding the supposed capacity of music to express the emotions of its makers and proposing to make poetry more like it, more sensuous, more affective, more "organic" in its form. There are some marvelous ironies in this development. First, the philosophers and poets who now embraced music as a model were at least as ignorant of the actual sources of musical eloquence as the English Augustan poets, whose ignorance had emerged as hostility. They imagined, for example, that music proceeded by a loose, associative logic, and consequently sought in their own poems a more fluid syntax, avoiding the grammatical precision of "strong sense"; on the formal side, they had similar objections to the constraining symmetries of the closed couplet. All this in the name of "musical poetry." But as Charles Rosen has shown, the actual music of this period was becoming *more* rigorous in its harmonic syntax, thanks to "a new emphatic polarity between tonic and dominant," *more* balanced in its rhythmic organization, thanks to "a heightened, indeed overwhelming, sensitivity to symmetry."[14] So the advocates of musical poetry were proposing that poetry imitate their myths about music, not the developments actually taking place in the work of Haydn and Mozart. And while the Romantics obviously differed from the Augustans, their similar ignorance of musical realities led both groups to employ similar language about music. If Pope imagined that the Italian opera was an effeminate "harlot," Goethe was eager to embrace music as the embodiment of the *"ewig-Weibliche,"* the "eternal feminine" which, as Michael Cooke has shown, became a locus of value in Romantic thought.[15] However successful its literary results, the Romantic striving after the formless, the associative, and the "feminine" was not in any strict sense an imitation of music—cer-

14. *The Classical Style,* pp. 26, 58. All references to Rosen in this chapter refer to this book.

15. See especially chapter 3, "The Feminine as the Crux of Values," in Cooke's *Acts of Inclusion.*

tainly not an imitation of the music being written by the Viennese classical composers, who regarded their art as formal, grammatical, and manly.

But composers soon learned that they were being valued for their emotions, not for their technique, and a reverse imitation took place: from 1825 on we hear composers speaking a more Romantic language, even claiming that their music expresses their own powerful emotions. The various arguments advanced to account for the greatness of Beethoven show the penetration of literary ideas into musical thought. Despite Beethoven's painstaking craftsmanship, he acquired the mythic character of a "tone-poet." The popular belief was that he had made the expression of poetic feelings a fundamental principle, thus overturning the rules of harmony and form; the mildly programmatic movement titles of his "Pastoral Symphony" provided precedents for the elaborate experiments of Berlioz and other composers of program music. As we can now see, the expressive and imitative devices of Beethoven's music actually operate within a rigorously logical system of construction and tonal harmony, but the next generation of composers, seeking to emulate their own literary and Romantic version of Beethoven, performed operations on musical syntax strikingly similar to those performed on literary syntax by the earlier Romantic poets. The tonally ambiguous "diminished seventh chord," for example, which provided a shortcut to distant keys, infected the harmonic language of Liszt and Chopin, ultimately helping to subvert the hierarchy of triads which had been fundamental to the tonal system. Wagner's Prelude to *Tristan und Isolde*, in which the dominant seventh, previously employed as the penultimate harmony of a cadence, becomes itself a goal or endpoint, represents such a loosening of tonal syntax that theorists still debate about whether the piece is in a key at all. But while these composers were undermining tonal syntax, a system whose deep resemblances to poetic syntax had not been grasped by poets, they were enthusiastically embracing the idea of program music, an overtly imitative system of composition which seeks musical equivalences for poetic plots or "programs." Berlioz and Liszt published such programs with many of their works; Wagner, through the device of the *leitmotif*, made programmatic representation a central part of the *Gesamtkunstwerk,* the union of music and poetry of which he dreamed. Imitation had not disappeared; if anything, it had widened its meaning.

Apprenticeship, "Natural Genius," and Music's "Nameless Graces"

That much by way of an aerial view. We may start a slower journey through this tangled material by remembering that imitation of the classics was already a central concept in the Renaissance, indeed, as we have seen, the principal means by which the early *literati* justified and authenticated their leaning toward an active, persuasive, kinetic rhetoric. As G. W. Pigman suggests, the meaning of the term was already complicated and various:

> Writers discuss imitation from so many different points of view: as a path to the sublime ("Longinus"), as a reinforcement of one's natural inclinations (Poliziano) or a substitute for undesirable inclinations (Cortesi), as a method for enriching one's writing with stylistic gems (Vida), as the surest or only way to learn Latin (Delminio), as providing the competitive stimulus necessary for achievement (Calcagnini), and as a means of "illustrating" a vulgar language (du Bellay).[16]

The most obvious and important thing these characteristic Renaissance definitions of imitation have in common is their implied view of the modern writer as a man who binds himself apprentice to the ancients in order to perfect his craft. There are, in this view, no short cuts to Parnassus; imitation is the only route, and it requires labor, as W. K. Wimsatt makes clear in discussing Ben Jonson, "the first English man of letters to exhibit a nearly complete and consistent neo-classicism":

> Jonson's stout and craftsmanly common sense about imitation, shown even more convincingly in his practice than in his precepts, may be taken as the key to a theory of poetry which stressed hard work—imitation, practice, study, art (and with these but one poor pennyworth of *ingenium.*) [17]

16. "Versions of Imitation in the Renaissance," *Renaissance Quarterly* 33 (1980): 2.
17. *Literary Criticism, A Short History,* p. 181.

Perhaps, as Wimsatt suggests, Jonson's poems show us more about this view of imitation than do his critical precepts. But the view of imitation as apprenticeship led inevitably to some emphasis on precepts: a good master would not instruct his apprentice exclusively by example; he would also lay down rules. Accordingly, the reputation of Aristotle, master rule-giver of antiquity, was enhanced by frequent translations of and commentaries upon the *Poetics*. In seventeenth-century France, literary theory and practice reflected a passion for rules; the rule of the three unities which Scaliger had fabricated from Aristotle's undogmatic observations became an absolute orthodoxy, so much so that both Corneille and Racine worried in print about their minute deviations from these norms. Lyric poetry reflected a similar fixation on "correctness," conformity to rules derived (more or less) from the ancients. Virgil and Horace were particularly useful as sources from which to derive rules, as Boileau's *Art Poétique* (1674) demonstrates, but not all ancient authors could be so easily accommodated to the interest in correctness and regularity: Boileau's other publication of 1674 was *Du Sublime*, a translation of Longinus, whose emphasis on subjective and irregular genius makes him, in Wimsatt's witty phrase, "the Trojan horse in the camp of neo-classicism" (p. 285).

In England, the Longinian notion of prodigious natural genius was frequently opposed to the Horatian and French emphasis on apprenticeship and rules. As early as 1622, Henry Peacham had made a surprisingly strong statement of this view:

> The Poet, as that Laurell *Maia* dreamed of, is made by miracle from his mothers wombe, and like the Diamond only polished and pointed of himselfe, disdaining the file and midwifery of forraine helpe. . . . And Experience daily affordeth vs many excellent yong and growing wits, as well from the Plow as the Pallace, endued naturally with this Diuine and heauenly guift, yet not knowing (if you should aske the question) whether a *Metaphore* be flesh or fish.[18]

This sounds for all the world like a prediction of the career, more than a century later, of Stephen Duck, the Thresher Poet! The

18. *The Compleat Gentleman*, p. 78.

same idea of natural genius takes a more explicitly Longinian turn, with references to Homer and the Old Testament, in Addison's *Spectator* on genius (1711):

> Among great Genius's, those few draw the Admiration of all the World upon them, and stand up as the Prodigies of Mankind, who by the mere Strength of natural Parts, and without any assistance of Art or Learning, have produced Works that were the delight of their own Times and the Wonder of Posterity. There appears something nobly wild and extravagant in these great natural Genius's, that is infinitely more beautiful than all the Turn and Polishing of what the *French* call a *Bel Esprit,* by which they would express a Genius refined by Conversation, Reflection, and the Reading of the most polite Authors. The greatest Genius which runs through the Arts and Sciences, takes a kind of Tincture from them, and falls unavoidably into Imitation.
>
> Many of these great natural Genius's that were never disciplined and broken by Rules of Art, are to be found among the Ancients, and in particular along those of the more Eastern Parts of the World. *Homer* has innumerable Flights that *Virgil* was not able to reach, and in the Old Testament we find several passages more elevated and sublime than any in *Homer.* [19]

We need not seize upon such phrases as "nobly wild and extravagant" or "*falls* unavoidably into Imitation" as reasons to imagine that Addison was unusually "pre-Romantic." In fact, as Bertrand Bronson has established, this emphasis on natural genius was a common strain in literary thought at the beginning of the eighteenth century. Addison's disparaging glance at French opinion suggests one reason: there were political points to be scored by constrasting the "liberty" of English genius, with appropriate references to Shakespeare, to the "servile imitation" of French practice.[20]

---

19. *Spectator* 160 (3 September 1711). This and all citations follow the edition of Gregory Smith; I, 482-83.

20. In his important revisionist article, "When Was Neoclassicism?," in *Studies in Criticism and Aesthetics,* ed. Anderson and Shea, pp. 13-35, Bronson "hazard[s] the generalization that there can hardly be such a phenomenon as primary, original classicism," pointing

   This patriotic analogy was useful to the advocates of "natural genius," as was the authority of Longinus. A third argument, also frequently encountered, was based on a questionable analogy to music. In the passage above, Addison's phrase "stand up as Prodigies" suggests the image of a musical prodigy, "draw[ing] the admiration of all the world" by his natural genius, and English responses to foreign virtuosi did often use similar terms. The diarist John Evelyn referred to Nicola Matteis as "that stupendous violin, Signor Nicholao . . . , whom I never heard mortal man exceed on

---

out that "by the time we met conscious formulations of aesthetic principle, it is always Neoclassicism that we confront" (p. 14). He proceeds with a trenchant account of "all those signs and signals of 'Romanticism' that complicate the *opening* of the Age of Reason" (p. 35). Perhaps this is a convenient place to remark that *all* the standard period labels after the Renaissance tend to confuse our subject. Historians of music, though frequently complaining about its inappropriateness, employ the term "baroque" as a catchall term for music from about 1600 to 1750; Claude Palisca, among others, would argue for an even earlier beginning. Manfred Bukofzer, in his standard work, *Music in the Baroque Era*, frequently cited below, subdivides the period into early, middle, and late baroque, but it is clear to him and most other musicologists that the music of the "late baroque," including Bach, has few stylistic features in common with the painting and architecture normally called baroque. Some German scholars have attempted to substitute the more technical term *"Generalbassepoch,"* which has the advantage of describing an actual compositional device introduced at the beginning of this period and disappearing at its end. In literary studies, the term "baroque" has been more frequently employed in discussions of Italian and Spanish poetry than in discussions of English poetry, and in any case its chronological limits are quite different: Harold B. Segel, author of *The Baroque Poem*, gives these as 1580-1680; the early pages of his book are a useful summary of the literary use of the term, with references to René Wellek and others who have championed its use. The situation is even more confusing when we consider the term "classical" and its hedging partner "neoclassical." Bronson argues that the prefix of the second term is "tautological" (p. 17). In any case, French literary historians have treated the seventeenth century as their "classical" period; "neoclassicism" in England is supposed to have flourished in the first half of the eighteenth century; and the term "classical" in music is now generally applied to the Viennese school of Haydn, Mozart, and Beethoven, i.e., to the period 1775-1825. On the late appearance of these terms, see René Wellek, "The Term and Concept of 'Classicism' in Literary History," in *Aspects of the Eighteenth Century*, ed. Wasserman, pp. 104-28. The term "Romantic," whatever it has to do with romance, normally describes a literary period which begins at least thirty years before the supposed beginning of "Romantic" music. And I have not even mentioned the similar conflicts in the use of transitional terms ("rococo" or "pre-Romantic"). As I hope to show in this chapter, these conflicts in terminology reflect not only the separation between the modern academic disciplines of musicology and literary history (not to mention art history, which employs these terms in still different ways), but the increasing separation between music and poetry from the Renaissance on. For some acute comments on the political metaphor by which "genius" was equated with "liberty," see David B. Morris, "Civilized Reading: The Act of Judgement in *An Essay on Criticism*," in *The Art of Alexander Pope*, ed. Erskine-Hill and Smith, p. 137.

that instrument,"[21] and similar suggestions of miraculous or su-
perhuman feats are common in contemporary accounts of other
successful instrumentalists.

We may see both sides of this argument brought deftly together in the first part of Alexander Pope's *Essay on Criticism*
(1711). After describing how Virgil, seeking to imitate Nature,
discovered that Nature and Homer were the same, checked his
bold design, and confined himself to Aristotelian rules, Pope endorses the idea of deriving rules from the ancients:

> Learn hence for Ancient *Rules* a just Esteem;
> To copy *Nature* is to copy *Them*. (139–40)[22]

But then comes a verse paragraph on *"Licences"* which uses the
analogy to music as a graceful transition to a Longinian excursus
on genius which even includes an appeal to wild or irregular landscape:

> Some Beauties, yet, no Precepts can declare,
> For there's a *Happiness* as well as *Care*.
> *Musick* resembles *Poetry*, in each
> Are *nameless Graces* which no Methods teach,
> And which a *Master-Hand* alone can reach.
> If, where the *Rules* not far enough extend,
> (Since Rules were made but to promote their End)
> Some Lucky LICENCE answers to the full
> Th' Intent propos'd, *that Licence is a Rule*.
> Thus *Pegasus*, a nearer way to take,
> May boldly deviate from the common Track.
> Great Wits sometimes may *gloriously offend*,
> And *rise* to *Faults* true Criticks *dare not mend;*
> From *vulgar Bounds* with *brave Disorder* part,
> And *snatch a Grace* beyond the Reach of Art,
> Which, without passing thro' the *Judgment*, gains
> The *Heart*, and all its End *at once* attains.
> In *Prospects*, thus, some *Objects* please our Eyes,

---

21. See John Evelyn's *Diary* for 19 November 1674; for an account of Matteis and
others, see J.A. Westrup, "Foreign Musicians in Stuart England," *Musical Quarterly* 27
(1941): 70-89.

22. This and all citations of Pope follow the text of *The Twickenham Edition of the Poems
of Alexander Pope*, ed. John Butt et al.

> Which *out of* Nature's *common Order* rise,
> The shapeless *Rock,* or hanging *Precipice.* (141–60)

The *"nameless Graces"* Pope admires in music, glancing perhaps at the normal practice of ornamentation (since "graces" was one of the many names for improvised embellishments), are analogous to the *"Grace* beyond the Reach of Art" to which "Great Wits" in poetry may rise. Poets, by this account, may learn from musicians how to achieve effects which will gain the heart "without passing thro' the *Judgment.*"

But in the actual music of Pope's period, not even the "graces" were "nameless." Bach, Couperin, and others worked out careful tables of ornaments, with precise instructions for their execution. Printed methods were available describing violin technique or keyboard improvisation from figured bass. And the training of composers required the completion of exercises in voice-leading in which the rules for the resolution of dissonances were not those employed in contemporary practice, but a more rigorous set of rules derived from the music of the late Renaissance, especially that of Palestrina. Like the shadowy literary figures of antiquity, Palestrina acquired a prestige based in part on myth. Indeed, as Manfred Bukofzer puts it, "the more the actual knowledge of Palestrina's music faded away, the more powerful became the legend of the alleged savior of church music." Like Scaliger fabricating rules from Aristotle, baroque composers and theorists "eternalized in their rules a fictitious strict style which bears the semblance of renaissance music, but which, in fact, is subtly infected with modern licenses" (p. 3). Nonetheless, training in the *stile antico* defined by these rules became at least as imperative for composers as training in the classics was for poets. And the analogy between the two kinds of training is explicit in the most important textbook of the *stile antico,* the *Gradus ad Parnassum* (1725) published at the end of a long career by the Viennese court composer Johann Joseph Fux.

Fux's treatise borrows its style and tone from similar compendia of literary rules. Even the title had been used in 1687 for a dictionary of Latin versification,[23] and the myth to which it al-

---

23. See the notes to the English translation of the first part of the *Gradus ad Parnassum,* published as *The Study of Counterpoint,* tr. Alfred Mann, p. 144. All citations of Fux are from this translation.

ludes, the step-by-step ascent of the mountain of the muses, was a poetical commonplace. Pope's *Essay* makes the same connection between rules and steps up the mountain.

> Hear how learn'd *Greece* her useful Rules indites,
> When to repress, and when indulge our Flights:
> High on *Parnassus'* Top her Sons she show'd,
> And pointed out those arduous Paths they trod,
> Held from afar, aloft, th' Immortal Prize,
> And urg'd the rest by equal Steps to rise. (92–7)

Fux emphasizes the idea of apprenticeship by casting his treatise in the form of a dialogue between a master named Aloysius (for Palestrina) and a student named Josephus (for himself); toward the end Josephus complains of the difficulty of the exercises, and Aloysius replies by combining the myth of the ascent of Parnassus with the practical analogue of apprenticeship:

> *Aloysius:* I can understand your complaint, my dear Josephus, and I sympathize with you. But the mountain of the muses is to be reached only by a very precipitous path. There is no craft—however modest it may be—to which the novice does not have to serve an apprenticeship of at least three years. What should I say then about music, which not only surpasses the simpler crafts and arts in ingenuity, difficulty and richness, but, in fact, cannot be rivaled by any of the liberal arts? The benefits your efforts may bring you; the hope of success; the facility in writing which you will gradually acquire; and finally, the firm confidence that what you are writing is well written, may encourage you. (p. 138)

Fux's attitude, as this passage suggests, is certainly closer to the Jonsonian notion of imitation as hard work than to the looser notion of inspired improvisation which one might extrapolate from Pope's phrase about "*nameless Graces* which no Methods teach." Deliberately casting himself in the role of a conservative preserver of earlier standards, Fux complains in his foreword that "music has become almost arbitrary and composers refuse to be bound by rules and principles, detesting the very name of school and law like death itself" (p. 17). He might have modified this grumbling had he lived to see the immense influence of his treatise. Telemann announced a German translation and, when he did not carry out the project, Bach's student Lorenz Mizler produced one, with annotations, in 1742. Forkel records Bach's own admiration for Fux and use of his methods. Nor did Fux's influence cease with the baroque period; indeed, as his most recent translator argues, "his foremost disciples were Haydn, Mozart, and Beethoven." Griesinger's early biography records Haydn's careful study of *Gradus ad Parnassum,* and the master's own heavily annotated copy was extant until World War II. A similarly annotated copy belonging to Mozart's father Leopold is still extant, and we know that Mozart himself used Fux's exercises when teaching the English composer Thomas Attwood. Beethoven also used the *Gradus,* and wrote an introduction to it in which he occasionally took even more stringent positions than Fux. A French edition including Beethoven's introduction and annotations was published in 1833; among the subscribers were Cherubini, Berlioz, Meyerbeer, Chopin, Rossini, Auber, Paganini, Hummel, and Liszt.[24] And the basic courses in "species counterpoint" taught today in American universities are still based upon Fux, employing many of his terms, rules, and exercises.

The idea that an artist may acquire technique by learning the rules of an older style, although originally borrowed by musicians from literary men, has thus persisted longer in musical than in literary practice. Pope was the last English poet to undertake a career modelled on Virgil's, beginning with pastorals because Virgil had done so and constructing those pastorals from materials drawn from the whole earlier tradition of such poems because he believed that such an apprenticeship would train him for larger tasks. In the years after Pope's career, the triumph of a poetic aesthetic based on "genius" and "originality" has been such that no college student today would expect the first requirement of his course in "Creative Writing" to be the composition of a Virgilian pastoral. But in music, beginning composers still start, like Fux's Josephus, with the harmonization in two parts, note against note,

24. For details, see Mann's Introduction, pp. xi-xiv. Forkel's biography of Bach (1802) is translated in *The Bach Reader,* ed. David and Mendel, pp. 294-356; the reference to Fux is on p. 335. Griesinger's *Biographische Notizen über Joseph Haydn* (1810) is now available, along with the biography by Dies, in *Haydn, Two Contemporary Portraits,* tr. Vernon Gotwals; the account of Haydn's study of Fux is on p. 10. For more information about Haydn's annotations of his copy, which were preserved by Carl Pohl, and which involve references to the theorist Kirnberger as well, see F. Sumner, "Haydn and Kirnberger: A Documentary Report," *Journal of the American Musicological Society* 28 (1975): 530-39.

of an ancient *cantus firmus*. And the notion that such training is essential persists even among composers of twentieth-century music, whose compositional language is wholly unlike that of Fux. Arnold Schönberg spent years writing a highly Fuxian textbook of theory, and Krysztof Penderecki recently remarked that he would consider himself unqualified as a composer if he could not write a perfect chorale.[25] The ironic aspects of this apparent modern disparity between musical and poetic attitudes toward technique may be seen in the eighteenth-century origins of that rift. The successful establishing of a set of rules for musical composition was, as Fux's very title shows, an imitation of a literary ideal. The earlier attempt of the Renaissance musical humanists to derive rules from actual ancient music had also been literary in its origin, but had failed because the ancient materials were too scrappy and too distant from the musical language of the sixteenth century. Fux succeeded in establishing "Palestrina" as a substitute "ancient" model because it proved possible to derive from Palestrina a coherent set of rules, and because the study of those rules had practical results: it gave young composers a facility in part-writing which they could carry over into the composition of "modern" music, in which the treatment of dissonances was freer. The idea that novices should school themselves in the rules of an obsolete style, badly damaged in poetic theory by the notion of "natural genius," has survived in music on the strength of its practical utility. But the very idea of "natural genius," in its eighteenth-century struggle against the ideas of apprenticeship and rule-following, drew life from a false analogy to music. Literary proponents of "natural genius" liked to suppose that prodigious composers provided an example of *"nameless Graces which no Methods teach,"* apparently unaware that those prodigious composers had usually acquired their facility by a patient apprenticeship to the methods of Fux.

Musical Imitation and the Meaning of Tonality

The word imitation had a particular musical meaning as well; in Fux's treatise it is the general term for those methods of compo-

25. In a conversation at the Aspen Institute, August, 1977.

sition in which one part follows the lead of another. Fux treats imitation as the general principle of which canon and fugue are more strictly defined variants. His examples of imitation are much like the examples of musical "anaphora" collected by Burmeister (see above, ch. 4): they show one part following the beginning of another, but then going its own way. Imitation is thus freer than canon, in which the second part must follow every note of the first, and less harmonically restricted than fugue, in which (according to Fux) the entire piece must follow modal principles.[26] His example of imitation at the interval of the fourth shows both kinds of freedom: the upper part follows the lower for only five notes, and as the student Josephus is quick to point out, the example "begins in C and ends in G" (p. 79).

By this account, musical imitation is a structural principle which insures that separate parts begin as real polyphony. It is also, though I am hardly claiming Fux was aware of this, a formal or abstract emblem of the procedures followed by poets imitating the classics in the eighteenth century. Pope's Horatian series, in which the Latin original and the English "imitation" are printed on facing pages, is strikingly parallel: like the composer writing a second line in imitation of a first, Pope tends to establish the principle of imitation at the beginning of these poems; he then feels

26. After the first example of imitation, Josephus remarks that not all the notes of the first part are repeated in the second, and Aloysius explains that that procedure "would be the function of a canon, not of imitation, [in which] it is enough if a few notes follow those of the opening part." Imitation, as a general principle, operates "without any regard for the scale or mode in which the parts move," as opposed to fugue, defined two pages later as arising "when a succession of notes in one part is taken over in another part, with due regard for the mode, and especially for the position of whole- and half-tone steps." I quote the translation of these sections by Alfred Mann, which appears along with translations of other important documents (by Marpurg, Albrechtsberger, and Martini) in *The Study of Fugue*, pp. 78, 80. Mann has also edited the entire treatise in Latin, as vol. VII/Band I of Fux's *Sämtliche Werke*.

free to depart from strict or canonic imitation, even to modulate to a more personal key. In Dryden's famous classification of kinds of translation (paraphrase, metaphrase, and imitation), imitation is the freest and most personal; it is no accident that Dryden describes such imitation with a musical analogy about "run[ning] division on the groundwork."[27]

But of course playing "divisions" above a repeating bass or "ground" is not the same musical technique as Fux's plastic "imitation," and no poet or theorist of the period seems to have been aware of an emblematic resemblance between the musical principle of imitation and the writing of poetic imitations of ancient models. In practice, the effect of the musical principle of imitation was to increase the independence of music by building purely musical kinds of meaning into instrumental pieces. Fux ends his discussion of musical imitation with a reference to the simpler meaning of imitation as practice or apprenticeship by advising the student to spend some time "imitating these examples" in order to acquire facility before moving on to the more difficult task of composing fugues. His much longer section on fugue, beginning on the next page, defines fugue as a compositional method in which stricter forms of imitation—canon, inversion, retrograde, sequence, diminution, and augmentation—are controlled by a larger harmonic design. Conservative in his terminology, Fux uses the Renaissance language of modes in discussing fugue, but his examples show the influence of the tonal syntax of key relations which was being used everywhere in the music of his time, and which had been hailed as the basis of music three years earlier in Rameau's *Traité de l'Harmonie* (1722). Rameau establishes triads as the basis of his system, discusses seventh chords as chords, and even argues that melodies arise from the motion from chord to chord.[28] Fux and other advocates of linear, contrapuntal thinking would never accept these radical assertions, but in practice the confluence of the linear and imitative procedures taught by Fux

27. In the Preface to his translation of Ovid, in the California edition, vol. I, pp. 114-15.

28. Strunk translates some of the most important sections of Rameau's treatise in *Source Readings in Music History*, pp. 564-74. See especially chapter 19, "in which it appears that melody arises from harmony" (p. 570).

and the chordal harmonic syntax taught by Rameau was a productive one; as Bukofzer explains, that confluence "resulted in the harmonically saturated or 'luxuriant' counterpoint of the late baroque period, which began with Corelli and culminated in the works of Bach" (p. 221).

> Bach lived at a time when the declining curve of polyphony and the ascending curve of harmony intersected, where vertical and horizontal forces were in exact equilibrium. This interpenetration of opposed forces has been realized only once in the history of music, and Bach is the protagonist of this unique and propitious moment. His melodies have the maximum of linear energy, but are at the same time saturated with harmonic implications. His harmonies have the vertical energy of logical chord progressions, but are at the same time linear in all their voices. (p. 303)

So rich was the saturation that is is unnecessary to produce a polyphonic example; Bach wrote single lines which implied two or more parts *and* clear chordal progressions. The suites for unaccompanied violin are frequently cited as examples, but they occasionally exploit the ability of the violin to produce double stops; an even purer example of a single-line implied polyphony is the Partita for unaccompanied flute in A minor (BWV 1013). I quote the conclusion of the "Corrente":[29]

The unequivocal harmonic implications of this brilliant passage, achieved by the use of chromatic alterations which clarify dominant relationships, may be seen in this polyphonic analysis by Samuel Baron:[30]

29. This and all citations of Bach are from the *Neue Bach Ausgabe*, vol. VI/Band 3, p. 7.
30. By permission of Mr. Baron, from unpublished analytical notes on this work.

The sequential, linear, imitative logic of the passage coincides exactly with its harmonic structure. The second and third bars repeat, in sequence and in each case a third lower, the pattern of the first bar; the fourth bar begins as another such repeat, but abandons that pattern when it reaches the dominant (E) in root position; the abandoning of the sequence and consequent slowing of harmonic rhythm signal the final V-I cadence.

In a careful discussion of meaning in music, the modern composer Roger Sessions concedes that "a musical motif, or even a phrase, means nothing in itself," and outlines two kinds of "association" by which music can acquire meaning:

> The music may be brought into association with words or dramatic gestures, and these elements will give it meaning. . . . [Or] when there is nothing of a not strictly musical nature to contribute this element of association, it must be supplied from within the music itself. The music must, to state it cautiously, supply some element of repetition.[31]

The canonic and sequential devices developed in the Middle Ages and the Renaissance, classified by Fux under the general rubric of "imitation," provide one such element of repetition, a linear one that helps us anticipate the direction of a musical line and signals its arrival at some important point by altering its pattern. Thus in our excerpt the sequences give the music an energetic drive toward the cadence, and the sequential pattern is emphatically interrupted (in the middle of one of its repetitions) when we reach that cadence. But we also anticipate that arrival point as an arrival point because it is the dominant, because it is a fundamental element of the chordal syntax of the tonal system. That system, as Rameau liked to claim, also provides meaning,

31. *The Musical Experience of Composer, Performer, and Listener*, p. 63.

but in this case the element of repetition is structural. In this movement, the dominant has been, as in any tonal piece, a frequent goal of harmonic motion. The first emphatic cadence (bar 4) is on the dominant, and several large sections may be regarded as in the "key" of the dominant; this last statement of the dominant at the end of the series of sequences is thus predictable, satisfying, meaningful. When a single line, not to mention a more fully harmonized piece, could thus entail two clear, logical principles of repetition, two compelling kinds of musical meaning, the need for verbal associations was bound to seem less pressing. Rameau took this position when he "emphatically stated that the logic of harmony and of part-writing [were] phenomena independent of any but musical explanations."[32]

Sound, Sense, and Structure

But neither philosophers nor poets were ready to accept such claims of musical autonomy, nor was there any immediate rush by composers to write only instrumental music. The importance of instrumental music increased steadily in the eighteenth century, but even Bach's influential and profound instrumental music constitutes a relatively small percentage of his output; in the bulk of his work, his church cantatas and passions, Bach employed texts. So did the composers of operas in Italy and France (including Rameau); so did Handel in England, turning to oratorios with English texts when his Italian operas failed. In all these kinds of vocal music, there was considerable emphasis on yet another kind of imitation, the "word-painting" devices which had survived the strictures of the musical humanists, and which flourished not only in recitatives, but in arias and choruses as well. Baroque examples of these devices are too familiar to require elaborate illustration; the extended rising sequence on the word "exalted" in the familiar tenor aria of Handel's *Messiah* will suffice as an example. As in most obvious cases of musical imitation of words, this example involves the idea of motion; as we have already seen in examining the origin of these techniques in the Italian madrigal, it was easier for composers to find musical equivalents for words associated

32. Lang, "The Enlightenment and Music," p. 103.

with motion (such as "speed, slowness, ascent, descent, height, depth, jumping, stepping, duration, shortness"[33]) than for any other category of words. Other conventional devices, such as falling half-steps for the word "dying," proceeded by analogy.

Poets, although their resources were more limited, were similarly attracted to words dealing with motion when practicing this kind of local imitation. Thus Pope, in the *Essay on Criticism:*

> When *Ajax* strives, some Rocks' vast Weight to throw,
> The Line too *labours,* and the Words move slow;
> Not so, when swift *Camilla* scours the Plain
> Flies o'er th' unbending Corn, and skims along the Main.
> (370–73)

The first of these lines may stand as an example of the maximum possible slowing of a line by consonant clusters ("xstr" is but one instance); and the last line, despite Dr. Johnson's attempt to show that its effects were merely imaginary, attempts to encourage a rapid reading. But as Irvin Ehrenpreis has argued, these effects are "coarse and showy," and have a potential for damaging the larger movement and structure of any poem:

> Except in a few masterpieces, Pope made large sacrifices in order to secure his beauties; and I suspect it must always be so. For instance, a devotion to expressive effects relieves an author from more profound demands of structure, whether narrative or expository. A series of discrete items lends itself to aural refinements as a well-told story or coherent argument does not.[34]

Indeed, the very frequency with which teachers of literature quote these lines of Pope and other similar examples of local sound-sense imitation suggests the ease with which such lines detach themselves from their poems, and this problem can also be acute in music.

When Dryden's "Song for St. Cecilia's Day, 1687" was set to music by the Italian keyboard player Giovanni Baptista Draghi,

---

33. This list appears in Bukofzer's classic article, "Allegory in Baroque Music," *Journal of the Warburg and Courtauld Institute* 3 (1939-40): 4.

34. "The Style of Sound: The Literary Value of Pope's Versification," in *The Augustan Milieu,* ed. H. K. Miller et al., pp. 234, 233.

the composer paid close attention to word-painting. In "The Soft
Complaining Flute," for example, Dryden's phrase about "dying
notes" receives this shockingly dissonant treatment:[35]

But this colorful chromaticism occurs only here; it cannot become
a part of the structure of the piece because Draghi has chained
himself to a static "ground bass" as a principle of structure. These

35. The music is extant in two manuscripts, one considerably more detailed than the
other, both at the Royal College of Music in London; I quote my own transcription from
microfilm. At the Eastman School of Music, in 1978, I conducted the first modern performance of this music of which I have knowledge. Tantalizing excerpts from Draghi's
setting were published by Ernest Brennecke in his fine study, "Dryden's Odes and Draghi's
Music," *PMLA* 49 (1934): 1-34, conveniently reprinted in *Essential Articles for the Study of
John Dryden,* ed. H. T. Swedenberg, pp. 425-65. I hope someday to publish an edition of
the complete score.

"dying notes," like the later dotted figure for the "warbling lute," remain, in Ehrenpreis' words, "a series of discrete items." They cannot acquire a larger musical meaning because Draghi, adopting a conservative English style, is unable to direct his chromaticism toward modulation; haunted by modality, this aria never even cadences on the dominant. Its musical structure and its imitations are entirely unconnected.

But poets and composers of the first rank, especially composers exploiting the tonal system, found ways to use devices which originated as local imitation in a more structural way, thus overcoming the tendency of such devices to subvert the larger shape of a whole piece or poem. Ehrenpreis "conclude[s] that Pope composed his greatest works when he invented a comprehensive structure that could hold—without contradictions or incongruities—the whole range of his expressive devices," and gives, as one example, the climax of the *Rape of the Lock*:

> When the Baron cuts Belinda's lock, Pope introduces a feminine rhyme to signal the catastrophe, and starts the second line of the couplet with a pyrrhic foot so that the gap will be obvious.
>
> > [The meeting Points the sacred Hair dissever
> > From the fair Head, for ever and for ever!
> > (III,153–4)]
>
> But he also places this supremely important action at the centre of the poem; and because the mode of the work is sympathetic comedy, he profits from the humorous connotation of feminine rhymes. (p. 244)

Impressive as this placement of a clever piece of local imitation at the climax of the poem is, it cannot compare with the ability of Bach to use musical materials originating from local imitations as the fundamental building blocks for a whole piece. Paul Henry Lang says of successful vocal composers that they "respond to word stimuli in such a manner that the musical logic almost automatically coincide[s] with the verbal,"[36] and Bach's vocal works abound with brilliant examples. We may single out for

---

36. "The Enlightenment and Music," p. 107.

analysis the soprano aria from the *St. John Passion, "Ich folge dir gleichfalls mit freudigen Schritten"* (I follow you also with joyful footsteps). Here is the first entrance of the vocal line:

The flowing, scalar idea Bach uses to set *"folge"* (follow) lends itself easily to canonic treatment, and the flute and soprano "follow" each other throughout the piece with various canonic and musically imitative devices derived from that scalar idea. The deliberate eighth notes with which Bach represents the *"Schritten"* (footsteps) become the motif of the bass line. Here is the same passage in its full setting; like the aria as a whole, this music has been made almost exclusively from the melodic and rhythmic materials Bach devised as ways of imitatively setting the text of the first line:

In the Renaissance we saw abstract constructive devices turned into means of expression; here we see expressive, imitative devices employed as means of construction, and there are less obvious examples. Later in the same aria, the word *"schieben"* (shove) is illustrated by a striking chromatic line:

The speaker is asking Christ to help him on his path, even to shove him, and the hesitant chromatic line, strongly contrasting with the easily flowing scales of the rest of the aria, emphasizes the difficulty of shoving a sinner onto the right path. But again Bach finds a musical, structural use for even this tiny piece of word-painting: these two bars extend the length of a phrase we would otherwise expect to last four bars to six bars, delaying and emphasizing an important cadence, and the same figure occurs, with the same effect, just before the final cadence of the middle section of the aria, immediately preceding the return of the opening music in the home key. A chart of the large phrasal structure of the piece may help to clarify the organizing effect of these "extra" bars:

Large sections (length in bars)	Subsections (length in bars)	Scoring	Cadence on	
	16	flute ritornello	B-flat	(I)
	4	voice and flute	F	(V)
A 48	4	flute ritornello	B-flat	(I)
	16	voice and flute	F	(V)
	8	flute ritornello	F	(V)
	18 [= 16+ 2 "schieben"]	voice and flute (1 bar overlaps here)	G minor (VI)	
B 64	12	flute ritornello	G minor (VI)	
	34 [=32+ 2 "schieben"]	voice and flute	D minor (III)	
	4	flute ritornello	F	(V)
	4	voice and flute	F	(V)
A' 52	4	flute ritornello	B-flat	(I)
	32	voice and flute	B-flat	(I)
	8	flute ritornello	B-flat	(I)

On its first occurrence, we hear the imitative effect of the sliding chromatic line, and the musically expressive way it delays and emphasizes an important event, the first minor cadence in the piece. But by repeating it, Bach gains symmetry and structure from what seemed at first an asymmetrical factor. The word "*schieben*" occurs five times, but only in these two precisely placed instances does Bach use the imitative chromatic phrase. That much a listener might be expected to hear, at least at some level. But the four "extra" bars produced by the two uses of the "*schieben*" phrase also have a structural effect which cannot be heard: because of their presence the proportion of the two major-key A sections to the piece as a whole is 100: 164, which reduces to 0.61, the proportion called the "golden section." If we apply the golden section to this aria in a linear way, taking the shorter segment first, we would divide the piece at bar 64, which is precisely where the first "*schieben*" phrase occurs! A successful imitative phrase designed to express a verb of motion thus serves not only the audible structural function of delaying and emphasizing two symmetrically placed cadences, but the recondite mathematical function of helping Bach construct this aria by the golden section, as he did many others. Sometimes Bach used symbolic numbers related to the text in the same way: a cantata whose text alludes to the ten commandments states its chorale melody ten times; another cantata for the New Year uses the calendar numbers 30, 31 and 365.[37]

These hidden numerical schemes, perceptible only to the eyes of someone patiently analyzing a score, raise all the aesthetic questions we considered when examining their ancestors in the mathematical music of the Middle Ages; they also indicate the stubborn survival of the Pythagorean view of music as mathematical mystery. And they point up in a particularly acute way the difference between musical and literary materials, even when

37. On the cantata with the ten chorale entrances (BWV 77), see Bukofzer's essay on allegory, especially pp. 15-18. On the New Year's Day cantata, see Lang, p. 96. For typical recent discussions of the general importance of number in Bach, see Henry Hahn, *Symbol und Glaube im I. Teil der Wohltemperierten Klavier von J.S. Bach,* and Randolph N. Currie, "A Neglected Guide to Bach's Use of Number Symbolism," *Bach* 5 (1974): 23-32; 36-49. Fifteen years ago, as an undergraduate, I played the flute part of an earlier version of this aria for a tape recording to be used by Arthur Mendel; that earlier version, in which the flute repeats the entire ritornello at the end, so that the piece has 172 bars, is printed in the appendix to vol. II/Band 4 of the *Neue Bach Ausgabe,* edited by Mendel (pp. 197-202): the version analyzed here appears on pp. 32-36. Mendel and three other distinguished musicologists—Donald Grout, E. T. Cone, and Edward Lippman—contributed essays to a symposium on this aria printed in *College Music Symposium* 5 (1965): 63-96. Of particular relevance to the issues I raise are Mendel's remarks on the various versions of the aria, pp. 63-7, and Cone's excellent account of its structure, pp. 77-87. Cone also offers a chart (p. 87), considerably more elaborate than mine, but his analysis places less emphasis than mine on the structural function of the chromatically imitative "*schieben*" phrases.

both involve local imitations. In praising Pope's approximately centered placement of the lines about the scissors, Ehrenpreis speaks of a poetic structure that can successfully *incorporate* or *accommodate* locally imitative effects. But we have just seen how Bach could use imitative effects as materials from which to *derive* a large structure. It would be unreasonable to expect such feats from Pope, whose materials are much less flexible than Bach's: his words are not merely phonemes, distinguishable sounds that can be arranged in patterns, but morphemes as well, sounds with lexical meaning. Bach's notes, if associated with a text, may temporarily acquire such a precise meaning, but if dissociated from a text, they retain their abstract musical meaning; they remain parts of chords, steps in lines with musical direction, signals of larger key relationships. Thus this aria could easily be performed as a trio-sonata movement, with the voice part taken by a violin.[38] "The Soft Complaining Flute," by contrast, would make less sense as an instrumental movement, since the devices there are more successful as witty imitations of words in the text than as musically coherent ideas. Deprived of the text, Draghi's devices would seem absurd, but the analogous devices in the Bach aria make sense as purely musical ideas, even though no listener to an instrumental version could be expected to hear them as representations of following, stepping, or shoving.

With the triumph of the tonal system, it was increasingly apparent that this abstract, purely musical meaning was the most important kind of meaning a musical phrase could have. Imitation of a text might temporarily provide a more precise meaning, but even when carried to the virtuoso extremes of this aria, could be eliminated without destroying the music. In poetry, the opposite situation obtained: the precise, lexical meaning of the words was essential; the imitative strengthening of that meaning by devices of sound was more temporary or ornamental. Nonetheless, at least one English poet made a truly remarkable attempt to derive a large poetic structure from locally imitative effects: John Dryden, in the poem whose setting we have already examined. Dryden's subject here is music, and his assignment was to write a

---

38. Bach in fact often employed as instrumental pieces works originating as vocal pieces; see Bukofzer's essay, p. 10.

text to be set to music; doubtless this combination of factors spurred on his attempt to structure his poem in ways closely resembling those we have seen in Bach. But it is still fascinating that for Dryden, as for Bach, the resulting abstraction of form shades into numerical proportion and symbolism of a recondite and medieval kind.

One kind of local sound effect in this poem, instead of imitating motion, imitates the sounds of musical instruments. Thus the drum, with an insistent rhythm and a recurring, dull vowel:

> The double double double beat
> Of the thundring DRUM . . .

Or the violins, with a fast tempo, feminine rhymes, and syncopated accents achieved by the alliteration of initial P, D, and F sounds:

> Sharp VIOLINS proclaim
> Their jealous Pangs, and Desperation,
> Fury, frantick Indignation,
> Depth of Pains, and height of Passion,
> For the fair, disdainful Dame.

Brilliantly effective as these passages are, their imitative effects, like others we have considered, are too specialized to become a structural or unifying principle for the poem. Dryden treats these sound effects with obvious concern for design, however, concentrating them in the central four stanzas (iii-vi), which describe, by alluding to these and other instruments, the passions music can "raise and quell."

But in the first stanza, Dryden finds a locally imitative effect which *can* function as a principle of structure, a complex pattern of rhyming which is surely meant to represent the matter of the stanza: the ordering of chaos by the "tuneful Voice" of Creation. The first six lines, of varying metrical length, appear unrhymed; but with the command that Chaos order itself, each finds a rhyme, and the rhyming lines also match their partners in length. Here is the stanza, with a diagrammatic analysis by Earl Wasserman; the numbers indicate length in feet, the letters rhymes:[39]

---

39. Wasserman's discussion of this poem is found in an essay on "Pope's *Ode for Musick*," *ELH* 28 (1961): 163-86. The chart appears on p. 167, as part of Wasserman's argu-

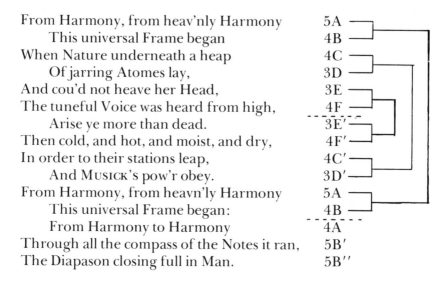

From Harmony, from heav'nly Harmony   5A
     This universal Frame began   4B
When Nature underneath a heap   4C
     Of jarring Atomes lay,   3D
And cou'd not heave her Head,   3E
The tuneful Voice was heard from high,   4F
     Arise ye more than dead.   3E'
Then cold, and hot, and moist, and dry,   4F'
In order to their stations leap,   4C'
     And MUSICK's pow'r obey.   3D'
From Harmony, from heavn'ly Harmony   5A
     This universal Frame began: 4B
          From Harmony to Harmony   4A
Through all the compass of the Notes it ran, 5B'
The Diapason closing full in Man.   5B''

Not only is this pattern of rhyming a poetic way of bringing order
out of apparent chaos; it is also, by means of an even more locally
imitative pun, a "universal Frame." This framing shape is replicated in various ways throughout the poem: by explicit repetitions
of lines, similarly shaped rhyme schemes, and thematic pairings
of symmetrically corresponding stanzas. Thus in the first stanza,
the explicit repetition of lines 1 and 2 as lines 11 and 12 enforces
the frame shape made inside it by the rhymes. In the second
stanza, the first line, "What Passion cannot MUSICK raise and
quell," is explicitly repeated at the end, framing the seven lines
describing Jubal, the Old Testament inventor of music. In the
fifth stanza, describing the violins (quoted above), the rhyme
scheme (*a bbb a*) again replicates the frame shape. The same structural device applies to the poem's large-scale organization. The
eighth and final stanza is cunningly unnumbered because it is an
octave, and thus symbolically the first again; that eighth stanza,
the "GRAND CHORUS," describes the Last Judgement, as the first

ment that Dryden, in this poem, is "organizing as though he were composing a piece of
music" (p. 165). Other important discussions of Dryden's poem, on all of which my summary depends, include Jay Arnold Levine, "Dryden's 'Song for St. Cecilia's Day, 1687,'"
Philological Quarterly 44 (1965): 38-50; D. T. Mace, "Musical Humanism, The Doctrine of
Rhythmus, and the Saint Cecilia Odes of Dryden"; and John Hollander, *The Untuning of
the Sky*, pp. 405-10.

had described the Creation, and Dryden hints at the mystic identity between the two by quoting the command of Creation, "Arise ye more than dead," not from Genesis but from Revelation. Stanzas ii and vii, the next pair as we move inside the frame, are similarly matched in matter and form. Orpheus and Cecilia, in stanza vii, correspond as classical and Christian models to Jubal as an Old Testament model. But here formal abstraction shades into numerical proportion: stanzas ii and vii, framing the four central stanzas on instruments and passions, have, respectively, 9 and 7 lines; the whole poem has 63 lines, the product of those numbers. Stanzas iv, v, vi, and vii have, respectively, 4, 5, 6, and 7 lines. And these are only the most obvious numerical features of this poem; Fowler and Brooks, in an elaborate article, suggest many other mathematical symbols, devices, and correspondences.[40]

We now confront the same aesthetic problem raised by numerical devices in Bach's music, and by numerical devices in medieval music and poetry: the problem of mode of perception. Clearly, the features of Dryden's poem I have just summarized are more obvious to someone studying a text than to someone listening to a reading, much less a sung performance. Indeed, when the poem was set to music, Draghi's close attention to locally imitative effects often obscured the structure Dryden had built into the poem. In the first stanza, for example, Draghi set the first two lines as a chorus, and repeated that setting exactly when the lines recurred, thus strengthening the outer parts of Dryden's frame. But he set lines 3–6 as a recitative for a remarkable bass named Gostling, giving him a low C on "underneath" and a high D on "heard from *high.*" Line 7, "Arise ye more than dead," he assigned to the presumably angelic voice of a boy soprano. The next three lines, about the elements leaping to their stations, he set as a vocal trio in imitative polyphony. All these devices are effective and dramatic, and Draghi's setting deserves to be published and performed, but the music obscures, as it must, the rhymes, the

---

40. Alastair Fowler and Douglas Brooks, "The Structure of Dryden's *A Song for St. Cecilia's Day, 1687 ,*" in their collection, *Silent Poetry,* pp. 185-220. This essay, crammed with musical and numerological lore, may well claim for Dryden kinds of knowledge which he did not have and kinds of mathematical intent which he did not consciously exercise. But its argument cannot be lightly dismissed. Even if one accepts, as I do, only about half of the mathematical hypotheses here offered, the resulting aesthetic problem of the poem remain the same.

grouping of the lines in pairs, and the metrical structure by which Dryden had made his own imitative "setting" of his matter, and from which he derived his larger structure. The numerical proportions, already obscure in the text alone, are of course utterly distorted by the musical setting.

Thus Dryden achieved in this poem a maximum application to poetry of a technique far better suited to music, the expansion of locally imitative ideas into structural principles, only to have music itself bury that virtuoso accomplishment under well-intended but structurally destructive local imitation. The poem and its setting may stand as a particularly rich and ironic instance of the general conflict between perceptible local imitative effects and the less perceptible use of such effects on a larger scale.

The Threat of the Visual Aesthetic

Seven years later, in 1694, Dryden wrote a poem exploring a kind of imitation which differed in many respects from the musical kinds we have been considering, and which was destined to become an important concern for writers during the next century. This poem addresses Sir Godfrey Kneller, the royal portrait painter who was later friendly with Pope; it is a typically inclusive Dryden performance, in which civil compliments to Kneller's abilities are undercut by wry intimations of jealousy at his economic success; its importance for our purposes lies in the accuracy with which it identifies the threat to literature (and thus to music) of aesthetic principles based on the visual arts as a normative model.

In painting, the concept of imitation at first seems simpler, more direct, less metaphorical than in literature or music. Artists have traditionally been praised for the precision, accuracy, or realism of their representations of external objects; indeed, when those objects are animate, the praise has even emphasized the "lifelike" qualities of the painting. If this kind of accuracy is established as a criterion, neither poetry nor music can compete with painting, as Addison points out in his visually oriented series of papers on the "Pleasures of the Imagination":

> *Description* runs yet further from the things it represents than Painting; for a Picture bears a real Resemblance to its Origi-

nal which Letters and Syllables are wholly void of. . . . It
would be yet more strange to represent visible Objects by
Sounds that have no Ideas annexed to them and to make
something like Description in *Musick*.
(*Spectator* 416; III, p. 291)

Dryden, writing some fifteen years earlier, already recognizes
the threat to poetry represented by a simple-minded application
of a visual norm, and sets about weakening the strength of the
argument from verisimilitude, even while ostensibly praising
Kneller. His poem begins with a conventional, epigrammatic description of a beautiful woman, "the fairest of her kind," left
dumb by an admiring Nature who "forgot her Tongue"
but "transferr'd it to her Eyes," giving them the capacity to speak.
This opening leads immediately to what looks like a compliment
to Kneller's realism:

> Such are thy Pictures, *Kneller:* Such thy skill
> That Nature seems obedient to thy Will:
> Comes out, and meets thy Pencil in the draught:
> Lives there, and wants but words to speak her thought.
> (7–10)

So far, only the word "seems" functions to qualify the apparent
admiration for Kneller and for the idea of "speaking pictures."
But now Dryden complicates the issue with a more serious qualification:

> At least thy Pictures look a Voice; and we
> Imagine sounds, deceiv'd to that degree,
> We think 'tis somewhat more than just to see. (11–13)

The grammatical awkwardness of the phrase "look a Voice" emphasizes the artificiality made explicit by "Imagine" and "deceiv'd":
even Kneller's skillful paintings are reductions to a flat surface of
three-dimensional reality, dead illusions of living models. We admire them because we participate willingly in their conventions,
just as we participate willingly in the conventions of poetry, or
those of imitative music.

The next verse paragraph works both sides of that conflict,
undercutting the realism of Kneller's paintings by comparing
them to shadows, then insisting, with an extravagant comparison,
that they are "alive" after all:

> Shadows are but privations of the Light,
> Yet when we walk, they shoot before the Sight;
> With us approach, retire, arise and fall;
> Nothing themselves, and yet expressing all.
> Such are thy Pieces; imitating Life
> So near, they almost conquer'd in the strife;
> And from their animated Canvass came,
> Demanding Souls; and loosen'd from the Frame. (14–21)

By stating both sides so strongly, a typical procedure in his poetry, Dryden emphasizes the unavoidable problem inherent in a visually centered aesthetic.[41] Even though paintings can make more obvious imitative claims than poems or musical pieces, they are not and cannot be identical with the objects they imitate. Nor, finally, would we want them to be. We expect artists to select from Nature those objects they will depict, to generalize, improve, and order them, just as we expect poets to follow rules which are, in Pope's later words, "*Nature* still, but *Nature Methodiz'd.*" A later passage in the poem to Kneller makes precisely this point, for both arts:

> A graceful truth thy Pencil can Command;
> The fair themselves go mended from thy hand:
> Likeness appears in every Lineament;
> But Likeness in thy Work is Eloquent:
> Though Nature, there, her true resemblance bears,
> A nobler Beauty in thy Piece appears.
> So warm thy Work, so glows the gen'rous frame
> Flesh looks less living in the Lovely Dame.
>   Thou Paint'st as we describe, improving still,
> When on wild Nature we ingraft our skill:
> But not creating Beauties at our Will. (104–14)

By this point in the poem, Dryden has succeeded in shifting the definition of imitation from simple replication to selection and

---

41. On Dryden's ability to accommodate apparently conflicting attitudes in the same poem, see A. D. Hope, "Anne Killigrew, or the Art of Modulating," in *The Cave and the Spring*, pp. 129-43, also in *Dryden's Mind and Art*, ed. Bruce King, pp. 99-113. The poem to Kneller ought also to be compared to Dryden's lengthier prose examination of the same issues, the "Parallel of Poetry and Painting" which he wrote as a preface to Du Fresnoy's *De Arte Graphica* (1695), available in *Essays of John Dryden*, ed. W. P. Ker, vol. II, pp. 115-53.

improvement; with this revised definition as a criterion, he can compare poetry favorably to painting, as he does in the last three lines of this passage, where the verb "ingraft" strengthens the case for poetry.

Addison, in the very essay which credits pictures with a "real Resemblance to [their] Original[s]," moves in a similar direction in closely related language:

> Words, when well chosen, have so great a Force in them, that a Description often gives us more lively Ideas than the Sight of Things themselves. The Reader finds a Scene drawn in Stronger Colours, and painted more to the Life in his Imagination, by the help of Words, than by an actual Survey of the Scene which they describe. In this Case the Poet seems to get the better of Nature; he takes, indeed, the Landskip after her, but gives it more vigorous Touches, heightens its Beauty, and so enlivens the whole Piece, that the Images which flow from the Objects themselves appear weak and faint, in Comparison of those that come from the Expressions.

The emphasis here on the reader recurs in a later paper, where Addison explicitly develops another important qualification of the criterion of visual imitation: not only should poets select and improve Nature, but they should do so in a way calculated to arouse the passions of the reader:

> There is yet another Circumstance which recommends a Description more than all the rest, and that is, if it represents to us such Objects as are apt to raise a secret Ferment in the Mind of the Reader, and to work, with Violence, upon his Passions. For, in this Case, we are at once warmed, and enlightened, so that the Pleasure becomes more Universal, and is several ways qualified to entertain us. Thus, in Painting, it is pleasant to look on the Picture of any Face, where the Resemblance is hit, but the Pleasure increases, if it be the Picture of a Face that is beautiful, and is still greater, if the Beauty be softened with an Air of Melancholy or Sorrow.
> (*Spectator* 418; III, p. 297)

That last sentence provides, in effective order, the qualifications we have been considering: accurate imitation is pleasing; imitation of beautiful objects is more pleasing; and imitation of beautiful objects with emotional meaning is most pleasing of all.

The Affektenlehre *and the* Persona

When this kind of thinking was applied to music, the emphasis naturally fell on the last concept. Music was and is obviously limited in its ability to imitate external objects. It cannot imitate a stationary, silent object (say a house) at all; when it imitates moving or sounding objects, it imitates their motion or their sound (the rippling of a stream, the song of a bird). And those imitations, like the similar imitations of words dealing with motion, are arbitrary and conventional. As Brigid Brophy puts it, in a witty and insightful aphorism, "almost the only thing music can represent unambiguously is the cuckoo—and that it can't differentiate from a cuckoo-clock."[42] Even composers devoted to various forms of imitation have usually qualified their advocacy of imitation by admitting that the resulting music must remain pleasing or beautiful. But the concept of a beautiful artwork that arouses the emotions had had a long history in music before Addison employed it in 1712; along with fugally imitative techniques and "word-painting" techniques, eighteenth-century composers had inherited from the Renaissance a tradition of procedures for imitating emotions in dramatic characters and arousing them in audiences. It was this supposed capacity of music to "raise and quell" the passions that Dryden celebrated in the central stanzas of his "Song," equating the stylized Renaissance "humours"—choler, melancholy, phlegm, and sanguinity—with various kinds of instrumentation and rhythmic motion. In the work of eighteenth-century composers and theorists, especially in Germany, this kind of emotional imitation was greatly expanded and minutely codified: it became the *Affektenlehre,* an extensive musical thesaurus of conventional melodic, rhythmic, and harmonic equivalents for various finely discriminated passions.

The central metaphor upon which the *Affektenlehre* was based was an equation of motion and emotion.[43] Daniel Webb's *Observa-*

---

42. Quoted in Nat Shapiro's amusing *Encyclopedia of Quotations about Music,* p. 8.
43. See Lang, "The Enlightenment and Music," which offers as a "principal postulate

tions on the Correspondence Between Poetry and Music (1769) provides a late but otherwise typical example of this doctrine:

> As we have no direct nor immediate knowledge of the mechanical operations of the passions, we endeavour to form some conception of them from the manner in which we find ourselves affected by them: thus we say, that love softens, melts, insinuates; anger quickens, stimulates, inflames; pride expands, exalts; sorrow dejects, relaxes: of all which ideas we are to observe, that they are different modifications of motion, so applied, as best to correspond with our feelings of each particular passion. From whence, as well as from their known and visible effects, there is just reason to presume, that the passions, according to their several natures, do produce certain proper and distinctive motions in the most refined and subtle parts of the human body. What these parts are, where placed, or how fitted to receive and propagate these motions, are points which I shall not inquire into. . . .
>
> I shall suppose, that it is in the nature of music to excite similar vibrations, to communicate similar movements to the nerves and spirits. For, if music owes its being to motion, and, if passion cannot well be conceived to exist without it, we have a right to conclude, that the agreement of music with passion can have no other origin than a coincidence of movements. (pp. 4–7)

As Webb's reference to "each particular passion" suggests, the *Affektenlehre* followed the Cartesian notion that the passions were separate, classifiable motions of the mind, expressible by separate, classifiable, more or less rhetorical musical devices. We have already seen how composers seeking to imitate specific words in sung texts usually fixed on words describing motion; the same musical devices, now more widely applied, came to be used to make entire pieces express a mood of anger or sadness. Imitation of words was the basic source for musical ideas to express the passions, but some theorists sought to distinguish sharply between the two kinds of imitation. Du Bos argued that

---

of the Enlightenment" the following: "Music is an art of motion in time, and as such it is akin to the motions of the human soul, from which it follows that music is able to apprehend and convey the impulses and moods of the human soul" (p. 96).

... the expression of a word can never affect us as much as that of a sentiment, unless a sentiment be contained in this single word. If a musician pays some regard to the expression of a word, he ought to do it without losing sight of the general purport of the phrase which he has set to music.[44]

If the notion of particular musical equivalents for particular, sharply defined passions was old-fashioned and rhetorical, the broadening of the process of musical imitation by detaching it from the single word was a step toward a more expressive aesthetic. Indeed, the whole *Affektenlehre* may be seen as a transitional doctrine, embodying old and new ideas: its workmanlike emphasis on classification and arrangement of passions and their musical equivalents, an attempt to methodize Nature, suggests Renaissance beliefs and procedures; but its broad interest in the passions, especially when that interest extended beyond the passions of singers and their hearers to those of the composer himself, led to more revolutionary later developments.

We may see such a combination of the old and new in the chapter on *Erfindung* or *inventio* in Mattheson's *Der Vollkommene Capellmeister* (1739). The format of this treatise, with its elaborate organization and short, numbered paragraphs, suggests a textbook of rhetoric, and there are significant ways in which Mattheson is the heir of Burmeister. In this chapter alone, he refers to *dispositio, elaboratio, decoratio,* and many other Latin rhetorical terms, redefining them for musical purposes; his footnotes include references to Weissenborn's *Einleitung zur Teutschen und Lateinischen Oratorie,* a standard rhetorical textbook. But the emphasis on orderly rules and hard work is qualified, from the outset, by a recognition of the importance of natural ability and even emotional inclination. Thus the first paragraph declares that the man who brings no natural qualities and abilities to the composition of melody will be unable to profit from the instructions given in the chapter, and the third paragraph says that the most important source of invention is an innate disposition, though it is also important to spend time and effort. Mattheson admits that ideas

44. I quote the influential English translation by Thomas Nugent, which adds the subject of music to the title: *Critical Reflections on Poetry, Painting, and Music,* vol. I, pp. 373-74.

may not always come when the composer sits down to his work, that they may come unbidden and suddenly; on the other hand, he recognizes that the possibility of praise or even monetary reward may be a powerful spur to invention.

The same inclusiveness continues as the chapter moves on to specific rules and examples. Mattheson moves without a major break from ways of inventing a melody we would consider constructive (such as inversion or ornamentation of a known older tune) to ways we would consider more personal or emotive; he calls the first group of techniques *locus notationis* and the second *locus descriptionis*. But he is careful to point out that the mechanical and canonic operations described in the first section can be stimuli to the imagination and creativity of the composer, just as he attempts to provide systematic rules for the more affective techniques of the second section. The beginning of that second section is worth quoting in full; its internal contradictions indicate the transitional nature of Mattheson's work:

> The second finding-place in order, namely the *locus descriptionis,* prompts us to notice that, next to the first, it really provides the richest source, indeed in my small opinion, the surest and most meaningful guidance to Invention, in that here the so-called bottomless sea of human inclinations of spirit applies, as these are to be described or painted in notes; except that, precisely because of the multitude and nature of these varied and mixed passions, it is much harder to supply clear and certain rules for this writing-source than for the other. (II, iv, 43; p. 127)

Notice how, in the very process of trying to supply an orderly and rational guide for the musical representation of the passions, Mattheson uses a disorderly and Romantic image, the bottomless sea, to describe those passions. His discussion continues by explaining that this kind of composition is easier when there is a text, but by no means impossible in instrumental music; the examples given are largely mechanical and rhetorical.

But in the last paragraph of the chapter, Mattheson returns to the idea of sudden, unexpected inspiration, and lists as one of its sources the passions of the composer himself. It is, he says, an aid to sudden inspiration

... if one presses himself strongly into a passion, and sinks himself entirely in it, as if one were in actuality pious, in love, angry, scornful, distressed, overjoyed, etc. This is certainly the surest way to entirely unexpected inventions. (II, iv, 85; p. 132)

This method of invention bears a striking resemblance to the Stanislavsky technique; Mattheson, in effect, advocates that a composer assume a *persona*, imagine a "subtext," sink himself into a passion in order to express it. Such claims of psychological realism were not uncommon in comments on the eighteenth-century theatre: Steele's first *Tatler*, in an essay purporting to be written from Will's Coffee-house, mentions a theatrical performance for the benefit of the aged actor Thomas Betterton, and claims that even the gamblers who now frequent Will's

... have been so much touched with a Sense of the Uncertainty of Humane Affairs, (which alter with themselves every Moment) that in this Gentleman, they pitied *Mark Antony* of *Rome*, *Hamlet* of *Denmark*, *Mithridates* of *Pontus*, *Theodosius* of *Greece*, and *Henry* the Eighth of *England*. It is well known, he has been in the condition of each of those illustrious Personages for several Hours together.[45]

When Betterton died, just a year later, Steele wrote a longer essay in his praise, in which he quoted the Roman actor Roscius as saying that *"The Perfection of an Actor is only to become what he is doing."* To validate this claim for Betterton, Steele praised his "wonderful Agony" as Othello, his ability to "betray in his Gesture such a Variety and Vicissitude of Passions" *(Tatler* 167; pp. 73–74). Steele seems to have believed that Betterton's success was due to his ability to "become what he [was] doing," to be "in the condition" of the person he was portraying. Betterton's acting, if we could see it, would doubtless strike *us* as stylized and rhetorical; he was, after all, not far removed in time from a period when treatises on acting showed various stylized postures as exact equivalents for various stylized passions. But within that tradition, if Steele's testimony may be credited, he succeeded in operating with greater

45. *Tatler* 1, following the text given in Daniel McDonald's handsome anthology, *Selected Essays from "The Tatler," "The Spectator," and "The Guardian,"* p. 9.

fluidity and grace; Mattheson, in the midst of a textbook on the *Affektenlehre* whose affinities with those Renaissance treatises on acting are obvious, drops the psychological hint we have been considering as a similar small gesture in the direction of a less rigid or rule-bound expression.

Even in non-dramatic poetry, the conventions so carefully acquired by apprenticeship to the classics were sometimes modified by similar role-playing. In Pope's Ovidian heroic epistle, *Eloisa to Abelard*, for example, the female speaker (or writer) has a *persona* quite carefully constructed from the conventions of the Ovidian model, and uses a pointed, antithetical rhetoric borrowed from the so-called "she-tragedies" briefly popular in the Restoration. But as I have argued at length elsewhere, Pope worked his way into her role by drawing on his own frustrating experiences with women, a process which may be traced in part by comparing phrases in his early letters to ladies with phrases employed in Eloisa's epistolary poem. To Martha Blount, Pope even acknowledged this process:

> The Epistle of Eloise grows warm, and begins to have some Breathings of the Heart in it, which may make posterity think I was in love.[46]

Thomas Gray, some forty years later, could overtly claim that he "identified" with his poetic creations: describing his state of mind when composing his rhapsodic ode "The Bard," he claimed that he felt himself the bard.[47]

Once poets and composers, instead of merely drawing on conventional melodic or rhetorical equivalents for discretely defined passions, began, like actors, to draw on their own real emotions as a way of imagining and expressing the emotions appropriate to a *persona*, the way lay open for the eventual Romantic redefinition of poets and composers not merely as people with unusual skill and training, but as people with unusual sensibility, whose feelings, somehow bodied forth in verse or melody, were considered a primary locus of value. John Stuart Mill, in 1833,

---

46. See *The Correspondence of Alexander Pope*, ed. George Sherburn, vol. I, p. 338. For the whole argument, see my essay, "Pope Plays the Rake: His Letters to Ladies and the Making of the *Eloisa*," in *The Art of Alexander Pope* , ed. Erskine-Hill and Smith, pp. 89-118.

47. See R. W. Ketton-Cremer, *Thomas Gray: A Biography*, p. 134.

defined poets as "those who are so constituted, that emotions are the links of association by which their ideas, both sensuous and spiritual, are connected together";[48] this radical redefinition claims for emotions the connecting and structural functions previously performed by rhetoric, syntax, and form. Constructive craft, imitation of tradition, even rhetorical swaying of an audience in the old sense become less important than authenticity. As M. H. Abrams puts it, himself adopting a Romantic idiom, "the mirror held up to nature becomes transparent and yields the reader insights into the heart and mind of the poet himself."[49]

A Language of Passions or a Grammar of Harmonies?

We are talking, of course, about the astonishing change in attitudes and assumptions we now usually call Romanticism. Its origins and causes are many: the Lockean associative psychology overtly expressed in the quotation from Mill, the social triumph of a bourgeoisie ignorant of and impatient with classic tradition, the questioning and eventual overturning of received truths which had animated poetry for centuries, to name but a few. My purpose in pushing my narrative toward these general concerns is to allege that we must add to this list of factors leading to Romanticism those changes in poetry brought about by attempts to make it aspire, in Pater's famous phrase, "to the condition of music." I also mean to argue that the condition aspired to was a myth, an inaccurate notion of music as an immediate language of the passions without syntactical or formal restraints. Schopenhauer's definition of the composer as a hypnotized somnambulist performing an act his reason cannot understand may serve as an extreme example of this myth; its complete discontinuity with everything we know about the painstaking compositional methods of the leading composers of his time points the irony.

The facts of the case are these: the materials of music, as we have had frequent occasion to notice, are more plastic than those of poetry; they can acquire their meaning entirely from musical context, while poetic materials, though greatly affected by poetic

48. See Mill's *Dissertations and Discussions,* vol. I, p. 80.
49. *The Mirror and the Lamp* , p. 23. This classic work remains the finest account of the shift from mimetic to expressive theories of poetry.

context, bring their dictionary meanings with them into the poem. In the Renaissance, where the word had unassailable prestige, most thinkers concluded from that difference between musical and poetic materials that poetry was superior: more rational, more precise, more manly. And as we have seen, the attempt of the musical humanists to reform music was, in part, an attempt to make notes more like words; hence the humanist hostility to such uniquely musical devices as polyphony. But as the central concepts of Renaissance thought began to weaken, the absence of fixed meaning in music began to seem "natural" or advantageous to a number of thinkers, including, at times, Mersenne. We might usefully compare the Renaissance biological doctrine of the fixity of species, ultimately overturned by the more fluid concept of evolution, or the Renaissance literary doctrine of the fixity of genres, overturned, as Pope laments, by a confused miscegenation in which "Farce and Epic get a jumbled race" (*Dunciad* I, 70). Even more closely connected to the changing conception of music is the Renaissance notion of the passions as fixed entities or "humours" —visible in Elizabethan stage characters, still useful to Dryden in his St. Cecilia poem, somewhat modified by the thought of Descartes, but surviving into the eighteenth century in the *Affekten-lehre* of German music and the "ruling passions" of Pope's poetic characters—which eventually gave way to the more fluid and personal notions of "sentiment" and "association." We have just seen the beginning of that shift in the works of Pope and Mattheson themselves, where rhetorical classification of the emotions is modified by the idea of role-playing.

But at the very moment when its plasticity was beginning to be appreciated, indeed celebrated for making it a "natural language of the passions," music was becoming more precise in its musical meaning, achieving the logic denied it by Renaissance thinkers. With the triumph of tonality, notes and chords took on meanings we may usefully describe as grammatical. As George Springer points out in a theoretical essay on language and music,

> ... grammatical meaning always implies formal relationships. Thus, grammatical meaning corresponds directly to such musical categories as "leading tones," "passing tones," "dominants," and "tonics." These concepts of musical gram-

mar define certain structural relationships in terms of "permissible," i.e. predictable, context.[50]

Springer's examples are drawn, of course, from the tonal system, in which a dominant is as surely a dominant as an accusative in an inflected language is an accusative. With the establishing of that system, chromatic alteration, which had served an expressive or colorful function for Renaissance composers like Gesualdo and even for the conservative Draghi, could now serve a logical and constructive function, as we have already seen in our example of Bach's "saturated" counterpoint. The clarity of tonal grammar was, I believe, the single most important factor in the growing independence and appeal of instrumental music in the eighteenth century. It was intimately related to the growth of such purely musical forms as the trio sonata and the instrumental concerto, and to the triumph in opera itself of musically ordered forms, especially the *da capo* aria. In all of these forms, whose flexibility was in all periods much greater than the rigid accounts in elementary music textbooks would suggest, arrivals at keys reached by strong tonal progressions helped to define the large-scale form. The strong progression from dominant to tonic became, as Charles Rosen explains, not only a locally important cadence, but a powerful structural device:

> The polarity of tonic and dominant was affirmed by modulation, which is the transformation of the dominant (or another triad) temporarily into a second tonic. . . . It is not until the eighteenth century, with the full establishment of equal temperament, that the possibilities of modulation could be completely articulated. (p. 26)

The articulation of these possibilities by eighteenth-century composers involved a special kind of compositional virtuosity: the building of structures with elaborate but purely musical meaning, many of which were also superb vehicles for the instrumental virtuosi whose purely musical popularity was a threat to mimetic theories of art. Du Bos, in 1719, recognizes the danger; after a long account of the imitative powers of instrumental "sympho-

---

50. "Language and Music: Parallels and Divergencies," in *For Roman Jakobson: Essays on the Occasion of his Sixtieth Birthday*, ed. Morris Halle, p. 509.

nies," he refers with disapproval to those listeners for whom this music has a different appeal:

> I speak here of the generality of men. For there are a great many, who being too susceptible of the impressions of music, attend to nothing but the charms of the modulation, and the richness of the harmony, and insist on the composer's sacrificing everything to these beauties.

A few pages earlier, with a hint of hysteria, he insists that compositional technique *must* serve imitative purposes:

> As the beauties of execution in poetry and painting ought to be employed in displaying the graces of invention and the strokes of genius which paint the object imitated; so the richness and variety of concords, the charms, and novelty of modulations should be applied to no other use in music but that of drawing and embellishing the imitation of the language and passions of nature. That which is called the knowledge of composition, is a handmaid (to make use of this expression) which a musical genius ought to entertain in his service, in the same manner as a poet's genius should keep the knack of rhiming. He is undone (to continue the figure) if the maid makes herself mistress of the house, and has liberty to dispose of it according to her own fancy and pleasure.[51]

English Literary Opposition to Opera: The Charms of the "Harlot Form"

On the continent, the development du Bos feared took place: the "handmaid," music as music, became the "mistress of the house." But in England, whose musical culture after the death of Purcell was essentially imported, the idea of imitation remained powerful, and literary men remained suspicious of music. The opera, where some kind of collaboration was necessary, was the most obvious battleground for a struggle between composers and poets, and on the continent, the composers were victorious: librettists learned to provide composers with the kinds of texts they (and the audience) wanted. As early as 1691, the Italian librettist Giuseppe Salvadori issued the following "warnings for librettists unfamiliar with music":

51. In Nugent's translation, pp. 385, 374.

Modern composers are men of power whose textual changes it is useless to resist. A prudent librettist familiarizes himself with the talents of the singers who will perform his work, and he collaborates wherever possible with the composer. Since arias are what the public most desires, it is senseless to emulate those who try to include in their works as many as three or four scenes devoid of arias. . . . Lengthy scenes should be avoided, as should aria texts whose accented syllables involve vowels other than "a" and "o."[52]

But in the same year, in England, John Dryden was writing a preface to the opera *King Arthur,* with music by Purcell himself, in which he complained that

> . . . the Numbers of Poetry and Vocal Musick, are sometimes so contrary, that in many places I have been oblig'd to cramp my Verses, and make them rugged to the Reader, that they may be harmonious to the Hearer.

In the next sentence, Dryden explains that operas are spectacles designed to appeal to the eye and the ear (and therefore, presumably, not to the reason); within this context, he is able to compliment Purcell graciously, and even to make the apparent concession that "in Reason my Art, on this occasion, ought to be subservient to his."[53]

But this is no real concession. Dryden allows music a controlling position only in an art form he has already defined as an empty appeal to the senses. In a longer preface to the opera *Albion and Albanius* (1685), with music by Louis Grabu, Dryden had made some less polite assertions about the constraints under which a poet collaborating with a composer must operate:

> . . . The nature of an *Opera* denies the frequent use of . . . poetical Ornaments: for Vocal Musick, though it often admits

52. This useful summary of the concluding pages of Salvadori's *Poetica toscana all' uso* comes from Robert Freeman's wide-ranging essay, "Apostolo Zeno's Reform of the Libretto," *Journal of the American Musicological Society* 21 (1968): 323.

53. Following the text given in *The Dramatic Works,* ed. Montague Summers, vol. VI, p. 242. Dryden also paid Purcell the compliment of doing a piece of ghost-writing for him, a preface to the music from *The Prophetess,* published as by Purcell but extant in Dryden's handwriting, in which, not surprisingly, music is favorably compared to poetry and painting. See the California edition, vol. XVII, pp. 324-26; 509.

a loftiness of sound: yet always exacts an harmonious sweetness; or to distinguish yet more justly, The recitative part of
the *Opera* requires a more masculine Beauty of expression
and sound: the other, which (for want of a proper *English*
Word) I must call *The Songish Part,* must abound in the soft-
ness and variety of Numbers: its principal Intention, being to
please the Hearing, rather than to gratify the understanding.
(vol. XV, pp. 3–4)

Like the Renaissance musical humanists from whom his opinions
must ultimately derive, Dryden praises the recitative, the most literary part of any opera, the part in which the text has its greatest
power, as "masculine." Arias, by this account, are feminine, even
effeminate, and (as Dryden slyly insinuates by ostensibly lamenting the lack of an English word to describe them) foreign. The
suspicion of music in this passage, metaphorically expressed as
sexist and nationalist snobbery, emerges a few pages later as open
hostility:

> The same reasons which depress thought in an *Opera,*
> have a Stronger effect upon the Words: especially in our Lan-
> guage: for there is no maintaining the Purity of *English* in
> short measures, where the Rhyme returns so quick, and is so
> often Female, or double Rhyme, which is not natural to our
> Tongue, because it consists too much of Monosyllables, and
> those too, most commonly clogg'd with Consonants: for
> which reason I am often forc'd to Coyn new Words, revive
> some that are Antiquated, and botch others: as if I had not
> serv'd out my time in Poetry, but was bound 'Prentice to some
> doggrel Rhymer, who makes Songs to Tunes, and sings them
> for a livelyhood. 'Tis true, I have not been often put to this
> drudgery; but where I have the Words will sufficiently show,
> that I was then a Slave to the composition, which I will never
> be again: 'Tis my part to Invent, and the Musicians to Hu-
> mour that Invention. I may be counsell'd, and will always fol-
> low my Friends advice, where I find it reasonable; but will
> never part with the Power of the Militia. (p. 10)

Here we hear the irritated voice of the poet threatened by music,
insisting, in a thoroughly Renaissance way, on the rational superiority of his own art. There are echoes of the xenophobia and

misogyny we noticed in the earlier passage, some strong new metaphors of servitude ("bound 'Prentice," "drudgery," "Slave") by which Dryden asserts his unwillingness to serve music, and a monarchial claim of military power in the last sentence. In declaring that the composition of the text ought to precede the composition of the music, Dryden arrogates to poetry the power of "invention"; perhaps in the notion that the musician's part is to "Humour that Invention" there is even an echo of the psychological theory of "humours," a suggestion that the composer's task is to animate the text with music expressing the appropriate passions.

All the attitudes toward music polemically expressed here— that music is foreign, effeminate, destructive of sense, and successful only when imitating the passions—lived on in English poetry and criticism throughout the eighteenth century. The Italian operas produced between 1710 and 1737, principally by Handel, provided a convenient target. Their texts and singers were foreign, their musical style elaborately ornamented, their staging lavish, their dramatic content ludicrous; their most important stars were *castrati*, on whom the charges of effeminacy, unnaturalness, foreignness, and dramatic absurdity could be concentrated. As a compact sample of these charges, we may examine an anonymous poem which appeared in Steele's *Poetical Miscellanies* for 1714:

ON NICOLINI 's *leaving the Stage*.

Begon, our Nation's Pleasure and Reproach!
Britain no more with idle Trills debauch;
Back to thy own unmanly *Venice* sail,
Where Luxury and loose Desires prevail;
There thy Emasculating Voice employ,
And raise the Triumphs of the wanton Boy.

Long, ah! too long the soft Enchantment reign'd,
Seduc'd the Wise, and ev'n the Brave enchain'd;
Hence with they Curst deluding Song! away!
Shall *British* Freedom thus become thy Prey?
Freedom, which we so dearly us'd to Prize,
We scorn'd to yield it——But to *British Eyes*.

Assist ye, Gales; with expeditious Care
Waft this prepost'rous Idol of the Fair;
Consent, ye Fair, and let the Trifler go,
Nor bribe with Wishes adverse Winds to blow:
Nonsense grew pleasing by his *Syren* Arts,
And stole from *Shakespear's* self our easie Hearts.[54]

The most immediately striking thing about this silly and incompetent poem is its shrill tone: why, we might wonder, is the poet taking so many cheap shots at a vulnerable and departing target? The answer, also fairly obvious in the text, is that the poet, like the society he represents, is attracted to the singer he seems so eager to banish. Nicolini is acknowledged as "our Nation's Pleasure" before he is criticized as its "Reproach." He may represent "Luxury and loose Desires" of a kind the speaker is anxious to separate from his own more proper desires, indicated by the little joke about *"British* Eyes," but his singing has enchanted exactly those women to whom the speaker is willing to yield his precious "Freedom." The phrase about "his *Syren* Arts" may be meant as another reference to Nicolini's sexual ambiguity, but it reminds us as well of the power of the sirens' song: not only "the Fair," but "the Wise, and ev'n the Brave" have been "seduc'd" and "enchain'd" by the "soft Enchantment." Nicolini has made nonsense pleasing: for a hearer who did not know Italian, the texts of the operas in which he performed would have been "nonsense," and for a hearer who did know it, not much better; the poet may also be using the conventional Renaissance notion that music could not mean anything specific. But again we notice his discomfort; the aesthetic rules he is attempting to impose upon the opera are

---

54. In the original printing with the misprinted date (MDDCXIV for MDCCXIV), pp. 44-5. I owe my copy to the generosity of Mr. and Mrs. Edwin Wolff. Pope was also a contributor, and may have remembered some phrases from this poetry years later: in Book IV of the *Dunciad,* the youth on the Grand Tour arrives at Nicolini's native Venice.

But chief her shrine were naked Venus keeps,
And Cupids ride the Lyon of the Deeps;
Where, eas'd of Fleets the Adriatic main
Wafts the smooth Eunuch and enamour'd swain. (307-10)

He comes home, appropriately enough, "With nothing but a Solo in his head." For some interesting information about Nicolini's acting, see Joseph R. Roach, "Cavaliere Nicolini: London's First Opera Star," *Educational Theatre Journal* 28 (1976): 189-205.

failing him. If Nicolini's performance, a purely musical one for most London ears, has no rational content, it must be nonsense, and yet, as the poet has to admit, this nonsense is so pleasing that the opera has stolen audiences from the legitimate theatre. The ranting criticisms ("Curst deluding Song," "prepost'rous Idol of the Fair") cannot conceal the attraction that Nicolini represents. The musical appeal of his singing (and he was a splendid singer by all accounts) is entirely at odds with the British, masculine, literary, rational values the speaker so desperately tries to assert, but it is undeniably real.

The ideas about music of which this poem provides such pointed examples, including the ambivalence about its appeal, occur in the writings of major figures as well. Addison, in a witty essay on an opera in which Nicolini fought a combat with a lion, also pokes fun at Nicolini's castration and glances disparagingly at musical conventions:

> Many . . . were the Conjectures of the Treatment which this Lion was to meet with from the Hands of Signor *Nicolini;* some supposed that he was to subdue him in *Recitativo,* as *Orpheus* used to serve the wild Beasts in his time, and afterwards to knock him on the Head; some fancied that the Lion would not pretend to lay his Paws upon the Hero, by reason of the received Opinion, that a Lion will not hurt a Virgin: Several, who pretended to have seen the Opera in *Italy,* had informed their Friends, that the Lion was to act a Part in *High-Dutch,* and roar twice or thrice to a *Thorough Base,* before he fell at the Feet of *Hydaspes.* (*Spectator* 13; I, pp. 40–41)

This is good witty journalism, but it does not represent Addison's complete attitude toward music, opera, or even Nicolini. In his Oxford St. Cecilia poem of 1694, he had made serious use of the myth of Orpheus and the wild beasts:

> When *Orpheus* strikes the trembling Lyre,
> The streams stand still, the stones admire;
> The list'ning savages advance,
>   The Wolf and Lamb around him trip,
>   The Bears in awkward measures leap,
> And Tigers mingle in the dance. (33–38)

And if the essay on Nicolini, like Addison's more general remarks in a number of other essays, seems hostile to opera, dubious of its dramatic absurdities and extravagant staging, these doubts did not stop him from attempting an English opera *(Rosamond,* 1707). In a poem praising Addison for that opera, which was a commercial failure, his satellite Thomas Tickell refers to the Italian opera as "Nonsense well-tun'd, and sweet stupidity," and contrasts Addison's

> . . . artful song,
> Soft as *Corelli,* but as Virgil strong.
> From words so sweet new grace the notes receive,
> And Musick borrows helps, she us'd to give.[55]

Inaccurate as a description of *Rosamond,* these lines are probably an accurate account of Addison's intent: like so many English figures, he still hoped for an accommodation between music and poetry, a more literary and reasonable opera. And he was generous enough to Nicolini to recognize his acting abilities; the essay about the lion recommends the *castrato* as a model for English actors:

> I have often wished, that our Tragoedians would copy after this great Master in Action. Could they make the same use of their Arms and Legs, and inform their Faces with as significant Looks and Passions, how glorious would an *English* Tragedy appear with that Action, which is capable of giving a Dignity to the forced Thoughts, cold Conceits, and unnatural Expressions of an *Italian* Opera. (pp. 42–43)

Addison's views on music and opera, while full of the usual prejudices, are much less hysterical than those of the anonymous poet in Steele's anthology: the Italian opera and its singers, while open to all kinds of criticism, may actually offer lessons to English actors and poets. The man who had admired music for its "unsuspected eloquence" was also sensitive to the gestural eloquence of Nicolini's acting. But all of Addison's comments on music remain within an essentially mimetic frame and bespeak a compla-

---

55. Guthkelch reprints Tickell's verses (1709) and the entire text of *Rosamond;* the lines quoted here are on p. 295.

cent amateurism. Unaware of the technical developments that were making the music of his time a stronger language, Addison at one point writes with what seems real hostility to technique:

> Musick, Architecture and Painting, as well as Poetry and Oratory, are to deduce their Laws and Rules from the General Sense and Taste of Mankind, and not from the Principles of those Arts themselves; or in other Words, the Taste is not to conform to the Art, but the Art to the Taste. Musick is not designed to please only Chromatick Ears, but all that are capable of distinguishing harsh from disagreeable Notes. A Man of an ordinary Ear is a Judge whether a Passion is expressed in proper Sounds, and whether the Melody of those Sounds be more or less pleasing. (*Spectator* 29; I, p. 89)

But all over Europe, people *were* conforming their taste to new developments in the art of music, learning how to have "Chromatick Ears," and judging instrumental music on other grounds than its expression of passions. In his resistance to this kind of hearing, his insistence on accounting for the power of music in mimetic or psychological terms, and his continuing belief in the primacy of texts, Addison exhibits a particularly British strain of thought.

Alexander Pope was probably less interested in music than Addison, though the stories suggesting that he was entirely insensitive to it have now been exposed as myths.[56] He too wrote a St. Cecilia poem (1713) and apparently helped solicit subscriptions for an edition of the musical works of the composer Bononcini, Handel's chief rival, who was his Twickenham neighbor in the summer of 1721.[57] He had apparently forgotten his own efforts

56. For an excellent summary of the gossip on which this myth was based, and of the evidence suggesting its falsehood, see Appendix A of Morris R. Brownell's sumptuous study, *Alexander Pope and the Arts of Georgian England*, pp. 368-71.

57. Pope's enemy Edmund Curll printed, in one of his unauthorized editions of Pope's correspondence, an authentic-looking letter in which Pope informs the Duchess of Buckingham that he has taken the liberty of adding her name to the list of subscribers for Bononcini's works. Pope never reprinted the letter, perhaps because he came to regret his activities on Bononcini's behalf when the Italian was attacked as a plagiarist, or simply because he had come to a position more firmly opposed to opera. But George Sherburn, who accepts the letter as authentic and gives it the conjectural date [27 January 1721/2], suggests that the presence on Bononcini's subscriber list of a large number of Pope's aristocratic friends indicates "notable activity" by Pope on his behalf. See Sherburn's edition

on behalf of an operatic composer by the time he wrote the lines attacking opera in *Dunciad* IV,

> When lo! a Harlot form soft sliding by,
> With mincing step, small voice, and languid eye;
> Foreign her air, her robe's discordant pride
> In patch-work flutt'ring, and her head aside (IV, 45–48),

and the note explaining that

> The attitude given to this Phantom represents the nature and genius of the *Italian* Opera; its affected airs, its effeminate sounds, and the practice of patching up these Operas with favourite Songs, incoherently put together. These things were supported by the subscriptions of the Nobility.

The passage continues by praising Handel's oratorios as superior to these empty operas; indeed, as Deborah Knuth has recently shown, Handel is one of a very few heroic figures in the whole fourth book, and his "banishment" to Ireland constitutes one more proof of the fall of "Universal Darkness."[58] But Handel is praised for allowing his music to "borrow aid from Sense," a phrase quite close to the one Tickell used to praise Addison, and one revealing a similar bias: music is still being judged by literary and mimetic criteria. If Handel's instrumental music appealed to Pope, and there is some epistolary evidence that it did, he was not able to acknowledge that appeal in a poem; he could not admit that any instrumental music could have the logic, form, coherence, and syntax which, for him, were properties of words. The result, as for Addison, was an ambivalent attitude: Pope was obviously impressed by Handel, but only able to praise him by recourse to a set of aesthetic principles not wholly applicable to his work.

Swift's *Cantata,* marvelously set by John Echlin, seems at first an unambivalent attack on music. It attacks the mimetic conventions of text-setting by cramming into a few lines a large number of words for which composers had conventions, for example:

---

of the *Correspondence,* vol. II, p. 99. For a full account of Bononcini's fall from popularity, see Lowell Lindgren, "The Three Great Noises 'Fatal to the Interest of Bononcini'," *Musical Quarterly* 61 (1975): 560-83.

58. "Pope, Handel, and the *Dunciad,*" *Modern Language Studies* 10 (1980), in press.

Here the poetry trails off into nursery-rhyme nonsense, and the conclusion of the cantata does so even more absurdly:

> See, see, Celia Celia Dies,
> Dies, Dies, Dies, Dies, Dies, Dies, Dies,
> While true Lovers Eyes
> Weeping Sleep, Sleeping Weep, Weeping Sleep.
> Bo peep, bo peep, bo peep, bo peep, peep, bo bo peep.[59]

Swift's satiric message in these passages is a conservative one: if, in the words of the opening lines, you "Suit your Words to your

59. For the complete cantata, see *The Poems of Jonathan Swift,* ed. Harold Williams, vol. III, pp. 956-61; my excerpts follow Williams' text and music, reprinted from Faulkner's edition of 1746.

Musick well," your words will become like music in the worst possible way: they will lose their meaning and become interchangeable sounds, like "Sleeping" and "Weeping" in the penultimate line, deprived of their meaning by arbitrary interchange, or like "bo" and "peep" in the last line, infantile nonsense without meaning at all. But Swift—the inveterate punster, the inventor of languages, the lover of alogical rhymes—delighted in depriving words of their ordinary meaning; as any reader of the *Journal to Stella* knows, infantile nonsense had a powerful appeal for him. Like the poem attacking Nicolini, though in a much more subtle and private way, this cantata against cantatas betrays affection for the art it attacks. But the main aspect of music attacked, mimetically literal text-setting, was in its origins a Renaissance technique, and the notion of music as nonsense, even if nonsense was privately attractive to Swift, was a Renaissance criticism of music no longer remotely applicable to the actual music of Swift's time.

Treatises on Poetry and Music

For Addison, Pope, Swift, Johnson, and numerous other English literary figures, ignorance of musical technique, when it did not lead to simple hostility to music, led to discussions of music couched in shopworn Renaissance commonplaces. Even the authors of articles and treatises about music, who were surely less ignorant than the poets, continued to use these tired ideas, despite the continental triumph of a tonally coherent instrumental music. Journalistic appreciations of Handel, the leading imported composer of the century, stressed his success in setting texts (especially the English texts of the oratorios) and his mastery of the *Affektenlehre*. His virtuosity at the organ and in instrumental composition, while universally acknowledged, fell outside the mimetic conceptual frame within which much British commentary on the arts remained. As Herbert Schueller points out, English theorists continued to use such mimetic conceptions as the *Affektenlehre* long after they had lost their relevance to the work of leading composers:

> While the theory [of the *Affektenlehre*] haunted British thought about music between 1750 and 1800, it was already dead for

musicians, and its relevance to the live music that was coming to England from the Continent [including, late in the century, Haydn's symphonies] was far from clear.[60]

Yet English theorists, haunted not only by the theory of the *Affektenlehre* but by the Renaissance humanist dream of a reunion of music and poetry as well, wrote in those fifty years an unprecedented number of treatises on the two arts, in the pages of which we may see humanist attitudes blurring into Romantic ones without the reexamination of musical logic that contemporary developments in music would seem to have demanded.

We may begin with *A Dissertation on the Rise, Union, and Power, the Progressions, Separations, and Corruptions of Poetry and Music* (1763) by John "Estimate" Brown, a well-written, opinionated treatise which betrays its argument in its title. Brown, generalizing from reports about North American Indians, posits a unified ancient origin for dance, music, and poetry, and explains how literacy and other forces tended to separate them. In his curious account of the Renaissance, about which he was obviously ill-informed, Guido d'Arezzo becomes the inventor of counterpoint (a myth frequently encountered elsewhere in the eighteenth century), and both arts are described as drifting away from the dramatic expression which is their true purpose:

> In the Revival of Learning . . . the Misfortune was, that even *Tragedy* and *Ode,* whose end is to shake the Soul with Terror, Pity, or Joy, by a *theatrical Exhibition,* and the *Powers* of *Music;* —even these, in many Instances and in different Periods, were *divorced* from their *Assistant Arts,* and became the *languid Amusement* of the *Closet.* . . . For now *instrumental* Music, having assumed a new and more inviting Form, and being ennobled by the principles of a complex and varied Harmony, was introduced as being of itself a compleat Species, independent of Poetry or Song. This gave it an artificial and laboured Turn; while the composer went in Quest of curious Harmo-

---

60. "'Imitation' and 'Expression' in British Music Criticism in the 18th Century," *Musical Quarterly* 34 (1948): 546. See also Schueller's other articles on ideas about literature and music in eighteenth-century England, in *Philological Quarterly* 26 (1947): 193-205; *Journal of the History of Ideas* 13 (1952): 73-93; and *Journal of Aesthetics and Art Criticism* 8 (1950): 155-171; 11 (1953): 334-59.

nies, Discords, Resolutions, Fugues, and Canons; and prided himself (like the Poet) in a pompous Display of Art, to the neglect of *Expression* and true *Pathos.* And thus modern Music, on its first Rise, was in a manner divorced from *Poetry, Legislation,* and *Morals.* (pp. 196, 198)

This account, of course, has less to do with Guido and the Renaissance than with Brown's discomfort about the music of his own period. A few pages later, in discussing the origins of opera, Brown reveals some of the reasons why opera finally failed in an England still in the grip of exclusively literary expectations about drama:

Again, as the Separation of the Poet's from the Musician's Art produced an *improper Poetry;* so the Separation of the Musician's from the Poet's Character was productive of improper and *unaffecting Music:* For the Composer, in his Turn, intent only on *shining,* commonly wanders into unmeaning Division, and adopts either a delicate and refined, or a merely popular music, to the Neglect of true musical Expression. Hence, too, the *Da Capo* had its natural Origin: A Practice which tends only to tire and disgust the Hearer, if he comes with an Intent of being *affected* by the *tragic Action,* or with any other View than that of *listening* to a *Song.* (p. 205)

As Brown, like Addison before him, was reluctant to admit, the lovers of opera came for the purpose of *"listening* to a *Song,"* so that the ornamented repetition of the first part of every *da capo* aria, however ludicrous dramatically, was musically attractive to them, as, for that matter, were the pastiche performances in which favorite arias from various operas were weakly linked together. Brown, rejecting opera because of the controlling power music now had over it, proposed an academy to explore the reunion of music and poetry in English songs, tragic choruses, anthems, and odes. He had no room in his academy for instrumental music, and little hope of a complete reunion, because, as he explains in an insightful passage, the technical complications of the arts now precluded anyone's knowing both:

The *Poet's* and *Musician's* Office cannot probably be again united in their full and general Power. For in their present refined State, either of their Arts separately considered, is of such *Extent,* that although they may incidentally meet in one Person, they cannot often be found together. . . . The Arts, in their present refined and complicated State, separately demand such continued Application and various Qualities, as seldom meet in the same Person. (pp. 223–24)

Brown's emphasis on the "continued Application" necessary to acquire musical technique suggests the extent to which serious music had become an art practiced by professionals and merely listened to by others, including poets. The participatory musical culture of the Renaissance, in which a gentleman was trained in music as a part of elementary education,[61] sang a part in a madrigal if he expected to hear it, and used musical terms accurately if he employed them in poetry, was giving way to a musical culture centered in opera houses and concert halls, a culture in which Addison could set up "a Man of an ordinary Ear" as a judge, and in which not one English poet of the eighteenth century was a really competent musician. Even Gay, who was something of an amateur flute player, needed help from Anne Arbuthnot and from the professional foreigner Dr. Pepusch in order to mount *The Beggar's Opera.*[62] And if Rousseau, in France, was considerably more competent, able to compose the music for his pastoral operetta *Le Devin du village* (1752), even he seems to have shared the suspicion of technique we find in Brown and other English writers. Praising his own music for its very simplicity, Rousseau boasts:

> . . . Nothing in my operetta goes beyond the elementary rules of composition with regard to learning and technique; a student of three months could write the "Devin," whereas a learned composer would find it hard to embark upon a course of such decided simplicity.[63]

61. See Hollander's summary of the use of music in the educational theory of Spenser's teacher Richard Mulcaster *(The First Part of the Elementarie,* 1582), in *The Untuning of the Sky,* pp. 115-16.

62. For a facsimile of the music as it appeared in the 1729 edition, including a full score of the overture composed by Pepusch, see the lovely paperback edition from Dover Books.

63. Quoted and translated in Edward Lowinsky's fascinating article, "Taste, Style, and Ideology in Eighteenth-Century Music," in *Aspects of the Eighteenth Century,* ed. Earl Wasserman, p. 201. Lowinsky prints generous excerpts from Rousseau's music.

In fact, as Edward Lowinsky points out, Rousseau's kind of musical simplicity, a concentration on "melodiousness, homophony, symmetry, regularity in phrase structure and in rhythm and accent," was a leading feature of the musical style now called rococo, in which Bach's sons and Mozart's father were important composers. No longer interested in the contrapuntal complexities of J. S. Bach, these *galant* composers concentrated on constructing melodies which would outline and emphasize clear tonal progressions. Much of their music may now strike us as shallow, but "such shallowness is often inseparable from a break with tradition. It takes a new simplicity, and even simpleness to arrive at a new profundity" (p. 202). And it took a real composer, trained in *opera seria,* to exploit the profound dramatic and expressive possibilities of a style devoted to melody: Gluck's *Orfeo,* produced in Vienna in 1762, was the revolutionary work. Rousseau and the other literary objectors to the stylized and ornamental aspects of *opera seria* stand in relation to Gluck as Peri, Caccini, and the academic humanists stand in relation to Monteverdi. In both cases, the polemicists mounted a broad attack on compositional technique, but the true realization of their expressive aims was achieved by an artist firmly grounded in that technique.

As we shall see, the rococo motion away from counterpoint was a brief episode in musical history, but a convenient one for British speculators about music and poetry, whose basic suspicion of technique could now be directed against a weakened adversary. In 1769, we find Daniel Webb coupling counterpoint and ancient hexameter; a footnote quotes a parallel passage from the *Saggio sopra l'opera in musica* (1755) of Francesco Algarotti, the elegant bisexual whose admirers included Frederick the Great, Lord Hervey, and Lady Mary Wortley Montagu:

> The music of the hexameter is noble, vigorous, sublime; but in this, as in our modern counterpoint, the specific impressions are sunk in the general effect. All refinements have a tendency to efface the principles of the art into which they are introduced. Were the counterpoint to take intire possession of our music, we should lose every ideal of its original destination, and the sole object of the art would be to flatter the ear. (pp. 118–19)

This could hardly be more wrong. Webb supposed that dactylic hexameter must have been a late and literary "improvement on the simplicity of . . . primitive measures," and a dubious improvement at that, but it is one of the most ancient poetic systems of which we have knowledge. Along with many others, he believed that "the origin of verse was from the impression of sentiment," and that the original language in which this verse was spoken, far from being a "refined" inflected tongue like ancient Greek, "must have been barren of words, rude of sound, of the simplest construction, and abounding with monosyllables" (pp. 117, 115–16). But modern linguistic study has shown, of course, that the evolution of language is away from inflection, not toward it; the languages spoken by some very primitive peoples have highly complex grammars. Webb could not have known this, any more than he could have known the true facts about the origins of counterpoint. For him, as for many other thinkers of his period, the myth of the origin of music or poetry or both in the crude, passionate cries of primitive man was a logical and attractive one: it followed the fragmentary testimony of observers of North American "savages," and it justified the suspicion of musical technique which we have been noticing among many literary thinkers. In Germany, Herder's *Origin of Language,* which extended this theory even further, was enormously influential: Wagner's decision to abandon rhymed verse in favor of a condensed, alliterative poetry rich in "root syllables" derives directly from Herder.[64]

Webb reached similar conclusions some seventy years earlier. Here are his objections to rhymed couplets:

> The constant and even tenor of the couplet secures it from falling into [prosaic] relaxations; a security, however, in which the poet hath little reason to triumph, while the perpetual returns of similar impressions lie like weights upon our spirits, and oppress the imagination. Strong passions, the warm effusions of the soul, were never destined to creep through monotonous parallels; they call for a more liberal rhythmus; for movements, not balanced by rule, but measured by sentiment, and flowing in ever new yet musical proportions. (p. 113)

64. For details, see Jack M. Stein, *Richard Wagner and the Synthesis of the Arts,* pp. 69-70.

According to the Wordsworthian imagery of this passage, poetry originates in the "warm effusions of the soul," flows in liquid patterns "measured by sentiment," and must avoid regular or monotonous patterns, lest "similar impressions" begin to "oppress the imagination." As M. H. Abrams points out, the word "expression," at least as common as Webb's "impression" in this period, usually meant what Webb seems to mean by "impression," the power of poetry or music to arouse passions in the listener, not yet the capacity of those arts to express the sentiments of their makers.[65] But Webb's double definition of music as an art of imitation *and* impression (quoted in the introduction to this chapter) attempts to combine two essentially incompatible aesthetic theories. The myth of the primitive outcry, with its emphasis on an inarticulate and irregular outpouring of emotion, worked against imitative ideas as it worked against formal rules and technical complexities. We may see popular manifestations of its power in the promotion of such supposed primitives as Stephen Duck, the Thresher Poet, and in the "primitive" pastoral setting of Rousseau's operetta, with its self-consciously simple music.

But one aspect of this simple music, as of the rococo style generally, was an extreme regularity of phrase length; in seeking simplicity, Rousseau and others produced a rhythm characterized by the "monotonous parallels" Webb objected to in poetic couplets. There was some loose talk of emotion among composers of rococo music: Carl Philipp Emanuel Bach declared that it was necessary to compose from the soul, and the modish *crescendi* of the Mannheim orchestra (a departure from the "terraced" dynamics of the baroque style) were sometimes credited with an exciting impact on the sentiments.[66] But even the rococo style, for all its simplicity, for all its eschewing of counterpoint, was not the formless outcry described by literary myth-makers. The rococo was really a period of consolidation, in which composers simplified their textures in order to master the harmonic possibilities of tonality; as Lowinsky points out, the simplification was not permanent:

65. *The Mirror and the Lamp*, p. 92. Abrams offers apposite quotations from Charles Avison's *Essay on Musical Expression* (1753) and other similar treatises.

66. Again, Webb provides an example: "An even and continued swell from the piano into the forte . . . , in music, is attended with a high degree of pleasure: . . . [which] proceeds from the spirits being thrown into the same movement as when they rise from sorrow into pride, or from an humble into a sublime affection" (p. 45).

... The deepening of Haydn's and Mozart's music was insep-
arably tied to their discovery of the music of [J. S.] Bach, who
had been rejected by the "progressives" of his own generation. In 1781, the year of Haydn's new thematically conceived
quartets (op. 33), and the year in which Mozart heard Bach's
music for the first time in the house of the Viennese patron
of music, Baron von Swieten, the stylistic revolution had
come full cycle. The new style was well established. And great
musicians such as Haydn and Mozart, and later Beethoven,
were now able to appreciate—across the boundary of styles—
the immense musicality of Bach's genius. (p. 202)

The result of this appreciation, in which von Swieten's collection
of manuscript works of Bach played an important role, was the
reintegration of counterpoint into the new style. Even in his operas, Mozart's most striking pieces are his ensembles, where contrapuntally constructed parts dramatize the relations between the
characters; as modern critics have shown, his first-act finales,
where the tonal grammar of key-relations works to organize a
number of arias and ensembles into a coherent whole, are among
his greatest accomplishments.[67]

But none of this could possibly have been grasped by English
theorists, who heard a haphazard selection of imported serious
music which they frequently regarded with suspicion, and who
showed, in the closing decades of the eighteenth century, considerable interest in folk ballads, Methodist hymns, and other
"primitive" effusions.[68] Even Anselm Bayly, who was a Sub-Dean
of the Chapel Royal and could write with some authority on matters of vocal technique, was content with a pious version of the
prevailing myth: he alleged, in 1789, that the original purpose of
music must have been "to animate by the simplicity of sounds in
divine worship," as that of poetry was "to civilize mankind with
sentiments." In modern music, whose improvements Bayly, like
Brown, credits to Guido,

... the simplicity of air is often spoiled by the redundance of
variations and graces; nature is outraged in imitations, and

67. See, for example, Kerman, ch. 3-4; Rosen, ch. V, part 3.
68. For a useful account, with citations of Wesley's pamphlet on music (e.g. "What has
counterpoint to do with passion?"), see Bertrand Bronson, "Some Aspects of Music and
Literature in the Eighteenth Century," pp. 46-55.

the ear is perplexed, if not lost, in a croud of harmony, or tired with everlasting repetitions of the subject.[69]

From the context, I suspect that the "imitations" by which "nature is outraged" are canonic or contrapuntal imitations, but it hardly matters. *All* the kinds of imitation we considered in the first part of this chapter—modeling oneself on a master, following rules, manipulating lines canonically, and matching sound to sense (whether at the level of the individual word or in the more generalized form of the *Affektenlehre*)—were losing their appeal to literary minds. The once powerful notion that music and poetry were similar in being imitative arts, though still often ritually recited, had been displaced by the notion that they were similar in expressing sentiments. The "correspondences" between the arts advertised in Webb's title turn out to be neither imitative nor formal, but dramatic:

> The truth is, music borrows sentiments from poetry, and lends her movements. . . . A dramatic spirit must be the common principle of their union. This spirit is not confined to the regular drama; . . . it may govern every mode of composition in which the poet assumes a character, and speaks and acts in consequence of that character. (pp. 131–32)

Romantic Ideas and "Musical" Syntax

The idea of role-playing, here made central to a new subjective theory of the relations between music and poetry, shaded easily into the idea of passionate self-expression. The weakening of mimetic criteria was an important part of this shift, as was the growing power of the myth of a passionate, formless, primitive origin for both arts. In Germany, where mimetic notions, at least as regards music, died sooner than in England, "music came to be the art most immediately expressive of spirit and emotion, constituting the very pulse and quiddity of passion made public."[70]

69. *The Alliance of Music, Poetry and Oratory*, pp. 3-4. The suspicion of modern music here is surprising, coming as it does from a man whose sections on singing show a thorough acquaintance with Italian treatises on the subject, but there is something conservative, even prudish, about Bayly, most humorously obvious in his contention that "vicious gratifications may ruin [a boy's *contralto* voice] before the age of manhood" (p. 51).

70. Abrams, p. 50.

The earliest music, Herder wrote in 1769, expressed passion; and this expression, when ordered and modulated, "became a wonder-music of all the affections, a new magical language of the feelings." . . . And Herder turns to music, as earlier critics had turned to painting, in order to specify the character of poetry. Unlike painting and sculpture, poetry "is the music of the soul. A sequence of thoughts, pictures, words, tones is the essence of its expression; in this does it resemble music." (p. 93)

Versions of these ideas were repeated by Wackenroder, Novalis, Schlegel, and Schopenhauer, and with the emergence of a full-blown Romanticism in England, we encounter them there as well. Hazlitt, in 1818, was calling poetry "the music of language, answering to the music of the mind," and offering as an example of the "near connection between music and deep-rooted passion" the fact that "mad people sing."[71]

Like Schopenhauer's account of the composer as an unconscious sleepwalker, this elevation of the presumably formless singing of the insane exemplifies one obvious feature of the Romantic embracing of music as a model: unlike their Renaissance forbears, who saw resemblances between music and poetry along a rhetorical axis, and who therefore selected for comparison highly crafted music, the Romantics saw resemblances along an emotional axis, and therefore selected for comparison (and emulation) the artless music of the savage, the madman, and the peasant. We may see all these notions at work in Wordsworth's "Power of Music" (1807), which celebrates the fiddling of a blind beggar:

> He stands, backed by the wall;—he abates not his din;
> His hat gives him vigour, with boons dropping in,
> From the old and the young, from the poorest; and
>   there!
> The one-pennied Boy has his penny to spare.
>
> O blest are the hearers, and proud be the hand
> Of the pleasure it spreads through so thankful a band;
> I am glad for him, blind as he is!—all the while
> If they speak 'tis to praise, and they praise with a smile.

71. "On Poetry in General," following the text of Hazlitt's *Complete Works*, ed. Waller and Glover, vol. V, p. 12.

> The tall Man, a giant in bulk and in height,
> Not an inch of his body is free from delight;
> Can he keep himself still, if he would? Oh, not he!
> The music stirs in him like wind through a tree.[72]

Perhaps it is unfair to lay much weight on the features of such a palpably weak poem, but some of the contradictions in Romantic thought about music appear here with a kind of crude clarity.[73] Neither the fiddling of the beggar nor the motion of the poem resembles the ideal of Webb ("warm effusions of the soul, ... movements not balanced by rule, but measured by sentiment, and flowing in ever new yet musical proportions"). Indeed, one of the weaknesses of the poem is its anapestic rhythm, which produces at least as monotonous an effect as that Webb complains of in couplets. Nor can we imagine that the blind beggar's playing flowed in "ever new proportions"; doubtless it fell into the repetitive dance rhythms of folk music. Philosophically, the Romantics identified the idea of the primitive with a magical expression of emotion, free from the constraints of syntax and form; but their attempts to reproduce the folk-like, the primitive, the innocent (like Rousseau's operetta or this poem) fell naturally into the all too regular rhythms of actual folk-song and ballad.

A more interesting misunderstanding of music lies behind Romantic innovations in syntax, innovations which characterize poems more worthy of our attention than "Power of Music." Stylistic analyses of the differences between Romantic and Augustan poetry have most often emphasized the Romantic rejection of conventional "poetic diction" in favor of "the language of conversation in the middle and lower classes of society," to quote Wordsworth himself,[74] and this democratic motion toward a simpler diction, obviously related to the affection for the primitive that we have been examining, is of course one of the clearest attributes of

72. Following the text of Wordsworth's *Poetical Works,* ed. Thomas Hutchinson, rev. Ernest de Selincourt, p. 150.

73. John Hollander, in an essay friendly to Wordsworth and partly concerned with his more interesting poem "On the Power of Sound," refers to "Power of Music" as "a very bad poem." See p. 5 of his wide-ranging lecture, *Images of Voice: Music and Sound in Romantic Poetry.*

74. In the *Advertisement* to the *Lyrical Ballads* of 1789, following the text given in the edition of Brett and Jones, p. 8. For an illuminating discussion of the diction issue, see ch. 16 of Wimsatt, *Literary Criticism, A Short History.*

English Romantic verse. But an equally important and less frequently emphasized change occurred in poetic syntax, a change influenced by the notion of "organic form" and by the ideal of an associative ordering of materials, which we have already encountered in Herder's assertion that music and poetry resemble each other in being "a sequence of thoughts, pictures, words, tones," and in Mill's later claim that "emotions are links of association by which [poets'] ideas . . . are connected." Donald Davie, after explaining the importance to the Augustans of the active, clear, tightly patterned syntax they called "strong sense," stresses the motion of the Romantics away from that ideal:

> Once the idea of "organic form" was broached, poetic syntax began to move into the orbit of music and away from "strong sense." Wordsworth's revision of *The Prelude* is . . . , among other things, a movement from syntax to pseudo-syntax.[75]

Davie is perfectly correct about Wordsworth's revision, and about the general tendency of Romantic poets to order their poems by associations of ideas and images. The long apostrophes to mysterious Powers, questioning or conditional subjunctive verbs, dangling participles, adverbial clauses, incomplete sentences, and other loose constructions so typical of English Romantic verse encourage us to read in an associative way, and discourage us from seeking the central meaning of a sentence in the relations between its main subject, verb, and object. W. K. Wimsatt calls this development "a step toward the directness of sensory presentation, . . . a structure which favors implication rather than overt statement."[76] Changes in form took a parallel course: the preference for blank verse or the more distant rhyming of various "ode" stanzas on the part of the English Romantics was a motion away from the antithetical tightness of the couplet, which had helped Augustan poets reinforce their syntax, or (in witty or

75. In his insufficiently appreciated study, *Articulate Energy*, p. 61. Davie makes good his claim with an analysis of parallel passages from the two versions, pp. 112-16. Another factor in this motion toward "pseudo-syntax," besides the idea of "organic form" and the misunderstanding of music, was the immense influence of a certain kind of Miltonic syntax. As Milton's diction had haunted the eighteenth century, his grammar haunted the nineteenth.

76. In "The Structure of Romantic Nature Imagery," now most readily available in *The Verbal Icon*, p. 116.

ironic poems) worked contrapuntally against that syntax. But these formal and syntactic changes in the direction of a more vaguely associative, emotionally fluid kind of poetry did not in fact bring poetry "into the orbit of music," however much the poets themselves may have believed that it did. The Romantic account of music as a loosely associative sequence of emotional effusions, still very much alive in the twentieth century,[77] is a myth with no applicability whatsoever to the music being composed when the myth was concocted: the brilliantly syntactic and symmetrical music of the Viennese classical school. Nor is that myth applicable to the European folk-music so admired by the Romantics, which exhibits, in a much simpler way, the same clear polarity of tonic and dominant, the same symmetrical structure of phrases as the composed music of the classical period—a similarity proved by the fact that folk-like tunes composed by the Viennese masters passed quickly into the folk-culture and were accepted there.[78]

But myths may be productive, and the Romantic loosening of syntax and form, derived at least in part from that misunderstanding of music, often had notable poetic results. Consider, for example, these lines from Wordsworth's *Prelude;* I quote both the version of 1805 and the version of 1850.

[1805]	[1850]
Imagination! lifting up itself	Imagination—here the Power so called
Before the eye and progress of my Song	Through sad incompetence of human speech,
Like an unfather'd vapour; here that Power,	That awful Power rose from the mind's abyss
In all the might of its endowments, came	Like an unfathered vapour that enwraps,
Athwart me; I was lost as in a cloud,	At once, some lonely traveller. I was lost;

77. For example, in the influential work of Susanne Langer, *Feeling and Form,* whose influence Davie acknowledges in his various discussions of "syntax as music." Langer believes that music reflects "the morphology of feeling," rather than specific feelings, and her analysis is more learned and supple than the Romantic ideas from which it is nonetheless descended.

78. See Rosen, pp. 332-33.

Halted, without a struggle to break through.	Halted without an effort to break through;
And now recovering, to my Soul I say	But to my conscious soul I now can say—
I recognise thy glory; in such strength	'I recognise thy glory:' in such strength
Of usurpation, in such visitings	Of usurpation, when the light of sense
Of awful promise, when the light of sense	Goes out, but with a flash that has revealed
Goes out in flashes that have shewn to us	The invisible world, doth greatness make abode,
The invisible world, doth Greatness make abode,	There harbours; whether we be young or old,
There harbours whether we be young or old.	Our destiny, our being's heart and home,
Our destiny, our nature, and our home	Is with infinitude, and only there;
Is with infinitude, and only there;	With hope it is, hope that can never die,
With hope it is, hope that can never die,	Effort, and expectation, and desire
Effort, and expectation, and desire,	And something evermore about to be.
And something evermore about to be.	

(VI, 525–42)	(VI, 592–608)[79]

Not only does the revision enact the drift away from "strong sense" identified by Davie; that drift is its central subject. In the second line, the replacement of the primly Augustan phrase about the "progress of my Song" with the much more apposite acknowledgement of the "sad incompetence of human speech" gives us the very idea that made the Romantics turn to music as a possible model for the expression of the unsayable. At the end of both versions, the emphasis on "Effort, and expectation, and de-

79. The 1850 text follows the edition of Hutchinson, p. 535; that of 1805 follows the separate edition of *The Prelude*, ed. Ernest de Selincourt, pp. 99-100.

sire, / And something evermore about to be" shows us why a poet like Wordsworth needed to move away from the finality of statement toward a syntax of fluid becoming. At the emotional center of the passage, imagination and greatness appear "when the light of sense / Goes out," a moment filled, in Romantic thought, with the strains of music.

The changes in grammar and punctuation display this process at the level of technique. By a change of punctuation, the second version attaches one adverbial clause ("whether we be young or old") to the clause that follows it instead of the clause that precedes it, but this change hardly matters: the adverbial clause was already floating pretty freely between the two independent clauses, modifying either or both with equal plausibility. Wordsworth has organized his poem in the way Herder claimed music was organized, as a sequence of images flowing into each other, and the second version increases the fluidity by making precise parsing so difficult that we abandon it. The central climax, "when the light of sense / Goes out," places a maximum strain on the syntax by occurring during a breath-holding parenthesis interrupting the main clause: "in such strength . . . doth greatness make abode." And while the second version shortens the parenthesis by eliminating a needless phrase ("in such visitings / Of awful promise"), it makes the grammar more difficult by providing a choppier rhythm and a more muscular phrasing for the idea of the revealing flash. If we have forgotten, by the time we reach the resolution of the main clause, where it is that greatness makes abode, we have nonetheless associated greatness with the invisible world, the revealing flash, usurpation, glory, imagination, and a certain smearing of syntax.[80] This kind of poetry does not invite the reader to make a mental diagram of its grammar; indeed, it strongly discourages that kind of reading by blurring the relations between its nouns until "Imagination," "Power," "vapour," "glory," "greatness," "destiny," and "infinitude" all seem aspects of the same fluid concept. And this synthesizing effect is precisely what the poem describes.

But we should recognize that to praise these lines for achiev-

---

80. I borrow the term "smear" from an illuminating account of similar tendencies in Shelley's *Mont Blanc* in Michael Cooke's *Acts of Inclusion*, pp. 189-92.

ing such a happy confluence of manner and matter is to apply yet another version of a mimetic aesthetic: Wordsworth has found a syntax which imitates or enacts his subject, just as earlier poets found sounds which imitated the motion described in their lines. We should also acknowledge that this motion away from "strong sense," undertaken in part for the purpose of making poetry more like music, involved losses as well as gains. In embracing a syntax whose ambiguities avoid resolution, Wordsworth and his Romantic allies were shutting themselves off from another set of poetic possibilities, already brilliantly exploited by their Augustan predecessors, in which temporary ambiguities *within* a tight syntactic system explode into meaning in witty resolutions. The familiar zeugmas of Pope ("Or stain her Honour, or her new Brocade") provide compact examples. Longer versions of this kind of wit often involve repetition and variation of some crucial grammatical motive. Consider, for example, this passage from the *Epistle to a Lady,* in which the varied formula is "too much [noun] to [verb]."

> Flavia's a Wit, has too much sense to Pray,
> To toast our wants and wishes, is her way;
> Nor asks of God, but of her Stars to give
> The mighty blessing, 'while we live, to live.'
> Then all for Death, that Opiate of the soul!
> Lucretia's dagger, Rosamonda's bowl.
> Say, what can cause such impotence of mind?
> A spark too fickle, or a Spouse too kind.
> Wise Wretch! with Pleasures too refin'd to please,
> With too much Spirit to be e'er at ease,
> With too much Quickness ever to be taught,
> With too much Thinking to have common Thought:
> Who purchase Pain with all that Joy can give,
> And die of nothing but a Rage to live. (87–100)

Of these fourteen lines, ten contain either the word "too" or the word "to" or both. The first line announces Pope's judgement of Flavia, and establishes the grammatical method by which he will amplify that judgement: Flavia, who fancies herself a refined Epicurean, "has too much sense to Pray." Immediately the wonderful capacity of that construction for irony is clear: the speaker evidently believes that if Flavia had the right amount of the right kind of sense, she would be praying to God, not toasting her wants and appealing to the stars. Pope points these constrasts by careful placement of the infinitives which form one part of the basic construction: "to Pray" immediately precedes "to Toast," while "to give" and "to live" form a couplet rhyme. Then come Flavia's theatrical posturings toward a Roman suicide, inflated by an epic question ("Say, what can cause," as if she were Juno), deflated by the speaker's awareness that these histrionics represent "impotence of mind." But the real deflation comes in the answer to the epic question, stated by means of the other half of the key construction, the superlative, which has a capacity for irony all by itself. Flavia, we learn, is threatening daggers and poison because of "A spark too fickle, or a Spouse too kind." The implication, that women like Flavia want not only devoted lovers but cruel husbands, is delicious. Having demonstrated what infinitives and superlatives can do apart, Pope now recombines them, in four consecutive lines employing the central construction. Yet even within this emphatic repetition there is variation: the first and last of the lines employ nouns and verbs with common roots ("Pleasures . . . please," . . . "Thinking . . . Thought"), producing a highly compressed irony; the second and third lines employ noun-verb pairs with more opposed meaning. Pope might have concluded the portrait with one more repetition ("And die at last of too much Rage to live"), but he does better than that; by substituting "nothing but" for "too much" in the final line, he confirms the ironic implication the construction has had all along: "too much sense to Pray" is no sense at all, and too much "Rage to live" is "nothing but" empty mental impotence. This kind of poetry evidently demands attention to its grammar; its most important meanings are built into its precise construction.

The witty modulations of the classical composers, especially Haydn, in which a note or phrase we first hear in one tonal context suddenly reveals a new meaning in another context, a new grammatical function, are much closer to Pope's kind of syntax than to Wordsworth's, despite the dates. Charles Rosen gives as an example Haydn's String Quartet in B-flat (opus 33, no. 4), in which "the modulation to the dominant is a joke, . . . a surprising change of nonsense into sense" (pp. 97-98).

As Rosen explains, the phrase,

repeated at the ends of bars 8, 10, 11, and 12, is ambiguous because it is always stated in unison (or, in the last case, by the solo
cello), so that its harmonic function only becomes clear with the
chord in bar 13, which reveals that the D with which the little
phrase ends is the root of the dominant of G minor. The syntax
called the tonal system is as necessary for this musical joke as the

syntax called English grammar is for Pope's couplet wit. A music which actually proceeded by the kind of loose association believed in by Romantic poets and philosophers could not have achieved this kind of wit, and when that literary myth passed into the thinking of composers, as it eventually did, the musical result was a weakening of tonal syntax, an abandonment of wit and logic in favor of sentiment and ambiguity. Modulation became "slower and more gradual, . . . at times so heavily chromatic that the two keys blend into each other . . . Wit was swamped by sentiment."[81]

The ironies of these developments are worth recapitulating. The Romantic poets loosened their syntax in the name of a more "musical" poetry, a stylistic change which made their poetry *less*, not more, like the music of their contemporaries the Viennese classical composers, arguably the most syntactical music in Western history. In its capacity to resolve ambiguities with a punning wit, in its essentially comic style, the music of Haydn and Mozart was much more analogous to the poetry of the Augustans. But the Augustans, deaf to the growing tonal logic of the music of *their* time, had pilloried music for its ambiguity, its fluidity, its "femininity." Despite their public protests against it, however, the "Syren Art" held secret charms for Addison, Pope, and even Swift, and by the end of the eighteenth century, music was being openly embraced by poets and philosophers as a model for all art. At this time, the music of the leading composers might easily have been praised for its logic, coherence, and wit, but when poets celebrated music it was for the very qualities Dryden had scorned as tending to "depress thought"—its ambiguity, fluidity, and "femininity." In Goethe's *Faust*, for example, the various embodiments of the "eternal feminine" make their appearances surrounded by explicit music or musical imagery. Yet Beethoven, in a compact statement of the masculine prejudice he shared with other classical composers, told Bettina von Arnim, in 1812: "Emotion suits women only; (forgive me!) music ought to strike fire from the soul of a man."[82] Finally, however, the Romantic literary myth about music affected music itself, and when it did, the resulting music came to cherish and prolong harmonic ambiguity in much

81. Rosen, p. 98. I have used Rosen's convenient transcription of the music.
82. *Beethoven's Letters*, tr. Lady Wollane, vol. I, p. 110.

the way that Romantic poetry had celebrated and enacted syntactic ambiguity. The Romantic fascination with prolonged pursuit of the unattainable, of "something evermore about to be," found musical expression in the vaguer modulations of the composers in the generation after Beethoven. The literary myth about music had made itself a musical reality.

Literary Ideas and Romantic Music

A central tenet of this myth, as we have seen, was the notion that music moved by loosely associative connections from idea to idea; by combining this misconception of music with the myth of the primitive outcry and the psychological doctrine of the association of ideas, the Romantic poets arrived at the belief that a more fluid kind of organization would make a poem more moving, more productive of sentiment than a tighter formal or syntactic scheme. Musicians were initially resistant to this idea: in an account of his compositional method recorded by his earliest biographer, Haydn acknowledges the importance of emotions in the generation of melodic material (a function earlier assigned to them by Mattheson), but emphasizes his concern for construction and coherence in developing that material; he criticizes younger composers who employ looser structures as failing their listeners *at an emotional level:*

> I sat down [at the clavier], began to improvise, sad or happy according to my mood, serious or trifling. Once I had seized upon an idea, my whole endeavor was to develop and sustain it in keeping with the rules of art. Thus I sought to keep going, and this is where so many of our new composers fall down. They string out one little piece after another, they break off when they have hardly begun, and nothing remains in the heart when one has listened to it.[83]

Even when the adjective "romantic" began to be applied to composers, there was no immediate retreat from Haydn's ideal of development and continuity: E. T. A. Hoffmann—poet, composer, and influential essayist—claimed Haydn, Mozart, and Beethoven

---

83. In Griesinger's *Biographische Notizen,* tr. Gotwals, p. 61.

as "romantics," but was still particularly anxious to defend Beethoven from the charge of incoherent construction.

For Hoffmann, "romantic" was a heroic epithet, a vaguely defined but numinous way of praising the composers he valued. Here are some typical phrases from his essay on Beethoven's instrumental music (1813):

> [Music] is the most romantic of all the arts—one might almost say, the only genuinely romantic one—for its sole subject is the infinite. . . . Romantic taste is rare, romantic talent rarer still, and this is doubtless why there are so few to strike that lyre whose sound discloses the wondrous realm of the romantic.
>
> . . . Beethoven's music sets in motion the lever of fear, of awe, of horror, of suffering, and wakens just that infinite longing which is the essence of romanticism. He is accordingly a completely romantic composer.[84]

The idea that "infinite longing . . . is the essence of romanticism" may remind us of Keats, who gave that idea memorable form just seven years later:

> Bold Lover, never, never canst thou kiss,
> Though winning near the goal—yet, do not grieve;
> She cannot fade, though thou hast not thy bliss,
> For ever wilt thou love, and she be fair![85]

Like the passage from Wordsworth we examined before, these lines exemplify one of the ways poets expressed that "infinite longing," a suspended, ambiguous syntax: the syntactic break at the dash in the second line enacts the suspension of the lover's pursuit of the woman, and the poem as a whole achieves its unity by the association of a sequence of telling metaphors, not by tight, logical statement. This kind of poetry would soon have an effect on compositional technique, but Hoffman goes out of his way to rebuke those "knowing critics" who say that Beethoven ". . . no longer bothers at all to select or shape his ideas, but, following the so-called daemonic method, . . . dashes everything off exactly as

84. In Strunk, pp. 775, 777.
85. "Ode on a Grecian Urn," lines 17-20, following the text of Keats' *Poetic Works*, ed. Paul D. Sheats, p. 135.

his ardently active imagination dictates to him." How wrong this account is we know from the voluminous sketches Beethoven left behind, and Hoffmann, even without personal knowledge of Beethoven's methods, had the musical intelligence to grasp the care with which his pieces were constructed. He taunts the critics with the possibility that the fault may be in their ears, not in Beethoven's scores:

> Yet how does the matter stand if it is *your* feeble observation alone that the deep inner continuity of Beethoven's every composition eludes? (pp. 777–78).

What did Hoffmann mean by Beethoven's "deep inner continuity"? If he meant the way Beethoven's harmonic and formal techniques of development logically extend those of Haydn and Mozart, he was employing an aesthetic standard not unlike that of Haydn himself, and praising an aspect of Beethoven's genius whose ultimate results, the late piano sonatas and string quartets, he would not live to hear. But these highly abstract late works, so important to twentieth-century composers, were not adequately understood by nineteenth-century commentators, who eventually enshrined Beethoven as a Romantic revolutionary, a brave destroyer of outmoded forms, and a "tone-poet" whose Pastoral Symphony legitimized the idea of program music which came to fascinate so many of them. By this account, the continuity of Beethoven's works is emotional, "organic," or literary, and among the most amusing products of nineteenth-century music criticism are the plots or "programs" for various works of Beethoven concocted by his admirers. Of course, as Alfred Einstein reminds us, these ideas about Beethoven were incorrect, but like the equally incorrect notions about music cherished by the Romantic poets, they affected later art:

> The Romantics were of the opinion that in his last works—in the piano sonatas from Op. 101 to Op. 111, and especially in the last quartets—[Beethoven] had "burst form asunder"; and from this illustrious model they developed the idea that it was permissible or justifiable that they themselves should deal as freely as possible with form. As a matter of fact there is not—even in these last works of Beethoven—a single movement, a single measure, that does not rest on the strictest,

immanent musical logic, and that even in the most minute detail would call for extra-musical justification.[86]

In the essay we have been considering, Hoffmann tries to have it both ways. First he praises Beethoven's harmonic technique as an example of heroic self-control:

> The truth is that, as regards self-possession, Beethoven stands quite on a par with Haydn and Mozart and that, separating his ego from the inner realm of harmony, he rules over it as an absolute monarch.

But the next sentence uses a loaded analogy to Shakespeare and a full-blown statement of the metaphor of organic form to make what seems a quite different claim:

> In Shakespeare, our knights of the aesthetic measuring-rod have often bewailed the utter lack of inner unity and inner continuity, although for those who look more deeply there springs forth, issuing from a single bud, a beautiful tree, with leaves, flowers, and fruit; thus, with Beethoven, it is only after a searching investigation of his instrumental music that the high self-possession inseparable from true genius and nourished by the study of the art stands revealed. (p. 778)

In these juxtaposed incompatible accounts of the continuity of Beethoven's music, we may see the seeds of the musical debates of the next half-century. Was it intellectual craft or emotional energy that most accounted for Beethoven's greatness? Could an external referent—whether a single metaphor or a complex novelistic "program"—be as valid a method for organizing a piece as the tonal and formal methods of the late eighteenth century? Was program music, as F. A. Gelbcke argued in 1841, actually more "classic" than "romantic" in its attempt to depict objects?[87] Or was

---

86. *Music in the Romantic Era*, p. 66. Cf. pp. 81-85, a fuller account of the Romantic interpretation of Beethoven.

87. For an account of Gelbcke's heterodox article and Schumann's response to it, see the useful study of Leon Plantinga, *Schumann as Critic*, pp. 106-07. Plantinga's larger discussion of the different ways the term "romantic" was used (pp. 100-110) is instructive; we learn, for example, that Schumann declared himself "heartily sick of the term romantic, though I have not spoken it ten times in my entire life" (p. 104). A more opinionated discussion, on a somewhat larger scale, is the "interchapter" on "The Century of Romanticism" in Jacques Barzun's *Berlioz*, vol. I, pp. 369-98.

it, in its relative freedom from tonal and formal syntax, its use of an "organic" or "expressive" sequence of musical ideas, the closest musical equivalent to Romantic poetry?

While these issues were being debated, with considerable po-lemical passion, in the pages of such journals as Schumann's *Neue Zeitschrift für Musik,* practical developments strengthened the hand of the advocates of program music. The orchestra, which had been growing steadily in size and variety since the days of Stamitz's Mannheim ensemble, became even more powerful and versatile with improvements in bows, in woodwind construction, and in the level of playing. In the hands of a master like Berlioz, the increased dynamic and coloristic range of the orchestra made possible many fresh sounds and combinations, whose thrilling ef-fects could easily be exploited in the service of a literary program. All over Europe, concert halls were built to accommodate these large new orchestras and the larger audiences who came to hear them—audiences whose expectations differed dramatically from those of the aristocratic connoisseurs who had supported Haydn. As the French authority François Joseph Fétis pointed out, in a passage later quoted approvingly by Liszt, the expectations of these listeners were an important factor in the rise of program music:

> With the large audience, coloring will always pass as expres-sion, for unless it consist of individuals capable of forming an abstract ideal—something not to be expected of a whole au-ditorium, no matter how select it may be—it will never listen to a symphony, quartet, or other composition of this order without outlining a program for itself during the perform-ance, according to the grandiose, lively, impetuous, serenely soothing, or melancholy character of the music.[88]

Since such programmatic hearing was, in Liszt's opinion, inevi-table, he concluded (like Berlioz and a number of other compos-ers) that the right course was to exploit that tendency in the au-dience by providing explicit printed programs, as he did in the "symphonic poems" composed between 1849 and 1858.[89] He

88. In Strunk, p. 868.
89. See Einstein, pp. 69-70, 142-49.

came to believe that these pieces achieved a deep *union* of music and poetry, while song and opera were merely *combinations* of the two. And he criticized composers not employing programs as "mere musicians":

> The difference between the tone-poet and the mere musician is that the former reproduces his impressions and the adventures of his soul in order to communicate them, while the latter manipulates, groups, and connects the tones according to certain established rules and, thus playfully conquering difficulties, attains at best to novel, bold, unusual, and complex combinations. Yet, since he speaks to men neither of his joys nor of his sorrows, neither of resignation nor of desire, he remains an object of indifference to the masses and interests only those colleagues competent to appreciate his facility.[90]

The lineal descent of these opinions from Bardi's polemic against counterpoint and Addison's emphasis on the "Man of an ordinary Ear" should be clear; what is surprising is that the apparent disdain for compositional technique, at least for "established rules" and "complex combinations," comes now from a technically skillful composer, not from a musically naive poet.

Nor was the battle against rules, which Liszt and Berlioz thought of themselves as fighting in music, entirely over in literature. The French theatre, where the seventeenth-century rules had held sway longer than anywhere else, finally yielded, in 1830, to a play without Aristotelian structure, and with a richer panorama of scenes and characters, Victor Hugo's *Hernani*. Among the hirsute squadron of supporters who helped insure the success of this play was, appropriately enough, Hector Berlioz. Indeed, W. K. Wimsatt's generalization about Hugo's play might just as well have been written about Berlioz's music:

One concerns too, that

> An art formed on the principle of a vast assemblage of diversely interesting parts will tend to promote a certain looseness of relationship among such parts and in the parts themselves a certain extravagance of local coloring.[91]

90. In Strunk, pp. 861-62.
91. *Literary Criticism, A Short History*, p. 343. On Berlioz' support of Hugo, see Barzun, I, pp. 127-30.

434, in Knopf edition

The perceptible "looseness" of Romantic music is not only a matter of freer large-scale structure and coloristic orchestration; more fundamentally, it involves a loosening of harmonic syntax much like the loosening of verbal syntax we noted in Romantic poetry. To take but one example: the so-called diminished seventh chord, a pile of minor thirds capable of resolving plausibly in many different directions, becomes in Romantic music, most excessively in that of Liszt, a means for rapid, unstable, ambiguous modulation. Any classical composer would normally have moved from D major to C minor as follows:

Liszt and others in his generation were more likely to do so in this fashion:

The second chord of the first example, a dominant seventh, makes the third chord all but inevitable; but the second chord of the second example, a diminished seventh, might lead with equal plausibility to a resolution in E-flat major or A minor:[92]

A harmonic language in which diminished sevenths are as frequent as triads produces such displays of directionless energy as the following, from Liszt's *Bravour-Studien für Pianoforte* (1837–38):[93]

92. The different spellings of the diminished seventh chord do not alter its sound on the piano (thanks to equal temperament), and even in orchestral pieces, Romantic composers treated enharmonic equivalences (e.g. F-sharp and G-flat) very freely.

93. No. 7, "Eroica," as edited by Busoni for Liszt's *Musikalische Werke; Pianowerke* II, p. 44.

Tempo di Marcia. (Un poco meno.)

un poco marcato il canto

poco   *cresc.*

The only evidence that this piece is in a key is that it proclaims itself in one by means of a signature. When we finally reach E-flat, the announced key, at the "Tempo di Marcia," we reach it in 6-4 position, without root support, and after a crashing climax on B seventh, a chord which would, in tonal practice, have preceded E major, not E-flat. Even composers who did not flaunt chromatic ambiguity in this fashion, such as Schumann, whose language was much more triadic, nevertheless displayed a similar ambiguity about key relationships. Charles Rosen comments acutely:

> Schumann's music is not exceptionally chromatic, and yet there is an ambiguity of tonal relationships in his work that has no precedent in the half-century from 1775 to 1825. The opening piece of the *Davidsbündlertänze* shifts so rapidly and so frequently from G major to E minor as to destroy any clear feeling for a tonal center. . . . This lack of a central reference arises, like Chopin's chromaticism, from a weakening of the tonic-dominant polarity. There are phrases by Beethoven, particularly in the *Diabelli* Variations and in the late quartets, which display a chromaticism as radical as anything outside Gesualdo, but they all imply a firm diatonic structure as a background. With Chopin it is the background that shifts chromatically as well. In such a fashion, even the classical harmonic pun—the violent fusion of two different harmonic contexts—is no longer possible, as the context no longer has sufficient clarity of definition.[94]

We have already seen the earlier poetic analogue of this process, the way that the Romantic loosening of syntax rendered impossible the grammatical wit that had characterized Augustan poetry. The diminished seventh chord was to music what the adverbial clause beginning "where" or "when" was to Romantic poetry: a smoothly plausible way of continuing motion, a means to juxtapose and associate images or key-areas without committing oneself to one unequivocal grammatical relation between

---

94. *The Classical Style*, pp. 453-4. Perhaps this is the best point at which to add my voice to the chorus of praise for Rosen's extraordinary book, and to acknowledge a larger debt to him than even my frequent quotations may indicate. Anyone who wants to think seriously about Haydn, Mozart, and Beethoven must grapple with Rosen, whose skills as pianist, thinker, and writer inform every page of his work.

those elements. But it is a striking final irony that the composers who were using such means to blur the harmonic and formal conventions of the classical style, thus destroying its strong resemblances to poetry along the axis of construction and rigor, often did so in the name of programmatic expression, an attempt to make music resemble poetry along the axis of emotional or narrative communication. Over and over again in the writings of Liszt, Berlioz, Wagner, and Schumann we hear the names of Dante, Shakespeare, Goethe, and other writers invoked,[95] but the writerly successes aspired to by these composers are not rhetorical at all, though Dante and Shakespeare, as we have seen, were masters of rhetoric. Instead, the Romantic composers speak of the ability of these writers to cast a spell, to hypnotize, to carry us away into their fictional worlds. Scorning the harmonic and formal rigor of the classical style as slavish rule-following, though that style had given music an intrinsic grammatical meaning, they strove instead for a freer expression which would attain the ability of literature to tell moving stories.

Richard Wagner is the ultimate example of this process. His Prelude to *Tristan und Isolde* is sometimes described as the first atonal piece because of its extension of the techniques of harmonic ambiguity we have noted in other Romantic composers; the previous meanings of tonal harmonies are so transformed in this piece that dominant seventh chords become points of arrival. Yet the composer who could write this and other landmark works, the man whose purely musical innovations haunted at least two subsequent generations of composers, devoted much of his career to the idea of a *Gesamtkunstwerk,* a union of the arts, especially music and poetry, in the form of a great "music drama" whose "endless melodies" would express the high truths of the poetry he wrote himself. In the process of working out these ideas, in theory and in practice, Wagner necessarily retraced the steps of many earlier poets and composers; he also frequently contradicted himself. One could easily write a book about his various solutions to the basic problem of joining words and music; fortunately Jack

95. Berlioz wrote works inspired by Virgil, Shakespeare, Goethe, and many other writers; Liszt and Schumann, among others, also wrote works involving Goethe's *Faust.* Berlioz called Shakespeare, Goethe, and Beethoven the inspirers of the "great drama" of his life (see Barzun, vol. I, pp. 84-89).

Stein has already done so. Without pretending to anything like complete coverage, we may briefly indicate Wagner's place in our story by glancing at the development of his ideas on that topic.

Wagner's earliest critical essays express his contempt for Weber's close attention to details of prosody and instrumentation, and his preference for the more general melodic expressiveness of Bellini—a position that may remind us of the humanist critique of detailed word-painting and intricate counterpoint, and a position he soon abandoned. As late as 1840, in a dialogue modeled on the work of Hoffmann, he was maintaining that music could not express concrete ideas, and he was consequently rejecting program music, but in 1846 he published a fictional "program" for Beethoven's Ninth Symphony loosely based on Goethe's *Faust*, and praised Beethoven for turning to words in that work. In the operas of the 1840s—*The Flying Dutchman, Tannhäuser*, and *Lohengrin*—the texts move in and out of rhyme and metrical regularity, while the music begins to blur the distinction between recitative and aria. In *Tannhäuser*, some individual words receive imitative treatment; here is Tannhäuser, soaring along above the chorus:[96]

Der Lenz, der Lenz, mit tau-send hol-den Klängen zog ju- -

- -belnd in die See- - le mir!

[The spring, the spring, with a thousand pleasing sounds, came rejoicing into my soul!]

The word-painting on *"jubelnd,"* rejoicing, makes the conventional identification of motion and emotion we remember from the *Affektenlehre*. *Lohengrin*, by contrast, avoids such devices in favor of an obsessive replication of speech rhythm. As Stein concludes,

96. I follow the text edited by Natalia MacFarren. This is one of five instances of word-painting in *Tannhäuser* noted by Stein (see pp. 47-48), whose account of Wagner's early development as composer and poet, unscrupulously condensed here, is admirable. See especially pp. 12-13, 26, 40-41.

"Wagner was subordinating the music to the words at this period more fully than at any other time in his career" (p. 53).

But the impulse toward word-painting and the impulse toward accurate declamation were potentially in conflict, since imitative devices applied to a single word tend to distort its accentuation. One possible compromise had already been worked out by the composers of German *Lieder* in the generation before Wagner; their imitative devices usually took the form of repeating patterns in the accompaniment, not isolated colorations of individual words. Familiar examples in Schubert's settings of Goethe include the triplet figure in *"Erlkönig,"* for the galloping horse, and the busy sixteenth-notes in *"Gretchen am Spinnrade,"* representing the spinning wheel. Even when the voice participates in the imitation, the pattern extends beyond the single word, as in the beginning of another Schubert setting of Goethe, *"Die Spinnerin"*: [97]

97. I follow the text of *Schubert's Songs to Texts by Goethe,* ed. Eusebius Mandyczewski, adapting slightly the English translation by Stanley Applebaum given there. The other songs mentioned in this paragraph appear in the same collection. For some acute commentary, see the first two chapters of E. T. Cone, *The Composer's Voice.*

[While I spun quietly and peacefully, without any hindrance . . .]

A madrigal composer, even a Draghi, might have been especially careful to give the voice some busy notes on the verb *"spann,"* but Schubert can maintain the poetic form with a long note on that word, continuing the sixteenth-notes in the piano, because he has done at the level of the whole piece what word-painting composers tended to do locally. We have already seen the theoretical origins of this kind of expression in the preference of du Bos for imitation of sentiment rather than words. Schubert also had at his disposal the power of harmony: the sequence of keys in a cycle like *Die Schöne Müllerin* is at once a large tonal structure and an imitation of a sequence of emotions.

Wagner's solution, though boldly proclaimed as a new and original synthesis, was in one sense a grand extension of this basic compromise. By locating his imitative effects in the orchestra, Wagner avoided the rhythmic disruption of the vocal line by word-painting, and was able to give his singers rhythms close to those of speech. By eliminating entirely the division of an opera into separate numbers—recitatives, arias, duets, and so forth—he was able to organize his music-dramas on a much larger scale, not, as Mozart had, by a tonal sequence of keys, but by the repetition of brief programmatic phrases intended to depict a theme or image ("fire," "love," and the like). Although Wagner never used the term, these units came to be called *leitmotifs;* they remain one of the most controversial parts of his operatic technique. We may recognize them as a fulfillment of some of the goals of the *Affektenlehre.*

Wagner did not arrive at this solution in private. Instead, he paused in mid-career to write a series of tendentious and polemical works—*Art and Revolution* (1849), *The Work of Art of the Future* (1849), *Opera and Drama* (1850–51)—in which he insisted, directly contradicting his own earlier position, that music and poetry were inadequate by themselves, and had to be organically fused and combined. One part of the argument involved the claim that Beethoven's career had moved steadily toward words; another claim, which will again remind us of the musical humanists, was that Greek tragedy had been a perfect synthesis of the arts, a *Ge-*

samtkunstwerk which Wagner would now restore. But perhaps the most important theme in Wagner's prose of this period is the emphasis on emotion: feeling, not pictorial imitation or metrical exactness, is the basis on which words and music are to be united.[98] As Stein points out, "this premise made possible the adjustment of the relative importance of the poem and the music . . . for it brought with it automatically a significant increase in the importance of music, the language of emotions par excellence" (p. 69). In theory, there were two kinds of musical units in which the feelings were to be represented, the "motifs of reminiscence and presentiment," as Wagner called them: the "motifs of reminiscence" were conceived as recognizable phrases which, when repeated, would remind the audience of the words with which they had first appeared; the "motifs of presentiment," by contrast, had no verbal origin, though Wagner nonetheless trusted them to affect his hearers psychologically. In the emotionally charged, organically continuous stream of the *Gesamtkunstwerk,* regular rhymed verse could have no place, and Wagner now rejected it in language much like that Webb had used to attack couplets.

Such, in summary, was the theory. But when Wagner set out to put these new principles into effect, in the great "music-dramas" on which his reputation still rests, purely musical concerns forced some modifications. As Stein explains,

> . . . his practice departed almost at once from his theory. . . . About half of the motifs in *The Rhinegold* resemble the theory closely enough to be considered genuine motifs of reminiscence. *The Valkyrie* and *Siegfried* show a rapid departure from the technique. With *Tristan and Isolde* the phenomenon of leitmotif no longer bears much resemblance to the theoretical model. (p. 75)

For all Wagner's talk about fusing words or sentiments with music, the *leitmotif* technique actually brought the opera into the orbit of the Romantic symphony. Joseph Kerman, in an account of *Tristan* sensitive to its many virtues, makes this point quite forcefully:

> Wagner carried the organic ideal to a monstrous climax: a single, pulsing, theme-ridden ostensible continuity over four

---

98. For some intelligent generalizations about Wagner's theory and its importance for our culture, see Bryan Magee, *Aspects of Wagner.*

hours—over four evenings, even. Once opera in the nineteenth century had interested an *avant-garde* German composer like Wagner, it was bound to become strongly symphonic; for the motivic texture of the symphony
(characteristically the texture of the first-movement development section) dominated musical thought in Wagner's time as
melody did in the time of Handel, and declamation in the
time of Monteverdi. . . . Like Berlioz's symphonies, Wagner's
operas break down into passages of great eloquence and
power, loosely bound together. . . . Short suggestive motives
are the necessary material from which Wagner constructs his
dense symphonic web. They are always present, always busy,
recombined, reorchestrated, reharmonized, rephrased, developed. . . . [Such] material can be pushed too far. Wagner
was especially prone to this kind of bathos on account of the
arrogant length to which he pursued the technique. . . . In
Tristan und Isolde an added danger came from the family likeness of all the music within the lovers' sphere; it was fatally
easy to produce an overall impression of gum. (pp. 206–09)

Among many possible literary analogues, we might recall the way
virtually all the nouns in our pasage from Wordsworth's *Prelude*
become versions of each other. We might also remark that the
revolutionary harmonic modulations of *Tristan,* for all their organic and fluid effect, deprive the composer of any opportunity
to signal structure by tonal key-relations.

Combined and developed in essentially musical ways, the *leit-
motifs* in *Tristan* do not finally have much poetic meaning, though
their dramatic effect is often impressive. Jacques Barzun, in his
biography of Berlioz, makes this point with his usual destructive
wit, claiming that Wagner "repeat[ed] these fragments so tirelessly
that any character they might acquire by association was chewed
out of them as by the reiteration of a common word" (vol. II, p.
195). Stein makes the same point even more effectively by quoting
the climax of the love-duet, where we find Tristan and Isolde singing simultaneously and in canon, so that the text is obscured by
the simultaneous singing of different words.[99]

All this might simply be another ironic instance of the power
of music to transcend attempts to subordinate it to poetry, were it

99. *Richard Wagner and the Synthesis of the Arts,* pp. 141-44.

not for the way cultured Europeans were trained to hear these operas. Urged on by Hans von Wolzogen and other self-appointed guides, people actually tried to memorize all the *leit-motifs,* to acquire a kind of musical card file so that they could hear the repetitions and metamorphoses of the *leitmotifs* not simply as musical events but as parts of a complex programmatic or psychological meaning. Again, Barzun's account is amusing:

> Certainly no one had ever had to acquire such an apparatus of information for the enjoyment of any art as was required by Wagner's system, yet within fifteen years of Ludwig II's conversion to it, all educated Europeans were conscientiously cramming. Printed guides, magazines, societies, schools, and lectureships flourished; "leitmotif" was a new word in every language and the habit everywhere accepted of being *led* by motives not only through music but through literature, philosophy, and religion. (vol. II, p. 192)

The idea of imitation had taken on yet another form. We may wonder what Mersenne or Bach or Daniel Webb might have thought, had any one of them lived to see German ladies in opera boxes thumbing through their *"leitmotif"* charts in order to learn what passion was being portrayed in the orchestra below.

6

The Condition of Music

Introduction

Wagner's ideas, not to mention his success and his arrogance, were bound to produce opponents, whose works, whether in music or in words, were just as certain to be dismissed as reactionary by his convinced followers. So when Eduard Hanslick published his slender volume *Vom Musikalisch-Schönen (The Beautiful in Music)* in 1854, it was possible for Wagnerites to dismiss it as mere polemic, the product of Hanslick's known antipathy to Wagner and friendship for Brahms. But the importance of Hanslick's work transcends not only these personal relations but the immediate concerns of nineteenth-century music as well; as Morris Weitz argues, "it is to music what Hume's *Inquiry Concerning Human Understanding* is to speculative philosophy, a devastating critique of unsupportable views and an attempt to state clearly and precisely the territories and boundaries of the areas they discuss."[1] More than that: *The Beautiful in Music* separates and dismisses the various imitative and emotive notions about the function of music which Romantic thought had impressionistically blurred together; it boldly insists on music's autonomy, its independence not only from words (a battle already won in the eighteenth century) but from verbally definable feelings as well. The aesthetic position it stakes out is not only fundamental to twentieth-century thought about music, but strikingly similar to the literary aesthetics of I. A. Richards and the American New Critics.

For musicians, the idea of autonomy would prove a means of

---

1. In his introduction to the translation of Gustav Cohen, p. vii. All citations of Hanslick are from this edition.

liberating themselves from all kinds of imitative demands; as the coherence of classical Viennese instrumental music had given the quietus to the Renaissance claim that music's function was to serve or express words, Hanslick's doctrine would still the Romantic claim that its function was to express or imitate some specific emotion. Thus, in the course of his argument, Hanslick finds the recitative, the legacy of the Musical Humanists, a particularly convenient target:

> In the recitative, music degenerates into a mere shadow and relinquishes its individual sphere of action altogether. Is not this proof that the representing of definite states of mind is contrary to the nature of music, and that in their ultimate bearings they are antagonistic to one another? Let anyone play a long recitative, leaving out the words, and inquire into its musical merit and subject. (p. 40)

Two birds with one stone: not only does music "degenerate" when it makes itself the slave of words, but "the beautiful tends to disappear in proportion as the expression of some specific feeling is aimed at."

Poets, too, were interested in autonomy, though the word necessarily had a different meaning for them. As Hanslick proclaimed the independence of music from the demands of words or specific emotions, Edgar Allan Poe, in an essay first published in 1850, "allude[d] to the heresy of *The Didactic*," the claim that "the ultimate object of all Poetry is Truth."[2] The old doctrine that poetry had a duty to instruct as well as to please, like the doctrine that music had a duty to imitate something, took a variety of forms in the nineteenth century; W. K. Wimsatt distinguishes three—"the Shelleyan and Carlylean rhapsodic retort to scientism," a vigorous assertion that poetry also dealt in truth; "the Arnoldian neo-classic idealism," a prophecy that poetry would assume the functions of religion and philosophy; and "the socio-realistic propagandism" that would eventually harden into Soviet demands for "socialist realism."[3] Concerned to make a quite differ-

---

2. "The Poetic Principle," following the text of *The Complete Works of Edgar Allan Poe*, ed. James A. Harrison, vol. XIV, p. 271. All citations of Poe are from this volume.

3. *Literary Criticism, A Short History*, p. 476.

ent claim for poetry, Poe argues that it has nothing to do with truth:

> The demands of Truth are severe. She has no sympathy with the myrtles. All *that* which is so indispensable in Song, is precisely all *that* with which *she* has nothing whatever to do. It is but making her a flaunting paradox, to wreathe her in gems and flowers. In enforcing a truth, we need severity rather than efflorescence of language. We must be simple, precise, terse. We must be cool, calm, unimpassioned. In a word, we must be in that mood which, as nearly as possible, is the exact converse of the poetical. (p. 272)

A familiar ancient distinction, if one more or less absent from Western aesthetics since the Renaissance; it might be Plato or Augustine on music and rhetoric, with the striking difference that Poe chooses Song rather than Truth. His Greek and patristic forbears, arguing that eloquence and melody were incompatible with truth, had sought in vain to control the claims of beauty, even in their own writings, but Poe "define[s]. . . the Poetry of words as *The Rhythmical Creation of Beauty.*" And like many who would follow him, including (in their several ways) Pater, Wilde, Mallarmé, Verlaine, Pound, and Auden, Poe links poetry to music in the same gesture with which he separates it from didacticism:

> Contenting myself with the certainty that Music, in its various modes of metre, rhythm, and rhyme, is of so vast a moment in Poetry as never to be wisely rejected—is so vitally important an adjunct, that he is simply silly who declines its assistance, I will not now pause to maintain its absolute essentiality. (p. 274)

Twenty-three years later, in an essay on the painter Giorgione, Walter Pater would maintain that *"all art constantly aspires towards the condition of music."* [4]

There were powerful conceptual similarities between the musical and literary movements toward "autonomy." Central in both cases was the positing of some aspect of the mind between intel-

---

4. "The School of Giorgione," in *The Renaissance*, following the text of *The Works of Walter Pater*, vol. I, p. 135. All citations of Pater are from this volume.

lect and feeling, a three-part scheme where older accounts had only two. Thus Hanslick:

> It is rather curious that musicians and the older writers on aesthetics take into account only the contrast of "feeling" and "intellect," quite oblivious of the fact that the main point at issue lies halfway between the horns of this supposed dilemma. A musical composition originates in the composer's imagination and is intended for the imagination of the listener. (p. 11)

And Pater:

> Art . . . is always striving to be independent of the mere intelligence, to become a matter of pure perception, to get rid of its responsibilities to its subject or material; the ideal examples of poetry and painting being those in which the constituent elements of the composition are so welded together, that the material or subject no longer strikes the intellect only; nor the form, the eye or the ear only; but form and matter, in their union or identity, present one single effect to the "imaginative reason," that complex faculty for which every thought and feeling is twin-born with its sensible analogue or symbol. (p. 138)

Yet even in these obviously similar passages we see equally important differences: Hanslick is concerned to *separate* the imagination from feeling on the one side and intellect on the other, to establish an area of the mind from which music can be said to arise in the composer and to which it can be said to appeal in the listener, without either the claim that music is an intellectual language or the claim that it is a language of the feelings. Pater, by contrast, is concerned to *fuse* intelligence and sensuality, the mind and the ear, to produce his "imaginative reason." The movement toward musical autonomy was a movement toward abstraction, a declaration of independence from imitative demands; the movement toward poetic autonomy saw and admired in music not only its physical sensuality, but its abstraction as well. For Pater, music "most completely realises" his combining ideal, the "perfect identification of form and matter"; therefore "music, . . . and not poetry, as is so often supposed, is the true type or measure of perfected art" (p. 139). Hanslick, denying the capacity of musical form to express an external subject, makes a simpler claim: "the form (the musical structure) is the real substance (subject) of music—in fact is the music itself" (p. 92).

Hanslick's definition of autonomy can be more abstract than Pater's because the art he describes is finally more abstract; he can claim that structure simply *is* meaning, while Pater must necessarily talk about "welding" the two together. If, with Hanslick, we define the condition of music as the abstraction resulting from the essential neutrality and plasticity of its materials, we must recognize, as Pater's verb suggests, that poetry may *aspire* to that condition but cannot reach it. Words, as we have repeatedly seen, resist attempts to empty them of their ordinary morphemic content. I may write a poem in which the word "swan" comes to function as a symbol for some larger abstraction, but even a reader who understands my method will find it hard to read that word without some notion, however fleeting, of a large, white bird with a curved neck. By contrast, I may change utterly the meaning of a note or even a chord in a composition; I may do so within a theoretical system or (more radically) by changing the entire system. The note G may be the tonic of one tonal piece, but in another piece in another key, it will take on another function; and since, in music, function *is* meaning, the fact that G has been the tonic of some other piece will be entirely irrelevant. As Hanslick compactly puts it,

> The fundamental difference consists in this; while sound in speech is but a sign, that is, a means for the purpose of expressing something which is quite distinct from the medium, sound in music is the end, that is, the ultimate and absolute object in view. (p. 67)

W. H. Auden, in a poem entitled "The Composer," makes the same distinction from a poet's point of view:

> All the others translate: the painter sketches
> A visible world to love or reject;
> Rummaging into his living, the poet fetches
> The images out that hurt and connect.

> From Life to Art by painstaking adaption,
> Relying on us to cover the rift;
> Only your notes are pure contraption,
> Only your song is an absolute gift.[5]

Just how absolute or pure music could be has been proved in our century by a development Hanslick only dimly foresaw: the waning of the tonal system. Hanslick does acknowledge the speed with which music "uses up" its forms:

> Modulations, cadences, intervals, and harmonious progressions become so hackneyed within fifty, nay, thirty years, that a truly original composer cannot well employ them any longer, and is thus compelled to think of a new musical phraseology. (p. 58)

But he imagines, as anyone would have in 1854, that triads "will ever remain the indestructible foundation upon which all future development must rest" (p. 107). The first perception proved more accurate than the second: as a result of the harmonic innovations of Hanslick's arch-enemy Wagner, among others, triadic progressions, stable keys, and ordinary cadences began to seem "hackneyed." By the turn of the century it was possible to hear, in the music of composers all over Europe (Debussy and Scriabin, for example) such powerful motion away from tonality that triadic conclusions, when employed, seemed hollow gestures toward convention. And by 1910, Arnold Schönberg was announcing his abandonment of tonality in language which still echoes Pater's notion of a fusion of expression and form, and which sounds positively Romantic in its acknowledgement of an "inner compulsion":

> With the *George* songs I have for the first time succeeded in approaching an ideal of expression and form which has been in my mind for years. Until now, I lacked the strength and confidence to make it a reality. But now that I am conscious of having broken through every restriction of a bygone aesthetic; and though the goal toward which I am striving appears to me a certain one, I am, nonetheless, already feel-

5. "The Composer" (1938), following the text of Auden's *Collected Poems*, ed. Edward Mendelson, p. 148. All citations of Auden's poetry are from this edition.

ing the resistance I shall have to overcome; I . . . suspect that even those who have so far believed in me will not want to acknowledge the necessary nature of this development. . . I am obeying an inner compulsion which is stronger than any upbringing.[6]

The revolutionary changes wrought by Schönberg and others exposed as never before the limitations of the metaphorical description of music as a language. As Charles Rosen explains in his little book about Schönberg,

> The so-called "breakdown of tonality" at the end of the nineteenth century revealed to what extent this exterior stability [of the tonal system] was an illusion; more precisely, it was a construction that depended substantially on the individual works of music much more than a linguistic system depends on individual acts of speech. Music is only metaphorically a language; a single work of music may transform and even create an entire musical system, while no act of speech may do more than marginally alter language.
> If an individual work of music may alter and even create "language," then the conditions for understanding it must—at least partially—be made evident in the work itself.[7]

Thus, to adopt for a moment the famous distinction of the linguist Saussure,[8] the relation between a *parole*, an individual speech act, and the *langue*, or larger system, is quite different in poetry and in music. A word in a particular *parole*, even if that *parole* is a poem, will seem to most readers to refer inevitably to its dictionary meaning in the *langue*. But in music, each *parole*, each piece, must establish *within itself* the "conditions for understanding it." This was actually as true for Mozart as for Schönberg, but

6. Schönberg's program notes for the first performance of the *George-Lieder (Das Buch der Hängenden Gärten)*, as given in Willi Reich, *Arnold Schoenberg: A Critical Biography*, tr. Leo Black, p. 49.

7. *Arnold Schoenberg*, p. 19. Rosen's book is not only the most compact introduction available to the significance of Schönberg, but one of the most provocative books on twentieth-century music. All citations of Rosen in this chapter refer to this book.

8. Ferdinand de Saussure, *Course in General Linguistics*, tr. Wade Baskin, especially pp. 7–20.

the familiarity of the tonal *langue* implied by Mozart's *parole* made it possible to adopt the comforting but false assumption that the tonal system was a stable language in which individual pieces might be written. One could thus believe that even if music did not express words or feelings, it followed dependable syntactic rules, and thus had some kind of extrinsic referent. Atonal music, by depriving us of the comfort of triads and cadences, scalar and chordal relations, all that Rosen aptly terms "prefabricated material," forces us to confront and acknowledge the uniqueness of each piece. It fully validates Hanslick's claim that musical structure is musical meaning.

Hanslick's prophetic assertions, especially as validated by the ever more apparent autonomy of individual musical works, would thus seem to indicate a final unbridgeable gap between poetry and music. But in the very crisis brought on by the abandonment of "prefabricated material," Schönberg drew on poetic form to solve the urgent problems of length and organization. And when he finally solved those problems in a more purely musical way by devising the "twelve-tone" or "serial" method of composition, he employed some procedures closely related to older kinds of poetic construction: the retrograde, for example, one of the basic operations performed upon a twelve-tone row, is the "crab" or backwards ordering we noticed in the music of Machaut, which Schönberg heard in an early revival and praised for its constructive craft, a craft precisely paralleled in the anagrammatic devices of Machaut's poetry.

In poetry itself, Pater's words have not lost their validity: many of the nameable movements in French and English poetry of the late nineteenth and twentieth centuries may be usefully described as attempts to attain various metaphorical versions of the condition of music, motions toward musical technique along various axes; the poets and theorists of these movements, though not all of them have understood music with real precision, have usually acknowledged their desire to make poetry more like it.

The Parnassian poet Théodore Banville, for example, believed that poets should recover intricate medieval forms—rondels, rondeaux, ballades, and villanelles—forms with such demanding technical requirements that content would become subservient to "the implacable richness of the rhyme."[9] Since rhyme depends upon an accidental likeness between words, not a syntactic or morphological one, the French Parnassians and their English admirers were aspiring to the condition of music along the old axis of construction, the axis along which Schönberg would later proceed in borrowing formal hints from poetry. Writing a rondel necessarily entails choosing words for their rhymes and adjusting both syntax and content to accommodate words thus chosen; Swinburne's rondels provide some familiar examples of the possibilities and limitations of this kind of aspiration toward music, but it has been a method infrequently employed in the twentieth century, where the ideal of "sincerity" has made it difficult for poets to accept the constraints of intricate forms. But W. H. Auden, perhaps the preeminent virtuoso among modern English poets, not only mastered numerous older forms but invented equally difficult new ones, some of which show curious affinities with serial techniques; these poems demonstrate the continuing possibility for a technical influence between music and poetry, the usefulness of "contraption" even in a century whose characteristic poetic style is, as Auden admits, "Good Drab."[10]

The much more important Symbolist movement placed even greater emphasis on sound; James Robinson argues that "Mallarmé went on from Banville to conclude that the value of poetry lay more in the sound of words than in their sense,"[11] but Mallarmé's position was much more revolutionary than Banville's: given a choice between suggestiveness and clarity, Mallarmé chose suggestiveness; he even attacked the Parnassians as "deficient in mystery," apparently because their poems sometimes named objects:

> The Parnassians take something in its entirety and simply exhibit it; in so doing, they fall short of mystery; they fail to give our minds that exquisite joy which consists of believing that we are creating something. To *name* an object is largely to

9. See James K. Robinson, "A Neglected Phase of the Aesthetic Movement: English Parnassianism," *PMLA* 68 (1953): 740.

10. In his Salzburg Festival speech for 1968, published (in German, English, and French) under the title *Worte und Noten*, p. 37.

11. "English Parnassianism," p. 740.

destroy poetic enjoyment, which comes from gradual divina-
tion. The ideal is to *suggest* the object. It is the perfect use of
this mystery which constitutes symbol.[12]

For the Symbolists, the poem becomes a closed system, whose elements derive their meaning as much as possible from their place
in that single formal structure, as little as possible from their
everyday functions as names of things. Small wonder that Paul
Valéry described Symbolism as the "intention of several groups of
poets (not always friendly to one another) to recover from music
the heritage due to them."[13] In its fascination with sound, its hostility to ordinary syntax, and most of all its attempt to make the
poem a self-contained world, Symbolism was one of the most
thorough and serious attempts in history to push poetry in the
direction of music. The final, summarizing document of the
movement is aptly entitled *Four Quartets*.

So argues Hugh Kenner, explaining how Eliot and Pound,
both influenced by the Symbolist movement, developed in different directions:

> One poet moved out of Symbolism, one deeper into it.
> Commencing from the post-Symbolist nineties, Pound worked
> his way clear of systematized suggestiveness until his chief
> point of contact with 19th-century French verse was Théophile
> Gautier of the direct statement ("Carmen is thin") and his
> most Symbolist procedure an isolating of single words, not
> necessarily English. Eliot . . . worked more and more deeply
> into the central Symbolist poetic.[14]

But Pound's hygienic program for clearing away the Symbolist
mists was the use of the "image" (later the "vortex"), which he
defined as "that which presents an intellectual and emotional
complex in an instant of time."[15] In that definition we may still

---

12. In "The Evolution of Literature," an interview with Jules Huret published in
1891, following the text of *Mallarmé: Selected Prose Poems, Essays, and Letters*, tr. Bradford
Cook, p. 21. All citations of Mallarmé's prose are from this edition.

13. *Avant-Propos á la Connaissance de la Déesse* (1926); I quote the translation appearing
in Wallace Fowlie, *Mallarmé*, p. 268.

14. *The Pound Era*, p. 133.

15. In Pound's *Literary Essays*, ed. T. S. Eliot, p. 4.

hear the voices of Hanslick and Pater, the idea of an instantaneous fusion of intellect and emotion in a single image. Simultaneity is the axis along which this kind of poetry—whether we call it Imagism, Vorticism, or (more simply) the procedure of Pound—aspires to the condition of music. Pound's fascination with Chinese ideograms, beyond their alleged visual expression, lay in the fact that one ideogram might be made out of several others like a chord out of several notes. Joyce's *Finnegans Wake*, forging new words (new chords) from disparate linguistic elements, strains toward this kind of harmony, and Pound's *Cantos*, assembling the melodies of many times and tongues, strain toward a more contrapuntal simultaneity. Again Kenner has caught it: "A polyphony, not of simultaneous elements which are impossible in poetry, but of something chiming from something we remember from earlier, earlier in this poem and out of earlier poems, such is Arnaut's way—and such Pound's."[16]

As Kenner's aside acknowledges, actual polyphonic simultaneity is impossible in poetry, but the results of Pound's search for an equivalent are often impressive, as are the results of Mallarmé's attempt to make the poem a closed system, or the results of Auden's formal virtuosity. Hanslick's claim that music is not finally a language is correct, but these poets (like many of their predecessors) have seen in the musical possibilities for simultaneity, density, and design attractive models for poetry.

Similarly, the greatest of twentiety-century composers, while convinced of the autonomy of music, have not by any means cut themselves off from the expressive possibilities we associate with poetry. At the simplest level, we ought to remember that the revolutionary works of Schönberg's "Expressionist" period—the *George Lieder, Erwartung,* and *Pierrot Lunaire*—all employ texts, and that the *Sprechstimme* introduced in *Pierrot Lunaire,* while it dramatizes the difference between speech and song, acknowledges the expressiveness of spoken poetry by incorporating its shifting and uncertain pitch into a carefully designed musical setting. Schönberg was neither naive nor sentimental about the relations between music and poetry; many of his pronouncements on the subject

16. *The Pound Era*, p. 370.

sound the orthodox Hanslickian doctrine of autonomy. But his greatest scorn was reserved for music he took to be empty of expression; he was no cold-blooded mathematician.

The other giant among twentieth-century composers, Igor Stravinsky, chose a path often followed by poets: the renewal of past techniques. Reaching back past Romanticism, he regained some of the compression, wit, and irony of eighteenth-century art. But even when writing in a strictly diatonic idiom, Stravinsky manages to indicate that that idiom is a mask, a *persona;* he is arguably the most rhetorical composer who ever lived. Because older music was more frequently heard in the twentieth century than in the nineteenth, thanks to recording and greatly expanded publication, neo-classic procedures which had been available to poets for centuries—allusion, parody, burlesque—were newly available to twentieth-century composers, a situation brilliantly exploited by Stravinsky. But like Pound and Eliot, similarly eclectic poets, Stravinsky remains recognizably himself no matter what mask he assumes. The ultimate example of the power of his compositional personality to transcend convention is the marvelous twelve-tone music he wrote after the death of Schönberg, music in which he masters a new idiom just as deftly as he had earlier mastered the idioms of Gesualdo, Haydn, and American jazz. And if, like Schönberg, Stravinsky made severe claims for musical autonomy, he too continued to set texts. His *Shakespeare Songs,* for example, are at once explorations of serial technique and witty examples of imitative word-painting.

Indeed, the great danger for poets and composers in our time may be the tendency to respond to our recognition of the gap between music and poetry by exaggerating it, by withdrawing into isolation. The weakest twentieth-century music, the dead academic serialism of the 1950s, results from a rigorous working out of constructive principles and an ascetic disregard for expression; in aleatoric music, where some elements are determined by chance, this asceticism has become a kind of despair. The weakest twentieth-century poetry, the self-indulgent amoebic "free verse" of the little magazines, so values its supposed expressive "authenticity" that it abhors even minimal craft and construction. If there is one central lesson in the history traced in this book, it is that great music and great poetry invariably involve both construction

and expression. The healthy and accurate recognition by modern
theorists of the fundamental gap between the two arts—the fact
that music has by nature greater constructive resources, and poetry greater expressive resources—need not mean that analogies
between musical and poetic procedures are pointless. The pursuit
of such analogies, whether true or false, has been a factor in the
making of great works in both arts, and may in turn enrich our
understanding of them.

Versions of Autonomy: Hanslick and the New Critics

Richard Wagner's enterprise, as Hanslick recognized, was not a
pursuit of analogies between distinct arts but a thoroughgoing
attempt to merge the arts in a *Gesamtkunstwerk*. In a pointed personal version of the myth of Beethoven as "tone poet," Wagner
argued that Beethoven finally turned to texts, specifically to
Schiller's "Ode to Joy" in the final movement of the Ninth Symphony, because he had come to recognize that only the word
could give music the precise expressive meaning for which (according to Wagner) his earlier work had been searching.[17] With
reverent gestures in the direction of ancient Greek tragedy, Wagner declared that the music of the future must be combined with
poetry and dramatic spectacle. His opinions, as we have seen,
sometimes resembled those of the Renaissance musical humanists, though there is no evidence that Wagner knew their work; in
any case, Wagner was a much more influential spokesman for
these ideas than Bardi or Baïf: not only was he an able propa-
gandist, but he was an important composer whose significant musical innovations suggested that his opinions should be taken seriously.

For Hanslick, however, Wagner's operas were a "violation of
music by words,"[18] and the metaphor of rape seems intentional.

17. See the excerpts from "The Music of the Future," in Strunk, *Source Readings in
Music History*, pp. 886–99. Hanslick answers this argument in a long footnote (pp. 68–69);
Debussy, in one of the essays in *Monsieur Croche the Dilettante Hater* ("The Symphony"), in
which he argues that "there was not an ounce of literature in Beethoven," and that
"Schiller's lines can have only been used for their appeal to the ear." See *Three Classics in the
Aesthetics of Music*, pp. 16–17.
18. In *Aus meinem Leben*, quoted and translated in Stewart Deas, *In Defence of Hanslick*,
p. 20.

In order to explain his opposition to Wagner without seeming merely personal, Hanslick constructs a careful and skeptical philosophy of music, a philosophy whose main points are negative: he denies the validity of a number of conventional ways of discussing music, insisting instead on an aesthetic perspective which acknowledges music's autonomy and discusses music in musical terms. Some of his main points reappear in the equally skeptical, negative, and liberating literary aesthetics of the so-called New Critics.

Romantic composers of program music, like the Musical Humanists of the Renaissance, couched much of their talk about music in the language of emotion; they spoke of the power of music to express a composer's emotions or to arouse a listener's emotions. Hanslick, while quite careful to acknowledge that "music operates on our emotional faculty with greater intensity and rapidity than the product of any other art" (p. 77), nonetheless insists that "definite feelings and emotions are unsusceptible of being embodied in music" (p. 21). He separates and rejects what the New Critics would call the "intentionalist" and "affectivist" arguments:

> On the one hand it is said that the aim and object of music is to excite emotions, i.e., pleasurable emotions; on the other hand, the emotions are said to be the subject matter which musical works are intended to illustrate.
>
> Both propositions are alike in this, that one is as false as the other. (p. 9)
>
> Aesthetic investigations must above all consider the beautiful object, and not the perceiving subject. (p. 8)

Even though Hanslick claimed (perhaps disingenuously) that the principle of concentration on the object had already been established in the aesthetics of the other arts, it took many years for literary critics to achieve a similarly rigorous insistence on separating the aesthetic object from the responses of its perceiver or the intentions of its maker. And when Monroe Beardsley and W. K. Wimsatt gave those principles their most exacting formulation—in the essays on "The Intentional Fallacy" and "The Affective Fallacy"[19]—they acknowledged their indebtedness to Han-

19. Now most conveniently available in Wimsatt's *The Verbal Icon*, pp. 3–39.

slick by choosing as an epigraph for the latter essay a cutting *reductio ad absurdum* from Hanslick's attack on musical affectivisim: "We might as well study the properties of wine by getting drunk" (p. 13). The essay on intentionalism contains no explicit quotations from Hanslick, but closely follows the opinions he expressed in passages like these:

> The beautiful, strictly speaking, aims at nothing. (p. 9)
>
> In music there is no "intention" that can make up for "invention." (p. 59)
>
> The limits to which a musical composition can bear the impress of the author's own personal temperament are fixed by a preeminently objective and plastic process. (p. 75)

Neither Hanslick nor his New Critical heirs would want to deny that poets and composers have intentions, or that their works may affect us powerfully; they are united in recognizing that neither of these phenomena "possesses the attributes of inevitableness, exclusiveness, and uniformity that a phenomenon from which aesthetic principles are to be deduced ought to have" (p. 15).

Hanslick takes a similar position about pleasure; he acknowledges its occurrence but denies its relevance to aesthetic investigation:

> If the contemplation of something beautiful arouses pleasurable feelings, this effect is distinct from the beautiful as such. I may, indeed, place a beautiful object before an observer with the avowed purpose of giving him pleasure, but this purpose in no way affects the beauty of the object. The beautiful is and remains beautiful though it arouse no emotion whatever, and though there be no one to look at it. (pp. 9–10)

Here the most striking literary analogue comes in the *Principles of Literary Criticism* of I. A. Richards (1928):

> It is no less absurd to suppose that a competent reader sits down to read for the sake of pleasure, than to suppose that a mathematician sets out to solve an equation with a view to the pleasure its solution will afford him. The pleasure in both cases may, of course, be very great. But the pleasure, however great it may be, is no more the aim of the activity in the course of which it arises, than, for example, the noise made by a motor-cycle—useful though it is as an indication of the way

the machine is running—is the reason in the normal case for its having been started.[20]

For both Hanslick and Richards, pleasure is at least as unsatisfactory a basis for aesthetic principle as intention or affect; it is a by-product of musical or poetic objects they would advocate studying in a more purely analytical way.

But Hanslick's most important point was one which could have no literary analogue: the denial of past and present attempts to describe music as a language. In a passionate conclusion to a long discussion of this point, Hanslick points to the "mischievous practical consequences" of

> . . . those theories which try to impose on music the laws of development and construction peculiar to speech, as in former days, Rameau and Rousseau, and in modern times the disciples of Richard Wagner, have endeavored to do. In this attempt the life of the music is destroyed, the innate beauty of form annihilated in pursuit of the phantom "meaning." One of the most important tasks of the aesthetics of music would, therefore, be that of demonstrating with inexorable logic the fundamental difference between music and language, and of never departing from the principle that, wherever the question is a specifically musical one, all parallelisms with language are wholly irrelevant. (p. 70)

This stringent denial of all metaphorical attempts to describe music as a language is central to Hanslick's stated purpose: the establishing of musical "autonomy." But advocates of poetic "autonomy," as we have seen, made much of metaphors comparing poetry to music; here we confront a semantic inconsistency at least as ironic and revealing as those conflicting definitions of "imitation" in the eighteenth century. For Hanslick and the twentieth-century musicians who came to accept his doctrine, musical autonomy meant an escape from the extraneous requirement that music "mean" something which might be verbalized; for Poe, Wilde, and Pater, poetic autonomy meant an escape from a criticism centered on subject matter, and one of the most common and powerful ways to express what that escape might mean for

---

20. This and subsequent citations follow a later edition (1955), p. 97.

poetry was to talk of aspiring to the condition of music. Even Richards, whom we hardly think of as a pale aesthete, sounds very much like Poe in drawing a clear line between poetry and truth:

> It is evident that the bulk of poetry consists of statements which only the very foolish would think of attempting to verify. . . . Even when they are, on examination, frankly false, this is no defect. (p. 272)

And in seeking to explain why T. S. Eliot's poems were misread by those seeking a logical or intellectual structure, he falls back on the analogy to music:

> If it were desired to label in three words the most characteristic feature of Mr. Eliot's technique, this might be done by calling his poetry a 'music of ideas.' The ideas are of all kinds, abstract and concrete, general and particular, and, like the musician's phrases, they are arranged, not that they may tell us something, but that their effects in us may combine into a coherent whole of feeling and attitude and produce a peculiar liberation of the will. (p. 293)

Ironically, the analogy leads Richards into an affectivist account of music that Hanslick would surely have rejected: another example of the tendency for poets and critics marching under the banner of autonomy to encourage loose analogies to music, while musicians marching under a similarly labeled banner have discouraged descriptions of music as a language. This inconsistency is not merely amusing; it ultimately confirms a basic difference between the arts, as does the fact that Hanslick's position has become something like orthodoxy among twentieth-century composers, while the tough Hanslickian positions of Beardsley and Wimsatt have met a constant and ingenious opposition from poets and literary critics.[21] To put it as simply as possible, most people cling more tightly to intentional and affective claims as ways of discussing poetry than as ways of discussing music, and they think of subject matter as a primary category for describing a poem. If you tell me that you have just read an interesting poem, I am

21. For a summary of replies to "The Intentional Fallacy," with a vigorous rebuttal, see the essay entitled "Genesis: An Argument Resumed" in Wimsatt's posthumous collection, *Day of the Leopards*, pp. 11–39.

likely to ask you what it was "about," and your answer may well include some remarks about what the poet was "trying to do" and how the poem moved you; if you tell me that you have just heard an interesting piece of music, I cannot so easily inquire about its subject matter, and your only satisfactory answer to such an inquiry would be to sing or whistle some remembered portion of the musical material. Nor would claims about the composer's intentions or the music's emotional impact on you tell me very much about the piece; its notes would remain "pure contraption." And even the coiner of that phrase, for all his respect for composers, recognized the limits on poetry's aspirations toward music, its ultimate duty to say something. In "The Cave of Making," he admits to the ghost of Louis MacNeice:

> I should like to become, if possible,
> a minor atlantic Goethe,
> with his passion for weather and stones but without his silliness
> re the Cross: at times a bore, but,
> while knowing Speech can at best, a shadow echoing
> the silent light, bear witness
> to the Truth it is not, he wished it were, as the Francophile
> gaggle of pure songsters
> are too vain to. We're not musicians: to stink of Poetry
> is unbecoming, and never
> to be dull shows a lack of taste. (pp. 522–23)

Poetry, by this account, is not truth, but its aspirations toward truth-telling are as much a part of its problematic identity as its aspirations toward musical purity. Auden is making at the level of the whole art the same point Hanslick made earlier at the level of fundamental materials: that notes are plastic and neutral, while words mean things, even if we wish they did not.

Pure Contraption

Hanslick's insistence that music means itself has gained its wide acceptance not merely because of his logic and passion, but because the actual development of twentieth-century music has confirmed as never before the autonomy of that art. Just as it took the development of a successful, independent instrumental music to invalidate the old claim that music's true function was to express specific words, it now took the development of a serious

music free from the conventional literary associations of tonal materials to invalidate the more stubborn claim that music's function
was to express or arouse specifiable emotions. In 1911 Ferruccio
Busoni spoke for many composers in complaining about the severe limitations of the major and minor modes, and of their conventional characters:

> Upon the two Series of Seven, the major key and the
> minor key, the whole art of music has been established; one
> limitation brings on the other.
>
> To each of these a definite character has been attributed;
> we have learned and have taught that they should be heard
> as contrasts, and they have gradually acquired the signifi-
> cance of symbols:—Major and Minor—Maggiore e Minore—
> Contentment and Discontent—Joy and Sorrow—Light and
> Shade. The harmonic symbols have fenced in the expression
> of music, from Bach to Wagner, and yet further on until to-
> day and the day after tomorrow. *Minor* is employed with the
> same intention, and has the same effect upon us now, as two
> hundred years ago. Nowadays it is no longer possible to "com-
> pose" a funeral march, for it already exists, once for all.[22]

Busoni's proposed solutions, which include 113 new scales and
plans for a microtonal notation, have not been widely followed,
but his sense of the problem tallies with the complaints of many
other composers around the turn of the century. As Wagner's music seemed to demonstrate, the traditional means for achieving
expressive effects within tonality, increased chromaticism, could
so weaken tonality as to deprive the composer of his traditional
means of construction, the sense of a key. Roger Sessions sums up
the impasse:

> As the cadence, in the early years of this century, came to
> acquire for composers more and more the aspect of a cliché,
> and as the composers found themselves more and more
> obliged to discover other means of achieving musical articu-
> lation, they found themselves obliged to discover new prin-
> ciples of contrast as well. They discovered that in the absence

22. In his intriguing *Sketch of a New Esthetic of Music*, also in *Three Classics in the Aesthetics of Music*, pp. 90–91.

of strictly triadic harmony it was virtually impossible to establish a feeling of key sufficiently unequivocally to make possible a genuine and definitive change of key, and that hence
tonality was for them no longer sufficient as a principle of
structure.[23]

The situation Sessions describes is not merely a matter of theory
or history. Many actual pieces of music dramatize the crisis, none
more impressively than Alban Berg's one-movement piano sonata, op. 1 (1904). Haunted by *Tristan*, as was so much of the music in its period, this remarkable work seeks a way to continue the
expressive development of chromaticism without abandoning
tonal grammar. As Eric Salzman points out, "the real structure of
the piece derives from the extreme prolongation of expected
resolution,"[24] but the final triadic conclusion in B minor seems an
empty and despairing gesture. It is reached, to be sure, by a version of tonal voice-leading, but it is only in the narrowest sense a
resolution; no tonal cadence could satisfactorily resolve the ener-
gies generated by the kind of dissonance reached at the climax of
the development, shown on the facing page.[25] And Berg acknowledged that truth; this composition is his last tonal piece. Anyone
who still wonders why composers had to abandon the tonal system
can receive a complete answer, an answer superior to any verbal
analysis, simply by listening to this piece with open ears. The mu-

23. "Problems and Issues Facing the Composer Today," in *Problems of Modern Music*,
ed. Paul Henry Lang, pp. 26–27.

24. In his excellent liner notes for the fine recording by Beveridge Webster on the
Dover label; the record number is HRC-ST-7285.

25. Following the text of the Universal Edition, p. 7.

sical structure of Berg's sonata is its true subject, as Hanslick had postulated of music in general, and that structure demonstrates the final limits of tonality.

It also demonstrates, as do the revolutionary developments of the ensuing decades, the limits of any description of music as a language. A poet seeking to emulate Berg's sonata might have written despairingly about the sad incompetence of human speech, as Wordsworth had, but in order to make his poem enact that impasse as Berg's work enacts the crisis of tonality, he would have had to risk incomprehensibility; as we shall see, various versions of this problem recur in twentieth-century poetry. But no group of poets could do what Schönberg, Berg, and Webern did: alter profoundly and decisively the fundamental procedures of their art with a few individual pieces. Poetic change is limited by the relative stability of the ordinary prose language from which most of a poet's words must be drawn; but in music, as the Viennese composers proved by abolishing at a stroke a system which had been considered a language, there really is no exterior language. Describing music as a language, as this book has often done, can have some pedagogical utility, but as Hanslick insisted and Schönberg demonstrated, that useful metaphor, if taken too far, may blind us to the real and serious differences between the two arts. The reactionary protest, "this is not music," which has been hurled at many important works (including Beethoven's late quartets), has a peculiar irony when applied, as it still is, to the music of the Vienna School, for there is a particular sense in which these composers have demonstrated what music *is* more powerfully than ever before.

Many composers came to see the necessity for moving beyond tonality; abandoning scales, and cadences, and "prefabricated material" was doubtless, as Schönberg acknowledged, an irresistible compulsion; but it must also have been terrifying. Not only were these composers stepping off into an abyss where the conventional expressive values of, say, major and minor would no longer be available, but they were leaving behind as well the constructive utility of keys and modulations, the organizing principle of the tonic-dominant polarity, even the comforting capacity of harmony to control rhythmic events. As Rosen points out:

The renunciation of the symmetrical use of blocks of elements in working out musical proportions placed the weight
on the smallest units, single intervals, short motifs.

The expressive values of these tiny elements therefore
took on an inordinate significance; they replaced syntax.
(p. 21)

But without a larger system to organize them, these tiny elements
could not sustain a large structure; small wonder that, as
Schönberg later explained, his first atonal pieces, and those of
Berg and Webern, were characterized by "extreme expressiveness
and . . . extraordinary brevity."[26] Schönberg's first solution to this
problem involved explicit dependence on the structure of chosen
poetic texts: "a little later," he writes, "I discovered how to construct larger forms by following a text or a poem" (p. 106). In the
George Lieder and *Pierrot Lunaire,* for example, the lines and stanzas of the poems mark out sections of the musical setting, as key
areas or symmetrical phrase lengths had normally marked out
sections in tonal music. In both these works, changes in musical
character (density of texture, complexity of rhythm) tend to coincide with line-breaks in the poem, not because Schönberg is setting the matter of the poem in any doggedly imitative fashion, but
because he has chosen to let its form order his musical material.

But this solution, however fascinating as another example of
the kind of relations we have been studying throughout this book,
was doomed to be temporary. The problems of length, structure,
and comprehensibility posed by the escape from tonality had to
be solved in a purely musical way, and in the 1920s Schönberg
solved them in a way that has proved decisive for twentieth-
century music: he devised a system of composition based on a
series of twelve tones. This is not the place for a complete exposition of his complex and frequently misunderstood technique, to
which there are a number of excellent guides,[27] but a few basic

26. In his essay on "Composition with Twelve Tones," available in *Style and Idea,* tr.
Dika Newlin, p. 105.

27. Chapter IV of Rosen is a convenient starting place; George Perle, *Serial Composition and Atonality,* is a standard basic book; for the mathematically literate, Milton Babbitt's
essay "Twelve-tone Invariants as Compositional Determinants," in the Lang collection, pp.
108–21, gives a precise description. All have aided the discussion which follows.

points may help us understand why this development was so important.

1. In twelve-tone composition, the composer devises a particular ordering of the twelve pitch-classes; here, for example, is the row for Schönberg's Piano Suite, op. 25:

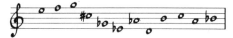

This series of pitches may be stated melodically, but it is not a melody in the traditional sense of having a fixed contour. It is an order of pitch-classes, not an order of pitches; i.e., the octave in which any pitch-class is stated is not fixed, so that this is an equally satisfactory statement of the same row:

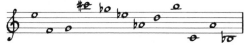

From this row may be derived three other related orderings: the inverse, in which each of the intervals is inverted (so that the rising half-step with which the row begins, for example, becomes a falling half-step),

the retrograde, in which the original pitches are stated in reverse order,

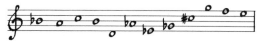

and the retrograde-inverse, which is the retrograde of the inverse

The composer may also use any one of these forms in any transposition; i.e., he may begin on a different pitch and proceed with the same series of intervals. There are thus 48 possible versions of the row, and the one we call the "original" has no real priority, since any one of the other versions would generate the same 48 versions if put through the same operations.

2. In mathematical terms, the twelve-tone system is permu-

tational, whereas the tonal system had been combinational. That is, in the tonal system, the notes of the chosen key are the norm; notes outside the key ("accidentals") occur less frequently and normally require resolution. But in the twelve-tone system, no matter what the chosen row, all twelve tones are equal: the universe of any twelve-tone piece is total chromatic space; the ordering of that space which the composer enforces by devising a row is one of factorial twelve (i.e., 12 x 11 x 10 . . . x 1) possible permutations.[28] And even that one unique permutation, as we have seen, generates 48 distinct series, a rich and organically connected source from which a composer may generate melodic material, *and* an equally fertile source for the structural relations needed to sustain longer pieces.

3. "Composition with twelve tones," wrote Schönberg, "has no other aim than comprehensibility,"[29] and in practical terms, composers have learned that *limiting* the materials they use makes their pieces more accessible. Poets, with their vast resources of vocabulary, have long understood this aesthetic principle; as David Thorburn puts it, "all serious literature is grounded in the paradox that variety, fullness, and resonance are achieved by strategies of constraint and exclusion."[30] The history of twelve-tone technique is a history of such strategies of exclusion: a composer may limit the number of transpositions used, as Schönberg does in op. 25, where he employs only the transposition at the interval of the tritone; he may "partition" the row into six-note "hexachords" or even smaller fragments in order to explore intensely the relations among a smaller group of pitch-classes; he may devise a row with special internal relationships, for example one whose second hexachord is a transposition of the first.[31]

The fact that we need mathematical and technical terms to achieve even this simplified account of twelve-tone technique confirms its freedom from literary associations of the nineteenth-century sort. Not only did the new system invalidate the literary analogies conventionally applied to instrumental music; it also de-

28. See Babbitt, pp. 109–10.
29. "Composition with Twelve Tones," p. 103.
30. In the introduction to his anthology, *Initiations*, p. vii.
31. Such a row has the property of "combinatoriality," widely explored by Schönberg after 1930 and others since his death; see Rosen, pp. 90–91.

cisively altered the setting of texts in vocal music. The functions tonal harmony and scalar melody had served in text-setting, expressive and constructive, had to be replaced by new relations, newly worked out. One basic approach, doubtless suggested by the mathematical rigor of the new system, was to seek relations with poetry along the old axis of construction, rediscovering patterns like those we examined in medieval music.

We may see the change with poignant clarity in Berg's two settings of a poem by Theodor Storm, *"Schliesse mir die Augen beide."* The first version, a tonal piece written in 1900 (before the piano sonata), may remind us of Schumann; the second, written in 1925, is Berg's first exercise in twelve-tone composition, employing the same row he later used for the Lyric Suite.[32] Here is the opening of the setting of 1900:

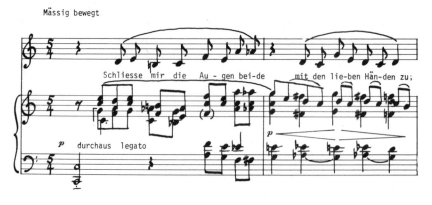

32. See the appendix by H. F. Redlich to the Universal Edition, from which this excerpt is taken.

[Close my two eyes with your beloved hands; all I suffer turns to peace beneath your touch.]

The piano part is in every sense an accompaniment: its predictable cadences on the dominant and the relative minor at the ends of the lines confirm the poetic form, as do the symmetries of the melodic contour. The E reached on the first syllable of "*deiner Hand*," your hand, is the highest vocal pitch in the whole song, a deft piece of expression for an altogether gentle, even sentimental love long. In 1925, all is changed utterly:

No comforting cadences, peaceful harmonies, or easy symmetries. The piano begins by arpeggiating the pitches of the second half of the row while the voice is stating the first half melodically; the syncopations in bars 3 and 4, contradicting the rhythm of the voice, suggest an equivalent rhythmic independence. The voice reaches the twelfth pitch of the row on the low B-natural of the second syllable of *"lieben"*; the leap from that note to the high F, the widest of many wide leaps in the voice part, strongly separates the first two statements of the row, but it also separates an adjective (*"lieben,"* dear) from its noun (*"Händen,"* hands). Considered from the point of view of traditional expression, the relations between the text and its setting seem highly arbitrary; one wonders whether the composer has considered the text at all in making his musical decisions.

But a closer look at the whole piece reveals some intricate correspondences along the old axis of construction. The complete text, 8 lines of poetry with 7 or 8 syllables per line, totals 60 syllables, and Berg has set it with 5 statements of a twelve-tone row, 60 pitches. A chart may illustrate how the two systems of ordering meet at the end:

line 1	Row I	8 syllables
line 2	Row II 4 3	7 syllables
line 3		8 syllables
line 4	Row III 1 6	7 syllables
line 5	Row IV 6 1	7 syllables
line 6		8 syllables
line 7	Row V 3 5	8 syllables
line 8		7 syllables

The close affinities between this kind of construction and the isorhythmic techniques of Philippe de Vitry (see above, ch. 3) are obvious: the poetic line-length here functions as a *talea;* the row

as a *color*. Two years earlier, Schönberg, who had declared his admiration for Vitry and Machaut, had set up similar relations between poetic lines and twelve-tone rows in his Serenade (opus 24).
In the fourth movement of that piece, Stefan George's German
version of a Petrarch sonnet is set as a bass solo. The 14 lines each
have 11 syllables, and the pitches of the voice part are repetitions
of a row, but since each line requires one pitch less than a complete row, each line begins on a different pitch, until the cycle
repeats at line 13; Schönberg signals this repetition by repeating
for that line the exact pitches of line one, not merely the pitch-
classes.

These pieces are not isolated examples. Even when not setting texts, modern composers have tended to find analogies between their technique and poetic technique along constructive
lines. Ernst Krenek, for example, accurately identifies the sestina
of Arnaut Daniel as "a serial form of poetry [whose] essential
principle is rotation."[33] The idea of a retrograde, another basic
serial procedure, has a poetic analogue in the palindrome; grammatical "inversion," in most Western languages, helps poets manipulate their materials to achieve symmetry, chiasmus, or rhyme;
and the triple ballade of Compiègne (discussed above in ch. 3)
provides a close poetic analogue to the principle of "partitioning."
At an even more basic level, the fundamental tension in poetic
form, in which syntactic units (phrases, clauses, sentences) do or
do not conform to formal units (lines, couplets, stanzas), is reen-
acted in twelve-tone music, whether or not a text is employed.
Phrase-lengths dictated by motivic or rhythmic or even expressive
considerations can force enjambments of various statements of
the row, just as poetic line-lengths do in the examples we have
been considering. Indeed, a twelve-tone piece in which each complete statement of the row was a complete phrasal unit would be
as deadly as a fully end-stopped poem.

The Axis of Construction

When modern poets have sought to emulate music along constructive lines embracing various kinds of formal complexity, they

33. In his essay on "Extents and Limits of Serial Techniques," in the Lang collection,
p. 85.

have often wished to escape critical fixations on the politics, morality, truth, or "sincerity" of their subject matter. We have already
seen how that kind of analogy to music helped Poe attack "the
heresy of *The Didactic,*" and in France, where Poe's influence was
to prove most powerful, Gautier had declared as early as 1835
that "form is everything." A group of poets called the Parnassians,
formed in the 1860s, built an entire aesthetic theory on that principle. Reaching back to Villon and Ronsard, as Schönberg later
reached back to Machaut, Théodore Banville devoted himself to
virtuoso forms ultimately derived from the troubadour tradition.[34] The title page of his *Améthystes* (1862) describes the contents as "composed according to the rhythms of Ronsard,"[35] and
since those rhythms were musical in origin, we may think of Banville as cheerfully writing new words to an old tune, insisting on
the primacy of form in order to deflect critical attention from the
contents of such lines as these:

> Vois, sur les violettes
> Brillent, perles des soirs,
> De fraîches gouttelettes!
> Entends dans les bois noirs,
> Frémissants de son vol,
> Chanter le rossignol.
>
> Reste ainsi, demi-nue,
> A la fenêtre; viens,
> Mon amante ingénue;
> Dis si tu te souviens
> Des mots que tu m'as dits
> Naguère, au paradis! (pp. 20-21)

[Look, on the violets / Sparkle, pearls of the evening, / Fresh
dewdrops! / Hear from the dark woods, / Trembling in his

---

34. See Robinson, "English Parnassianism," pp. 738–40. Gautier's declaration came
in his book on Victor Hugo, and took another form in 1857 in his famous poem "L'Art."
35. "Composées sur des rhythmes de Ronsard." This and subsequent citations follow
the original edition, the first of whose three title pages frames the word AMETHYSTES with
four logos consisting of the inverse of Banville's initials (i.e., ꞁꓭ).

flight, / The nightingale singing. // Stay that way, half-naked, / At the window; come, / My innocent lover; / Say if you remember / The words you said to me / Before, in paradise!]

In the troubadour tradition, as we have seen, a similar concentration on form produced a similar freezing of content, but in Victorian England, where the moral criticism of Arnold and Ruskin was dominant, the issue was not the conventional emptiness of the first stanza but the "indecency" of the second, for which the perfection of the rhyme between *"demi-nue"* and *"ingénue"* was no justification. When Swinburne, among others, began to employ such old French forms, he did so (as Robinson puts it) "defiantly, with accusations of indecency and atheism exploding in his ears." Tennyson referred to the intricate stanzas as "poisonous honey stol'n from France,"[36] a phrase in which we may hear not only Victorian prudishness but a distant echo of eighteenth-century British attitudes toward seductive "foreign" music; this suspicion of continental "art for art's sake" was apparently still alive in 1964, when Auden glanced disparagingly at the "Francophile gaggle of pure songsters."

But the real aesthetic issue raised by Parnassian poetry is neither moral nor national: it is the poetic imbalance between form and content produced when a poet commits himself to a stanza requiring repeated rhymes on the same syllable. Under these circumstances, the poet must find not only a number of words for each of his rhyming sounds, but a structure of meaning in which he may logically use the rhymes he has found; as Banville's phrase about the "implacable richness" of rhyme suggests, formal considerations may alter or even control the poem's content.[37] The metaphor of "organic form," plausible enough when applied to Wordsworth's blank verse, cannot apply to any rondel, though the successful rondel will minimize the strain between form and meaning. Consequently, such poems often work best when taking

36. See Robinson, pp. 738, 733. Tennyson's phrase comes in the "Epilogue to the Queen" (1873).

37. For a very full discussion of this point, see John Crowe Ransom's famous essay, "Wanted: An Ontological Critic" (1941), in his collection, *Beating the Bushes*, especially pp. 13–41. Ransom's categories, "determinate" and "indeterminate" sound and meaning, are precise and helpful.

poetic form itself for a subject, as in this example of Swinburne at
his best:

The Roundel

A roundel is wrought as a ring or a starbright sphere,
With craft of delight and with cunning of sound unsought,
That the heart of the hearer may smile if to pleasure his ear
   A roundel is wrought.

Its jewel of music is carven of all or of aught—
Love, laughter, or mourning—remembrance of rapture or fear—
That fancy may fashion to hang in the ear of thought.

As a bird's quick song runs round, and the hearts in us hear
Pause answer to pause, and again the same strain caught,
So moves the device whence, round as a pearl or tear,
   A roundel is wrought.[38]

Here Swinburne's own craft and cunning make the rhymes successful; even "tear," perhaps the word most distant from the basic
subject of the poem, is neatly worked in through the witty, almost
"Metaphysical" play on its roundness. But the claim of the second
stanza, that a rondel may accommodate any subject, even strong
emotion, is not borne out in Swinburne's other poems in this
form. The series on the death of a baby, in which the ingenuity of
the form makes the expression of grief almost grotesque, exemplifies the problem. Here is the worst of those poems:

Etude Réaliste

A baby's feet, like sea-shells pink,
 Might tempt, should heaven see meet,
An angel's lips to kiss, we think,
 A baby's feet.

---

38. From his collection, *A Century of Roundels*, following the text of *Swinburne's Collected Poetical Works*, vol. II, p. 575. This uneven collection includes a poem on "The Death
of Richard Wagner" (pp. 549–50) and "Two Preludes" subtitled "Lohengrin" and "Tristan
und Isolde" (pp. 551–52). Subsequent citations are from this volume.

>Like rose-hued sea-flowers toward the heat
>They stretch and spread and wink
>Their ten soft buds that part and meet.

>No flower-bells that expand and shrink
> Gleam half so heavenly sweet
>As shine on life's untrodden brink
> A baby's feet. (p. 565)

Here the strain to rhyme is everywhere evident; the extended comparison to flowers is forced by the need to accommodate such implausible words as "heat" and "wink," which seem tenuously connected to a baby's feet despite the metaphor, and the superfluous phrase "we think" in the first stanza serves only to slip in a rhyme.

Our sense of a poor fit between the formal music of this poem and its sentimental matter is analogous to the discomfort we may feel in the church music of Haydn and Mozart, where a solemn text like the *Kyrie* is frequently set as a bright operatic quartet. But in that case, we can ignore the inappropriateness of the setting and enjoy the music on its own terms, while we cannot (alas) ignore the content of Swinburne's poem. The demands of meaning constrain the constructive ingenuity of poets, but also make possible their most dazzling feats of virtuosity; we are impressed with "The Roundel" because it succeeds where it might easily have failed. During the tonal period, harmonic demands provided similar constraints and opportunities for composers employing canonic constructions; the thrill of a Bach fugue lies in the way the strictly canonic lines nonetheless produce plausible voice-leading and clear harmony. An atonal canon, by contrast, free from the requirements of tonality, is somewhat one-dimensional. As Rosen puts it, "the ingenuity of design of Schönberg's canons may dazzle and charm, [but] the virtuosity . . . has vanished with the disappearance of tonal harmony" (p. 55).

If poets could escape from meaning as composers had escaped from tonality, they might gain a similar freedom of construction, while risking a similar loss of virtuosity. Not surprisingly, there were such experiments among the Dadaists: in 1913 the Russian Futurist poet Kruchonykh published a series of vowels entitled "Heights (Universal Language),"[39] and a few years later Hugo Ball, leader of the Zurich Dada circle, published a number of poems containing virtually no words in any language. Here is one:

> Seepferdschen und Flugfische
> [Sea-horses and Flying Fish]
>
> tressli bessli nebogen leila
> flusch kata
> ballubasch
> zack hitti zopp
>
> zack hitti zopp
> hitti betzli betzli
> prusch kata
> ballubasch
> fasch kitti bimm
>
> zitti kitillabi billabi billabi
> zikko di zakkobam
> fisch kitti bisch
>
> bumbalo bumbalo bumbalo bambo
> zitti kitillabi
> zack hitti zopp
>
> tressli bessli nebogen grügrü
> blaulala violabimini bisch
> violabimini bimini bimini
> fusch kata
> ballubasch
> zick hiti zopp[40]

Much of the charm of this poem is purely musical. It has strong rhythm ("bumbalo bumbalo bumbalo bambo"), marked cadences ("zack hitti zopp"), variation ("flusch . . . prusch. . . fusch"); we might even describe it as an imprecisely notated, percussive,

---

39. For texts in Cyrillic and Roman letters, see the *Primer of Experimental Poetry* 1 (1870–1922), ed. Edward Lucie-Smith, pp. 68–69.

40. Following the text given in Lucie-Smith's *Primer*, p. 71.

vaguely pitched piece of minimal music. But even this radical attempt to attain the condition of music cannot escape problems of meaning: it has a title; it includes at least one real word ("fisch"); its coinages (e.g., "violabimini") frequently suggest real words; and it even includes a poetic allusion ("leila" and "blaulala" sound like distortions of the song of Wagner's Rhine maidens, "Weialala leia").[41] It is at least as impure as a piece of program music; we are encouraged to seek for some kind of meaning, despite the obvious lack of syntax. And this "impurity" is inevitable, for meaning in poetry, unlike tonality in music, is not a system which can be replaced, but a central and inescapable element.

The contemporary inheritors of the Dadaists and the Parnassians, the OuLiPo group in Paris, seem for the most part to recognize this fact. Their leader, George Perec, claims to "reject the noble image of literature as a divine inspiration," preferring to believe that "language is a kind of putty that we can shape," but Perec's shapes, which include a 5,000-letter palindrome and a substantial novel *(La Disparition)* without a single occurrence of the letter *e*, have meaning; indeed, some reviewers of the novel failed to notice its technical trick. Another production from the same group, *Cent Mille Milliards de Poèmes* by Raymond Queneau, shows obvious affinities with serial methods in music. It is a book containing 10 sonnets, each cut into 14 one-line strips; by turning over these strips, the reader may produce 10^{14} different poems, all making sense! Machaut and Compiègne would be proud, for this kind of production is more like their work than like that of Hugo Ball; its ultimate accomplishment is intelligibility.[42]

Despite their ingenuity and charm, the constructive experiments we have been examining were not and are not part of the main stream of Western poetry, in which there has been, on balance, a turning away from virtuosity of all kinds. In 1968, W. H. Auden spoke at the opening of the Salzburg festival, acknowledging his great fondness for music and opera. He said in part;

---

41. Did T. S. Eliot, who explicitly quoted Wagner's refrain at the conclusion of part III of *The Waste Land*, also know Ball's poem, which was published in 1916? The "Song of the Thames-daughters," with its short lines and fragmentary syntax, may owe something to the rhythm of Ball's lines.

42. See the unsigned article entitled "Perverbs and Snowballs," *Time* (10 January 1977): 55.

... In the contemporary world, opera is the only art-form involving words which can still employ the High or Sublime Style. In days gone by, the poet could write in a High Style all by himself. This seems to be no longer possible. The characteristic style of modern poetry, or of the modern poetry I admire, is what Professor C. S. Lewis has termed Good Drab. It is a quiet intimate tone of voice, the speech of one person addressing one person, not a large audience: whenever a modern poet raises his voice, he seems phoney, like a man wearing elevator shoes.[43]

The nostalgia for the High Style here is as real as the recognition of its difficulties. And if Auden seems to be thinking mainly of diction, we should remember that choice of words powerfully affects form and meter, as Edward Sapir argues in a seminal essay on "The Musical Foundations of Verse":

Whatever be our favorite theory of the nature of diction in poetry, it must be granted unreservedly that any lexical, grammatical, or stylistic peculiarity that is not current in prose helps to accentuate the rhythmic contour if only because the attention is more or less forcibly drawn to it.[44]

Constrained by his perception of modern life to employ a vocabulary and grammar "current in prose," Auden was not unlike Schönberg, who was constrained by his perception of musical truth to abandon the tonality he loved.

But neither composer nor poet yielded to the formless. We have seen how Schönberg eventually won through to a music at once highly formal and uncompromisingly modern, in part through renewing old techniques, in part through inventing new ones. Auden's career involved parallel achievements. He could imitate Anglo-Saxon alliterative verse, Skelton, Swift, or Hardy; he could write short lines, long lines, or lines scanned syllabically; he made such forms as the *ballade*, the *rondeau*, the *villanelle*, the *sestina*, and the *canzone* his own without producing a sense of artificial High Style, using them to accommodate wryly modern comments on politics, theology, and sex.[45] He was rarely guilty of

43. In *Worte und Noten*, p. 37.
44. *Journal of English and Germanic Philology* 20 (1921): 226.
45. Some examples, drawn in part from a lecture by A. Walton Litz, page numbers

an empty line, preferring the true virtuosity in which formal song
enhances expression to the hollow chiming of the "Francophile
gaggle of pure songsters." And in a century where, as Sapir complains, "only a very small number of possible forms have been at
all frequently employed" (p. 222), Auden invented a number of
stanza-forms and rhyme-schemes, some of them as intricately new
as serial procedures in music.

Consider this poem; I have marked the rhymes to avoid a
lengthy exposition:

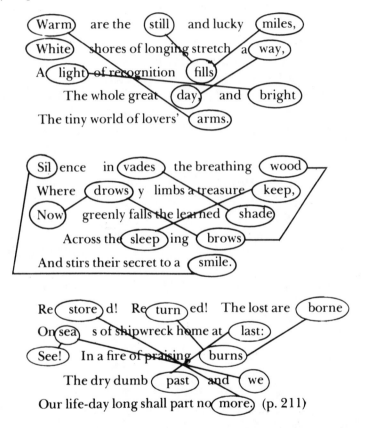

from Mendelson's edition: Anglo-Saxon, "The Wanderer" (p. 62); Skelton, "Easy Knowledge" (p. 44); Swift, "New Year Letter" (159); Hardy, "A Summer Night" (p. 103); short
lines, "For What as Easy" (p. 59); long lines, "The Aliens" (p. 637); syllabic scansion, "Moon
Landing" (p. 632); *ballade*, Stephano's song from *The Sea and the Mirror* (p. 318); *rondeau*,
"The Hidden Law" (p. 209); *villanelle*, "Alone" (p. 243); *sestina*, "Kairos and Logos"
(p. 238); *canzone*, "Canzone" (p. 256).

Auden achieves his formal complexity without resorting to the diction of the High Style; "greenly," "borne," and "life-day" are the most unusual words, but they are not archly "poetic," and the first stanza in particular adheres closely to the language of ordinary speech. Nor does the poet parade his virtuosity: the rhymes are perhaps more obvious than medieval anagrams or Renaissance numerology, but they are less obvious than conventional end-rhymes, and are probably perceived by many a reader as merely a pleasant, not very definite chiming, in the same way that most people hear recurring intervals in a twelve-tone piece without becoming acutely conscious of the row. Despite its original form, the poem is not detached from the English poetic tradition; indeed, I suspect Auden remembered another *aubade*, John Donne's "The Good-Morrow," which this poem resembles in its imagery: Donne also celebrates the way love "makes one little room an everywhere" (cf. "The tiny world of lovers' arms"); he mentions "snort[ing] in the Seven Sleepers' den," the landscape of Auden's second stanza; and he proclaims his lack of envy for "Sea-discoverers" who seek out "new worlds," an image perhaps related to Auden's "seas of shipwreck." In a similar way, some twelve-tone pieces allude effectively to the tonal past: Berg's violin concerto quotes Bach's chorale *"Es ist genug"* as a logical extension of a row rich in tonal implications. Most important of all, Auden's poem never suggests an attitude of cold calculation on the part of its maker; like the best works of the Vienna School, it is an intense and personal utterance which happens to take a rigorous form.[46]

The Axis of Symbolism

It is another striking irony that the most thoroughgoing modern attempt to push poetry in the direction of Hanslick's kind of autonomy was perpetrated by a group of poets devoted to his enemy Wagner. In 1887 a group of French Symbolists, normally a mild-mannered lot, actually engaged in a street riot when a performance of *Lohengrin* was forbidden by the police.[47] As early as 1861, when Baudelaire published an admiring essay on *Tannhäuser*,

46. William Meredith introduced me to this poem and its mysteries in 1965.
47. See Fowlie, *Mallarmé*, pp. 261–62.

there had been interest in and enthusiasm for Wagner among French poets. Wagner's *Lettre sur la Musique* (also 1861), a greatly condensed and somewhat misleading statement of his aesthetic principles, seems to have been the main point of contact, though there were occasional performances of his works in France. Some poets traveled to Germany to hear the operas or meet the great man: Villiers de l'Isle-Adam was such an enthusiast, visiting Wagner in 1869 and 1870. And when Wagner died in 1883, his mythic stature was assured: in the next year Edouard Dujardin organized a new periodical to be called the *Revue Wagnérienne* and secured a promise of a contribution from Stephane Mallarmé.[48]

Mallarmé's contribution, entitled *Richard Wagner, Revery of a French Poet*, appeared in August, 1885; five months later, Mallarmé distilled from its already suggestive imagery a dense and mysterious sonnet on Wagner. In these works, and in the poet's famous Oxford speech, *Music and Literature* (1894), we encounter in all its complexity the "simultaneous need for, and distrust of, music" which Bradford Cook has identified as an important part of the Symbolist movement.[49]

There were real affinities between Wagner and Mallarmé: Mallarmé's interest in producing an all-embracing, dramatic work of art, thought of simply as *"L'OEuvre,"* the work, suggests Wagner's grandiose concept of the *Gesamtkunstwerk;* Wagner's dissolution of tonality and embracing of a fluid and continuous chromaticism suggests Mallarmé's extraordinary treatment of French syntax. But Mallarmé seems not to have understood the drive toward mimesis and literary precision apparent in the device of the *leitmotif;* indeed, his praise of Wagner suggests a view of music somewhat closer to Hanslick's:

> Now at last we have music which is obedient only to its own most complex laws, above all to the vague and the intuitive. (p. 75)

If the sentence ended at the word "laws," we would have a plausible statement of autonomist doctrine, but Mallarmé goes on to celebrate "the vague and the intuitive" as *laws.* This attitude, ap-

---

48. See the helpful chapter entitled "Homage to Wagner" in Haskell M. Block, *Mallarmé and the Symbolist Drama*, pp. 52–82.

49. In the notes to his translation, p. 135.

plied to language, lies at the heart of the Symbolist movement, as Hugh Kenner perceives:

> Mallarmé and Valéry and Eliot felt words as part of that echoing intricacy, Language, which permeates our minds and obeys not the laws of *things* but its own laws, which has an organism's power to mutate and adapt and survive, and exacts obligations from us because no heritage is more precious. The things against which its words brush are virtually extraneous to its integrity. . . . By the end of the [nineteenth] century, in France, whole poems have been made "too subtle for the intellect," held together, as effects are, by the extrasemantic affinities of their words.[50]

Ignoring the musical attempt to name or describe objects, the *leitmotif*, Mallarmé praised Wagner's music, and music in general, for its imprecise, evocative effects. He had attacked the Parnassians for naming objects in poetry, and he heard in music the suggestiveness he hoped to achieve in words. The speech on *Music and Literature* includes a typical statement of this theme:

> It is not *description* which can unveil the efficacy and beauty of monuments, seas, or the human face in all their maturity and native state, but rather *evocation, allusion, suggestion.* (p. 45)

The Symbolist movement reenacts and extends the Romantic tendency to celebrate and emulate the supposed vagueness of music; Kenner contends that "Symbolism is scientific Romanticism" (p. 130), and the scientific thoroughness with which the Symbolists explored "extra-semantic" devices of sound, undermined syntax, and sealed off their poems from the exterior world of things bears out his claim. In all these activities, the Symbolists imagined that they were moving closer to music.

At the level of basic materials, Mallarmé laments the fact that the sounds of words are not always appropriate to their meaning:

> I am disappointed when I consider how impossible it is for language to express things by means of certain keys which would reproduce their brilliance and aura—keys which do exist as a part of the instrument of the human voice, or

---

50. *The Pound Era*, p. 123.

among languages, or sometimes even in one language. When compared to the opacity of the word *ombre* [shadow], the word *tenebres* [darkness] does not seem very dark; and how frustrating the perverseness and contradiction which lend dark tones to *jour* [day], bright tones to *nuit* [night]! We dream of words brilliant at once in meaning and sound, or darkening in meaning and so in sound, luminously and elementally self-succeeding. (p. 38)

In poetic practice, this longing for a more musical language led Mallarmé, Valéry, and most of all Verlaine to an intense emphasis on sound. Like older poets, they employed imitative devices: in Mallarmé's sonnet on Wagner (of which more presently), the hero makes his entrance in a noisy fanfare of trumpets achieved by crowding the line with dentals and plosives:

> Trompettes tout haut d'or pâmé sur les vélins . . .

[Trumpets high of gold fainted on velum . . .][51]

But Symbolist manipulation of sound moved well beyond mere onomatopoeia. In Mallarmé's mature work, subtle patterns of organization by sound are more important than syntax. These patterns are not complex and orderly constructions of the kinds we examined in the last section, but unique and particular creations in whose mysterious power to suggest and evoke Mallarmé believed intensely. It is difficult to provide examples because these effects, almost by definition, defy analysis. Perhaps the strongest evidence of their presence is the continued capacity of the best Symbolist poetry to move us, even when we cannot parse it. "Genuine poetry can communicate before it is understood," wrote T. S. Eliot in 1929, thinking of Dante, and in 1942 he applied that highly Symbolist principle explicitly to Mallarmé:

> One of the most obscure of modern poets was the French writer Stephane Mallarmé, of whom the French sometimes say that his language is so peculiar that it can be understood only by foreigners. . . . If we are moved by a poem, it has

51. For this line, and for the whole sonnet below, I follow the text given in Fowlie, *Mallarmé*, pp. 83–84, with the translation given in Fowlie's notes, p. 89.

meant something, perhaps something important, to us. . . .
If, as we are aware, only a part of the meaning can be conveyed by paraphrase, that is because the poet is occupied with
frontiers of consciousness beyond which words fail, though
meanings still exist.[52]

In its resistance to paraphrase, Symbolist poetry attains one
aspect of the condition of music. Its dependence on the specific
sounds of deliberately selected words, its distaste for naming objects and making statements, its fragmentation of syntax (far
more complete than the Romantic bending we noticed in the last
chapter), its tendency to employ words and phrases with a gestural rather than a lexical significance—all the features that make
it impossible to translate or paraphrase—produce a close poetic
analogue to that feature of music which Hanslick perceived so
clearly: that its sounds are not signs of exterior objects but objects
in their own right. Thus Cleanth Brooks:

> In the Mallarmean poem the words acquire something of the
> bulk and density of things; the poem is treated almost as if it
> were a plastic object with weight and solidity and with even a
> certain opacity. For the words are not *signs*, transparently re-
> dacting ideas. Instead they have acquired something like bulk
> and mass.[53]

The kind of bulk and mass, we might add, possessed by notes and
chords.

All these aspects of Symbolism appear in Mallarmé's sonnet
on Wagner:

> Le silence déjà funèbre d'une moire
> Dispose plus qu'un pli seul sur le mobilier
> Que doit un tassement du principal pilier
> Précipiter avec le manque de mémoire.
> Notre si vieil ébat triomphal du grimoire
> Hiéroglyphes dont s'exalte le millier
> A propager de l'aile un frisson familier!
> Enfouissez-le moi plutôt dans une armoire.
> Du souriant fracas originel haï

52. *The Music of Poetry*, pp. 14–15.
53. *Literary Criticism, A Short History*, p. 593.

Entre elles de clartés maîtresses a jailli
Jusque vers un parvis né pour leur simulacre,
Trompettes tout haut d'or pâmé sur les vélins,
Le dieu Richard Wagner irradiant un sacre
Mal tu par l'encre même en sanglots sibyllins.

[The silence already funereal of a veil / Covers with more than a fold over the furniture / Which a collapse of the principal pillar / Will efface with the loss of memory. // Our so old triumphant exercise of the conjuror's book, / Hieroglyphs with which the crowd is excited / At propagating on its wing a familiar thril / Rather hide it for me in a closet. // Hated by the original smiling noise / There burst forth from master lights / To the stage born for their representation, // Trumpets high of gold fainted on velum, / The god Richard Wagner radiating a consecration / Ill-silenced by the very ink in sibylline sobs.]

The Symbolist reluctance to name objects is evident here. A dark theatre is evoked without being overtly described; Mallarmé's embarrassment about the state of poetry appears obliquely in the desire to conceal the hieroglyphic conjuror's book; and Wagner appears less as a sound piercing the silence than as a light piercing the darkness. The climax of the poem is unquestionably the word *"Trompettes,"* but naming a musical instrument is the least important function of that word. The trumpets stand for Wagner; they delay still further the appearance of his name and stand in grammatical apposition to that name, which is the long-delayed subject of the poem's strongest verb (*"a jailli,"* burst forth); they are golden in color, so as to participate fully in the poem's most basic opposition, that between darkness and light; their gold, in the poem's strangest construction, has "fainted" onto parchment, and the force of that fainting or swooning surely attaches to the speaker as well, for whom Wagner's appearance in a flourish of trumpets is an overwhelming experience. One might mechanically line up the imagery of the poem this way: Wagner's music illuminates poetry as the "master lights" illuminate a dark theatre as gold trumpets illuminate an old manuscript. But the first part of that formula remains entirely unstated, and the other images are not discrete, one-to-one allegory but interpenetrating, fluid symbolism. Our paraphrase does violence to the poem by attempting to restate what Mallarmé evokes or suggests.

But we paraphrase because we need to find meanings in poems, just as, at the level of the individual word, we cannot entirely ignore the ordinary significance of *"Trompettes,"* even though that meaning is less important here than the unique symbolic meanings built into this poem, in which the trumpets represent Wagner, shine like gold, and burst forth from the stage lights. Symbolist poetry can effect this kind of shift or enrichment of a word's meaning because a symbolist poem, like a piece of music, is a closed system, in which context is a primary determinant of meaning. Thus T. S. Eliot, in *Four Quartets,* relentlessly repeats his central symbols ("fire," "rose") until we think of them primarily as compressed allusions to their previous contexts, not as names of elements or flowers. When the fire and the rose become one, in the last line of that poem, the effect is like a musical conclusion in which two previously separate themes are shown to be harmonically compatible. That musical effect, not some analogy by form to any particular piece, earns the poem its title. Once we get past the "file-card" approach to Wagner's operas, something quite similar can happen: we may hear a *leitmotif* less as a phrase arbitrarily designating some object or concept ("the sword," "fate") than as a phrase we have heard before in other contexts and are now hearing, aware of its past, in a new context.

Perhaps Mallarmé heard these effects in Wagner, despite his relative ignorance of musical technique. But even in the enthusiastic *Revery* there are uncertainties, jealousies, reservations. Mallarmé points to the "strange defiance hurled at poets by him who has usurped their duty," and to the way the music "penetrates, envelops, and joins [the drama] by virtue of the composer's dazzling will" (pp. 73, 75). And the conclusion, from which he drew some of the imagery of the sonnet, depicts the poet as climbing only part of the way up the mountain of abstraction, for a curious reason:

> Oh Genius! that is why I, *a humble slave to eternal logic,* oh Wagner!—that is why I suffer and reproach myself, in moments branded with weariness, because I am *not among those* who leave the universal pain and find lasting salvation by going directly to the house of your Art, which is their jour-

ney's end. . . . May I at least have my share in this delight? And *half-way up* the saintly mountain may I take my rest in your Temple, Whose dome trumpets abroad the most extensive dawning of truths ever known and, as far as the eye can reach from the parvis, urges on the steps of your elected as they walk upon the lawns?[54]

That Mallarmé, the chief celebrant of Symbolist aspiration toward music, should find himself, by contrast with Wagner, a slave to *logic* indicates that even he was finally aware of the limits of that aspiration. In the later speech, he describes literature as "our mind's ambition (in the form of language) to define things" (p. 49), and if the method of that defining, for Mallarmé and his inheritors, was a sonorous suggestiveness which owed much to music, the sonnet to Wagner, hazy as it is, achieves a degree of defining much more exact than that achieved by any piece of music—even a Wagnerian *leitmotif*. Eliot would later ". . . insist that a 'musical poem' is a poem which has a musical pattern of sound and a musical pattern of the secondary meanings of the words which compose it, and that these two patterns are indissoluble and one."[55] This definition, if somewhat clearer than any of Mallarmé's utterances on the subject, remains fundamentally Symbolist in its concentration on sound and secondary meaning; by implication, it also recognizes that *primary* meaning, with its capacity to define things, is the area where analogies between poetry and music fail.

The Axis of Polyphony

To review: a composer gives meaning to an otherwise neutral or meaningless note by giving it a function in a system: in tonal music, he chooses a key; in twelve-tone music, he devises a row. Sym-

54. In Cook, pp. 77–78, emphasis mine. Here is the original passage, to facilitate comparison with the sonnet; I follow the text of *Divagations*, pp. 159–60: "Voilà pourquoi, Génie! moi, l'humble qu'une logique éternelle asservit, ô Wagner, je souffre et me reproche, aux minutes marquées par la lassitude, de ne pas faire nombre avec ceux qui, ennuyés de tout afin de trouver le salut définitif, vont droit à l'édifice de ton Art, pour eux le terme du chemin. . . . Au moins, voulant ma part du delice, me permettras-tu de goûter, dans ton Temple, à mi-côte de la montagne sainte, dont le lever de vérités, le plus compréhensif encore, trompette la coupole et invite, à perte de vue du parvis, les gazons que le pas de tes élus foule un repos."

55. *The Music of Poetry*, p. 19.

bolist poets, seeking similar control over their words, loaded them with so many functions and meanings that their ordinary denotative functions were obscured, and became less important than particular functions taken on by words in a particular poetic context, a context held together by "extra-semantic affinities" of sound and suggestion. But when a tonal composer wants to alter the function of a note, he tends to isolate it, to state it without harmonic support, as Haydn denudes the little motif which served us as an example of classical wit (in ch. 5 above), while a Symbolist poet alters the meaning of a word by multiplying its secondary associations in order to drown out the dictionary definition, as Mallarmé turns *"Trompettes"* into an explosion of Wagnerian light. The Symbolist poet makes his words more flexible by turning them into simultaneities, polyphonic intersections of multiple meanings.

Twentieth-century advances in linguistics have made all of us more aware of the extent to which all words are simultaneities. A word has a history; it may once have meant something else; it may once have been more overtly or physically metaphorical; it has cousins in the great linked family of languages, brothers within its own. What the Symbolists were trying to do to words—to enrich them, to complicate them, to make them more flexible, to free them from one fixed significance—was an intuition of a feature now recognized as pervasive in language, a feature explored in all its complexity by a poet who treated all languages as a part of Language: Ezra Pound.

Symbolism was an important part of Pound's heritage, to be sure; it alerted him to these matters. Even when writing a brief for increased technical precision by poets, Pound makes a generously inclusive gesture toward Symbolist aesthetics:

> . . . I do not by any means mean that poetry is to be stripped of any of its powers of vague suggestion. Our life is, in so far as it is worth living, made up in great part of things indefinite, impalpable.[56]

But this genuine respect for the indefinite was affected, inevitably, by Pound's close study of troubadour poetry, which he under-

56. "I Gather the Limbs of Osiris." following the text given in Pound's *Selected Prose*, p. 33.

stood far more fully than Swinburne did. In the same essay, "I Gather the Limbs of Osiris" (1911–12), he recognizes the "polyphonic" quality of Arnaut's rhyming technique, as well as the fundamental difference between collaborations in which a composer sets a poem and those in which a poet writes words for a tune:

> It is my personal belief that the true economy lies in making the tune first. We all of us compose verse to some sort of tune, and if the 'song' is to be sung we may as well compose to a 'musician's' tune straight away.[57]

By 1918, echoing Dante, he has become quite dogmatic:

> Poetry is a composition of words set to music. Most other definitions of it are indefensible, or metaphysical. . . . Poets who will not study music are defective.[58]

During the same period, he was also learning about Chinese poetry, a poetry in which each word was a visible combination of meanings, not adequately describable in the Western notion of "parts of speech." His mentor, Ernest Fenollosa, had written:

> A true noun, an isolated thing, does not exist in nature. Things are only the terminal points, or rather the meeting-points of action, cross-sections cut through possible actions, snapshots. Neither can a pure verb, an abstract motion, be possible in nature. The eye sees noun and verb as one, things in motion, motion in things.[59]

The word as chord in a fused, organic fashion: if Symbolism was scientific Romanticism, the Imagism with which Pound briefly flirted in 1912 was compressed Symbolism. Heinrich Schenker, penetrating to the essence of tonality as tonal music waned, reduced sonata movements to statements of a triad; his analytical method distinguishes ruthlessly between "foreground" and "background" levels of composition, between decorative "passing tones" or "neighbor notes" and more essential or structural events. But Schenker's reductions appear as analytical charts, while Pound's similar reductions of Symbolism appear as poetry:

---

57. p. 37; the observation about Arnaut's "polyphonic rhyme" is on p. 27.
58. "Vers Libre and Arnold Dolmetsch," in *Literary Essays*, p. 437.
59. Quoted (without a citation) in *The Pound Era*, p. 157.

IN A STATION OF THE METRO

> The apparition of these faces in the crowd;
> Petals on a wet, black bough.[60]

A poem distilled from a much longer draft. The *Cantos* would carry this process further in one way, using Chinese characters and brief phrases in Greek, Italian, and Provençal as allusive reductions of other poetic and historical worlds. Kenner's assertion that this "isolating of single words, not necessarily English" was Pound's "most Symbolist procedure" identifies the source of the notion of the word as chord, but also acknowledges that Pound was to move beyond that notion, though not away from techniques derived from music; indeed, it was by means of his serious study of music that he progressed from the chordal, separate sonorities of Imagism to the intersecting melodic and contrapuntal lines of the *Cantos*. His opinions about music were as definite and cranky as his opinions about literature, and as honestly earned. Learning by doing, just as he taught himself languages by translating their literature and carpentry by building his own furniture, he composed a sort of opera *(Villon)*, attempted to play the bassoon (a perfect instrument for him, with its rich, often awkward assortment of overtones), and wrote in 1924 a "Treatise on Harmony" which Kenner has accurately identified as one of the important keys to the *Cantos*. [61]

The most important assertion of the "Treatise" is its Bach-like insistence on the primacy of the horizontal line: chords are not thought of as units (as in Rameau) but as intersections of contrapuntal lines:

> The early students of harmony were so accustomed to think of music as something with a strong lateral or horizontal motion that they never imagined any one, ANY ONE could be stupid enough to think of it as static; it never entered their heads that people would make music like steam ascending from a morass.[62]

60. Following the text of Pound's *Selected Poems*, ed. T. S. Eliot, p. 113.

61. In his earlier book, *The Poetry of Ezra Pound*, pp. 233, 279.

62. I quote the modern reprint of *Antheil and the Treatise on Harmony*, which has a sympathetic introduction by the composer Ned Rorem; otherwise, its pages reproduce the original printing of 1927; the passage is on p. 11.

This opinion represents more than a prejudice against nine-teenth-century chordal practice (though it is certainly that, as Pound's concurrent distaste for the piano and fondness for antique instruments suggests): properly understood, it explains why Pound eventually broke free from Symbolist practice to achieve a contrapuntal poetry. Chordal moments remain, as emphatic chords sometimes punctuate an otherwise linear fugue of Bach, but the *Cantos* are made from "strong lateral or horizontal motions," including the narrative line of the *Odyssey*, the sexual energy of Ovid and Arnaut, the correspondence of early American presidents, and the misguided economics of Mussolini. It is an index of Pound's achievement that no single sample can serve as a touchstone, any more than a few isolated bars can tell us much about a fugue; in both cases, the manipulation of the lines in the total construct is the central accomplishment.

Here as in other areas, Pound stands revealed as the quintessential modern, for twelve-tone music, relentlessly linear, recovers true polyphony from the chordal mists of Impressionism. In Chapter 3 we saw polyphony originating in the combining of distinct tunes, and no music centered on chords as chords has been able to sustain real development: Debussy's harmonies, as Schönberg realized, were "without constructive meaning" and so served only a "coloristic purpose."[63] Impressionist music, starved of linear motion, had to be outgrown, though even Schönberg profited from its lessons in the handling of color; Symbolist poetry, starved of linear statement, had to be outgrown as well, though Pound salvaged from it some of his most memorable techniques. James Joyce, in prose, moved in the opposite direction: *Ulysses* constructs a giant counterpoint of ancient myth and tawdry Dublin reality, but in *Finnegans Wake* those elements have been fused, at the level of the individual word, into chords. On the first page, "Sir Tristram, violer d'amores," arrives "from North Armorica . . . to wielderfight his penisolate war,"[64] and in one word we hear "penis," "penultimate," "peninsular," "isolate," and perhaps "desolate." Other Joycean coinages involve several languages, performing chordally the combinations the *Cantos* perform contrapuntally.

63. *Style and Idea* (cited above, n. 26), p. 104.
64. I quote the revised edition, p. 3.

The contrapuntal method, as we have seen, is the more authentically musical, not only in terms of the past, but in terms of the present: according to Roger Sessions, in 1960, "composers seem by and large no longer interested in chords as such,"[65] since atonality allows any vertical combination and finds its grammar in the ordering of intervals, not in chordal inflections. It is also a superior literary method, as we may discover by comparing the rewards of rereading the *Cantos* with those of rereading the *Wake:* rereading Joyce, we will gain local explosions of understanding, many of them comic, as we hear more of the component notes in the chordal words from which the work is forged; rereading Pound, we will begin to hear the "long lines" of thought, argument, and design which cross each other in every canto. For Pound had no Symbolist distaste for statement, narrative, opinion; like the Goethe Auden admired, he wished his poetry were truth: "I have tried," he confessed at the end, "to write Paradise."[66]

Expression in Modern Music:
Schönberg the Romantic, Stravinsky the Rhetorician

So we come all the way around to praising Pound for recovering expression, for restoring to literature the capacity to narrate, argue, and communicate that Romantic composers had envied. Twentieth-century composers, free of the illusion that music can or should achieve the condition of telling or describing, retain to a greater degree than one might suspect the literary desire to express themselves and persuade us.

On the first page of an essay called "The Relationship to the Text," Schönberg delivers what seems a solidly Hanslickian attack on programmatic listening:

> There are relatively few people who are capable of understanding, purely in terms of music, what music has to say. The assumption that a piece of music must summon up images of one sort or another, and that if these are absent the piece of music has not been understood or is worthless, is as widespread as only the false and banal can be.[67]

65. "Problems and Issues," p. 25.
66. *Canto* CXX, following the text of *The Cantos*, p. 803.
67. *Style and Idea*, p. 1.

But on the very next page he makes a generous judgement of Wagner's fanciful novelistic programs for the Beethoven symphonies: they may help "the average man." And in other essays we hear a highly Romantic account of creativity:

> I write what I feel in my heart, and what finally comes on paper is what first coursed through every fiber of my body. A work of art can achieve no finer effect than when it transmits to the beholder the emotions that raged in the creator in such a way that they rage and storm also in him.[68]

His biographers mention "his insistence upon working at high speed and his extraordinary reliance upon instinct and inspiration," and in his String Trio, op. 45, he actually tried to represent a terrifying episode in which his heart had temporarily stopped beating.[69]

It seems necessary to conclude that Schönberg's personal aesthetics did preserve a version of Romantic thought. He abandoned tonality because he thought it inadequate as an expression of himself and his modern situation; he scorned the composers of "pseudo-tonal" music as dishonest and insincere. He invented the twelve-tone system not so much to confirm expression as to give it constraints against which to struggle, so that there might again be a principle of dissonance, with its expressive possibilities.[70] And he turned again and again to texts: to the Symbolist lyrics of Stefan George for *Das Buch der Hängenden Gärten*, to a German translation of Albert Giraud's *Pierrot Lunaire* for that extraordinary work, to his own texts for *Erwartung* and *Moses und Aaron*. Nor was his relationship to these texts mechanical; he claimed to have "completely understood . . . the poems of Stefan George from their sound alone, with a perfection that by analysis and synthesis could hardly have been attained, but certainly not surpassed."[71] Another reversal: the claim to understand a work of art by osmosis was the way Romantic poets and philosophers talked about

---

68. Quoted (without an exact citation) by Joseph Machlis in a brief article on *The Early Vocal Works of Arnold Schönberg*, bound into the Columbia recording (M2L336/M2S736). Compare the very similar position in Schönberg's essay on "The Heart and the Brain in Music," in which an aphorism from Balzac plays an important part.

69. See Rosen, pp. 105, 94–95.

70. See Rosen's brilliant chapter on "Atonality," in which this is one basic point.

71. *Style and Idea*, pp. 4–5.

music, but here it is applied to poetry by a composer. In much the same way, *Sprechstimme,* Schönberg's special contribution to the history of text-setting, is a highly expressive, even Romantic device. Falling midway between speech and song (see List's chart in ch. 1 above), it renders the words of the text more audible than when they are sustained in normal singing,[72] and by making the voice *less* like an instrument, dramatically isolates the speaker. As the Romantic poets liked to believe they had stripped off the masks of "poetic diction" and formal rhetoric to achieve a more naked expression of self, the speaker in *Pierrot Lunaire* presents the text without the adornments of *sostenuto* and *vibrato,* and becomes, in turn, an emblem of Arnold Schönberg, stripping away the conventions of tonality to achieve the tortured and grotesque expression he considered necessary for our time.

Schönberg, in short, was a serious composer, and would have agreed with what Richard Lanham calls *"serious* premises":

> Every man possesses a central self, an irreducible identity.
> . . . When he is communicating feelings, success is measured
> by something we call *sincerity,* faithfulness to the self who is
> doing the feeling.[73]

For Schönberg, sincerity demands atonality, *Sprechstimme,* and a belief that "great art must proceed to precision and brevity," to "musical prose."[74]

But there are other options, other premises; thinking of Ovid, Rabelais, and Shakespeare, Lanham writes a description of rhetorical man that might have been tailor-made as an account of the career of Igor Stravinsky:

> Rhetorical man is an actor; his reality public, dramatic. His
> sense of identity, his self, depends on the reassurance of daily
> histrionic reenactment. . . . And his motivations must be
> characteristically ludic, agonistic. He thinks first of winning,
> of mastering the rules the current game enforces. He as-

---

72. Cf. Auden, "Notes on Music and Opera," in *The Dyer's Hand,* p. 473: "A Cambridge psychologist, P. E. Vernon, once performed the experiment of having a Campion song sung with nonsense verses of equivalent syllabic value substituted for the original; only six percent of his test audience noticed that something was wrong."

73. *The Motives of Eloquence,* p. 1.

74. *Style and Idea,* p. 72.

sumes a natural agility in changing orientations. He hits the
street already street-wise. . . . Nor is conceptual creativity, invention of a fresh paradigm, demanded of him. He accepts
the present paradigm and explores its resources. (p. 2)

When the "present paradigm" was Impressionism, the *Firebird;* a
few years later, with a more angular and troubled Expressionism
in the air, the *Rite of Spring;* after the first World War, a cool objec-
tivism announced in archly Hanslickian phrases:

My *Octet* is a musical object. The object has a form and that
form is influenced by the musical matter with which it is composed.
. . . My *Octet* is not an 'emotive' work but a musical composition based on objective elements which are sufficient in themselves.

And some years later, writing of the same piece,

Composition, structure, form, here all are in the line of the
18th-century masters.[75]

Except that no "eighteenth-century master" wrote a tango, and
the *Octet,* brilliantly comic throughout, ends with a tango; it stands
"in the line of" Haydn as the *Rape of the Lock* stands in the line of
Homer.

Stravinsky responded to the vastly increased knowledge of
older music in our century as the Renaissance *literati* had responded to the rediscovery of precious ancient manuscripts: he
tried on the rediscovered styles as possible masks. In his *Mass* we
hear the vocal architecture of the Middle Ages, in *Pulcinella* an
appropriation of the rococo, and so on. Finally, when atonality
was no longer the personal style of a California neighbor but a
widely diffused "present paradigm," he made it his own as well.
Commentators who had sought to describe twentieth-century music as a dialectical struggle between two masters misunderstood
this last change as a defection or apostasy, but it was as logical as
the other explorations of style.[76] Stravinsky had not been trying

75. Philip Ramey cites these remarks, dated 1924 and 1952 but not otherwise identified, in his liner notes to the Columbia recording, conducted by the composer (M30579).
76. See for example Paul Henry Lang, in his introduction to *Problems of Modern Music,*

to preserve tonality in a stubborn or reactionary way; in the 1920s, Rosen reminds us, he was already "treating tonality as if it were an archaic and foreign language" (p. 71), like Spenser making up a poetic language out of Chaucer. His admirers may have been sentimental about the vestiges of tonality they heard in Stravinsky's work, but Stravinsky was not. In his own discussion of the differences between himself and Schönberg, he sets up a chart, from which we may excerpt two particularly relevant entries:

STRAVINSKY:	SCHOENBERG:
Learns from others, a lifelong need for outside nourishment and a constant confluence with new influences.	An autodidact. After the early works, no influence from other composers.
'What the Chinese philosopher says cannot be separated from the fact that he says it in Chinese.' (Preoccupation with manner and style.)	'A Chinese philosopher speaks Chinese, but what does he say?' ('What is *style* ?')

Then, dismissing these comparisons as "a parlour game," he declares that "the parallelisms are more interesting," and lists, among others, these striking points:

> For both of us, numbers are things.
> Both of us were devoted to the Word, and each wrote some of his own librettos.[77]

In short, like all truly significant artists, both men were concerned with construction *and* expression.

---

pp. 10–11: "We have witnessed the most abject surrender only recently, when Stravinsky, always aloof, arrogant, used to command, bared his head before 'the three Viennese,' obediently accepting terms. . . . [Now] he, too, writes 'objective' serial music, cold, grim, and beautifully made." Theodor W. Adorno's *Philosophy of Modern Music*, first published in German in 1948, has done a great deal to promote the notion of twentieth-century music as a "dialectical" competition between Schönberg, whom Adorno honors as a progressive, and Stravinsky, whom he abuses as an infantile reactionary. Whatever the undoubted merits of Marx and Freud in their own fields, Adorno's attempt to use their categories as a way to describe composers is perverse.

77. For the whole discussion, see Stravinsky and Robert Craft, *Dialogues and a Diary*, pp. 107–09.

Texts set by Stravinsky include Russian nursery-rhymes, Latin Psalms, Hebrew narratives, and a Latin version of Sophocles' *Oedipus* with spoken interludes in the French of Cocteau. (Pound, whose first *Canto* gives us an episode from the *Odyssey* by way of a Renaissance Latin version, would have loved it.) As a rhetorical composer with a particular fondness for Gesualdo, Stravinsky could even indulge in rhetorical techniques of text-setting: the *Oedipus Rex* employs a "false relation" at the words *"falsus pater"* (false father).[78] And in one of his first forays into serial technique, in 1953, Stravinsky chose to set *Three Songs from William Shakespeare*, deliberately selecting texts inviting imitative word-painting: "Musick to heare" (Sonnet 8), with its relentless reference to singleness and harmony; "Full fadom five" (from *The Tempest*), with its clanging bell; and "When Daisies pied" (from *Love's Labour's Lost*), with its scolding cuckoo. In all three songs, Stravinsky derives his material from ideas originating as conventional, more or less tonal imitation; we are continually aware of a witty interplay in which he discovers intersections between Shakespeare's poetic technique and serial composition.

This process is clearest in "Full fadom five."[79] At the end of this song, the voice imitates the bell with the most conventional intervals imaginable:

From these intervals, Stravinsky derives a kind of row, breaking with twelve-tone practice by including only seven pitches and stating one of them twice; the row is restricted to the three intervals of the bell motif:

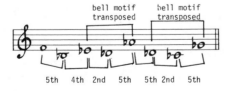

78. Stravinsky himself points out this device; see *Expositions and Developments*, p. 122.

79. All citations follow the text and music given in the vocal score (London: Boosey and Hawkes, 1953), pp. 6–7.

A transposition at the interval of a fifth adds only one new pitch:

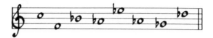

From this material is built the opening phrase: the viola plays the first five pitches of the row in half-notes; the flute plays the transposition at the fifth in quarter-notes (diminution); the voice states the entire row, beginning in eighth-notes, then slowing to quarters:

After this opening, rich in open, bell-like intervals both horizontally and vertically, Stravinsky rearranges the pitches of the row in an order with more close intervals:

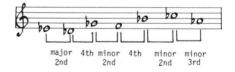

From this new series, with minor ornamental repetitions, is derived the rest of the vocal line. First the series:

Then its retrograde:

Those are pearles . . . that were . . . his eies, . . .

Then the inverse:

No - thing of . . him . . . . that . . . doth fade, . . .

Then the retrograde inverse, whose last two pitches are the same as the first two pitches of the original series, so that this phrase is musically enjambed at precisely the one unpunctuated line-end in the poem, its most notable enjambment:

But doth . . . suf - - fer a Sea-change In- - to some - - thing rich

and strange . . .

Meanwhile the three accompanying instruments (flute, clarinet, and viola) play parts based on the same canonic and transpositional procedures; the material we have been examining in linear sequence in the voice part occurs contrapuntally as well.

Like Bach in *"Ich folge dir gleichfalls,"* Stravinsky transcends the problem of imitation by making his imitative material organic to the construction of the entire song. That this kind of virtuosity could survive the death of tonality, a death recognized in part by this song itself and even more decisively in the stricter twelve-tone music of Stravinsky's last years, is another of the stubborn survivals we have been noticing throughout our history. That Schönberg conceived of his constructive innovations within a highly Romantic theory of creativity, acknowledging his break with tonality as the result of an "inner compulsion," is a similar survival. Neither poetry nor music can afford to be without master practitioners of both kinds: if the Wordsworths and Schönbergs alter the course of artistic development in obedience to an irresistible compulsion, the Popes and Stravinskys ultimately find an equally satisfying expression of self by wearing the masks of other makers.

Conclusion

Just as both arts need Romantics and rhetoricians, both need the renewal that comes from aspiration toward each other. Aesthetics is a notoriously imprecise and subjective area, and the relative consensus in the twentieth century about the distinctions between music and poetry is an example of progress; no composer I know of now advocates a return to program music, nor do poets aspire to a hidden medieval complexity of form. But the most characteristic modern problems in both arts may be described as withdrawals into their own conditions. Thus Ernst Krenek, an advocate of "total serialization," in which the composer abdicates his decision-making capacity and allows chance procedures to dictate pitches and rhythms, alleges that what composers have always called inspiration is really chance:

> Generally and traditionally "inspiration" is held in great respect as the most distinguished source of the creative process in art. It should be remembered that inspiration by definition is closely related to chance, for it is the very thing that cannot be controlled, manufactured, or premeditated in any way. This obviously answers the [dictionary] definition of chance as "the absence of any known reason why an event should turn out one way rather than another." Actually the composer has come to distrust his inspiration because it is not really as innocent as it was supposed to be, but rather conditioned by a tremendous body of recollection, tradition, training, and experience. In order to avoid the dictations of such ghosts, he prefers to set up an impersonal mechanism which will furnish, according to premeditated patterns, unpredictable situations.[80]

80. "Extents and Limits of Serial Techniques," p. 90.

This is the counsel of despair, and its results, whether generated by humans or machines, are contemptible.[81] Meaning in music is a profound mystery, not finally susceptible to verbal accounts, but surely the "body of recollection, tradition, training, and experience" that a composer brings to his work is a central part of the process that generates meaning. The success of composers like George Crumb in an eclectic, collage style that alludes explicitly to parts of that tradition is only one of many current attempts to leave behind the grimly academic music that resulted from the principles laid out by Krenek and his allies. Some have overreacted, alleging that only by a return to tonality can music regain emotional meaning; this is nonsense.[82] Expressive power in music has survived other changes of the musical language, as we have seen, and in the works of Schönberg and Stravinsky, it survives the death of tonality. Nor is the twelve-tone system the only possibility: the stunning music of Krysztof Penderecki is neither tonal nor Schönbergian, but it achieves a dramatic expression of its composer's "recollection. . . . and experience."

On the poetic side, the equivalent problems result from an exaggeration of Auden's healthy perception that the High Style is no longer possible. Some poets have evidently concluded that no style is possible, that a group of words becomes a poem when its author declares it one. The notion that formlessness guarantees authenticity, the apparent principle behind much "little magazine" verse, is as serious an abdication of artistic responsibility as Krenek's reliance on chance. An art that began as one part of *mousike* cannot so abandon its past as to break entirely with construction. Again there is a possible overreaction, the allegation that only a return to rhyme and regular metrics can save poetry; but this notion, like the equivalent advocacy of a return to tonality

81. Not everyone understands the important distinction between the electronic music composed by Milton Babbitt and others, in which the composer designs and controls every event, and resorts to electronic realization because of the limits of human and instrumental performance, and the quite different music *generated* by computers using procedures like those advocated by Krenek.

82. Leonard Bernstein's televised lectures on "musical semantics," published as *The Unanswered Question*, conclude, after much useful pedagogy, with an example of this kind of tonal mysticism: "I believe that from [the] Earth emerges a musical poetry, which is by the nature of its sources tonal" (p. 424). Mr. Bernstein thus installs the bias of his own compositional career as universal dogma.

for music, misses the point. If contemporary poetry has a serious need, it is the need for formal innovation, for *new* principles of construction which can help poets shape, order, and control the expression which is their high calling.

Finally, as I have tried to show here, analogies between poetry and music can help those of us who read and listen as well as those of us who create: by recasting poetic problems in musical terms, or musical problems in poetic terms, we may gain a fresh perspective. The naive student who demands of poetry a breathless enthusiasm, and so suspects any highly formal poetry of infidelity to feeling, may find it hard to cling to his reductive aesthetics if asked to apply them to music. And the advanced literary theorist may also profit from thinking about the relations we have been studying, as W. K. Wimsatt realized:

> A theorist of poetry, being inevitably a person who subscribes to metaphoric and analogical ways of thinking, is in a good position to avoid both the fault of running the arts confusedly together by metaphors which become literal and the opposite fault of cutting the arts off from one another too completely by the denial of all such relations. There are poetic dimensions which can never be described except metaphorically, and to keep open, if only tentatively, the time-honored metaphoric avenues may do something to prevent theoretical discussion from declining into the literalism of a quasi-scientific semantics.[83]

My purpose in this history has been to demonstrate the origins of those "time-honored metaphoric avenues" in the explicit intersections of the histories of music and poetry.

---

83. *Literary Criticism, A Short History*, p. 279.

Works Cited

Abert, Hermann. *Die Musikanschauung des Mittelalters.* 1905. Reprint. Tutzing: Hans Schneider, 1964.

Abrams, M. H. *The Mirror and the Lamp.* New York: Oxford University Press, 1953.

Addison, Joseph. *Miscellaneous Works,* ed. A. C. Guthkelch. London: Bell, 1914.

————. *The Spectator,* ed. Gregory Smith, London: Dent, 1945.

Adorno, Theodor W. *Philosophy of Modern Music,* trs. Anne G. Mitchell and Wesley V. Blomster. New York: Seabury Press, 1973.

Allen, W. Sidney. *Accent and Rhythm.* Cambridge: Cambridge University Press, 1973.

————. *Vox Graeca.* 2nd ed. London: Cambridge University Press, 1974.

Amerio, Franco. *Il 'De Musica' di S. Agostino.* Turin: Diadaskaleion, 1929.

Anderson, Gordon Athol. *The Latin Compositions in Fascicules VII and VIII of the Notre Dame Manuscript Wolfenbüttel Helmstadt 1099 (1206).* New York: Institute of Medieval Music, 1968.

Anderson, Howard, and John S. Shea, eds. *Studies in Criticism and Aesthetics.* Minneapolis: University of Minnesota Press, 1967.

Anderson, Warren. "Word-Accent and Melody in Ancient Greek Musical Texts." *Yale Journal of Music Theory* 17 (1973): 186–203.

Anglès, Higini. "Latin Chant before St. Gregory." In *The New Oxford History of Music,* vol. II, pp. 58–91.

————. "Gregorian Chant." In *The New Oxford History of Music,* vol. II, pp. 92–127.

Appel, Carl. "Zur Formenlehre des provenzalischen Minnesangs." *Zeitschrift für romanische Philologie* 53 (1933): 151–71.

Aristides Quintilianus. *De Musica,* ed. R. P. Winnington-Ingram. Leipzig: Teubner, 1963.

Aristoxenos. *Elementa Harmonica*, ed. Rosetta da Rios. Rome: Consilio Academiae Lynceorum. 1954.

Auden, W. H. *Collected Poems*, ed. Edward Mendelson. London: Faber and Faber, 1976.

———. *Worte und Noten*. Salzburg: Festungsverlag, 1968.

———. *The Dyer's Hand*. London: Faber and Faber, 1962.

St. Augustine. *De Musica*, trs. R. Catesby Talliaferro. Annapolis: St. John's Bookstore. 1939.

———. *Confessions*, trs. R. S. Pine-Coffin. Middlesex: Penguin, 1961.

———. *De Doctrina*, trs. D. W. Robertson. Indianapolis: Bobbs-Merrill, 1958.

———. *Epistvlae*, ed. Alois Goldbacher. *Scriptorum Ecclesiasticorum Latinorum*, vols. 34, 44, 57, 58. Prague: Tempsky, 1898.

Aurelian of Réomé. *Musica Disciplina*, trs. Joseph Ponte. Colorado Springs: Colorado College Music Press, 1968.

Babbitt, Milton. "Twelve-tone Invariants as Compositional Determinants." In *Problems of Modern Music*, ed. Lang, p. 108–21.

Bach, Johann Sebastian. *Neue bach Ausgabe*. Basel: Bärenreiter, 1957–.

Banville, Theodore. *Améthystes*. Paris: Poulet-Malassis, 1862.

Barbour, J. Murray. "The Principles of Greek Notation." *Journal of the American Musicological Society* 13 (1960): 1–17.

Barzun, Jacques. *Music into Words*. Washington: Library of Congress, 1953.

———. *Berlioz and the Romantic Century*. Boston: Little, Brown, 1950.

Bate, Philip. *The Flute*. London: Ernest Benn, 1969.

Bayly, Anselm. *The Alliance of Music, Poetry and Oratory*. London, 1789.

Beare, William. *Latin Verse and European Song*. London: Methuen, 1957.

Beethoven, Ludwig van. *Beethoven's Letters*, trs. Lady Wollane. 1867. Reprinted in facsimile. Boston: Longwood, 1978.

Berg, Alban. *Sonata for Piano*. Berlin: Universal, 1926.

———. *2 Lieder (Theodor Storm)*. English text by Eric Smith. Appendix by H. F. Redlich. Vienna: Universal, 1960.

Bernstein, Leonard. *The Unanswered Question*. Cambridge: Harvard University Press, 1976.

Besseler, Heinrich. *Die Musik des Mittelalters und der Renaissance*.

Potsdam: Athenaion, 1931–34.

———. "Studien zur Musik des Mittelalters." *Archiv für Musikwissenschaft* 7 (1925): 167–252.

Blackmur, R. P. *Language as Gesture.* New York: Harcourt Brace, 1952.

Block, Haskell M. *Mallarmé and the Symbolist Drama.* Detroit: Wayne State University Press, 1963.

Blom, Eric, ed. *Grove's Dictionary of Music and Musicians.* 5th ed. New York: St. Martin's 1954.

Booth, Stephen. *An Essay on Shakespeare's Sonnets.* New Haven: Yale University Press, 1969.

Booth, Wayne. *The Rhetoric of Fiction.* Chicago: University of Chicago Press, 1961.

Boswell, James. *The Life of Dr. Samuel Johnson,* ed. G. B. Hill, rev. L. F. Powell. Oxford: Clarendon, 1934.

Boulez, Pierre. *Notes of an Apprenticeship.* New York: Knopf, 1968.

Bowra, C. M. *Primitive Song.* Cleveland: World Publishing, 1962.

Bradbrook. M. C. *Shakespeare and Elizabethan Poetry.* London: Chatto and Windus, 1951.

Brennecke, Ernest. "Dryden's Odes and Draghi's Music." *PMLA* 49 (1934): 1–34. Reprinted in *Essential Articles for the Study of John Dryden,* ed. Swedenberg, pp. 425–65.

Bridgman, Nanie. "France and Burgundy: 1300–1500." In *Music from the Middle Ages to the Renaissance,* ed. Sternfeld, pp. 145–74.

Bronson, Bertrand. "Some Aspects of Music and Literature in the Eighteenth Century." Los Angeles: Clark Library Papers, 1953.

———. "When Was Neoclassicism?" In *Studies in Criticism and Aesthetics,* ed. Anderson and Shea, pp. 13–35.

Brown, John A. *A Dissertation on the Rise, Union, and Power, the Progression, Separations, and Corruptions of Poetry and Music.* London, 1763.

Brownell, Morris R. *Alexander Pope and the Arts of Georgian England.* Oxford: Clarendon, 1978.

Bukofzer, Manfred. *Music in the Baroque Era.* New York: Norton, 1947.

———. "Allegory in Baroque Music." *Journal of the Warburg and Courtauld Institute* 3 (1939–40): 1–21.

Bull, John. *Keyboard Music,* ed. John Steele and Francis Cameron.

Musica Britannica, vol. XIV. London: Stainer and Bell, 1960.

Burmeister, Joachim. *Musica Poetica*. Rostock, 1606. Reprinted in facsimile. Basel: Bärenreiter, 1955.

Busoni, Ferruccio. *Sketch of a New Aesthetic of Music*. in *Three Classics in the Aesthetics of Music*, pp. 75–102.

Caldwell, John. *Medieval Music*. Bloomington: University of Indiana Press, 1978.

Campion, Thomas. *Observations in the Art of English Poesie*, ed. G. B. Harrison. London: Bodley Head, 1925.

———. *Selected Songs*, ed. John Hollander. Boston: David Godine, 1973.

Cannon, Beekman C., Alvin H. Johnson, and William G. Waite. *The Art of Music*. New York: Crowell, 1960.

Carpenter, Nan Cooke. *Music in the Medieval and Renaissance Universities*. Norman: University of Oklahoma Press, 1958.

Cassirer, Ernst, Paul O. Kristeller, and John H. Randall, eds. *The Renaissance Philosophy of Man*. Chicago: University of Chicago Press, 1948.

Chamberlain, David. "The Music of the Spheres and *The Parlement of Foules*." *Chaucer Quarterly* 5 (1970): 32–56.

Chaucer, Geoffrey. *Works*, ed. F. N. Robinson. Boston: Houghton Mifflin, 1957.

Chaytor, H. J. *From Script to Print*. Cambridge: Heffer, 1945.

Cole, Thomas. "The Saturnian Verse." *Yale Classical Studies* 21 (1969): 3–73.

Cone, Edward T. *The Composer's Voice*. Berkeley: University of California Press, 1974.

———. "On the Structure of 'Ich Folge Dir.'" *College Music Symposium* 5 (1965): 77–87.

Cooke. Michael. *Acts of Inclusion*. New Haven: Yale University Press, 1979.

Crocker, Richard. *The Early Medieval Sequence*. Berkeley: University of California Press, 1977.

———. *A History of Musical Style*. New York: McGraw-Hill, 1966.

———. "Discant, Counterpoint, and Harmony." *Journal of the American Musicology Society* 15 (1962): 1–21.

———. Review of *Tonality and Atonality in Sixteenth-century Music*, by Edward E. Lowinsky. *Journal of Music Theory* 6 (1962): 142–53.

Currie, Randolph N. "A Neglected Guide to Bach's Use of Number Symbolism." *Bach* 5 (1974): 23–32; 36–49.

Dante Alighieri. *De Vulgari Eloquentia*, ed. Ludwig Bertalot. Frankfurt, 1917.

———. *Lyric Poetry*, ed. K. Foster and P. Boyde. Oxford: Clarendon, 1967.

David, Hans T., and Arthur Mendel, eds. *The Bach Reader*. Rev. ed. New York: Norton, 1966.

Davie, Donald. *Articulate Energy*. New York: Harcourt Brace, 1955.

Deas, Stewart. *In Defence of Hanslick*. Rev. ed. Westmead: Gregg, 1972.

Debussy, Claude. *Monsieur Croche the Dilettante Hater*. In *Three Classics in the Aesthetics of Music*, pp. 3–71.

Del Grande, Carlo. "I documenti musicali." In *Enciclopedia Classica*, sez. II, vol. V, tomo ii, pp. 435–76.

Demetrius. *On Style*, trs. W. Rhys Roberts. Cambridge: Cambridge University Press, 1902.

Deschamps, Eustache. *Oeuvres Complètes*, ed. Gaston Raynaud. Paris: Didot, 1891.

Dionysius of Halicarnassus. *On Literary Composition*, trs. W. Rhys Roberts. London: MacMillan, 1910.

Dronke. Peter. *Medieval Latin and the Rise of European Love-Lyrics*. Oxford: Oxford University Press, 1965–66.

Dryden, John. *Works*, ed. Edward H. Hooker, H. T. Swedenberg, et al. Berkeley: University of California Press, 1956–.

———. *Essays*, ed. W. P. Ker. New York: Russell and Russell, 1961.

———. *Dramatic Works*, ed. Montague Summers. London: Nonesuch, 1932.

Du Bos, Jean Baptiste. *Reflexions critiques sur la poésie et sur la peinture*. Utrecht, 1732. Trs. Thomas Nugent as *Critical Reflections on Poetry, Painting, and Music*. London, 1748.

Ehrenpreis, Irwin. "The Style of Sound: The Literary Value of Pope's Versification." In *The Augustan Milieu*, ed. H. K. Miller et al., pp. 232–46.

Einstein, Alfred. *Essays on Music*. New York: Norton, 1956.

———. *The Italian Madrigal*. Princeton: Princeton University Press, 1949.

———. *Music in the Romantic Era*. New York: Norton, 1947.

Eisenstein, Elizabeth. "The Advent of Printing and the Problem of the Renaissance." *Past and Present* 45 (1969): 19–89.

Eliot, T. S. *The Music of Poetry*. Glasgow: Jackson, 1942.

Ellinwood, Leonard. "The Fourteenth Century in Italy." In *The New Oxford History of Music*, vol. III, pp. 31–81.

Enciclopedia Classica. Turin: Società Editrice Internazionale, 1957–70.

Erasmus, Desiderius. *Opera Omnia*, ed. John Le Clerc. Leyden, 1703. Reprinted in facsimile. Hildesheim: Georg Olms, 1961.

Erskine-Hill, Howard, and Anne Smith, eds. *The Art of Alexander Pope*. Edinburgh: Vision Press, 1979.

Evans, Paul. *The Early Trope Repertory of Saint Martial de Limoges*. Princeton: Princeton University Press, 1970.

Evelyn, John. *Diary*, ed. E. S. de Beer. London: Oxford University Press, 1960.

Farmer, Henry George. "The Music of Ancient Egypt." In *The New Oxford History of Music*, vol. I, pp. 255–82.

Feaver, Douglas D. "The Musical Setting of Euripides' *Orestes*." *American Journal of Philology* 81 (1960): 1–15.

Ficino, Marsilio. *Opera omnia*. Basel, 1576. Reprinted. Turin: Bottega d'Erasmo, 1959.

Finney, Gretchen L. "A Musical Background for 'Lycidas.'" *Huntington Library Quarterly* 15 (1952): 325–50.

Fleming, John. *The "Roman de la Rose": A Study in Allegory and Iconography*. Princeton: Princeton University Press, 1969.

Fowler, Alastair, and Douglas Brooks. "The Structure of Dryden's *A Song for St. Cecilia's Day, 1687*." In *Silent Poetry*, ed. Fowler and Brooks, pp. 185–200.

————, eds. *Silent Poetry*. London: Routledge, 1970.

Fowlie, Wallace. *Mallarmé*. Chicago: University of Chicago Press, 1973.

Frank, Istvàn. *Répertoire métrique de la poésie des troubadours*. Paris: Champion, 1953–57.

Frank, Mortimer H. "Milton's Knowledge of Music: Some Speculations." In *Milton and the Art of Sacred Song*, ed. Patrick and Sundell, pp. 83–98.

Freeman, Robert. "Apostolo Zeno's Reform of the Libretto." *Journal of the American Musicological Society* 21 (1968): 321–41.

Fux, Johann Joseph. *Gradus ad Parnassum*, ed. Alfred Mann. *Sämtliche Werke*, Vol. VII, Band I. Graz: Fux Gesellschaft,

1967. Trs. Alfred Mann in two parts: *The Study of Counterpoint*. New York: Norton, 1965. *The Study of Fugue*. New Brunswick: Rutgers University Press, 1958.

Gay, John. *The Beggar's Opera*. London, 1728. Reprint. New York: Dover, 1973.

Gennrich, Friedrich. *Grundriss einer Formenlehre des mittelalterlichen Liedes*. Halle: Niemeyer, 1932.

———. *Troubadours, Trouvères, Minne-und Meistergesang*. Cologne: Arno, 1951.

Gerbert, M., ed. *Scriptores ecclesiastici de musica sacra*. St. Blaise, 1784. Reprinted in facsimile. Milan, 1931.

Gervais du Bus. *Le Roman de Fauvel*. Facsimile of the 1316 MS, ed. Pierre Aubry. Paris: Didot, 1907.

———. *Le Roman de Fauvel*, ed. Arthur Langfors. Paris: Didot, 1914–19.

Ghisi, Federico. "Italy: 1300–1600." In *Music from the Middle Ages to the Renaissance*, ed. Sternfeld, pp. 211–54.

Gilbert, Alan H. ed. *Literary Criticism: Plato to Dryden*. Detroit: Wayne State University Press, 1962.

Gmelin, Hermann. "Das Prinzip der Imitatio in den romanischen Literaturen der Renaissance." *Romanische Forschungen* 46 (1932): 88–360.

Gotwals, Vernon, trs. and ed. *Haydn, Two Contemporary Portraits*. Madison: University of Wisconsin Press, 1968.

Gray, Hanna H. "Renaissance Humanism: The Pursuit of Eloquence." In *Renaissance Essays*, ed. Kristeller and Wiener, pp. 199–216.

Gunther, Ursula. "The Fourteenth-Century Motet and its Development." *Musica Disciplina* 12 (1958): 27–58.

Gurlitt, Wilibald. "Musik und Rhetorik—Hinweise auf ihre geschichtliche Grundlageneinheit." *Helicon* 5 (1944): 67–87.

Hahn. Henry. *Symbol und Glaube im I. Teil der Wohltemperierten Klavier von J. S. Bach*. Wiesbaden: Breitkopf und Härtel, 1973.

Halle, Morris, ed. *For Roman Jakobson: Essays on the Occasion of his Sixtieth Birthday*. The Hague: Mouton, 1956.

Handschin, Jacques. "Trope, Sequence, and Conductus." In *The New Oxford History of Music*, vol. II, pp. 128–74.

Hanslick, Eduard. *The Beautiful in Music*, trs. Gustav Cohen. Indianapolis: Bobbs-Merrill, 1957.

Havelock, Eric. *A Preface to Plato.* Cambridge: Harvard University Press, Belknap Press, 1963.

Hazlitt, William. *Complete Works,* ed. A. R. Waller and Arnold Glover. London: Dent, 1902.

Henderson, Isobel. "Ancient Greek Music." In *The New Oxford History of Music,* vol. I, pp. 336–403.

Hieatt, A. Kent. *Short Time's Endless Monument.* New York: Columbia University Press, 1960.

Hill, Raymond Thompson and Thomas Goddard Bergin, eds. *Anthology of the Provençal Troubadours.* New Haven: Yale University Press, 1941.

Hollander, John. *The Untuning of the Sky.* Princeton: Princeton University Press, 1961.

———. *Vision and Resonance.* New York: Oxford University Press, 1975.

———. *Images of Voice: Music and Sound in Romantic Poetry.* Cambridge: Heffer, 1970.

Hope, A. D. "Anne Killigrew, or the Art of Modulating." In *The Cave and the Spring,* pp. 129–43. Adelaide: Rigby, 1965. Reprinted in *Dryden's Mind and Art,* ed. King, pp. 99–113.

Hoppin, Richard H. *Medieval Music.* New York: Norton, 1978.

Hughes, Dom Anselm. "The Birth of Polyphony." In *The New Oxford History of Music,* vol. II, pp. 270–86.

———. "Music in Fixed Rhythm." In *The New Oxford History of Music,* vol. II, pp. 311–52.

———. "The Motet and Allied Forms." In *The New Oxford History of Music,* vol. II, pp. 353–404.

Huglo, Michel. "L'auteur du 'Dialogue sur la Musique' attribué à Odon." *Revue de Musicologie* 55 (1969): 119–71.

Jammers, Ewald. "Rhythmische und tonale Studien zur Musik der Antike und des Mittelalters." *Archiv für Musikforschung* 8 (1943): 27–45.

Jaynes, Julian. *The Origin of Consciousness in the Breakdown of the Bicameral Mind.* Boston: Houghton Mifflin, 1976.

Josquin des Prez. *Werken,* ed. A. Smijers. Amsterdam: Vereniging voor Nederlandse Musiekgeschiedenis, 1969.

Jourdan-Hemmerdinger, Denise. "Un Nouveau Papyrus Musical d'Euripide." *Comptes Rendus de l'Académie des Inscriptions et Belles-Lettres* (1973) : 292–302.

Keats, John. *Poetic Works*, ed. Paul D. Sheats. Boston: Houghton-Mifflin, 1975.

Kelly, Douglas. *Medieval Imagination: Rhetoric and the Poetry of Courtly Love*. Madison: University of Wisconsin Press, 1978.

Kennedy, William. *Rhetorical Norms in Renaissance Literature*. New Haven: Yale University Press, 1978.

Kenner, Hugh. *The Poetry of Ezra Pound*. London: Faber and Faber, 1951.

———. *The Pound Era*. Berkeley: University of California Press, 1971.

Kerman, Joseph. *Opera as Drama*. New York: Vintage, 1959.

Ketton-Cremer, R. W. *Thomas Gray: A Biography*. Cambridge: Cambridge University Press, 1955.

King, Bruce, ed. *Dryden's Mind and Art*. New York: Barnes and Noble, 1970.

Kirk, G. S. *The Songs of Homer*. Cambridge: Cambridge University Press, 1962.

Knight, W. F. Jackson. *Accentual Symmetry in Vergil*. Oxford: Oxford University Press, 1950.

Knuth, Deborah. "Pope, Handel, and the Dunciad." *Modern Language Studies* 10 (1980), in press.

Krenek, Ernst. "Extents and Limits of Serial Techniques." In *Problems of Modern Music*, ed. Lang, pp. 72–94.

Kristeller, Paul Oskar. *The Philosophy of Marsilio Ficino*. New York: Columbia University Press, 1943.

Kristeller, Paul O., and Philip P. Wiener, eds. *Renaissance Essays*. New York: Harper, 1968.

Lang, Paul Henry. *Music in Western Civilization*. New York: Norton, 1941.

———. "The Enlightenment and Music." *Eighteenth-Century Studies* 1 (1967): 93–108.

———, ed. *Problems of Modern Music*. New York: Norton, 1962.

Langer, Susanne. *Feeling and Form*. New York: Scribner, 1953.

Langlois, E., ed. *Recueil d'Arts de la Seconde Rhétorique*. Paris: Imprimerie Nationale, 1902.

Lanham, Richard. *The Motives of Eloquence*. New Haven: Yale University Press, 1978.

Lasso, Orlando di. *Sämtliche Werke*. Leipzig: Breitkopf und Härtel, 1895.

Leichtentritt, Hugo. *Music, History, and Ideas.* Cambridge: Harvard University Press, 1947.

Levine, Jay Arnold. "Dryden's 'Song for St. Cecilia's Day, 1687.'" *Philological Quarterly* 44 (1965): 38–50.

Lewis, C. S. *The Allegory of Love.* 1936. Reprint. London: Oxford University Press, 1973.

Lindgren, Lowell. "The Three Great Noises 'Fatal to the Interest of Bononcini'." *Musical Quarterly* 61 (1975): 560–83.

List, George. "The Boundaries of Speech and Song." *Ethnomusicology* 7 (1963): 1–16.

Liszt, Franz. Musikalische Werke. Leipzig: Breitkopf und Härtel, 1911.

Longinus. *On the Sublime,* trs. W. Rhys Roberts. Cambridge: Cambridge University Press, 1907.

Lord, Albert B. *The Singer of Tales.* Cambridge: Harvard University Press, 1960.

Lowinsky, Edward. *Secret Chromatic Art in the Netherlands Motet,* trs. Carl Buchman. New York: Columbia University Press, 1946.

———. *Tonality and Atonality in Sixteenth-Century Music.* Berkeley: University of California Press, 1961.

———. "Music in the Culture of the Renaissance." *Journal of the History of Ideas* 15 (1954): 509–53.

———. "Taste, Style, and Ideology in Eighteenth-Century Music." In *Aspects of the Eighteenth Century,* ed. Wasserman, pp. 163–206.

Lucie-Smith, Edward, ed. *Primer of Experimental Poetry 1 (1870–1922).* London: Rapp and Whiting, 1971.

Machaut, Guillaume de. *Oeuvres,* ed. Ernest Hoepffner. Paris: Didot, 1911.

———. *Livre du Voir-dit,* ed. Paulin Paris. Paris: Société des Bibliophiles François, 1875.

Mace, Dean T. "Musical Humanism, The Doctrine of Rhythmus, and the St. Cecilia Odes of Dryden." *Journal of the Warburg and Courtauld Institutes* 27 (1964): 251–92.

———. "Marin Mersenne on Language and Music." *Yale Journal of Music Theory* 14 (1970): 2–31.

McClain, Ernest G. *The Pythagorean Plato.* Stony Brook: Nicholas Hays, 1978.

Machlis, Joseph. *The Early Vocal Works of Arnold Schoenberg* (notes for recording no. M2L336/M2S736). New York: Columbia, 1954.

McKinnon, James W. "The Meaning of the Patristic Polemic against Musical Instruments." *Current Musicology* 1 (1965): 69–82.

Magee, Bryan. *Aspects of Wagner.* London: Alan Ross, 1968.

Mallarmé, Stephane. *Selected Prose Poems, Essays, and Letters,* trs. Bradford Cook. Baltimore: Johns Hopkins Press, 1956.

———. *Divagations.* Paris: Charpentier, 1942.

Mari, Giovanni, ed. *I Trattati Medievali di Ritmica Latina.* Milan, 1899. Reprint. Bologna: Bibliotheca Musica Bononiensis, 1971.

Marlowe, Christopher. *The Complete Poems and Translations,* ed. Stephen Orgel. Harmondsworth: Penguin, 1971.

———. *Complete Plays,* ed. Irving Ribner. New York: Odyssey Press, 1963.

Mattheson, Johann. *Der vollkommene Capellmeister.* Hamburg, 1739. Reprinted in facsimile. Basel: Bärenreiter, 1954.

Mei, Girolamo. *Letters on Ancient and Modern Music,* ed. Claude Palisca. Rome: American Institute of Musicology, 1960.

Mendel, Arthur. "Documentary evidence concerning the aria 'Ich Folge Dir Gleichfalls' from Bach's 'St. John Passion.'" *College Music Symposium* 5 (1965): 63–67.

Mersenne, Marin. *Harmonie Universelle.* Paris, 1636. Reprinted in facsimile. Paris: Centre National de la Recherche Scientifique, 1963.

Meyer, Leonard B. *Emotion and Meaning in Music.* Chicago: University of Chicago Press, 1965.

Migne, Jacques P., ed. *Patrologia Latina.* Paris: Garnier, 1844–1903.

Mill, John Stuart. *Dissertations and Discussions.* London: Parker, 1859.

Miller, H. K., et al., eds. *The Augustan Milieu.* Oxford: Clarendon, 1970.

Milton, John. *Complete Poems and Major Prose,* ed. Merritt Y. Hughes. Indianapolis: Bobbs-Merrill, 1957.

Morris, David B. "Civilized Reading: The Act of Judgement in *An Essay on Criticism.*" In *The Art of Alexander Pope,* ed. Erskine-Hill and Smith, pp. 15–39.

Morris, R. O. *Contrapuntal Technique in the Sixteenth Century.* 1922.

Reprint. Oxford: Oxford University Press, 1944.

Murphy, James J. *Rhetoric in the Middle Ages.* Berkeley: University of California Press, 1974.

Nathan, Hans. "The Function of Text in French 13th-century Motels." *Musical Quarterly* 28 (1942): 445–62.

The New Oxford History of Music. London: Oxford University Press. Vol. I, *Ancient and Oriental Music*, ed. Egon Wellesz, 1957. Vol. II, *Early Medieval Music*, ed. Dom Anselm Hughes, 1954. Vol. III, *Ars Nova and the Renaissance*, ed. Dom Anselm Hughes and Gerald Abraham, 1960.

Norberg, Dag. *Introduction a l'étude de la versification latine médiévale.* Stockholm: Almquist and Wiskell. 1958.

Olson, Claire C. "Chaucer and Music of the Fourteenth Century." *Speculum* 16 (1941): 64–91.

Ong, Walter J. *Interfaces of the Word.* Ithaca: Cornell University Press, 1977.

Oras. Ants. "Milton's Early Rhyme Schemes and the Structure of *Lycidas.*" *Modern Philology* 52 (1954): 14–22.

Palisca, Claude. "The Beginnings of Baroque Music: Its Roots in Sixteenth-Century Theory and Polemics." Ph.D. dissertation, Harvard, 1954.

Pater, Walter. *The Works of Walter Pater.* London: Macmillan, 1900.

Paterson, Linda M. *Troubadours and Eloquence.* Oxford: Clarendon, 1975.

Patrick, J. Max. "Milton's Revolution against Rime, and Some of Its Implications." In *Milton and the Art of Sacred Song*, ed. Patrick and Sundell, pp. 99–117.

Patrick, J. Max and Roger H. Sundell, eds. *Milton and the Art of Sacred Song.* Madison: University of Wisconsin Press, 1979.

Peacham, Henry. *The Compleat Gentleman.* London, 1622.

Peck, Russell A. "Theme and Number in Chaucer's *Book of the Duchess.*" In *Silent Poetry*, ed. Fowler and Brooks, pp. 73–115.

Perle, George. *Serial Composition and Atonality.* Rev. ed. Berkeley: University of California Press, 1969.

"Perverbs and Snowballs." *Time* (10 January 1977): 55.

Petrarch, Francesco. *Le Familiari*, ed. Vittorio Rossi. Florence: Sansoni, 1934.

———. *De sui ipsius et multorum ignorantia*, trs. H. Nachod. In *The Renaissance Philosophy of Man*, ed. Cassirer et al., pp. 47–133.

———. *Le Rime*, ed. Giosue Carducci and Severino Ferrari. 1899. Reprint. Florence: Sansoni, 1957.

Pickard-Cambridge, A. W. *Dithyramb, Tragedy, and Comedy.* 2nd ed., rev. T. B. L. Webster. Oxford: Clarendon, 1962.

Pigman, G. W. "Versions of Imitation in the Renaissance." *Renaissance Quarterly* 33 (1980): 1–32.

Plantinga, Leon. *Schumann as Critic.* New Haven: Yale University Press, 1967.

Plato. *Phaedrus*, trs. B. Jowett. Oxford: Clarendon, 1953.

———. *Republic*, trs. Allen Bloom. New York: Basic Books, 1968.

Poe, Edgar Allan. *Complete Works*, ed. James A. Harrison. New York: Crowell, 1902.

Pope, Alexander. *The Twickenham Edition of the Poems of Alexander Pope*, ed. John Butt et al. London: Methuen, 1950–67.

———. *The Correspondence of Alexander Pope*, ed. George Sherburn. Oxford: Clarendon, 1956.

Pound, Ezra. *Selected Prose*, ed. William Cookson. New York: New Directions, 1973.

———. *Literary Essays*, ed. T. S. Eliot. Norfolk, CT: New Directions, 1954.

———. *Antheil and the Treatise on Harmony.* 1927. reprinted. New York: Da Capo, 1968.

———. *Selected Poems*, ed. T. S. Eliot. London: Faber and Faber, 1928.

———. *The Cantos.* New York: New Directions, 1972.

Ptolemy. *Die Harmonielehre Klaudios Ptolemaios*, ed. Ingemar Düring. Göteborg: Hogskolas Årsskrift, 1930.

Puttenham, George. *The Arte of English Poesie*, ed. Baxter Hathaway. Kent: Kent State Press, 1970.

Quintilian. *Institutia Oratoria*, trs. H. E. Butler. London: Heinemann, 1921.

Raby, F. J. A. *A History of Christian-Latin Poetry.* Oxford: Clarendon, 1927.

Ramey, Philip. Notes to recording of *Octet*, by Stravinsky (M30579). New York: Columbia, n.d.

Ransom, John Crowe. *Beating the Bushes.* New York: New Directions, 1972.

Reaney, Gilbert. "Ars Nova in France." In *The New Oxford History of Music*, vol. III, pp. 1–30.

————. "A Chronology of the Ballades, Rondeaux and Virelais set to Music by Guillaume de Machaut." *Musica Disciplina* 6 (1952): 33–38.

————. "Guillaume de Machaut: Lyric Poet." *Music and Letters* 39 (1958): 38–51.

————. "The Development of the Rondeau, Virelai, and Ballade Forms from Adam de la Hale to Guillaume de Machaut." In *Festchrift Karl Gustav Fellerer*. Regensburg: Bosse, 1962, pp. 241–47.

Reese, Gustave. *Music in the Middle Ages*. New York: Norton, 1940.

————. *Music in the Renaissance*. Rev. ed. New York: Norton, 1959.

Reich, Willi. *Arnold Schoenberg: A Critical Biography*, trs. Leo Black. New York: Praeger, 1971.

Reichert, Georg. "Das Verhältnis von musikalische and textlicher Struktur in den Motetten Machauts." *Archiv für Musikwissenschaft* 13 (1956): 197–216.

Richards, I. A. *Principles of Literary Criticism*. London: Routledge and Kegan Paul, 1955.

Roach, Joseph R. "Cavaliere Nicolini: London's First Opera Star." *Educational Theatre Journal* 28 (1976): 189–205.

Robertson, D. W. *A Preface to Chaucer*. Princeton: Princeton University Press, 1962.

Robinson, James K. "A Neglected Phase of the Aesthetic Movement: English Parnassianism." *PMLA* 68 (1953): 733–54.

Rokseth, Yvonne. *Polyphonies du XIIIe Siècle*. Paris: L'Oiseau-Lyre, 1935–39.

Rosen, Charles. *The Classical Style*. New York: Norton, 1972.

————. *Arnold Schoenberg*. New York: Viking, 1975.

Rubsamen. Walter H. *Literary Sources of Secular Music in Italy*. Berkeley: University of California Press, 1943.

Ruhnke, Martin. *Joachim Burmeister*. Basel: Bärenreiter, 1955.

Sachs, Curt. *Rhythm and Tempo*. New York: Norton, 1953.

Salzman, Eric. *Piano Music of Berg, Schoenberg and Webern* (notes for recording no. HCR-ST-7285). New York: Dover, 1968.

Sanders, Ernest H. "Polyphony and Secular Monophony." In *Music from the Middle Ages to the Renaissance*, ed. Sternfeld, pp. 89–144.

Sapir, Edward W. "The Musical Foundations of Verse." *Journal of*

English and Germanic Philology 20 (1921): 213–28.

Saussure, Ferdinand de. *Course in General Linguistics*, trs. Wade Baskin. New York: McGraw-Hill, 1966.

Scher, Steven. *Verbal Music in German Literature*. New Haven: Yale University Press, 1968.

Schönberg, Arnold. *Style and Idea*, trs. Dika Newlin. New York: Philosophical Library, 1950.

Schopenhauer, Arthur. *The World as Will and Idea*, trs. R. B. Haldane and J. Kemp. London: Kegan Paul, 1927.

Schrade, Leo. *Monteverdi, Creator of Modern Music*. New York: Norton, 1950.

———, ed. *Polyphonic Music of the Fourteenth Century*. Monaco: L'Oiseau-Lyre, 1956.

Schubert, Franz. *Schubert's Songs to Texts by Goethe*, ed. Eusebius Mandyczewski. New York: Dover, 1979.

Schubiger, Anselm. *Die Sängerschule St. Gallens*. Einsiedeln: Benziger, 1858.

Scott, J. E. "Roman Music." In *The New Oxford History of Music*, vol. I, pp. 404–20.

Schueller, Herbert M. " 'Imitation' and 'Expression' in British Music Criticism in the 18th Century." *Musical Quarterly* 34 (1948): 544–66.

———. "Literature and Music as Sister Arts: An Aspect of Aesthetic Theory in Eighteenth-century Britain." *Philogical Quarterly* 26 (1947): 193–205.

———. "The Use and Decorum of Music as Described in British Literature, 1700–1780." *Journal of the History of Ideas* 13 (1952): 73–93.

———. "Correspondences Between Music and the Sister Arts, According to 18th-century Aesthetic Theory." *Journal of Aesthetics and Art Criticism* 11 (1953): 334–59.

Segel, Harold B. *The Baroque Poem*. New York: Dutton, 1974.

Sessions, Roger. *The Musical Experience of Composer, Performer, and Listener*. Princeton: Princeton University Press, 1950.

———. "Problems and Issues facing the Composer Today." In *Problems of Modern Music*, ed. Lang, pp. 21–33.

Shakespeare, William. *The Poems*, ed. F. T. Prince. Vol. 18 of the Arden edition. London: Methuen, 1960.

————. *Sonnets*, ed. Douglas Bush. Baltimore: Penguin, 1961.

Shapiro, Nat, ed. *Encyclopedia of Quotations about Music*. Garden City: Doubleday, 1978.

Smoldon, W. L. "Liturgical Drama." In *The New Oxford History of Music*, vol. II, pp. 175–219.

Spenser, Edmund. *Poetical Works*, ed. J. C. Smith and E. de Selincourt. London: Oxford University Press, 1912.

Springer, George. "Language and Music: Parallels and Divergencies." In *For Roman Jakobson: Essays on the Occasion of his Sixtieth Birthday*, ed. Morris Halle, pp. 504–13.

Stäblein, Bruno, ed. *Monumenta Monodica Medii Aevi*. Kassel: Bärenreiter, 1956.

Stanford, W. B. *The Sound of Greek*. Berkeley: University of California Press, 1967.

Steele, Richard. *Selected Essays from "The Tatler," "The Spectator," and "The Guardian,"* ed. Daniel McDonald. Indianapolis: Bobbs-Merrill, 1973.

————, ed. *Poetical Miscellanies*. London, 1914.

Stein, Jack M. *Richard Wagner and the Synthesis of the Arts*. Detroit: Wayne State University Press, 1960.

Sternfeld, F. W., ed. *Music from the Middle Ages to the Renaissance*. London: Weidenfeld and Nicolson, 1973.

Stevens, John. *Music and Poetry in the Early Tudor Court*. London: Methuen, 1961.

Stravinsky, Igor. *Three Songs from William Shakespeare*. London: Boosey and Hawks, 1953.

————, and Robert Craft. *Expositions and Developments*. Garden City: Doubleday, 1962.

————. *Dialogues and a Diary*. London: Faber and Faber, 1968.

Struever, Nancy S. *The Language of History in the Renaissance*. Princeton: Princeton University Press, 1970.

Strunk, Oliver, ed. *Source Readings in Music History*. New York: Norton, 1950.

Suñol, Gregorio Maria, ed. *Liber Vesperalis*. Rome, 1939.

Swedenberg, H. T., ed. *Essential Articles for the Study of John Dryden*. Hamden, CT: Archon Books, 1966.

Swift, Jonathan. *The Poems of Jonathan Swift*, ed. Harold Williams. Oxford: Clarendon, 1958.

Swinburne, Algernon Charles. *Collected Poetical Works*. London: Heinemann, 1924.

Thorburn, David, ed. *Initiations*. 2nd ed. New York: Harcourt Brace, 1976.

Three Classics in the Aesthetics of Music. New York: Dover, 1962.

Treitler, Leo. "Homer and Gregory: The Transmission of Epic Poetry and Plainchant." *Musical Quarterly* 60 (1974): 333–72.

Turner, R. L. "A Note on the Word Accent in Greek Music." *Classical Review* 29 (1915): 195–96.

Unger, Hans-Heinrich. *Die Beziehungen zwischen Musik und Rhetorik in 16.–18. Jahrhundert*. Hildesheim: Georg Olms, 1969.

Van den Werf, Hendrik. *The Chansons of the Troubadours and Trouvères*. Utrecht: Oosthoek, 1972.

Vitry, Philippe de. *Ars Nova*, ed. Gilbert Reaney, André Gilles, and Jean Maillard. *Corpus Scriptorum de Musica*, vol. viii. Rome: American Institute of Musicology, 1964.

Vivell, Cölestin. "Die direkte Entwicklung des römischen Kirchengesang aus der vorchistlichen Musik." *Kirchenmusikalisches Jahrbuch* 24 (1911): 21–54.

Von den Steinen, Wolfram. *Notker der Dichter*. Bern: Francke, 1948.

Wagner, Richard. *Tannhäuser*, ed. Natalia MacFarren. New York: G. Schirmer, n. d.

Wahlström, Erik. "Accentual Responsion in Greek strophic poetry." *Commentationes Humanarum Litterarum* 47 (1970): 5–22.

Waite, William G. *The Rhythm of Twelfth-Century Polyphony*. New Haven: Yale University Press, 1954.

Walker, D. P. "Musical Humanism in the Sixteenth and Early Seventeenth Centuries." *The Music Review* 2 (1941): 1–13, 111–21, 200–27, 288–308; 3 (1942): 55–71.

———. *Studies in Musical Science*. London: Warburg Institute, 1979.

Walpole, A. S. *Early Latin Hymns*. Cambridge: Cambridge University Press, 1922.

Wasserman, Earl. "Pope's *Ode for Musick*." *ELH* 28 (1961): 163–86.

———, ed. *Aspects of the Eighteenth Century*. Baltimore: Johns Hopkins Press, 1965.

Webb, Daniel. *Observations on the Correspondence between Poetry and Music*. London, 1769.

Wellek, René. *Concepts of Criticism*. New Haven: Yale University Press, 1963.

————. "The Term and Concept of 'Classicism' in Literary History." In *Aspects of the Eighteenth Century*, ed. Wasserman, pp. 104–28.

Wellesz, Egon. "Early Christian Music." In *The New Oxford History of Music*, vol. II, pp. 1–13.

Westrup, J. A. "Medieval Song." In *The New Oxford History of Music*, vol. II, pp. 220–69.

————. "Foreign Musicians in Stuart England." *Musical Quarterly* 27 (1941): 70–89.

Williams, Sarah Jane. "An Author's Role in Fourteenth-century Book Production: Guillaume de Machaut's 'Livre ou je met toutes mes choses.'" *Romania* 90 (1969): 433–54.

Wimsatt, James. *The Marguerite Poetry of Guillaume de Machaut*. Chapel Hill: University of North Carolina Press, 1970.

Wimsatt, W. K. *The Verbal Icon*. Lexington: University of Kentucky Press, 1954.

————. *Day of the Leopards*. New Haven: Yale University Press, 1976.

————, and Cleanth Brooks. *Literary Criticism, A Short History*. New York: Vintage, 1957.

Winn, James A. "Pope Plays the Rake: His Letters to Ladies and the Making of the *Eloisa*." In *The Art of Alexander Pope*, ed. Erskine-Hill and Smith, pp. 89–118.

Winnington-Ingram, R. P. "Greek Music (Ancient)." In *Grove's Dictionary of Music and Musicians*. 5th ed. Vol. III, pp. 770–81.

————. *Mode in Ancient Greek Music*. Cambridge: Cambridge University Press, 1936.

Wolf, Johannes. *Geschichte der Mensuralnotation von 1250–1460*. Leipzig: Breitkopf und Härtel, 1904.

Woodridge, H. E. *The Polyphonic Period. The Oxford History of Music*, vol. II. Oxford: Clarendon, 1905.

Wordsworth, William. *Poetical Works*, ed. Thomas Hutchinson, rev. Ernest de Selincourt. Oxford: Oxford University Press, 1969.

————. *Lyrical Ballads*, ed. R. L. Brett and A. R. Jones. London: Methuen, 1965.

————. *The Prelude*, ed. Ernest de Selincourt. Rev. ed. London: Oxford University Press, 1960.

Wulstan, David. "Introduction: Ancient Greece." In *Music from the Middle Ages to the Renaissance*, ed. Sternfeld, pp. 27–58.

Yates, Frances. *The French Academies of the Sixteenth Century*. London: Warburg Institute, 1947.

Zuckerkandl, Victor. *Sound and Symbol*, trs. Willard R. Trask. New York: Pantheon, 1956.

Index